Digital Transformation Roadmap

In a world undergoing rapid technological evolution, this is your indispensable guide to thriving in the digital age. *Digital Transformation Roadmap: From Vision to Execution* offers a comprehensive exploration of the Fourth Industrial Revolution by presenting a roadmap for leveraging technology to revolutionize businesses, strategy, and innovation.

Embark on a journey that unveils the dynamic interplay between technology and business. Discover the evolution of tech life cycles, the significance of digital transformation, and the key domains of change reshaping industries. Explore strategies to gain competitive advantage, from reimagining business models to aligning digital visions with organizational goals. Experience a holistic approach to digital transformation. Learn how to empower employees, foster a culture of innovation, and navigate change adeptly. Delve into the world of emerging technologies such as AI, IoT, and blockchain, and harness their potential to open new avenues for growth.

From cybersecurity roadmaps to measuring system performance, uncover essential practices to ensure the resilience and success of digital initiatives. Master the art of delivering exceptional digital customer experiences and harnessing the value of data.

Whether you're a business leader, strategist, or tech enthusiast, this book equips you with actionable insights, practical strategies, and a forward-thinking mindset to drive change and thrive in the digital landscape.

Hamed Taherdoost is an Associate Professor and Chair of RSAC, University Canada West, Founder of Hamta Business Corporation, and R&D Director, Q Minded Tech. He is an award-winning research and development professional and methodologist with more than 20 years of experience in both industry and academia. He is a senior member of many organizations, including the IEEE, IAEEEE, IASED, IEDRC and HKSRA, and a fellow member of ISAC. He is also a working group member of IFIP TC 11 – Security and Privacy Protection in Information Processing Systems; Human Aspects of Information Security and Assurance and Information Security Management.

Digital Transformation Roadmap

From Vision to Execution

Hamed Taherdoost

CRC Press
Taylor & Francis Group
Boca Raton London New York

CRC Press is an imprint of the
Taylor & Francis Group, an **informa** business

Designed cover image: Background image from Freepik.com. This cover has been designed using assets from Freepik.com. iStock.com/rudall30

First edition published 2024
by CRC Press
2385 NW Executive Center Drive, Suite 320, Boca Raton FL 33431

and by CRC Press
4 Park Square, Milton Park, Abingdon, Oxon, OX14 4RN

CRC Press is an imprint of Taylor & Francis Group, LLC

ISBN: 978-1-032-74848-1 (hbk)
ISBN: 978-1-032-74053-9 (pbk)
ISBN: 978-1-003-47122-6 (ebk)

DOI: 10.1201/9781003471226

Typeset in Times
by SPi Technologies India Pvt Ltd (Straive)

To my dearest Hamta and Kiasha, you are the stars in the storybook of my life, illuminating every page with the brilliance of your laughter and the magic of your dreams. May this book be a testament to the transformative power of dreams, guiding you from visionary beginnings to the exhilarating execution of your own extraordinary narratives. Here's to navigating the uncharted with joy and curiosity.

Contents

Acknowledgments

Special recognition goes to my parents. My father, whose more than 50 years of engagement in the electrical industry, manufacturing switchgear panels, and overseeing numerous projects, has been a profound influence. My mother and brother, your unwavering support and encouragement are deeply appreciated. I want to express my heartfelt gratitude to my wonderful wife whose unwavering support and encouragement have been my anchor throughout the creation of *Digital Transformation Roadmap: From Vision to Execution*. Her patience, understanding, and insightful perspectives, shaped by her role in academia and industry, have been the driving force behind this endeavor.

I am deeply appreciative of the support and collaborative spirit from my colleagues at University Canada West. A special thank you to the innovative team at Hamta Business Corporation for fostering an environment of innovation and providing valuable insights that have contributed to the practical aspects explored in this book. A heartfelt thank you to the brilliant minds at Q Minded | Quark Minded Technology Inc., whose expertise and forward-thinking approach have indelibly marked the technological landscape explored within these pages.

A special shout-out to my incredible students, whose enthusiasm and curiosity have infused energy into my work. Your questions, discussions, and fresh perspectives have undoubtedly shaped the essence of this book.

And to you, dear readers, thank you for embarking on this transformative journey with me. May the roadmap ahead inspire and guide your own ventures.

With sincere thanks,

Hamed Taherdoost
Canada, Vancouver
October 2023

Introduction

The concept of "digital transformation" encapsulates the integration of digital technologies into various aspects of organizations and society, leading to profound changes in how businesses operate and how individuals interact with technology. Understanding the societal impact of technology is essential to grasp its trajectory fully. This concept emerged alongside technological advancements and the Internet's rise. Initially, computers were mainly used for data processing and automation, simplifying tasks, and boosting productivity. The advent of the Internet made information more accessible and communication more efficient, marking the onset of the digital revolution.

In today's rapidly evolving business landscape, digital transformation is driven by various challenges that companies encounter. These challenges include adapting to evolving customer expectations for seamless digital experiences, responding to disruptive innovations by competitors, and addressing inefficiencies that lead to errors and delays. Moreover, the accumulation of vast amounts of data and the demand for actionable insights have compelled businesses to embrace data analytics. Regulatory changes, globalization, and shifts in labor expectations toward digital technologies also significantly shape digital transformation. Updating legacy systems and adopting advanced technology is imperative for security and environmental sustainability amid cybersecurity concerns and calls for eco-friendliness.

Digital transformation is further motivated by the competitive edge of agile companies and the need for personalized customer engagement. Organizations must cater to employees' preferences for digital tools, keep pace with rapid innovation cycles in various sectors, and enhance supply chain processes for greater efficiency. The push for enhanced environmental sustainability encourages the use of digital solutions that minimize ecological impact. As the digital landscape evolves, businesses face opportunities and challenges that necessitate their digital evolution to remain competitive, efficient, and responsive to stakeholder demands.

Technological progress has brought about the development of new tools and platforms over time. The widespread adoption of smartphones, cloud computing, artificial intelligence (AI), and the Internet of Things (IoT) has expanded the scope of digital transformation. These technologies facilitate collecting and analyzing massive data volumes, leading to insightful knowledge generation and improved decision-making. Rapid advancements in 5G networks, edge computing, machine learning, and automation will significantly impact future digital transformation in the next five years.

Over the upcoming five years, digital transformation is predicted to exert a profound influence on businesses and society as a whole. Companies will increasingly leverage digital technology to streamline operations, enhance customer experiences, and foster innovation. Routine tasks are expected to become more automated, freeing time for creative and strategic endeavors. The convergence of machine learning and AI will give rise to more intelligent, personalized services.

The shift toward digital technology will also have a substantial impact on individuals. Accessibility to information and services will improve for everyone, regardless of location. The banking, education, and healthcare sectors will benefit from increased accessibility and efficiency. Innovations like telemedicine will enable remote medical consultations, benefiting people with limited mobility or those in remote areas. Online learning platforms will democratize education by offering continuous learning opportunities globally. The interplay between digital transformation and other technological advancements is evident; for instance, the IoT's connectivity potential generates vast data that can accelerate digital transformation initiatives when harnessed for insights. Furthermore, cybersecurity breakthroughs will be crucial to safeguard digital systems' privacy and integrity and maintain public trust in the digital transformation process.

In a time of remarkable technological advances and fast changes, businesses and society are experiencing a big transformation. The idea of changing to digital ways is spreading through different industries. This suggests a big change that could reshape how we live. *Digital Transformation Roadmap: From Vision to Execution* is not just a book; it is like a guide that helps us through this change. It gives a complete guide for understanding, planning, and carrying out digital changes in a rapidly changing world.

The fast advance of technology, the Fourth Industrial Revolution, has brought us to a time when the blending of physical and digital worlds is changing how things work. In this lively setting, making big changes in how we use technology is not just something we can choose to do or not—it is something we need to do to succeed. This book is based on the idea that digital transformation is more than a trendy word. It is like a special key that helps us develop new ideas, grab opportunities, and stay competitive in a world where change is always happening. The story told in these pages shows that it is not just about surviving anymore but about finding success in the Industry 4.0 era. It is like having a ticket to doing well in this new age.

The digital transformation process is like a journey of change where businesses, academics, and society are becoming increasingly involved with technology. This book is special because it connects two important areas: The business world and the world of academia and society. This book is like a map for people working in businesses and organizations. This map helps them understand how to make changes using technology. It gives them ideas, helpful information, and the best ways to do things so that they can navigate through the changes confidently. In academics and learning, this book is like a precious tool. It helps students, teachers, and researchers understand the ideas behind digital transformation. It talks about the theories and concepts that are the foundation of these changes.

Moreover, it also connects these theories to the real problems and chances people working in businesses face daily. So, this book is important for two reasons. First, it helps people make business changes by showing them the way. Second, it helps people studying and researching understand why these changes are happening and how they affect the real world. It is like a friendly guide and a smart helper for everyone in this digital transformation journey.

The *Digital Transformation Roadmap: From Vision to Execution* is a detailed guidebook. It helps people understand and do the digital transformation process, which is when companies use technology to improve their work. This guidebook mixes big ideas with practical plans, making it useful for thinking and doing. The main sections of the guidebook are like different themes, showing how everything fits together. Imagine building a house: You need a plan (the guidebook) with big design ideas and step-by-step instructions. The different parts of the plan (the chapters) focus on different parts of the house, like the kitchen, living room, and bedrooms. Similarly, the chapters in the guidebook focus on different aspects of digital transformation, making it easier to understand and follow.

- *Chapter 1 – Technology Transformation*: This chapter delves into the profound shifts brought about by the Fourth Industrial Revolution, exploring the current technological landscape's evolution and impact. It clarifies the concept of digital transformation and its significance and identifies the key domains experiencing transformative change.
- *Chapter 2 – Digital World Strategies*: Focusing on strategic aspects, this chapter emphasizes how technology can be a competitive advantage and how traditional business models need adaptation for the digital era. It guides readers through formulating effective digital strategies aligned with business goals and explaining strategic analysis in the context of digital transformation.
- *Chapter 3 – Digital Organization*: Addressing the challenges and opportunities of digital transformation, this chapter examines the factors influencing its success and guides organizations in overcoming barriers. It outlines the importance of linking strategy to execution, explains the digital marketplace's dynamics, and highlights customer experience and innovation as key components.
- *Chapter 4 – Digital Transformation Project Management*: Providing practical guidance, this chapter introduces the project management aspects of digital transformation. It covers project planning, development, and the crucial agile mindset required for successful adaptation. The Scrum methodology is also explored, offering insights into effective agile project management.
- *Chapter 5 – Emerging Technologies*: Diving into cutting-edge technologies, this chapter presents diverse innovations reshaping industries. From 3D printing to quantum computing, it offers succinct overviews of each technology's potential impact on various sectors.
- *Chapter 6 – Organizational Culture/Change Management*: Focusing on the human side of transformation, this chapter discusses the vital role of employees and organizational culture in the digital journey. It emphasizes cultivating a culture of innovation and change and provides insights into effective change management practices.
- *Chapter 7 – Digital Transformation Cybersecurity Roadmap*: This chapter addresses cybersecurity's pivotal role in Industry 4.0 in an increasingly interconnected world. It outlines risk assessment, planning, and enhancement strategies, offering a comprehensive roadmap to bolster cybersecurity in digital transformation.

- *Chapter 8 – Performance Assessment*: This chapter explores measuring system performance and resilience (performability), leveraging analytics for data-driven decision-making (analyticity), and creating user-centric digital experiences (usability). It underscores the importance of these elements in optimizing digital initiatives' outcomes.

What makes *Digital Transformation Roadmap: From Vision to Execution* special is its all-encompassing approach. This book goes beyond simple technical guides or theoretical discussions. Instead, it combines theories with practical applications, giving you a complete view of digital transformation. It brings together knowledge about technology, strategic planning, how people work together, and the skills to make things happen. By explaining how all these aspects are connected—technology, strategy, culture, and getting things done—this book provides a roadmap that's not just about ideas but also about taking real steps to create meaningful change. This book does not just talk the talk; it shows you how to walk the walk toward transformation.

The Fourth Industrial Revolution is coming, and it brings big changes. *Digital Transformation Roadmap: From Vision to Execution* is not just a regular book. It is like a tool that helps you navigate and understand these changes. It is like a map, a guide, and a mentor as you go through the exciting digital transformation journey. Whether you are an experienced leader, a curious student, or someone who wants to start a business, this book is like a helpful friend. It shows you how and helps you stay on track as technology changes.

Technology Transformation

1

1.1 THE FOURTH INDUSTRIAL REVOLUTION: UNDERSTANDING THE CURRENT STATE OF TECHNOLOGY

In today's fast-paced and connected world, it is crucial to understand the state of technology. Technology now plays a significant role in many parts of our lives, including communication, education, healthcare, business, and entertainment. We can utilize the potential of the most recent technical developments, make wise decisions, and successfully adjust to the changing environment by remaining educated about them. Understanding the condition of technology today is important for several reasoens, including how it affects communication. Technological breakthroughs have completely transformed the way we communicate and engage with one another. The way we communicate and share information has changed due to technology, which includes social networking platforms, instant messaging apps, video conferencing tools, and collaboration platforms. Knowing the most recent communication technology allows us to use them for more effective networking, collaboration, and outreach.

Additionally, technology is essential to schooling. Learning has become more participatory, interesting, and accessible due to the use of technology in classrooms. Technology has widened educational options beyond conventional bounds with online courses, e-learning platforms, instructional apps, and virtual reality (VR) simulations. By embracing these technologies and incorporating them into the learning process, educators, students, and parents can stimulate creativity and improve educational outcomes. This is made possible by clearly understanding the state of technology today. Technology has transformed medical procedures, research, and patient care in healthcare. Developing advanced medical technologies, electronic health records, telemedicine, and data analytics has greatly enhanced disease diagnostics, treatment, and monitoring. Healthcare personnel knowledgeable about the most recent developments in medical technology are better able to provide better patient care, streamline workflows, and stay at the forefront of medical innovation.

Technology also spurs innovation and company growth. Businesses of all sizes, from major multinationals to fledgling startups, rely on technology to streamline processes, boost productivity, and expand their client bases. Entrepreneurs and business executives may make strategic decisions, create competitive advantages, and adjust to changing customer needs by thoroughly understanding the status of technology today. This knowledge gives them insights into new trends, disruptive technologies, and market dynamics. Technology influences entertainment by introducing new ways to consume content and immersive experiences. Technology has completely changed how we amuse ourselves, from streaming services to VR gaming and from augmented reality (AR) experiences to artificial intelligence (AI)-generated content. Content producers, artists, and media professionals who keep up with technology advancements can use these technologies to give audiences worldwide unique, personalized experiences.

The preceding industrial revolutions marked a key turning point in human history marked by several technological developments and socioeconomic changes. The preceding industrial revolutions are summarized as follows:

- *The First Industrial Revolution (18th and 19th centuries)*: The "Mechanization Revolution," began in Britain in the late 18th century. It was powered by developing tools like the steam engine, transforming sectors including mining, transportation, and textiles. Urbanization and considerable societal changes resulted from transitioning from an agrarian economy to a factory-based manufacturing system.
- *The Second Industrial Revolution (late 19th–early 20th centuries)*: Also referred to as the "Technological Revolution," the Second Industrial Revolution occurred between the middle of the 19th and the beginning of the 20th centuries. Electricity and steel manufacturing innovations, as well as the development of the telegraph and telephone, were among its hallmarks. During this time, the railway network was expanded, mass production methods were created, and new industries like petroleum, autos, and chemicals emerged.
- *The Third Industrial Revolution (late 20th century)*: The "Digital Revolution," or the "Information Age," as the Third Industrial Revolution is known, started in the late 20th century. Digital technology advanced quickly, particularly in computers, telecommunications, and the Internet. Communication, commerce, and entertainment are just a few industries that the ubiquitous use of computers and the Internet has altered. As a result of the widespread use of digital technology to connect people and commerce, globalization also grew during this time.

These three industrial revolutions have profoundly altered society, the economy, and culture. They altered social institutions, changed the nature of employment, and brought forth new opportunities and difficulties. These revolutions have also had a cumulative effect, with succeeding ones building on the discoveries of the previous ones. The Fourth Industrial Revolution (Industry 4.0) increases organizational effectiveness by seamlessly integrating digital technologies with organizational processes and personnel. Figure 1.1 depicts how Industry 4.0 has developed.

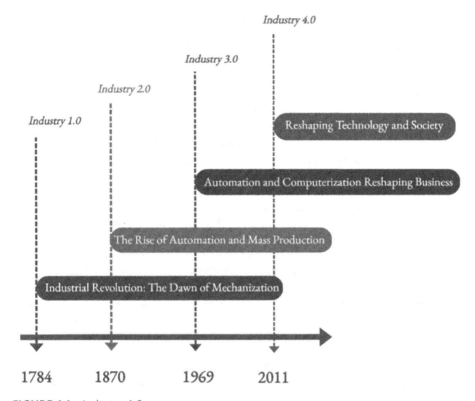

FIGURE 1.1   Industry 4.0.

The blending of digital, physical, and biological technologies defines the Fourth Industrial Revolution, which is currently taking place. It includes developments in biotechnology, nanotechnology, robotics, AI, and the Internet of Things (IoT). The Fourth Industrial Revolution can reshape markets and professions in previously unheard-of ways, altering how people live, work, and engage with the world. The past industrial revolutions profoundly altered many facets of human existence.

- *Economic Transformations*: With the transition from manual to machine-based manufacturing during the First Industrial Revolution, productivity rose and new sectors were created. During this time, factories proliferated, and industries, including coal mining, iron production, and textile production, were mechanized. Large-scale industrial corporations were founded due to the Second Industrial Revolution's introduction of mass production methods, assembly lines, and the division of labor. Industry digitalization, automation, and the emergence of e-commerce during the Third Industrial Revolution changed business structures and worldwide supply networks.
- *Urbanization and Social Changes*: During the Industrial Revolution, massive urbanization resulted from individuals moving from rural areas to cities in pursuit of employment. As a result of this rapid urbanization, there

are now social problems, unsanitary living conditions, and crowded living spaces. It also prompted labor movements, the fight for workers' rights, and the emergence of new social classes, including the urban middle class and the industrial working class.

- *Technological Advancements*: Technological advances were substantial with each industrial revolution. The First Industrial Revolution brought about the development of the railway system, steam power, and mechanized textile production. The widespread use of electricity, the development of the telephone, the growth of the steel industry, and improvements in transportation, such as the development of the automobile and the airplane, all occurred during the Second Industrial Revolution. With the advent of computers, the Internet, and mobile technology during the Third Industrial Revolution, instant communication and access to massive amounts of information became possible.
- *Impact on Workforce*: The Industrial Revolution significantly impacted the workforce. Due to the mechanization and centralization of skilled artisans' labor in factories during the First Industrial Revolution, many of them were displaced. In addition to creating new work opportunities in the industrial sectors that were expanding, the Second Industrial Revolution also contributed to labor exploitation and the expansion of labor unions and movements. Automation and automation of some jobs during the Third Industrial Revolution raised worries about job security, retraining, and upskilling requirements.
- *Globalization*: The world's connectivity increased with each industrial revolution. The steamship and railroad development during the First Industrial Revolution facilitated international trade and the flow of products and ideas. Global commerce networks were further developed during the Second Industrial Revolution, and the invention of telegraphy made it possible to communicate more quickly over large distances. With the development of the Internet and other digital technologies, the Third Industrial Revolution connected people and markets worldwide, spurring multinational corporations' emergence and globalization's acceleration.

Digital technologies' incorporation into all facets of our existence is what defines the Fourth Industrial Revolution as a disruptive period. It is altering society, economies, and industries at a never-before-seen rate.

The phrase "Industry 4.0" first appeared in the German manufacturing sector in 2011, when it was introduced at the CeBIT exhibition [1]. The objectives of Industry 4.0 continue to provide challenges to manufacturing and service organizations across all industries, and they will probably do so for some time to come. The following three ideas are the foundation of Industry 4.0:

- Cyber-physical systems combine current digital technology with actual physical processes and systems.
- The IoT links tiny embedded devices, typically sensors, actuators, or a combination.
- Universal connectedness is made possible by the presence of fast networking.

"Cyber-physical systems" could require a little more explanation:

Understanding cyber-physical systems is crucial for companies aiming to transition to Industry 4.0. In simple terms, these systems integrate physical components with computerized technology inorder to oversee and manage operations efficiently. Embracing digital transformation is imperative for businesses to thrive in the modern technological landscape.

The shift to Industry 4.0 is undoubtedly tricky. Organizations need to accept these issues and approach them methodically to execute a successful digital transition. This manual leads a company through this procedure to take advantage of the opportunities provided by Industry 4.0. A generic framework for Industry 4.0 adaption considers the insights learned from the link between design principles and supporting technologies. Companies should integrate and redefine intelligent products and innovative processes in their essential functions, such as product development, production, logistics, marketing, sales, and after-sale services, to adopt Industry 4.0. Accordingly, an intelligent product consists of three fundamental parts: (i) Physical part(s), such as a mechanical part; (ii) an intelligent part with sensors, microprocessors, an embedded operating system, and a user interface; and (iii) connectivity, which includes ports, antennae, and protocols [2]. All intelligent processes and products should be supported by a comprehensive technology infrastructure that connects to external sources and synchronizes data collecting, processing, and analytics within the product and services. Big data analytics allows for monitoring products and services and detecting changes in various environmental variables. Cloud technologies also ensure that production is coordinated and connected to distributed systems. Agent-based services, real-time analytics, and business intelligence (BI) systems increase compatibility with large data processing platforms, which is crucial for networking. Big data platforms and cloud systems can thus offer real-time data management to enable quick responses for data processing, management of data flow, and knowledge extraction to enhance the performance and usage of the overall product. By adjusting algorithms and iterative processes like self-learning and self-assessment, adjustments can be performed to differences between the current situation and intended needs. This intelligent data management should be supported by building a communication and networking infrastructure based on the Industrial Internet and cybersecurity for effective remote controlling and monitoring.

Rapid improvements in the marriage of manufacturing and computer technology led to a remarkable adaptation of connected and intelligent goods for value generation in manufacturing and other fields. Companies are looking for the best adaption of the term "Industry 4.0," which denotes more efficient and continuous systems. This circumstance demands that the implementation strategy be explained. Future directions suggest that the production, control, and monitoring of intelligent and connected devices will shift from a human-labor-centered production to a fully automated method based on the experiences of industrial firms. In this regard, the transition to Industry 4.0 calls for strategic workforce planning, the creation of an ideal organizational structure, the development of partnerships, and participation and sharing in technological standardization, all of which are crucial for advancing technology. According to the McKinsey Report 2017 [3], real-time supply chain optimization, human–robot collaboration, smart energy usage, digital performance management, and predictive maintenance would be the key implementation areas in the manufacturing sector. Additionally, incorporating nanotechnology and robotics into Industry 4.0 will increase the efficacy of supporting technologies. Additionally, increasingly advanced AI algorithms will be used to create self-organized, self-motivated, and self-learning systems, and shortly, the auto-creation of corporate processes will be observed.

1.1.1 Core Technologies of the Fourth Industrial Revolution

The merger of digital, physical, and biological technologies, which has dramatically impacted several industries and society, defines the Fourth Industrial Revolution. Several important technologies fostering innovation and changing how we live, work, and interact are central to this transformation. These foundational innovations include:

- *Artificial Intelligence (AI)*: The development of computer systems that can carry out tasks that would ordinarily need human intelligence is called AI. Subfields of AI, such as machine learning (ML), deep learning, computer vision, and natural language processing (NLP), have all made major strides. Healthcare, banking, transportation, and manufacturing are just a few sectors where AI is being used to revolutionize procedures, improve decision-making, and enable automation.
- *Internet of Things (IoT)*: The IoT is a network of interconnected physical objects, including cars, buildings, and other things, that can collect and exchange data because they are equipped with sensors, software, and network connectivity. This technology allows the digital and physical worlds to be seamlessly integrated. IoT applications improve efficiency, productivity, and resource utilization, varying from smart homes and cities to industrial automation and supply chain management.
- *Big Data and Analytics*: Social media, sensors, and connected gadgets are just a few sources of the enormous amount of data produced by the Fourth Industrial Revolution. Large amounts of structured and unstructured data are called "big data." Analytics is the process of drawing conclusions and patterns from such data. Organizations can now make data-driven decisions, optimize operations, and develop individualized experiences thanks to advanced analytics approaches like predictive analytics, data mining, and ML algorithms.
- *Robotics and Automation*: By automating laborious and repetitive operations, robotics and automation technologies are transforming various industries. Robots are becoming increasingly smart, able to complete difficult tasks precisely and effectively. These technologies, which include autonomous cars, drones, industrial robots, and collaborative robots (cobots), are revolutionizing manufacturing, logistics, healthcare, and other industries, resulting in higher productivity and increased safety.

- *Blockchain*: Blockchain is a distributed ledger system that enables safe, open, and independent data management and transactions. It increases efficiency and confidence by removing the need for intermediaries and creating a tamper-proof, auditable record of all transactions. Blockchain technology has a variety of uses, including voting systems, supply chain management, healthcare (protected patient data), and finance (cryptocurrencies and smart contracts).
- *3D Printing*: By layering materials according to a computer blueprint, 3D printing, sometimes referred to as additive manufacturing, enables the production of actual items. With the ability to produce items as needed, customize them, and produce less waste, this technology has the potential to transform the industrial industry. It enables quick prototyping and low-cost production in various industries, including aerospace, healthcare (medical implants and prostheses), and automotive.

1.1.2 Industries and Sectors Affected by the Fourth Industrial Revolution

The present wave of technology developments reshaping industries and sectors worldwide is known as the Fourth Industrial Revolution, or Industry 4.0. Digital technologies, automation, AI, robotics, the IoT, big data analytics, and other cutting-edge technologies are all integrated into it. This revolution is upending established business paradigms and changing how many industries function. The Fourth Industrial Revolution has a substantial impact on the following prominent industries and sectors.

1.1.2.1 Manufacturing

Industry 4.0 is revolutionizing manufacturing processes by adopting automation and smart technologies. Advanced robotics and AI-powered machines enhance factory efficiency, productivity, and precision. Smart factories equipped with IoT sensors and connectivity enable real-time data monitoring, predictive maintenance, and streamlined supply chains.

- *Healthcare*: The industry is undergoing a major transformation due to Industry 4.0. Medical professionals utilize digital health technologies, wearables, and remote monitoring devices to provide personalized care, improve patient outcomes, and reduce healthcare costs. AI and ML algorithms are used for disease diagnosis, drug discovery, and treatment planning.
- *Transportation and Logistics*: The Fourth Industrial Revolution revolutionized transportation and logistics through autonomous vehicles, connected infrastructure, and smart logistics systems. Self-driving cars, drones, and delivery robots are being deployed to optimize transportation networks and reduce congestion. Advanced tracking and data analytics technologies are enhancing supply chain visibility and efficiency.

- *Energy and Utilities*: The energy and utilities sector is experiencing significant changes driven by Industry 4.0. Integrating renewable energy sources, smart grids, and IoT devices enables efficient energy management, grid optimization, and demand–response systems. Big data analytics optimize energy consumption, predict maintenance needs, and improve sustainability.
- *Financial Services*: The financial industry is being transformed by digital technologies. Fintech companies leverage AI, blockchain, and data analytics to deliver personalized services, automate processes, and enhance security. Mobile payment systems, robo-advisors, and digital currencies are reshaping how people transact and manage their finances.
- *Agriculture*: Industry 4.0 is revolutionizing agriculture through precision farming techniques and smart agriculture solutions. IoT sensors, drones, and satellite imagery monitor crops, optimize irrigation, and detect diseases. AI-powered systems help farmers make data-driven decisions, improve crop yields, and reduce resource wastage.
- *Retail*: The retail sector is experiencing a significant shift due to Industry 4.0. E-commerce platforms, personalized recommendations, and VR shopping experiences reshape how consumers shop. Retailers leverage big data analytics to understand customer preferences, optimize inventory management, and deliver targeted marketing campaigns.
- *Education*: The Fourth Industrial Revolution impacts the education sector by introducing new learning models and technologies. Online learning platforms, virtual classrooms, and AI-powered tutors enhance access to education and personalized learning experiences. Educational institutions are incorporating emerging technologies to develop future-ready skills and competencies.

1.1.3 Socioeconomic Implications of the Fourth Industrial Revolution

Our society is changing in many ways, including the economy and the employment market, due to the Fourth Industrial Revolution, defined by the rapid growth of technology and automation. Although it presents numerous opportunities for innovation and development, it also has important social ramifications that must be properly explored. The effect on employment is one of the main worries. AI technologies and the automation of various operations have the potential to reduce the number of jobs available significantly. Jobs that are routine-based, repetitive, or easily automatable are particularly vulnerable. The difficulty in finding acceptable jobs for people lacking the requisite abilities to succeed in the new technology landscape may lead to unemployment and economic disparity. The disparity between highly skilled and low-skilled workers could increase, causing socioeconomic inequalities to worsen.

The Fourth Industrial Revolution also generates new work prospects; it is crucial to remember this. The need for talented personnel in developing industries like AI, robotics, data analytics, and cybersecurity is fueled by technological breakthroughs. Creative, problem-solving, and critical thinking-intensive jobs are less likely to be automated. Proactive steps to upskill and reskill the workforce are required to ensure a smooth transition by giving workers the skills they need to compete in the changing labor market. The fact that labor itself is changing is another implication. Increased connection and flexibility are characteristics of the Fourth Industrial Revolution, enabling platforms for the gig economy, digital entrepreneurship, and remote labor. While this may provide workers with more convenience and flexibility, it also raises questions about the stability of their employment, their legal rights, and their pay. Platform-based employment may undermine existing employment patterns and undercut labor safeguards, necessitating regulatory changes from legislators to promote fair working conditions and safeguard workers' rights.

Additionally, there is a chance that the Fourth Industrial Revolution will make socioeconomic disparities worse. Inequalities in technology and digital infrastructure access may make it difficult for marginalized communities to participate in the digital economy. The socioeconomic disparity might deepen, and disadvantaged communities may become even more marginalized due to the digital divide, preventing them from taking full advantage of technology improvements. By building up the digital infrastructure, encouraging digital literacy, and guaranteeing equal access to educational and employment opportunities, efforts need to be made to close this gap. The Fourth Industrial Revolution also prompts social and ethical issues. The growing reliance on AI and automation raises questions concerning privacy, security, and algorithmic bias. To deal with these problems and ensure that the advantages of technology are reaped responsibly and inclusively, it is essential to build strong governance frameworks and ethical standards.

Society will face opportunities and problems due to the Fourth Industrial Revolution. It could spur creativity, productivity, and economic expansion but also has huge socioeconomic ramifications. Investing in education and training, ensuring equitable access to technology, defending workers' rights, and promoting a responsible and inclusive approach to deploying emerging technologies are all proactive ways that policymakers, businesses, and individuals can address these issues. By doing this, we can work toward a time when everyone can profit from the Fourth Industrial Revolution.

1.2 TECH LIFE CYCLE: THE EVOLUTION OF TECHNOLOGY

The technology life cycle is the pattern of stages a technological product or innovation goes through from its inception to its eventual decline and obsolescence. This cycle begins with the inception of the product or innovation and ends with its obsolescence. It is a conceptual framework that aids in comprehending the development and implementation of technologies across various business sectors. The evolution of technology can be broken down into several distinct phases, each of which is distinguished from the others by varying degrees of invention, market expansion, and client acceptability. In most cases, these phases will consist of (Figure 1.2).

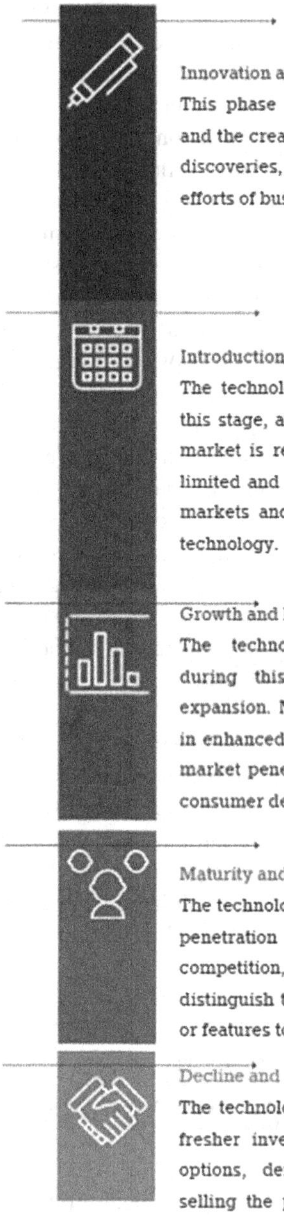

Innovation and Development

This phase consists of research, development, and the creation of novel technologies. Scientific discoveries, technological advances, and the efforts of businesspeople and inventors propel it.

Introduction and Early Adoption

The technology is introduced to the market during this stage, and early adopters begin to utilize it. The market is relatively small, and the product may be limited and expensive. Companies may target niche markets and collect customer feedback to advance technology.

Growth and Expansion

The technology obtains widespread acceptance during this phase and experiences exponential expansion. More companies invest in R&D, resulting in enhanced features, decreased costs, and increased market penetration. As the product gains popularity, consumer demand increases.

Maturity and Saturation

The technology reaches its pinnacle regarding market penetration and adoption. As a result of increased competition, the market gets saturated. Businesses distinguish their products and provide extra services or features to sustain their market share.

Decline and Obsolescence

The technology eventually ages or is superseded by fresher inventions. As consumers switch to newer options, demand declines. Companies may stop selling the product or spend heavily on significant redesigns to increase lifespan. In the end, the technology is phased out and becomes obsolete.

FIGURE 1.2   Phases of the tech life cycle.

1.2.1 Innovation and Development

The first stage of the technological life cycle is known as the innovation and development stage, and it is an essential stage since it is the stage in which groundbreaking ideas are translated into real products or services. This phase includes the ideation, research, and prototyping processes, which are responsible for laying the groundwork for future technical developments. During the era of innovation and development, the primary focus is on pushing the boundaries of existing knowledge, finding possible prospects, and exploring new avenues of possibility. It requires creative thinking, scientific investigation, and technical competence to create unique solutions to preexisting problems or fulfill unmet demands. Researchers and innovators engage in lengthy brainstorming sessions, market research, and feasibility studies throughout this phase of the process. This phase aims to find gaps in the existing technological environment and uncover opportunities for improvement. They immerse themselves in scientific literature, work closely with specialists in various sectors, and investigate cutting-edge technology to get new perspectives and ideas for their discoveries.

The process of development starts as soon as a concept that has potential has been found. During this step, the notion will be translated from its abstract form into a tangible prototype or proof of concept. Engineers, designers, and developers work together to improve the concept by refining it using various materials, technologies, and methods to bring it to life. There was significant experimentation and iteration during the time of invention and development. Several prototypes are developed and put through their paces, and the results of these processes are incorporated into subsequent product iterations. The viewpoints of potential customers and other stakeholders are solicited and considered while developing the structure and operation of the product or service in question.

Additionally, a large amount of capital needs to be invested in research and development (R&D) endeavors during this phase. To support the investigation and improvement of new ideas, funding can be gained through various ways, such as grants from the government, venture capital, or corporate investments. Because they understand how vital it is to maintain a leadership position within their respective industries, research institutions, newly founded businesses, and long-standing corporations actively participate in this phase.

The era of innovation and development is naturally fraught with peril because only some concepts will ultimately prove profitable or sustainable in the market. However, groundbreaking inventions can only be developed by taking risks and participating in experimental activities. Failures and other setbacks are seen as learning opportunities, which drive further iteration and progress. If an innovation is successful, it will advance to succeeding phases of the technology life cycle, such as introduction, growth, maturity, and eventually decline. The initial phase of the technology life cycle is called the emergence phase. The later phases include market penetration, scaling, and ongoing improvement. However, the phase of innovation and development determines the course that the entire life cycle will follow.

1.2.2 Introduction and Early Adoption

A technology's numerous stages can be broken down into distinct stages collectively called a technology's "life cycle." These stages can range from the technology's inception through its widespread adoption to its eventual demise. The second stage of the life cycle of a technology is referred to as the Introduction and Early Adoption stage. Technology has progressed to this stage when it has completed the earlier stages of its development and is currently being released into the market. During the Introduction and Early Adoption phase, the technology is often only accessible to a small subset of early adopters. These early adopters are prepared to take a chance on new and developing technologies. Early adopters are typically those with a significant interest in being on the cutting edge of technical breakthroughs, such as technology enthusiasts, professionals working in the field, or people working in related fields.

Gaining initial traction in the market and generating excitement about the technology are the primary goals of this process phase. Businesses often invest in marketing and promotional activities to increase brand awareness and entice early adopters. They might also form partnerships with people with much power in their sector or with industry experts to generate a positive perception among potential users and promote the technology. Building credibility and trust in the technology is one of the primary hurdles that need to be overcome at this phase. Potential users might be wary of its dependability, security, or practicality because it is still in its infancy and is yet to be well-tested. Companies have a responsibility to address these concerns by engaging in open and honest communication, presenting evidence of the efficiency of the technology, and providing guarantees or warranties to reduce risk.

The early adopters significantly impact the future direction the technology will go. They provide helpful input, report problems, and make suggestions for changes, all of which assist the companies in refining the technology and addressing any deficiencies. This recurrent feedback loop is critical to the development of the technology, which will allow it to mature and become more robust and user-friendly. As the technology acquires traction and demonstrates its worth, it shifts from the market for early adopters to a market that caters to a more general audience. This change signifies the beginning of the subsequent phase in the technology life cycle, which is referred to as the growth and maturation stage. During this stage, the technology will become easier to obtain, more economical, and more user-friendly, leading to increased adoption by mainstream consumers and enterprises.

1.2.3 Growth and Expansion

The next phase in the life cycle of technology is focused on growth and expansion. It refers to a period during which a certain product or technology is experiencing rapid development, greater adoption, and expanded market penetration. During this stage, the technology goes through a period in which it experiences considerable advances, universal acceptance, and a rise in demand. As a result, businesses already functioning in this field have substantial prospects for expansion. The rising number of consumers or users who accept the technology is fundamental to the growth and expansion phase. This phase follows the maturation phase. More people and companies will become interested in employing the technology as it becomes more well-known and exhibits its usefulness. This will allow them to improve their operations, increase productivity, or solve certain problems. The expansion of its customer base is fueling the expansion of the technology's commercial reach. In addition, while the business is growing and expanding, business owners and entrepreneurs invest significant money into R&D to improve and perfect the technology. They try to overcome constraints, enhance functionality, and maximize performance to cater to their clientele's ever-evolving requirements. This dedication to innovation contributes to consolidating the technology's position in the market and its advantage over other competitors.

During the growth and expansion phase, there is typically an increase in the level of competition since more competitors enter the market after realizing the potential of the technology. Established businesses risk being challenged by new startups or existing competitors trying to secure a larger portion of the expanding market. This competition encourages more innovation as businesses seek to separate themselves from one another by providing distinctive features, superior customer assistance, or lower prices. Another feature of this phase is the increased investment in resources and infrastructure to meet the ever-increasing demand for the product or service. For businesses to keep up with the ever-increasing demands of the market and the expectations of their customers, they will need to ramp up their operations, increase their manufacturing capacity, invest in marketing and distribution channels, and form strategic partnerships or alliances. Companies that are successful in this phase can successfully manage their resources, adjust their business models, and form strategic relationships to utilize synergies and keep a competitive edge.

For businesses functioning in the technology industry, a large amount of financial success can be achieved during the growth and expansion period if the phase is managed effectively. When technology is successful, it may see exponential revenue growth, increasing market share, and enhanced profitability. The ability to capitalize on this phase is frequently contingent on elements such as the timing of the market, efficient marketing and sales techniques, powerful leadership, and in-depth familiarity with customers' requirements. It is essential to emphasize that the growth and expansion phase will continue. The technology may enter the following phase of its life cycle, known as maturity or consolidation; as time passes, the technology will mature and the market will get saturated. During this phase, the growth rate will begin to slow down, market saturation will develop, and the focus will move toward retaining market share, improving efficiency, and exploring new avenues for innovation.

1.2.4 Maturity and Saturation

The terms "maturity" and "saturation" denote two distinct phases that a product or technology must pass through to progress and achieve widespread adoption in the context of the technological life cycle. Let us discuss these phases in more detail.

(A) **Maturity Phase**: After a product or technology has made it through the initial stages of introduction and growth without any major setbacks, the next phase is known as maturity. While this phase is taking place, the market will become more stable and the product's growth rate will plateau. The mature stage is characterized by several significant qualities, including:

- *Market Acceptance*: The product has garnered universal approval and is utilized by a sizeable proportion of the target audience. A bigger group of customers has joined the early adopters and enthusiasts already using the product.
- *Slowing Growth*: Compared to the tremendous growth seen during the introduction and growth stages, the pace of growth starts to slow down during the maintenance period. When this happens, so many people are interested in purchasing something that the market is considered saturated.
- *Competition*: As more businesses enter the market selling products or services that are comparable to those already available, there will be an increase in the level of competition. In order to preserve their market share, businesses concentrate on developing differentiated products and setting competitive prices.
- *Market Saturation*: The market is getting close to becoming saturated, indicating that most people who might buy the product have already purchased it. Replacements and improvements are the primary drivers of any further expansion.
- *Maturity of Technology*: The technology that underpins the product reaches a point of stability, resulting in more incremental improvements than major technological breakthroughs. R&D activities focus on improving existing capabilities and responding to customer comments and suggestions.
- *Consolidation*: Consolidating their position and gaining an advantage over their competitors can be accomplished by forming partnerships, mergers, or acquisitions by the respective companies. Because of the severe competition, some of the market's smaller participants might leave.

(B) **Saturation Phase**: The saturation phase is a subset of the maturity phase and denotes the point at which the market is completely saturated with offerings from all available suppliers. The following are some of the characteristics of this stage:

- *Market Plateau*: When this happens, there is a return to equilibrium in the market, and the number of new customers is either minimal or extremely low. The product has reached a point where many people use it, and future expansion will be difficult.
- *Replacement or Upgrade Focus*: Replacements and upgrades are the key contributors to revenue since existing customers constantly look for newer product iterations or alternate options. Companies place a strong emphasis on maintaining loyal customers.
- *Limited Innovation*: The rate of innovation within a product category tends to slow down due to businesses concentrating more on making incremental changes and keeping their existing customer base than on offering revolutionary new features.
- *Pricing Pressure*: Pricing pressures could result from intense rivalry and a lack of meaningful product differentiation. Businesses may provide price discounts or special deals to persuade clients to upgrade their services or switch to their products.

- *Market Decline*: It is possible for an already saturated market to see a fall as a result of the introduction of a new disruptive technology or rival product. Customers may change their preferences, and businesses that cannot adapt may have their sales decrease as a result.

1.2.5 Decline and Obsolescence

The decline and obsolescence phases of the life cycle of technology are both very important. Products and services inevitably reach a point where they are rendered obsolete, less desirable, or perhaps irrelevant due to the rapid pace of technological advancement. In the traditional progression of the technological life cycle, the decline and obsolescence phase comes right after the maturity period. During the decline phase, several variables contribute to the decreasing popularity of technology, resulting in fewer sales. The introduction of newer, technologically advanced alternatives is one key factor. Technological breakthroughs typically attract customers away from outdated technologies since these advancements typically bring higher features, improved performance, and increased user experiences.

Consequently, the demand for antiquated goods and services continues to fall. Alterations in consumers' tastes are yet another aspect that contributes to the decline phase. People's needs and aspirations shift along with the development of society. As a result, they look for novel solutions compatible with the alterations in their way of life and the requirements they face. This change in preferences might make older technologies less appealing, which can contribute to the downfall of those technologies.

In addition, the rapid pace of technological progress has the potential to hasten the onset of the decline phase. When paradigms evolve, or disruptive breakthroughs are introduced, certain technologies might be obsolete relatively quickly. For instance, the launch of smartphones brought about a revolution in the mobile sector and rendered traditional feature phones irrelevant in a relatively short time. When technology reaches the obsolescence phase, it has reached the point where it is no longer useful to consumers or generally backed by businesses. Due to the low level of demand or profitability, producers and developers have reached this point where they have decided to stop producing or supporting the technology. Customers who continue to utilize outdated technology may need help locating appropriate accessories, maintaining an up-to-date software suite, or obtaining adequate technical assistance.

There are a few different types of obsolescence, the most common of which are functional and economic obsolescence. Functional obsolescence is when technology becomes less useful or inefficient compared to recent alternatives. Economic obsolescence is when the expense of maintaining or upgrading the technology surpasses its benefits. On the other hand, it is essential to remember that one technology's decline and eventual obsolescence typically clear the path for the development and widespread use of newer, more cutting-edge technologies. The life cycle of technology is an ongoing process driven by innovation and the ever-changing requirements of consumers. In order to adapt and maintain their competitive edge, businesses and individuals alike need to be aware of the warning signals of deterioration and obsolescence. This can involve diversifying the products and services offered, investing in R&D, or switching to more recent technologies. By understanding the technology life cycle, businesses may improve their ability to make educated decisions and maintain relevance in the rapidly evolving technological context.

For the following reasons, people, corporations, and society need to comprehend how technology is evolving (Figure 1.3).

Strategic Planning

By understanding how technology evolves, businesses can develop effective strategies to adapt and stay competitive. They can anticipate trends, identify emerging technologies, and make informed investments, partnerships, and product development decisions.

Innovation and Research

Knowledge of technology evolution helps researchers and innovators identify gaps and areas for improvement. It allows them to build upon existing technologies and push the boundaries of innovation, leading to the development of new products and services.

Market Opportunities

Recognizing the trajectory of technology enables businesses to identify potential market opportunities. They can spot emerging trends and consumer demands, allowing them to enter new markets or create disruptive products that meet evolving customer needs.

Risk Mitigation

Technology evolution is often accompanied by risks and challenges. By understanding the life cycle of technologies, businesses can assess potential risks and plan mitigation strategies. They can adapt their business models, diversify their offerings, or invest in alternative technologies to minimize the impact of disruptive changes.

Consumer Adoption

Understanding how technology evolves helps individuals and consumers make informed decisions. It allows them to assess the value, risks, and long-term viability of adopting a particular technology. This knowledge empowers consumers to choose wisely and avoid investing in technologies that may soon become obsolete.

FIGURE 1.3 Reasons for understanding the technology is evolving.

1.3 DEFINING DIGITAL TRANSFORMATION: WHAT IT IS AND WHY IT MATTERS

Digital transformation has evolved as a critical idea that firms across many sectors need to adopt in order to be competitive and relevant in today's quickly changing technology landscape. This introduction will define digital transformation and emphasize the significance and relevance of it in the modern world. Employing digital technology to alter how businesses function fundamentally, provide value to customers, and accomplish their business goals is known as "digital transformation." It entails utilizing digital tools, technology, and data-driven insights to optimize operations, generate innovation, and expedite procedures. In order to fully utilize digital breakthroughs, digital transformation involves more than just implementing new technology. It also involves thoroughly rethinking and restructuring organizational cultures, business models, and strategies.

In today's world, digital transformation is essential for improving consumer experiences. By utilizing digital technologies, organizations may provide their customers with individualized, smooth, and practical experiences. Digital transformation enables organizations to meet the growing expectations and demands of digitally enabled customers, from online buying and mobile banking to personalized suggestions and real-time support. Increasing operational efficiency is an additional important component of digital transformation. Organizations can improve resource allocation, streamline operations, and decrease manual errors by integrating digital tools and automation into their processes. Organizations may increase their levels of productivity and efficiency thanks to digital transformation, which affects everything from inventory and supply chain management to data analysis and reporting.

Agility and innovation are crucial for staying one step ahead of the competition in a fast-paced, dynamic corporate environment. Organizations may experiment with new ideas, respond rapidly to market developments, and promote a culture of ongoing innovation thanks to digital transformation. Businesses can use it to spot new trends, grasp chances, and adjust their plans as necessary. Making decisions based on data is a crucial aspect of the digital revolution. Organizations have access to enormous amounts of data in the digital age. Making data-driven insights and sophisticated analytics-based business decisions are key components of digital transformation. Organizations can make strategic decisions that promote growth and profitability by utilizing the insights they can acquire from data on customer behavior, market trends, and operational efficiency. Organizations need to undergo a digital transformation to be competitive; it is no longer a choice. Businesses that successfully adopt digital transformation can outperform their more established competitors. It enables businesses to explore new markets, challenge established ones, and develop cutting-edge goods and services that meet changing consumer demands.

A thorough and diverse process called "digital transformation" allows firms to radically use digital technologies to alter their company operations, procedures, and strategy. Technology integration, process improvement, data-driven decision-making, customer focus, and change management are all part of this strategy approach. Let us examine the essential features and parts of the digital revolution:

- *Technology adoption and integration*: One of the fundamental aspects of digital transformation is adopting and integrating advanced technologies into existing business operations. This includes technologies such as cloud computing, AI, ML, IoT, big data analytics, and automation tools. The successful implementation of these technologies enables organizations to streamline processes, improve efficiency, and gain a competitive edge.
- *Process optimization and automation*: Digital transformation involves optimizing and automating existing business processes to eliminate inefficiencies and reduce human error. Organizations can automate repetitive and manual tasks by leveraging technologies like robotic process automation (RPA), allowing employees to focus on more strategic and value-added activities. Process optimization also involves reimagining workflows and reengineering processes to leverage the full potential of digital technologies.
- *Data-driven decision-making*: Data plays a pivotal role in digital transformation. Organizations need to collect, analyze, and derive insights from vast amounts of data generated by various sources. This requires implementing robust data analytics tools and techniques to make informed decisions. By harnessing the power of data, organizations can identify patterns, trends, and customer preferences, enabling them to optimize operations, personalize experiences, and identify new business opportunities.
- *Customer-centricity and user experience*: Digital transformation puts the customer at the center of the organization's strategy. It involves understanding customer needs, preferences, and behaviors to deliver personalized experiences and build strong relationships. By leveraging digital channels and technologies, organizations can engage with customers at every touchpoint, provide seamless interactions, and create differentiated experiences. This includes developing user-friendly interfaces, intuitive mobile applications, and omnichannel experiences to enhance customer satisfaction and loyalty.
- *Organizational culture and change management*: Digital transformation requires a shift in organizational culture and mindset. It involves embracing a culture of innovation, agility, and continuous learning. Change management is critical in guiding employees through the transformation journey, ensuring their readiness and acceptance. Effective change management strategies involve strong leadership, clear communication, employee training, and a supportive environment for experimentation and risk-taking.

Together, these essential features and factors of digital transformation promote creativity, drive corporate growth, and increase operational effectiveness in today's fast-paced and technologically-driven corporate landscape; organizations that effectively navigate the digital transformation journey position themselves for long-term success.

1.3.1 Why Digital Transformation Matters

Organizations need to go through the digital transformation process to fully harness the potential of technology and revolutionize their business models, operations, and customer experiences. Businesses need to adapt and embrace digital transformation in order to stay competitive and relevant in today's quickly changing digital landscape. Here are some main arguments in favor of digital transformation:

- *Enhanced Efficiency and Productivity*: Digital transformation enables businesses to streamline their processes and automate manual tasks, improving operational efficiency and increasing productivity. By implementing digital tools and technologies, organizations can eliminate redundant and time-consuming tasks, optimize workflows, and empower employees to focus on high-value activities.
- *Improved Customer Experience*: Digital transformation allows businesses to understand better and meet customers' evolving needs and expectations. By leveraging digital channels and data-driven insights, organizations can personalize customer interactions, deliver seamless experiences across various touchpoints, and provide faster and more convenient services. This enhanced customer experience leads to higher customer satisfaction, loyalty, and, ultimately, increased revenue.
- *Data-Driven Decision-Making*: Digital transformation enables organizations to collect, analyze, and derive valuable insights from vast amounts of data. Leveraging advanced analytics and BI tools allows businesses to make data-driven decisions, identify emerging trends, and uncover new growth opportunities. This data-driven approach helps organizations stay ahead of the competition and respond quickly to market changes.
- *Agility and Innovation*: Digital transformation fosters a culture of agility and innovation within organizations. By embracing digital technologies, businesses can adapt to market dynamics, rapidly prototype and launch new products or services, and experiment with innovative business models. This flexibility allows organizations to stay relevant in a fast-paced digital world and seize emerging opportunities.
- *Cost Optimization*: Digital transformation often leads to cost optimization by eliminating manual processes, reducing paperwork, and streamlining operations. By digitizing and automating various functions, organizations can achieve significant cost savings in time, resources, and infrastructure. Cloud-based solutions and virtualization also enable businesses to scale their operations efficiently and reduce capital expenditures.
- *Competitive Advantage*: Digital transformation can provide a significant competitive advantage to organizations. By embracing digital technologies strategically, businesses can differentiate themselves in the market, create unique value propositions, and disrupt traditional industry norms. Organizations that successfully undergo digital transformation are better positioned to adapt to evolving customer demands, outpace their competitors, and drive sustainable growth.

The widespread phenomenon of digital transformation has revolutionized business operations and customer interactions across various industries and sectors. Rapid technological development has paved the way for digital innovations, presenting new opportunities and challenges for businesses worldwide. Here, we will examine how the digital revolution has affected various industries and sectors.

- *Retail and E-commerce*: The retail industry has experienced a significant shift with the rise of e-commerce platforms. Digital transformation has enabled retailers to reach a global audience, personalize customer experiences, and provide seamless online shopping options. Brick-and-mortar stores have also embraced digital technologies by incorporating features like mobile payment systems, AR for virtual try-ons, and personalized recommendations based on customer data.
- *Healthcare*: Digital transformation has had a profound impact on the healthcare industry, enhancing patient care, diagnosis, and treatment processes. Electronic health records (EHRs) have replaced paper-based systems, improving the accessibility and security of patient data. Telemedicine has gained popularity, allowing patients to consult with healthcare professionals remotely. Advanced technologies such as AI, ML, and wearable devices have facilitated early disease detection, personalized treatment plans, and remote patient monitoring.
- *Banking and Finance*: The financial sector has witnessed significant changes due to digital transformation. Traditional banking processes have been digitized, allowing customers to perform transactions, manage accounts, and access financial services online. Fintech companies have emerged, offering innovative solutions such as mobile banking apps, peer-to-peer lending platforms, and robo-advisors. Blockchain technology has also disrupted the industry, enabling secure and transparent transactions, reducing fraud, and enhancing efficiency.
- *Manufacturing*: Digital transformation has led to the concept of Industry 4.0, characterized by automation, connectivity, and data exchange in manufacturing processes. IoT devices and sensors collect real-time data, optimizing production and supply chain management. Smart factories leverage robotics, AI, and big data analytics to improve productivity, reduce costs, and enable predictive maintenance. 3D printing and additive manufacturing have revolutionized prototyping and production, allowing for customization and faster time-to-market.
- *Education*: The education sector has embraced digital transformation to enhance learning experiences and expand access to education. Online learning platforms, virtual classrooms, and educational apps have made education more flexible, enabling self-paced learning and remote education. Digital tools facilitate interactive and personalized learning, adaptive assessments, and real-time feedback. Moreover, data analytics help educators monitor student progress and tailor teaching strategies accordingly.
- *Transportation and Logistics*: Digital transformation has revolutionized the transportation and logistics industry, streamlining operations and improving efficiency. GPS and fleet management systems optimize routes, reduce fuel

consumption, and enhance delivery tracking. E-commerce has created a surge in demand for last-mile delivery services, prompting the use of drones and autonomous vehicles. Blockchain technology is being explored for secure and transparent supply chain management, reducing fraud and counterfeiting.

* *Media and Entertainment*: The media and entertainment industry has experienced a seismic shift with the advent of digital transformation. Traditional media outlets have adapted to digital platforms, offering online streaming services, digital publications, and social media engagement. User-generated content and social sharing have become integral to entertainment consumption. AI and big data analytics are employed to personalize content recommendations and target advertising more effectively.

1.3.2 Key Drivers of Digital Transformation

"Digital transformation" describes how digital technologies are integrated into every part of an organization, profoundly altering how it functions and provides value to customers. Organizations are being compelled to launch digital transformation initiatives by several important factors. These factors influence how firms adapt to the digital age and maintain their competitiveness in a continually changing market. Following are some of the main forces for digital transformation:

* *Technological Advancements*: Rapid technological advancements, such as AI, ML, cloud computing, big data analytics, and the IoT, are major drivers of digital transformation. These technologies provide new opportunities for businesses to optimize processes, improve efficiency, and enhance customer experiences.
* *Changing Customer Expectations*: Today's customers have higher expectations regarding digital experiences. They demand personalized, seamless, and convenient interactions across multiple channels. To meet these expectations, businesses need to transform their operations and adopt digital strategies that enable them to engage with customers effectively and deliver exceptional experiences.
* *Competitive Pressure*: The digital landscape has leveled the playing field for businesses of all sizes. Startups and digital-native companies are disrupting traditional industries, forcing established organizations to rethink their strategies. To remain competitive, businesses need to embrace digital transformation to innovate, differentiate themselves, and stay relevant in the market.
* *Evolving Business Models*: Digital transformation enables businesses to explore new business models and revenue streams. Companies can leverage digital technologies to create innovative products and services, develop new distribution channels, and explore alternative monetization strategies. Organizations that fail to adapt may be disadvantaged as competitors seize these opportunities.
* *Data-Driven Insights*: Data has become a strategic asset for businesses. Digital transformation allows organizations to collect, analyze, and leverage vast amounts of data to gain actionable insights. By harnessing data,

businesses can make more informed decisions, identify trends and patterns, and optimize operations, ultimately driving growth and profitability.

- *Operational Efficiency*: Digital technologies streamline and automate business processes, increasing efficiency and productivity. By digitizing workflows, eliminating manual tasks, and implementing intelligent automation, organizations can reduce costs, improve operational speed, and enhance overall efficiency.
- *Regulatory and Compliance Requirements*: Changing regulations and compliance requirements have become a significant driver of digital transformation, particularly in industries such as finance, healthcare, and data privacy. Organizations need to adopt digital solutions and processes that ensure compliance while maintaining data security and privacy.
- *Employee Expectations*: Digital transformation impacts not only customers but also employees. Today's workforce expects a digital work environment that enables collaboration, flexibility, and access to the latest tools and technologies. Organizations prioritizing digital transformation are better positioned to attract and retain top talent and foster a culture of innovation.

1.4 DOMAINS OF DIGITAL TRANSFORMATION: UNDERSTANDING THE KEY AREAS OF CHANGE

A holistic approach, digital transformation involves many different organizational domains. It is part of utilizing digital technologies to boost consumer experiences, streamline corporate processes, and spur innovation. Understanding the critical areas of change or domains where digital transformation can significantly influence is essential for navigating the digital landscape effectively. Looking at five crucial domains of strategy, you can see how digital forces are changing them: Consumers, competition, data, innovation, and value (Figure 1.4). The environment of digital transformation for business today can be characterized by these five domains. Digital technologies are reinventing many fundamental strategies and guidelines businesses need to follow to flourish across these five domains. New opportunities are now open to us because many previous restrictions have been removed. Businesses founded before the Internet need to understand that many of their underlying presumptions now need to be changed.

1.4.1 Customer

Focusing on the customer is one of the main drivers of digital transformation across all industries and businesses. Businesses are realizing that it is critical to put the customer at the center of the operational strategies they use in today's constantly evolving digital landscape. This customer-centered approach enables organizations to more fully comprehend

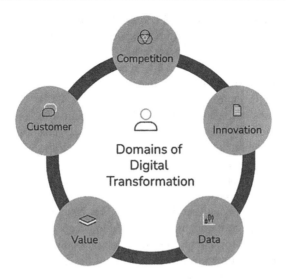

FIGURE 1.4 Domains of digital transformation.

and satisfy the needs of their target market, which in turn promotes growth, client loyalty, and profitability. A crucial part of digital transformation in customer experience is the use of technology and data to create seamless, customized, and engaging interactions throughout the customer journey. This covers a variety of touchpoints, including marketing, sales, customer support, and after-sale services. Businesses may gain important insights into their customers' behavior, preferences, and pain areas by utilizing digital tools and platforms. This makes it possible for businesses to build long-lasting relationships with clients by offering them experiences tailored to their requirements.

One of the key drivers of digital transformation in customer experience is the abundance of data generated due to interactions between customers and digital channels. By gathering, examining, and using this information, it is possible to gain a deeper understanding of the needs and preferences of customers. Businesses can use AI and ML algorithms to identify patterns and trends, predict customer behavior, and make personalized recommendations and offers. Additionally, digital transformation enables firms to create omnichannel experiences by seamlessly integrating various channels. Some of these outlets are websites, mobile apps, social networking platforms, and actual stores. Customers may interact with a brand through the channel of their choice, and no matter whatever touchpoint they select, they will always have a uniform and unified experience. This seamless connection makes customers' lives simpler, which boosts their pleasure and deepens their loyalty to the brand.

As a result of the digital transformation, customers may now access information, independently resolve issues, and independently make purchases. This further empowers businesses to take advantage of automation and self-service options. Digital tools that can answer frequent queries and offer quick support include chatbots, virtual assistants, and knowledge bases. Human agents are thus freed up to concentrate on more intricate customer demands. This automation increases productivity and ensures that customers will always receive accurate and timely help.

Additionally, including customer feedback mechanisms like surveys, ratings, and reviews is made simpler by digital transformation. Real-time feedback enables organizations to gain direct customer insights, which helps these businesses pinpoint areas where they can improve and make data-driven decisions. If businesses actively listen to the suggestions made by their customers, they will be able to continuously enhance their goods, services, and the entire customer experience.

Other interactions in the customer domain can benefit from digital transformation in addition to "business-to-consumer" (B2C) contacts. B2B (business-to-business) companies can gain by embracing a customer-centric approach to their operations as they work to meet the always-changing needs of their corporate clients. By utilizing digital tools and platforms, companies that sell to other companies can increase the effectiveness of their order management procedures, create customer-facing self-service portals, and offer specialized pricing and service bundles. For the consumer domain to undergo meaningful digital transformation, more is needed to accept digital tools and platforms merely. Businesses need to undergo an organizational culture change that embeds a customer-centric mindset throughout every aspect of the firm. In order to achieve this, procedures, tactics, and technology need to be coordinated such that they center on the needs, desires, and expectations of the customer.

A key element of the digital transformation happening in the customer sector is the concept of personalization. In today's environment, customers have grown to demand tailored experiences that respond to their interests and requirements. Organizations can get insights and create consumer profiles by using sophisticated data analytics and customer segmentation strategies. These methods provide tailored product offerings, focused marketing efforts, and personalized advice. Personalization not only promotes customer satisfaction but also client loyalty and customer advocacy. Integrating social media and online communities is another crucial element of digital transformation in the consumer arena. Thanks to the growth of social media platforms, customers now have a potent new platform to share their experiences, interact with brands, and voice their opinions. Social media is used by businesses embracing digital transformation to actively engage in conversations with their customers, respond to their questions and concerns, and listen to what they have to say. By creating a strong online presence and engaging in fruitful interactions with their customers, businesses may increase customer loyalty, enhance brand reputation, and foster trust in their company.

Additionally, digital transformation enables companies to take advantage of emerging technologies like AR and VR, enhancing the overall quality of the client experience. For instance, stores can offer customers the chance to virtually try items before buying them. Customers now get a chance to see how the products will appear on them. Similarly, real estate companies might provide virtual home tours so potential buyers can look at available homes from a distance. Businesses may bridge the gap between the physical and digital worlds by utilizing these immersive technologies, which enables them to offer clients unique and captivating experiences.

Digital change in the customer service sector further emphasizes giving clients a real-time response. Customers now expect quick and efficient service, and businesses can now meet these expectations thanks to digital tools. For instance, live chat support enables users to speak with customer service representatives right away and get answers to any queries they may have in real time. Additionally, organizations can utilize predictive analytics and ML algorithms to foresee client needs and proactively address any potential problems to resolve them before they arise. Real-time customer service increases consumers' satisfaction, builds their faith in the organization, and increases the likelihood of returning for more services. The extent of the digital revolution in the consumer space goes far beyond solitary transactions, to name just one such point. It emphasizes the creation of long-term partnerships and encompasses the whole client lifecycle. Firms can use customer relationship management (CRM) systems and marketing automation tools to successfully manage and grow their connections with clients. These technologies let firms manage customer data, track customer contacts, and send targeted communications to clients at different stages of their customer journeys. By forming intimate bonds with people and regularly providing them with pleasant experiences, businesses may turn customers into brand ambassadors who spread the word about their goods and services to others.

1.4.2 Competition

Any successful commercial setting requires the existence of strong competition. As businesses seek to preserve a competitive advantage in a constantly changing and evolving digital environment, rivalry has taken on a new dimension in this digital transformation era. Companies now compete to use technology and innovation to gain a competitive advantage in the digital transformation sector, which has grown into a war zone. Examples of how digital transformation has profoundly changed how businesses compete include the dissolution of traditional industry borders, redefining customer expectations, and facilitating new business models. It uses various technologies, including automation, cloud computing, the IoT, big data analytics, robotics, and AI. These technologies provide businesses with previously unheard-of opportunities to reinvent their goods and services, enhance business operations, and enhance consumer experiences.

The level of competition is fierce and merciless in digital transformation. Organizations need to evaluate the market regularly, spot emerging trends, and quickly adjust to stay relevant in their business. Firms that need help to keep up with these changes risk falling behind in the rapidly changing digital landscape. Therefore, to take a proactive approach against the threat of competition, organizations need to adopt a culture of ongoing learning, experimentation, and innovation. The importance given to the customer experience is a crucial element of effective competition in digital transformation. As a direct result of the expansion of digital channels and the volume of data, businesses now have access to crucial information regarding their customers' preferences, behaviors, and needs. Successful companies use this data to tailor their product and service offerings, carry out laser-focused marketing campaigns, and create outstanding client experiences. When businesses put the customer at the center of their digital operations, they may stand out from their rivals and gain sustainable competitive advantages.

Another essential component for succeeding in the digital transformation market is agility. Thanks to digital technologies, businesses can now respond to changes in the market and client demands more swiftly. Compared to their rivals that move more slowly in their respective industries, businesses that can quickly modify their processes, products, and business strategies enjoy a significant competitive edge. An agile organization needs to have a flexible organizational structure, use agile project management techniques, and be open to experimentation and iteration. Additionally, collaboration and partnership both play a significant part in the competition that occurs within the field of digital transformation. A single business cannot possess the information and assets required to succeed in every area of digital transformation. Companies work with technology partners, startups, and other industry players; they may expedite innovation, use complementary skills and abilities, and broaden their reach. When businesses form strategic alliances with one another, they can combine their resources and create synergies that enhance their competitive position.

The level of competitiveness in digital transformation is currently at an all-time high. With the introduction of digital technology, the playing field has been leveled, enabling even start-up companies to compete successfully with mature market leaders. Disruption is a recurring threat because ingenious newcomers outfitted with disruptive technologies and adaptable business strategies can quickly seize market domination. This dynamic has forced established organizations to reconsider their strategies and adopt digital transformation to preserve their competitive advantage. One of the main elements raising the level of competition in digital transformation is the concept of digital innovation. Organizations are pressured to innovate and provide cutting-edge digital solutions that address customer pain points and provide unique value propositions. This innovation extends beyond just the company's goods and services to business operations, operational effectiveness, and customer experience. Businesses using digital technology to provide innovative solutions have a substantial competitive advantage in the market.

Additionally, the growth of digital platforms has fundamentally changed the competitive landscape. Platforms have developed into potent intermediaries that link customers to other players in the digital ecosystem, such as goods, services, and other platforms. These platforms, which include social media platforms, app stores, and e-commerce marketplaces, have created new channels for businesses to interact with customers and vie for their attention. Businesses that can use these platforms can reach vast clientele and rapidly solidify their place in the market. Data has also become a key resource in the competition surrounding digital transformation. Large volumes of data can now be collected and analyzed by businesses, giving them new insights into consumer behavior, industry trends, and the efficiency of their operations. Businesses' capacity to use analytics and ML to enhance current tactics, customize consumer experiences, and identify new development opportunities has made using data to inform decisions essential to survive in today's fiercely competitive corporate climate. Utilizing data effectively has become one of the key differentiators in the field of digital technology.

Additionally, the pace of digital transformation has become a key element in the landscape of competition. One aspect that can affect a company's level of success is its capacity to adopt and integrate new technologies into its ongoing operations quickly. Companies that can quickly adapt to changing trends and implement innovative solutions have an advantage over rivals. Therefore, you need to foster a culture of adaptability and be willing to accept change. Businesses that put off or delay their digital transformation risk losing ground to more nimble rivals. Remembering that many different companies and organizations are competing in digital transformation is crucial. Companies need to be able to function within these broader contexts since digital disruption affects not only specific enterprises but also entire ecosystems. Collaboration and establishing partnerships are now crucial elements of every effective plan. If organizations work with businesses that complement one another, they can create synergies, pool resources, and accelerate innovation. Through the creation of strategic alliances with technology suppliers, startups, and other players in the industry, businesses can acquire specialized expertise and gain a competitive advantage.

1.4.3 Data

Data is crucial in digital transformation because it gives organizations the foundation to innovate, optimize operations, and make informed decisions. Data is the engine that powers the digital transformation process, enabling businesses to change their business models, operations, and consumer experiences. Data is the lifeblood that powers the entire digital transformation process. Gathering and aggregating data from many sources is one of the most crucial steps in the digital transformation process. The amount of data generated per second has increased due to the proliferation of connected devices, social media platforms, and online activities. This information, usually called "big data," consists of structured and unstructured data and can offer businesses priceless insights. If businesses are successful in capturing and integrating this data, they will be able to have a more thorough understanding of their operations, customers, and market trends.

However, the true value of data lies not just in its quantity but also in its quality and the ability to draw meaningful conclusions from it. The real worth of data can be discovered in this. Businesses need to leverage advanced analytics techniques like data mining, ML, and AI in order to acquire actionable insights. Organizations can use these technologies to find hidden data patterns, trends, and correlations. As a result, these technologies give firms crucial information that influences decision-making, enhances operations, and generates fresh business opportunities.

Additionally, the scope of data in digital transformation goes beyond the confines of the organization's internal data sources. Examples of external dataset businesses can use to extend their perspectives and strengthen their organizations' analytical capabilities include open data, industry benchmarks, and market research. Businesses can better understand customer behavior, market dynamics, and the competitive environment by combining data from internal and external sources. Thanks to this, they can sustain a competitive advantage in a constantly changing digital world.

Personalization and a focus on the customer are mostly driven by the data gathered in the context of the digital era. Businesses can gain profound insights into specific customers' preferences, actions, and needs by studying customer data. This enables the personalization of marketing initiatives, the creation of tailored product recommendations, and an improvement in the standard of the customer experience across a range of touchpoints. Data-driven personalization increases consumer satisfaction while bolstering customer loyalty and generating extra revenue. Effective data use is also essential for the growth of flexible and agile firms. Businesses can maintain a close check on their operations, monitor their key performance indicators (KPIs), and respond quickly to market changes using real-time data analytics. By employing data so that bottlenecks in processes can be found and removed and data-driven decisions can be made promptly, an organization can become more agile and better able to respond to changes in market dynamics.

Nevertheless, it is crucial to remember that the use of data in the context of digital transformation also poses challenges and risks. Organizations need to resolve privacy concerns, guarantee data security, and ensure that standards are followed to ensure the ethical and responsible use of data. Implementing data governance frameworks, data protection measures, and openness in data processes are essential for building trust with consumers and stakeholders. Organizations need to consider several crucial aspects when handling data in the context of digital transformation, in addition to any challenges and risks they may encounter:

- *Data Strategy*: Developing a comprehensive data strategy is essential for organizations to leverage data in their digital transformation efforts effectively. This strategy should encompass data governance, management, quality, and integration, among other aspects. It should align with the organization's overall business objectives and provide a roadmap for data-driven initiatives.
- *Data Infrastructure*: To handle the increasing volume, velocity, and variety of data, organizations need to invest in robust data infrastructure. This may involve adopting cloud-based storage and computing solutions, implementing data lakes or warehouses, and leveraging scalable data processing frameworks. A well-designed data infrastructure ensures data accessibility, availability, and security.
- *Data Talent and Skills*: Building a team with the right data skills is crucial for successful digital transformation. Data scientists, data engineers, and data analysts are some of the key roles organizations must fill. These professionals should understand data analytics techniques, statistical modeling, programming, and data visualization. Continuous training and upskilling programs should be implemented to keep the data team abreast of the latest advancements in the field.
- *Data Privacy and Security*: Protecting sensitive data and ensuring compliance with regulations such as the General Data Protection Regulation (GDPR) and the California Consumer Privacy Act (CCPA) is paramount. Organizations need to establish robust data privacy and security measures, including encryption, access controls, data anonymization, and regular audits. Transparency in data collection and usage practices is essential to maintain customer trust.
- *Data Collaboration*: Collaboration within and outside the organization is vital for maximizing the value of data. Data sharing and collaboration can foster innovation, drive industry-wide insights, and create new business models. Organizations can explore partnerships, data consortiums, and open data initiatives to tap into shared data resources and gain a broader perspective on industry trends and challenges.
- *Continuous Learning and Improvement*: As data and analytics evolve rapidly, organizations must foster a continuous learning and improvement culture. This involves regularly evaluating and updating data strategies, adopting emerging technologies and techniques, and learning from successes and failures. Organizations should embrace a data-driven mindset and encourage experimentation and innovation.

1.4.4 Innovation

Innovation is a crucial part of digital transformation and is important in driving businesses forward in the fast-evolving digital ecosystem of today. Businesses need to embrace innovation to maintain their competitive edge, seize new opportunities, and give their customers more value because technical advancement is occurring at a rate that has never been witnessed before. "Digital transformation" describes how an organization substantially changes how it operates and produces value by integrating digital technologies into every aspect of that business. It utilizes digital tools, data analytics, automation, AI, and other cutting-edge technologies to simplify operations, boost productivity, and promote growth.

Innovation is a change driver within the digital transformation framework, enabling companies to create new goods, services, and business models. To succeed, one needs to develop a culture of innovation and risk-taking, challenge conventional wisdom, and think creatively. Innovation in the context of digital transformation can take on various forms. It might entail the development of cutting-edge digital products, such as mobile applications, cloud-based platforms, or data-driven analytics systems, that enable companies to increase the effectiveness of their operations and offer tailored customer experiences. Disruptive technologies, another manifestation of innovation, have the power to alter several economic sectors completely. For instance, the emergence of blockchain technology, which has the potential to revolutionize industries like banking, supply chain management, and healthcare, and the proliferation of ride-sharing platforms, which caused a fundamental shift in the transportation sector, are both excellent examples.

Businesses need to foster an environment that encourages and fosters experimentation if they want to succeed in digital transformation. It might be essential to create dedicated innovation departments or labs, allocate funds for R&D, and promote cooperation among numerous groups and fields of study to achieve this goal. Businesses also need to adopt iterative processes, speed up prototyping, and adopt a more agile attitude in order to be innovative. As a result, they can quickly test ideas, gather feedback, and alter their solutions in light of new information learned from the actual world. Additionally, businesses should prioritize looking for chances to engage with outside innovators. This can entail joining industry ecosystems and innovation networks, collaborating with recently founded companies, or participating in open innovation projects. When businesses rely on the knowledge and various perspectives other sources provide, they can accelerate their innovation processes and stay one step ahead of the competition.

Innovation, as a facet of digital transformation, also includes "innovation at scale." It aims to establish an innovative culture throughout the company rather than focusing on isolated innovation centers within an organization. Businesses need to create a climate that encourages cross-departmental teamwork, collaboration, and information sharing if they want to grasp innovation's potential fully. Silos need to be dismantled to achieve this, and a culture where ideas can freely flow across departments and hierarchies needs to be established. Giving employees a chance to express their thoughts and insights enables businesses to draw from a wider pool of ideas and increases the likelihood of game-changing developments.

Additionally, implementing systems inside businesses that provide continuous learning and adaptation is necessary for innovation at scale. Potential moves in this direction include implementing feedback loops, performing routine evaluations, and basing decisions on data-driven insights. Organizations can swiftly identify what works and what does not by adopting a culture of learning and iteration, which helps them to refocus and alter their innovation initiatives. Organizations can interact more successfully when adopting a learning and iteration culture. In the context of digital transformation, "co-creation" is yet another aspect of innovation that may be investigated. This means collaborating with customers, business partners, and rivals to develop original answers to challenging issues. Co-creation allows companies to better understand their target audience's needs, increase product-market fit, and encourage customer-centric innovation.

Businesses also need to think about the ethical implications of any new digital technologies they use. As the usage of technology increases, worries about data privacy, security, and the possibility of algorithmic bias are becoming increasingly prominent. Integrating ethics and responsible innovation principles into the digital transformation process is essential for building trust with consumers, stakeholders, and society. In digital transformation, innovation is a process that unfolds throughout a journey rather than a singular occurrence. Enterprises must establish a mindset that values adaptation and agility to navigate the rapidly changing digital landscape successfully. If businesses keep an eye on emerging technology, industry trends, and customer wants, they can proactively discover opportunities for innovation and stay one step ahead of the competition.

1.4.5 Value

A key component of digital transformation is creating and delivering enhanced value propositions to customers, stakeholders, and the company as a whole. A crucial step in the digital transformation process is the value domain. In digital transformation, "value" refers to the advantages, benefits, and positive outcomes achieved via the thoughtful and effective application of digital technologies and technology. These can be achieved through overhauling an organization's operational procedures. One of the main goals of digital transformation is to use technology to create new value propositions or enhance existing ones. One method to achieve this goal is to reimagine business structures, procedures, products, and services to give customers more value. By embracing digital talents, which will enable them to find new sources of value, organizations may stand out in a market that is getting more competitive.

In the value domain, the process of digital transformation offers several opportunities. Through the use of data analytics and customer insights, it enables organizations to, first and foremost, gain a deeper understanding of the needs, preferences, and behaviors of customers. Due to their ability to adapt their offers and tailor their clients' experiences, businesses can eventually increase customer happiness and loyalty. Additionally, by implementing digital transformation, organizations may streamline their operations and boost productivity, eventually lowering operating expenses and boosting output. By optimizing processes, reducing bottlenecks, and allowing staff to focus on more crucial duties, automation, AI, and ML have the potential to improve workflows. This improves the efficiency of the company's internal operations and enables companies to provide their clients with faster and more dependable services.

Additionally, the digital revolution facilitates the development of fresh business strategies and revenue sources. Businesses can expand their consumer base, penetrate new markets, and offer cutting-edge goods and services to customers by utilizing digital platforms, e-commerce, and online marketplaces. Businesses leveraging digital channels and technologies can disrupt old markets and create entirely new value ecosystems. In digital transformation, stakeholders, or groups of people other than customers, are also involved in the value-creation process. Employees will benefit from improved collaboration tools, more remote work options, and educational opportunities, which can increase employee job satisfaction and retention rates. Value for partners and suppliers may increase due to greater integration, data exchange, and procedures. Greater partnerships and growth for both sides may follow from this.

However, meticulous preparation, strategic alignment, and a customer-focused mindset are necessary in order to appreciate the benefits given by digital transformation fully. Businesses need to prioritize investing in technologies that support their goals for creating value, and they also need to ensure that they have the infrastructure, know-how, and capabilities required to take advantage of digital tools fully. Additionally, the digital transformation process is an ongoing project requiring constant flexibility and adaptability. Businesses need to be at the forefront of innovation to preserve and enhance the value they offer while considering the reality that both technology and client expectations are always changing. This might entail accepting newly created technological forms, encouraging an environment where experimentation is welcomed, and having a mindset that stresses continuous improvement.

In digital transformation, value can be classified into different categories based on its nature and impact. Here are some common classifications of value:

- *Customer Value*: This category focuses on the value delivered to customers through digital transformation initiatives. It includes improved customer experiences, personalized offerings, faster response times, convenience, and enhanced product or service quality. Digital transformation enables organizations to understand better and meet customer needs, increasing satisfaction and loyalty.
- *Operational Value*: Operational value pertains to the internal benefits of digital transformation. It encompasses improved efficiency, streamlined processes, reduced costs, and increased productivity. By leveraging digital technologies, organizations can automate tasks, eliminate manual errors, optimize workflows, and make data-driven decisions, ultimately leading to operational excellence.
- *Strategic Value*: Strategic value refers to the broader impact of digital transformation on an organization's long-term goals and competitive position. It involves leveraging digital capabilities to drive innovation, enter new markets, and differentiate from competitors. Digital transformation enables

organizations to reimagine their business models, identify new growth opportunities, and position themselves as market leaders.

- *Financial Value*: Financial value focuses on the tangible financial benefits derived from digital transformation initiatives. This includes revenue growth, cost savings, increased profitability, and improved return on investment. By leveraging digital technologies effectively, organizations can drive revenue through new sales channels, pricing optimization, and targeted marketing while reducing costs through process efficiencies and resource optimization.
- *Social Value*: Social value encompasses the positive impact of digital transformation on society and communities. It includes digital inclusion, accessibility, sustainability, and social responsibility. Digital transformation can enable organizations to bridge the digital divide, create equal opportunities, reduce environmental impact, and contribute to social causes, thereby generating social value.

It is critical to remember that these classifications are not mutually exclusive and that firms may benefit from combining different classifications simultaneously. The company's objectives, the industry it works in, and the activities involved in digital transformation will all affect how value is precisely classified. When organizations have a solid understanding of the numerous dimensions of value in digital transformation and have categorized them appropriately, they can successfully plan, prioritize, and evaluate the results of their projects. This helps ensure a thorough approach to creating value, increasing the return on investment, and linking the transformation efforts with the strategic goals.

1.5 CONCLUSION

The Fourth Industrial Revolution, or Industry 4.0, signifies a transformative era marked by the seamless integration of digital technologies into various aspects of our lives. This revolution is reshaping industries, economies, and societies at an unprecedented pace. Key advancements such as connectivity and the IoT, AI and ML, big data and analytics, robotics and automation, blockchain technology, and cybersecurity are driving this revolution. The tech life cycle, encompassing stages of innovation, adoption, maturation, saturation, obsolescence, and replacement, illustrates the evolution of technology and the factors influencing its trajectory. Meanwhile, digital transformation has become imperative for organizations as it enables them to leverage digital technologies to drive fundamental changes in processes, strategies, and customer experiences. Embracing digital transformation is essential for businesses to thrive in the modern era and effectively navigate the ever-changing technological landscape. Table 1.1 summarizes the Fourth Industrial Revolution (Industry 4.0), the key advancements driving it, the tech life cycle, and the importance of digital transformation concisely and organized.

TABLE 1.1   Critical aspects of the Fourth Industrial Revolution and Digital Transformation

ASPECT	DESCRIPTION
Fourth Industrial Revolution (Industry 4.0)	The transformative era integrates digital technologies into various aspects of our lives.
Key Advancements	Connectivity, Internet of Things (IoT), artificial intelligence (AI) and machine learning, big data and analytics, robotics and automation, blockchain technology, and cybersecurity.
Tech Life Cycle	Stages: Innovation, adoption, maturation, saturation, obsolescence, and replacement.
Digital Transformation	Imperative for organizations to leverage digital technologies for fundamental changes in processes, strategies, and customer experiences.
Importance	Enables businesses to thrive in the modern era and navigate the ever-changing technological landscape.

REFERENCES

1. Majstorović, V.D., et al. Cyber-physical manufacturing in context of industry 4.0 model. In *Proceedings of 3rd International Conference on the Industry 4.0 Model for Advanced Manufacturing: AMP 2018 3*. 2018. Springer.
2. Porter, M.E. and J.E. Heppelmann, How smart, connected products are transforming companies. *Harvard Business Review*, 2015. **93**(10): pp. 96–114.
3. Manyika, J., et al., *A future that works: AI, automation, employment, and productivity*. McKinsey Global Institute Research, Technical Report, 2017. **60**: pp. 1–135.

2 Digital World Strategies

2.1 COMPETITIVE ADVANTAGE: USING TECHNOLOGY TO STAY AHEAD

A corporation is said to have a competitive advantage if it possesses unique qualities and abilities that enable it to outperform its competitors and achieve superior overall business performance. It is the primary factor that distinguishes a business in its industry and enables it to attract more customers, increase its market share, and increase its profitability. A competitive advantage can derive from a variety of sources, such as novel products or services, cost leadership, exceptional customer service, solid brand recognition, efficient supply chain management, proprietary technology, or similar factors. Businesses with a sustainable competitive advantage are better able to withstand market fluctuations, adapt to new circumstances, and remain one step ahead of competitors. Innovation is one of the most essential factors in gaining a competitive advantage. Customers are attracted to businesses that consistently differentiate themselves from competitors by developing new and superior products or services.

Companies can maintain a competitive advantage and remain ahead of the curve if they invest in R&D, cultivate a culture of creativity and experimentation, and monitor market trends. Innovation can result in enhanced product characteristics, enhanced quality, increased productivity, or the introduction of entirely new business models. All of these advantages are directly attributable to innovation. A further source of competitive advantage is the capability to command the industry in terms of costs. If a business is able to effectively manage its expenses and operate more efficiently than its competitors, it can sell its products or provide its services at a discount while still generating a profit. The economies of scale, the optimization of processes, the effective management of supply chains, and the implementation of innovative cost-cutting strategies are all methods for achieving cost benefits. Lower prices attract price-sensitive customers, thereby increasing market share and possibly discouraging new competitors from entering the market. Superior customer service can also provide a competitive advantage.

Businesses can cultivate loyal customer bases and encourage repeat purchases if they consistently provide exceptional customer experiences and work diligently to develop close relationships with their clients. Understanding a customer's requirements, quickly resolving their concerns or problems, providing unique solutions, and going

DOI: 10.1201/9781003471226-3

above and beyond the call of duty are all essential components of delivering excellent customer service. When customers have positive interactions with a business, it can lead to positive word-of-mouth, customer referrals, and a solid brand reputation; all of these factors contribute to a sustainable competitive advantage. A strong brand reputation can be a significant source of competitive advantage. Even in incredibly competitive markets, brands that are trusted, respected, and recognized for their quality, dependability, or distinct value proposition can attract customers. Developing a powerful brand requires sustaining a consistent message, delivering on the brand's promises, and establishing positive associations with the target audience. Customers may be reluctant to switch from a well-known and trusted brand to an unfamiliar alternative, making it challenging for new companies to enter the market and compete successfully. Last but not least, effective supply chain management can contribute to a competitive advantage. With a carefully designed and proficiently managed supply chain, it is possible to reduce costs, increase product availability, guarantee on-time delivery, and boost customer satisfaction. By optimizing their processes, working closely with their suppliers, and leveraging technology, businesses can gain a competitive advantage in terms of speed, flexibility, and responsiveness. If a company's supply chain is both adaptable and resilient, it can respond swiftly to fluctuations in market demand or disruptions. This provides these businesses a distinct advantage over rivals with less efficient or adaptable supply chains.

For both organizations and individuals, staying ahead in the technology world of today is crucial. Rapid technological breakthroughs are redefining business structures, disrupting sectors, and changing how we live and work. Here are some main arguments on why it is so important to stay ahead in this environment:

- *Competitive Advantage*: Technology has evolved into a major contributor to competitive advantage. It is possible for businesses to gain a competitive advantage over their competitors if they adopt and implement cutting-edge technologies. By implementing innovative solutions, optimizing business processes, and delivering superior digital experiences, businesses can expand their customer base, enhance their operational efficiency, and differentiate themselves from market competitors.
- *Market Relevance*: Technology is reshaping the expectations of customers as well as the dynamics of markets. Customers in the current market are technologically savvy and seek seamless digital experiences across all channels. Businesses that cannot adapt to consumers' changing preferences run the risk of becoming irrelevant. Keeping up with the ever-evolving technology landscape enables businesses to meet the evolving requirements of their customers better, maintain their relevance in the industry, and preserve their market advantage.
- *Increased Efficiency and Productivity*: Frequently, newly developed technologies contribute to increases in both productivity and efficiency. AI, data analytics, and automation-based tools have the potential to accelerate decision-making, reduce required human labor, and streamline operations. Businesses that are able to stay one step ahead of their competitors can use these technologies to improve processes, reduce costs, and increase overall productivity, giving them a significant competitive advantage over slower-moving businesses.

- *Innovation and Growth Opportunities*: The development of technology creates new opportunities for innovation and growth. Being at the forefront of technological development enables businesses to identify emerging trends, investigate innovative ideas, and seize opportunities that other businesses may overlook. If organizations consistently embrace innovation and stretch the boundaries of what is possible, they can generate new revenue streams, expand into new markets, and achieve sustainable growth.
- *Adaptability and Resilience*: By remaining at the forefront of the technological landscape, an organization's adaptability and resiliency can be improved. The disruption of businesses caused by technological advancements is unavoidable; however, companies that are proactive in embracing change are better equipped to manage challenging circumstances. Maintaining a culture of continuous learning, keeping up with the newest technologies, and monitoring industry trends enables businesses to quickly adapt to altering market conditions, capitalize on opportunities, and withstand unanticipated problems.
- *Talent Attraction and Retention*: Companies that are technologically innovative are more likely to attract the finest and most talented employees. Talented individuals are actively seeking opportunities to collaborate on creative initiatives and utilize cutting-edge technologies in today's extremely competitive job market. If businesses maintain a competitive advantage, they have a greater chance of attracting and retaining skilled personnel, who are essential for driving digital transformation and attaining long-term success.

2.1.1 Technology's Role in Creating Competitive Advantage

Technology has become a crucial aspect in achieving success and creating competitive advantage across a range of businesses. It has transformed market dynamics, customer interactions, and business processes. By automating operations, streamlining processes, and maximizing resource allocation, technology improves efficiency and production [1]. Employing tools like enterprise resource planning systems and workflow automation, organizations may offer goods and services more quickly than rivals while minimizing manual labor and errors. Innovation and the creation of new products are fueled by technology. Technologies like AI, IoT, and data analytics are advancing, giving organizations a chance to develop innovative solutions that meet client needs. Those that support technology-driven innovation are able to launch novel products, gain a competitive edge, and seize untapped market niches.

The customer experience is being transformed by technology. Technology enables businesses to provide greater consumer experiences, from online purchasing platforms to tailored marketing efforts. Businesses may provide tailored recommendations, focused promotions, and seamless omnichannel experiences by utilizing consumer data and analytics, which will increase customer loyalty and help them stand out from the competition. Technology also makes it possible to make decisions based on data. Large amounts of data can be gathered, analyzed, and used by businesses to help them make wise decisions. BI and data analytics solutions offer insights into consumer preferences, market trends, and operational efficiency. These insights enable businesses to adapt to market changes quickly, find growth opportunities, and enhance their strategy. Analyzing the competitive market is made easier by technology. Technology tools can be used by businesses to track rivals, examine market trends, and obtain useful insights into rivals' tactics and client attitudes. Platforms for competitor information, sentiment analysis, and social media monitoring assist firms in adjusting their own strategies, differentiating their services, and staying one step ahead of the competition.

Innovation is a vital driver of competitive advantage over the long term. By supplying tools and platforms for R&D, prototyping, and collaboration, technology enables companies to innovate. For instance, cloud computing enables businesses to access scalable computing resources and experiment with new concepts with minimal initial investment. In addition, emerging technologies such as IoT, blockchain, and ML can enable new business models and create opportunities for disruption (Table 2.1).

TABLE 2.1 Technological solutions for competitive advantage

TECHNOLOGY SOLUTION	DESCRIPTION
Enterprise Resource Planning	Integrated software system for managing business processes such as finance, HR, procurement, and inventory.
Supply Chain Management Software	Tools and platforms to optimize and manage the flow of goods, information, and finances across the supply chain.
Robotic Process Automation	Automation technology uses software robots to automate repetitive and rule-based tasks, improving efficiency and accuracy.
CRM	Software solution for managing customer interactions, capturing data, and analyzing customer behavior to enhance relationships and personalize offerings.
Advanced Analytics and AI	Techniques and algorithms that analyze large datasets and enable predictive modeling allow companies to make data-driven decisions and improve customer experience.
Cloud Computing	On-demand access to computing resources and storage via the Internet provides scalability, flexibility, and cost-efficiency for businesses.
IoT	Network of interconnected devices that gather and exchange data, enabling real-time monitoring, automation, and new service opportunities.
Blockchain	Distributed ledger technology ensures transparency, security, and trust in transactions, opening up possibilities for secure and efficient digital processes.
Machine Learning	Branch of AI that enables systems to learn and improve from data without explicit programming, supporting tasks such as pattern recognition, prediction, and optimization.

2.1.2 Using Technology to Gain a Competitive Advantage

Businesses need to adopt a comprehensive digital strategy to leverage technology and obtain a competitive edge. Here are some potential strategies (Figure 2.1).

When selecting technologies to align with business objectives and industry dynamics, several criteria need to be considered. Three essential criteria include scalability, flexibility, and compatibility; integration with existing systems and processes; and security and data privacy considerations. Let us explore each criterion in detail:

- *Scalability, Flexibility, and Compatibility*: The selected technologies should have the ability to scale and adapt to meet changing business needs and growth. Scalability ensures that the technology can handle increased workloads, user demands, or data volumes without significant performance degradation. Flexibility is crucial to accommodate evolving business processes and requirements. Compatibility is essential to ensure seamless integration with other systems, software, or platforms within the organization's ecosystem.
- *Integration with Existing Systems and Processes*: Compatibility and integration capabilities are vital when choosing technologies. The new technology should seamlessly integrate with existing systems, databases, and processes to avoid disruptions or data silos. This criterion is particularly important in industries where legacy systems are prevalent. A well-integrated technology stack enhances data flow, collaboration, and efficiency across the organization, leading to improved productivity and streamlined operations.
- *Security and Data Privacy Considerations*: Security and data privacy are critical factors, especially in an era of increasing cybersecurity threats and stringent regulations. The selected technologies should have robust security features, encryption protocols, access controls, and vulnerability management. Data privacy compliance is crucial to protect sensitive customer information and adhere to legal and regulatory requirements. Technologies that prioritize privacy and offer data protection mechanisms help build trust with customers and minimize the risk of data breaches or regulatory penalties.

In addition to these three criteria, other factors should also be considered when selecting technologies. These include:

- *Cost-effectiveness*: Evaluating the total cost of ownership, including implementation, maintenance, and training costs, is essential to ensure that the technology aligns with the organization's budget and provides a positive return on investment.
- *User-friendliness*: The technology should be intuitive and user-friendly to facilitate employee adoption and minimize the learning curve. Usability is crucial for maximizing productivity and minimizing resistance to change.
- *Industry Relevance*: Different industries may have unique technological requirements and compliance standards. It is important to select technologies

Embrace Innovation

Encourage experimentation, collaboration, and continuous learning to foster an innovative culture. Invest in R&D to investigate the potential implementations of emerging technologies in your industry.

Customer Experience Priority

Give customer experience a top priority by leveraging technology to personalize interactions, provide seamless omnichannel experiences, and anticipate customer requirements. Utilize data analytics to gain insights into consumer preferences and behavior, enabling targeted marketing and customized offerings.

Agile Operations

Adopt agile methodologies and practices to improve operational effectiveness, responsiveness, and adaptability. Automation, AI, and robotics streamline processes, reduce manual labor, and boost productivity.

Data Analytics and Insights

Invest in analytics capabilities to extract actionable insights from your organization's vast data. Utilize these insights to make informed decisions, identify market trends, and discover growth and innovation opportunities.

Strategic Partnerships

Collaborate with technology partners, entrepreneurs, and other industry participants to gain access to cutting-edge technologies and promote innovation. Strategic alliances can provide access to knowledge, resources, and complementary capabilities that can strengthen your competitive advantage.

FIGURE 2.1 Strategies for competitive advantage.

that are specifically designed or customized to meet the industry's needs and regulations.

- *Vendor Reputation and Support*: Evaluating the vendor's track record, reputation, and customer support capabilities is crucial. A reliable vendor with a proven track record can provide ongoing support and updates and resolve any technical issues that may arise.

By carefully considering these criteria and conducting a thorough evaluation, businesses can select the right technologies that align with their objectives and industry dynamics. This ensures optimal performance, operational efficiency, and the ability to capitalize on technological advancements for sustainable growth.

2.1.3 Implementing Technology for Competitive Advantage

It is important to evaluate the organization's present level of technology adoption before deploying new technologies. In order to do this, existing systems, software, and infrastructure must be assessed for efficacy and efficiency. A detailed image of the organization's technical strengths and shortcomings can be obtained by evaluating elements, including data management, communication tools, collaboration platforms, and customer-facing technology. This evaluation assists in identifying areas in which technology can be used for a competitive advantage. Determine possible areas for advancement and the incorporation of new technology based on the assessment. This can entail improving consumer experiences, streamlining internal procedures, advancing data analytics, or stepping up digital marketing initiatives. Take into account technologies that support the organization's strategic objectives and have the capacity to fill in gaps or solve problems. Prioritize areas for improvement based on how they will affect business results and whether they can be implemented. New technology implementation can offer difficulties that need thorough preparation and attention. These are the three main obstacles to overcome:

1. *Resource Allocation and Budgeting*: The incorporation of new technologies frequently necessitates the allocation of financial resources for the acquisition of software licenses, hardware upgrades, infrastructure enhancements, and qualified staff. In order to ensure that the implementation will be successful, it is crucial to allocate funds efficiently and obtain the necessary resources. It is important to take into account the organization's total cost of ownership, which includes the costs of implementation, maintenance, and training, in order to ensure that the budget is both practical and supportive of the organization's technology goals.

2. *Change Management and Employee Training*: When new technologies are implemented, it is common for existing workflows, processes, and staff roles to undergo transformations. Employees who are used to the current processes or who are afraid of losing their jobs can object to this change. It is important to have efficient change management techniques in place so that employees can be informed of the advantages of the new technologies, their concerns can be addressed, and they can receive training and assistance. For a successful implementation, ensuring a smooth transition and encouraging staff buy-in are both essential components.

3. *Risk Mitigation and Cybersecurity Measures*: Introducing new vulnerabilities and potential threats to data privacy and security can be a risk when using new technology. It is of the utmost importance to carry out exhaustive risk

assessments, put in place proper security measures, and train personnel on the best methods for ensuring data security. This includes putting in place stringent access controls, encrypting data, maintaining software updates on a regular basis, and educating employees. Continuous monitoring and proactive risk management are two important components in mitigating potential risks and protecting sensitive information.

Organizations have a better chance of effectively implementing new technologies and gaining a competitive edge if they take these obstacles and factors into account. For an implementation to be successful, it is necessary to engage in strategic planning, have strong leadership, and collaborate among business units, IT departments, and stakeholders. To ensure that the technologies that have been adopted continue to give a sustainable competitive advantage, regular evaluation and monitoring of technology performance as well as the influence that performance has on business objectives are required. Implementing new technology is a process that always continues. In order to maintain a competitive advantage in a market that is undergoing rapid change, it is essential to perform ongoing technology landscape assessments at the organization, investigate new technological developments, and cultivate an innovative culture. Innovation, improved customer experiences, increased operational efficiency, and a major competitive advantage can all be achieved by businesses that use technology as a strategic enabler in a way that is both successful and efficient.

2.2 BUSINESS MODELS: RETHINKING STRATEGY FOR THE DIGITAL AGE

The advent of the digital age has resulted in a significant rise in the significance of business models, which are now absolutely necessary for the achievement of business goals and the continued existence of businesses. The landscape of business has been significantly altered as a result of the rapid development of technology and the broad adoption of the Internet, which has resulted in the emergence of both new opportunities and new obstacles. In this scenario, having a business model that is both well-designed and flexible is very necessary in order to make effective use of digital capabilities and maintain a competitive edge in the market. The advent of the digital age has made traditional business models obsolete and given rise to new approaches to running a company. The value proposition that companies offer to clients and the methods through which they provide it to them need to be rethought. A business model is a blueprint that specifies the essential components of a company's strategy. These components can include the company's target market, income streams, and cost structure, among other things. Businesses are able to discover new and unique methods to offer value for their customers and differentiate themselves from their rivals by connecting these aspects with digital technologies.

Second, the advent of the digital era has contributed to the growth of decision-making that is based on data. Today's businesses have access to large volumes of data, which may offer them invaluable insights into the behavior of their customers, the trends in the market, and the effectiveness of their operations. Data analytics and the application of technology to the collection, analysis, and interpretation of data are essential components of successful business models. This enables companies to make educated decisions, tailor the consumer experience, maximize operational efficiency, and locate new prospects for growth. The advent of the digital age has made feasible new kinds of business models that did not previously exist. Traditional techniques for running a business have been challenged by the emergence of viable alternatives such as the sharing economy, platform-based models, and subscription-based services. These models make use of digital platforms in order to bring together buyers and sellers, make transactions easier, and generate value through the power of network effects. When businesses adopt these new models, it may be possible for them to enter previously unreachable markets, expand their client base, and generate other sources of revenue.

The advent of the digital era has had a profound impact on the expectations and habits of customers. These days, customers expect convenience, personalization, and continuity of experience across a variety of platforms and mediums. Having a solid business model gives firms the ability to comprehend and accommodate the shifting preferences of their customers. They are able to harness digital platforms, engage customers through tailored marketing and communication, and create experiences that are consistent across all channels as a result of this. Businesses may foster long-term client loyalty and generate sustainable growth if they connect their business models with the requirements of their target demographics. In conclusion, the advent of the digital era has led to an increase in competitiveness while simultaneously lowering the barriers to entrance. By introducing novel business models and making strategic use of available technology, startups and digital-native enterprises have the potential to cause disruption in established industries quickly. Established businesses have to always look for new ways to improve their business models so that they can remain competitive in the current environment. They need to be willing to embrace digital transformation, cultivate a culture of innovation, and be open to experimenting with new ideas and methods. The foundation for such innovation is provided by a business model that has been thoughtfully created, which enables businesses to adapt, maintain their agility, and embrace new opportunities.

In the digital age, the business landscape is undergoing a significant transformation. Traditional strategies that have long been successful are now facing challenges due to rapid technological advancements and the widespread use of the Internet. This section explores the need for rethinking traditional strategies and the importance of adapting to the digital age to ensure business success and sustainability.

- *Disruption and the Evolving Business Landscape*: The digital age has brought forth disruptive technologies that have reshaped industries. Companies need to recognize the impact of these disruptions and reevaluate their strategies. Traditional business models may need to be more effective in meeting the demands of digitally empowered customers and the changing market dynamics. It is crucial to understand the implications of these disruptions and adapt strategies accordingly.
- *Leveraging Digital Capabilities for Competitive Advantage*: To remain competitive, businesses must leverage digital capabilities. The Internet, data analytics, and emerging technologies provide unprecedented opportunities for companies to enhance their operations and customer experiences. Rethinking

traditional strategies involves embracing digital transformation and incorporating technology-driven solutions into business models. By doing so, companies can gain a competitive advantage, improve efficiency, and create new value propositions for their customers.

- *Embracing Innovation and Agility*: In the digital age, innovation and agility are paramount. Traditional strategies often rely on fixed processes and long planning cycles, which can hinder responsiveness to market changes. Rethinking strategies involves fostering a culture of innovation and embracing agile methodologies. By encouraging experimentation, embracing new ideas, and fostering collaboration, companies can adapt quickly to emerging trends and seize opportunities as they arise.
- *Customer-Centric Approaches in the Digital Era*: Customer expectations have evolved dramatically in the digital age. Customers now demand personalized experiences, convenience, and seamless interactions across multiple channels. Rethinking traditional strategies means shifting focus toward customer-centric approaches. By leveraging data analytics, businesses can gain insights into customer behavior and preferences, enabling them to tailor their products, services, and marketing strategies to meet individual needs.
- *Collaboration and Partnerships*: Collaboration and partnerships have become crucial in the digital age. Traditional strategies often focus solely on internal capabilities and resources. However, in the interconnected digital ecosystem, collaboration with external partners can lead to innovative solutions and access to new markets. Rethinking strategies involves seeking collaborations, forming strategic alliances, and embracing open innovation to leverage collective strengths and achieve mutual growth.

A conceptual framework that defines how a corporation generates, delivers, and ultimately "captures" value is referred to as a "business model." It encapsulates the fundamental components of a business's strategy and lays forth a road map for the manner in which an organization conducts its business and makes income. A business model that is well-designed will align the firm's resources, capabilities, and activities so that the company can effectively meet the demands of its customers, maintain its edge over its competitors, and achieve profitability.

2.2.1 Components of a Business Model

The "Components of a Business Model" encompass various essential aspects that define a company's operations and value delivery.

- *Value Proposition*: The value proposition represents a firm's unique advantages or benefits provided to clients or consumers. It encompasses products, services, and solutions addressing client needs, pain points, or competitive advantages. A robust value proposition sets the company apart and generates customer value.
- *Target Market*: The "target market" consists of specific client groups or market segments a firm aims to serve, as defined by the company. This involves identifying ideal customer traits, preferences, and behaviors. Thorough

knowledge of market demographics and purchasing habits enables efficient product alignment, marketing, and customer experiences.

- *Revenue Streams*: A business's "revenue streams" encompass avenues for converting goods or services into revenue. This includes various pricing structures, sales channels, and income sources. Revenue sources might include direct sales, subscriptions, licensing fees, advertising, and more. Diverse and sustainable revenue sources are crucial for financial stability and growth.
- *Key Activities*: "Key activities" refer to essential tasks and processes necessary for fulfilling a company's value proposition. These activities cover a wide spectrum, including production, distribution, marketing, R&D, customer service, and partnerships. Identifying vital activities streamlines operations, optimizes resource allocation, and ensures efficient product or service delivery.
- *Key Resources*: A company's "key resources" encompass assets, capabilities, and infrastructure required for delivering value to customers. These resources can be tangible, like physical assets and technology, or intangible, such as intellectual property and human capital. Properly managing and distributing crucial resources sustains competitiveness and supports the company's value proposition.
- *Channels*: "Channels" denote communication and distribution methods used by a business to reach and engage its clientele. This includes brick-and-mortar locations, online platforms, direct sales teams, digital marketing, and collaborations with distributors or retailers. Effective channel selection and management make goods and services accessible and provide seamless customer experiences.
- *Customer Relationships*: Customer relationships encompass all interactions and strategies for establishing and maintaining connections with clients. This involves understanding customer needs, delivering exceptional service, and fostering loyalty. CRM methods range from personal interactions to digital self-service platforms, depending on the business and target audience.
- *Cost Structure*: The cost structure outlines expenses and investments necessary for business operations and delivering the value proposition. It covers fixed costs, variable costs, overheads, as well as resource, technology, marketing, and infrastructure investments. A solid grasp of the cost structure and effective management are essential for achieving profitability and resource optimization.

2.2.2 Rethinking Strategy for the Digital Age

In the digital age, businesses must rethink their strategies to adapt to the changing landscape and seize the opportunities presented by technology and connectivity. Here are key considerations for rethinking strategy in the digital age:

- *Embrace Digital Transformation*: Digital transformation involves leveraging technology to change how a business operates and delivers value fundamentally. It requires a mindset shift and a willingness to embrace new tools, processes, and business models. Companies should assess their current operations and identify areas where digital solutions can enhance efficiency, improve customer experiences, and unlock new sources of value.

- *Understand Customer Behavior*: In the digital age, customers have more power and options than ever before. To stay relevant, businesses must deeply understand their target audience, their preferences, and their digital behaviors. Utilize data analytics, social listening, and market research to gain insights into customer needs and expectations. This understanding will enable companies to tailor their products, services, and marketing efforts to meet customer demands effectively.
- *Foster a Culture of Innovation*: Innovation is essential for survival in the digital age. Encourage a culture that values experimentation, creativity, and learning from failures. Empower employees to generate and explore new ideas and provide resources for prototyping and testing innovative concepts. Collaboration with external partners, startups, or academia can also bring fresh perspectives and accelerate innovation efforts.
- *Emphasize Agility and Adaptability*: The pace of change in the digital age demands agility and adaptability. Traditional long-term planning may need to be revised. Implement agile methodologies and frameworks that allow for iterative development and rapid response to market feedback. Regularly reassess strategies and make necessary adjustments to align with emerging trends and technologies.
- *Embrace Data-driven Decision-Making*: Data is a valuable asset in the digital age. Invest in data analytics capabilities and leverage data to drive strategic decision-making. Collect and analyze relevant data to gain insights into customer behavior, market trends, and operational performance. Use these insights to refine strategies, optimize processes, and identify new growth opportunities.
- *Leverage Digital Marketing Channels*: Traditional marketing channels are being supplemented or replaced by digital channels. Develop a strong online presence through websites, social media, search engine optimization, and digital advertising. Utilize personalized marketing strategies and automation tools to engage customers and deliver targeted messages. Harness the power of social media influencers and online communities to extend the reach and build brand advocacy.
- *Collaborate and Partner*: Collaboration and strategic partnerships can be instrumental in navigating the digital age. Identify complementary businesses, startups, or technology providers with whom you can collaborate to leverage synergies and access new markets. Explore partnerships that can enhance your digital capabilities, such as joint ventures, co-development projects, or technology licensing agreements.
- *Invest in Cybersecurity and Privacy*: The digital age brings new risks and vulnerabilities. Safeguard your business and customer data by implementing robust cybersecurity measures. Comply with data privacy regulations and build trust with customers by being transparent about data collection, usage, and protection practices.

In order to effectively rethink strategy for the digital age, one must take a holistic approach that takes into account not only technology but also customer-centricity, innovative thinking, and adaptability. Businesses have the ability to position themselves for success in the constantly shifting digital landscape by embracing digital transformation, understanding the demands of their customers, encouraging innovation, and exploiting data.

2.2.3 Business Model Varieties in the Digital Age

E-commerce has revolutionized business operations and consumer interactions. The relationship between different e-commerce business models is described in Figure 2.2. Diverse e-commerce business formats have emerged, including:

- *B2C (Business-to-Consumer)*: In this model, products or services are sold directly to individual consumers via online platforms. Online retailers such as Amazon and clothing firms with online stores are examples.
- *B2B (Business-to-Business)*: This model concentrates on providing products or services via online platforms to other businesses. It encompasses global supplier and manufacturer connecting platforms such as Alibaba.
- *C2C (Consumer-to-Consumer)*: This model allows individuals to sell goods and services directly to other consumers via online marketplaces. eBay and Etsy are examples of such platforms.
- *D2C (Direct-to-Consumer)*: Under this model, businesses sell their products or services directly to consumers without intermediaries. D2C brands reach consumers through digital marketing, online stores, and social media.

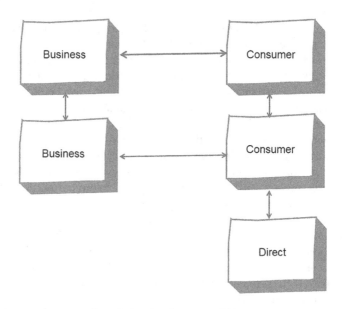

FIGURE 2.2   E-commerce: The relationship between different models.

Subscription-based business models: Subscription-based business models have become popular in the digital age. Customers pay a recurring fee to access products or services under these models. Examples include:

- *Software-as-a-Service (SaaS)*: This model provides subscription-based software applications over the Internet. Such businesses as Salesforce and Slack provide SaaS products.
- *Content Subscription*: Businesses like Netflix and Spotify offer subscription-based access to their libraries, allowing users to stream movies, television programs, and music.
- *Membership-based models*: Membership-based models, such as Amazon Prime, offer subscribers various benefits, including free shipping, exclusive discounts, and additional services.

2.2.4 Models for Sharing Economy Businesses

Traditional industries have been disrupted by the sharing economy, which facilitates the peer-to-peer exchange of products and services. Key business models in the sharing economy include:

- *Peer-to-Peer (P2P) Sharing*: Platforms such as Airbnb and Uber enable individuals to share their unused resources, including homes and vehicles, for a charge.
- *On-Demand Services*: Platforms such as TaskRabbit and Instacart connect customers with service providers who meet their immediate requirements, such as handyperson services and grocery delivery.

Platform-based business models: By connecting users, facilitating transactions, and generating network effects, digital platforms have transformed entire industries. Principal platform-based business models consist of the following:

- *Two-Sided Platforms*: These enable interaction between two distinct user groups. Examples include ride-hailing platforms that connect drivers and passengers, such as Uber.
- *Multisided Platforms*: These platforms facilitate the value creation of multiple user groups. Facebook and Instagram are social media platforms that connect consumers, advertisers, and content creators.
- *Data-driven Platforms*: Google and Facebook generate revenue by accumulating and utilizing user data to provide targeted advertising services.

2.2.5 Conceptualizing a Digital Business Model

To create a successful digital business model, organizations have to implement the following steps (Figure 2.3):

(A) **Study and Evaluation**: Conduct market research and analysis to comprehend the changing requirements of customers, emerging technologies, and competitive landscape. This will provide insight into future business model innovation opportunities.

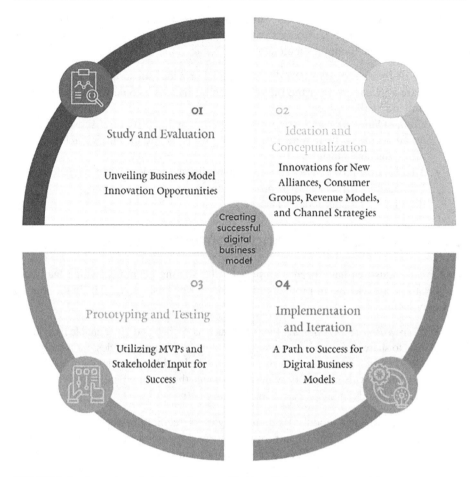

FIGURE 2.3   Four steps for designing an effective digital business model.

(B) **Ideation and Conceptualization**: Create fresh concepts for brand-new alliances, consumer groups, revenue models, and channel strategies. Evaluate and refine these ideas based on their viability, alignment with organizational objectives, and value-creation potential.

(C) **Prototyping and Testing**: Develop minimum viable products or prototypes to test and validate the viability of the proposed digital business model. Collect input from customers, partners, and internal stakeholders to refine the model and resolve its flaws.

(D) **Implementation and Iteration**: After a workable digital business model has been identified, gradually put it into practice, perhaps by launching a pilot or small-scale rollout first. Continually refine and optimize the model by monitoring performance, gathering data, and iterating based on customer feedback and market dynamics.

2.3 DEVELOPING A DIGITAL STRATEGY: ALIGNING TECHNOLOGY AND BUSINESS GOALS

In today's fast-paced digital environment, organizations in a wide variety of sectors are embracing digital transformation strategies to maintain their competitive edge, meet the expectations of their customers, and stimulate innovation. Businesses must have a comprehensive digital strategy to effectively use technology and align it with their more significant business objectives. This section takes an in-depth look at the fundamental components and processes that go into developing a digital strategy for a company. Such a strategy must combine commercial objectives with technological ones for a company to succeed in the digital environment.

2.3.1 Recognizing the Digital Environment

The digital world has permeated every aspect of our daily life in the 21st century. The digital era has radically changed how we connect with the outside world, changing everything from how we communicate and obtain information to how we do business and create our identities. Therefore, it is essential for individuals, corporations, and societies as a whole to recognize and comprehend this complicated environment.

Developing digital literacy is one component of understanding the digital world. Beyond simple computer abilities, digital literacy entails a deeper comprehension of how technology works, as well as the ability to assess online content and defend oneself against online threats critically. Being digitally literate is crucial for making informed decisions, taking part in civic discourse, and using the Internet responsibly in today's information-driven culture.

Recognizing the digital environment necessitates not only digital literacy but also an understanding of the ubiquitous influence of technology in numerous fields. Traditional industries have been disrupted by the digital age, which has also created new opportunities and difficulties. It has altered the way we watch television, shop, travel, and even meet love interests. Individuals and companies may adapt and take advantage of the potential advantages of the digital landscape by being aware of these developments. In the age of big data, governments and companies gather enormous amounts of personal data, which they then utilize to influence decision-making and create user experiences. Understanding these power relationships enables people to make more informed purchasing decisions, preserve their privacy, and promote openness and responsibility in digital practices.

Blockchain, VR, AI, and other advancements are still reshaping industries and altering societal systems. Individuals and organizations can proactively adapt, exploit opportunities, and handle possible problems in an ever-evolving digital ecosystem by staying up to date with these advancements. Addressing crucial concerns like digital equity and inclusion is part of recognizing the digital environment. Technology has the power to empower people and close gaps, but it may also amplify already existing inequities. Digital resources are not equally accessible to all people, and underprivileged communities may encounter obstacles that prevent them from fully engaging in the digital world. Building a more inclusive society requires acknowledging these differences and working toward fair digital access and opportunity.

2.3.2 Finding Technological Facilitators

The following step is to identify the technical enablers required to support the business goals. This involves looking at the current technology infrastructure, systems, and processes to identify gaps and areas that need improvement. It also calls for researching and evaluating cutting-edge technology having the potential to further specific corporate objectives. These technologies include blockchain, cloud computing, big data analytics, AI, and IoT. The basis for an organization's digital transformation path can be set by choosing the right technological enablers. Tools, platforms, or other technological solutions that facilitate and improve the execution of digital initiatives are known as technological facilitators. They are facilitators, enabling organizations to utilize technology to accomplish their targeted results. These facilitators can differ based on the particular industry, business strategy, and organizational goals. As part of creating a digital strategy, the following processes can be used to locate technological facilitators (Figure 2.4):

(A) **Define Your Business Goals**: Start by articulating your organization's objectives and goals. Understand what you want to achieve through your digital strategy, such as increasing market share, improving customer experience, or driving operational efficiency. This will provide a solid foundation for aligning technology with your business objectives.

(B) **Assess Your Current Technology Landscape**: Evaluate your existing technological infrastructure, applications, and systems. Understand their strengths, weaknesses, and limitations in supporting your digital strategy. Identify any gaps or areas for improvement that need to be addressed. This assessment will help you identify the technological facilitators required to bridge these gaps and enhance your digital capabilities.

(C) **Research Emerging Technologies**: Stay abreast of the latest technological trends and innovations relevant to your industry. Conduct thorough research on emerging technologies such as AI, blockchain, IoT, cloud computing, and data analytics. Identify how these technologies can potentially align with and support your business goals. Evaluate their potential benefits, risks, and feasibility for implementation.

(D) **Engage with Technology Vendors and Experts**: Collaborate with technology vendors, consultants, and experts who specialize in the areas of your interest. Engage in discussions, attend conferences, and participate in industry forums to gain insights into available technological facilitators. Seek expert advice on the most appropriate technologies and solutions for your organization. Leverage their expertise and experience to make informed decisions.

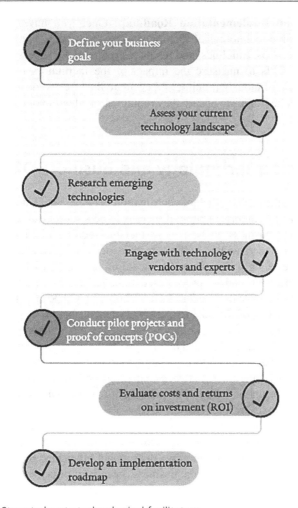

FIGURE 2.4   Steps to locate technological facilitators.

(E) **Conduct Pilot Projects and Proof of Concepts**: Before implementing a new technological facilitator organization-wide, consider conducting pilot projects or POCs. Test the technology's feasibility, scalability, and impact in a controlled environment. This approach allows you to assess its effectiveness and identify potential challenges or modifications required before full-scale implementation.

(F) **Evaluate Costs and Returns on Investment (ROI)**: Assess the financial implications of adopting different technological facilitators. Evaluate the costs associated with implementation, training, maintenance, and ongoing support. Consider the potential ROI, such as increased revenue, cost savings, or improved operational efficiency. Compare and prioritize the facilitators based on their potential value and alignment with your business objectives.

(G) **Develop an Implementation Roadmap**: Once you have identified the most suitable technological facilitators, create a comprehensive roadmap. Define the steps, timelines, and resources required for successful adoption. Establish KPIs to measure the impact of the facilitators on your digital strategy. Continuously monitor and evaluate the effectiveness of the implemented technologies to ensure they remain aligned with your evolving business goals.

2.3.3 Aligning Technology and Business Objectives

It is necessary for there to be efficient coordination between the IT department and the business department of an organization if there is to be a successful alignment of technological goals and business goals. This partnership requires that there be consistent communication, an understanding of the objectives of the project, and decision-making that is based on reaching a consensus. By including relevant business stakeholders in the planning and decision-making processes, companies can increase the likelihood that the actions and investments they undertake in technology will be closely linked with the objectives and priorities of the business. This alignment fosters an innovative culture within the firm. It ensures that technology is regarded as a facilitator rather than a separate entity by its employees rather than being considered an independent factor. Because it guarantees that technological efforts are not undertaken in isolation but as enablers of broader business goals, alignment between technology and business objectives is crucial to every successful business strategy. Several benefits can be gained when technological goals and business goals are aligned:

- *Enhanced Efficiency*: Technology can streamline business processes, automate repetitive tasks, and improve operational efficiency. By aligning technology initiatives with specific business objectives, organizations can target areas for improvement and achieve significant efficiency gains.
- *Competitive Advantage*: Technology can give organizations an edge by enabling innovative products, services, or business models. Aligning technology with business goals allows companies to identify strategic opportunities and leverage technology to gain a competitive advantage in the market.
- *Customer Satisfaction*: Technology plays a crucial role in enhancing the customer experience. By aligning technology initiatives with customer-centric business objectives, organizations can leverage digital tools to personalize interactions, deliver seamless experiences, and meet customer expectations effectively.
- *Agility and Adaptability*: In today's rapidly changing business landscape, agility and adaptability are essential. Technology can enable organizations to respond quickly to market shifts and evolving customer needs. By aligning technology and business goals, companies can ensure that their technology infrastructure is flexible, scalable, and capable of supporting business growth and adaptation.

2.3.4 Strategies for Achieving Alignment

Alignment is essential for success and effectiveness, whether it be achieved inside a team, an organization, or simply an individual. Alignment guarantees that everyone is collaborating effectively, understanding their roles and responsibilities, and working toward the same objectives. The following tactics can be used to achieve alignment:

- *Clear Communication*: Effective communication is the cornerstone of alignment. Clearly articulate the vision, goals, and expectations to all stakeholders involved. Provide regular updates, address concerns, and foster an environment where open and transparent communication is encouraged. Use multiple channels such as meetings, emails, and collaboration tools to ensure that information is disseminated effectively.
- *Establish Shared Goals*: Alignment requires a shared understanding of the overarching goals and objectives. Collaboratively define and communicate the goals, ensuring that they are specific, measurable, achievable, relevant, and time-bound (SMART). Involve all stakeholders in the goal-setting process to foster a sense of ownership and commitment.
- *Define Roles and Responsibilities*: Clearly define and communicate the roles and responsibilities of each individual or team involved. This ensures that everyone understands their specific contributions and avoids duplication of efforts. Clearly outline decision-making authority and establish channels for collaboration and coordination.
- *Foster a Collaborative Culture*: Encourage collaboration and teamwork to foster alignment. Create an environment where individuals feel comfortable sharing ideas, seeking input, and working together toward common goals. Promote a culture of respect, trust, and inclusivity, where diverse perspectives are valued and considered.
- *Regular Check-ins and Feedback*: Regularly check in with individuals or teams to monitor progress, address challenges, and provide feedback. This allows for course corrections and ensures that everyone stays on track toward alignment. Provide constructive feedback and recognize achievements to motivate and reinforce alignment efforts.
- *Continuous Learning and Development*: Promote a culture of continuous learning and development. Encourage individuals and teams to enhance their skills, knowledge, and capabilities relevant to their roles and goals. Provide opportunities for training, workshops, and mentoring to foster growth and alignment with changing needs and dynamics.
- *Embrace Technology*: Utilize technology tools and platforms that facilitate collaboration, communication, and project management. Project management software, shared document repositories, and communication tools can enhance alignment by providing a centralized platform for information sharing and coordination.
- *Foster Cross-functional Collaboration*: Break down silos and encourage cross-functional collaboration. Aligning different departments or teams

ensures that everyone is working toward a common purpose, avoids conflicts or duplications, and promotes a holistic approach to problem-solving and decision-making.

- *Lead by Example*: Leadership plays a crucial role in achieving alignment. Leaders should embody the desired behaviors and values, demonstrate commitment to the goals, and actively promote alignment efforts. By leading by example, leaders inspire others to align their actions and behaviors with the shared vision.
- *Regularly Evaluate and Adjust*: Regularly evaluate alignment efforts and make adjustments as needed. Monitor progress, assess outcomes, and solicit feedback from stakeholders to identify areas for improvement. Adapt the strategies and approaches based on lessons learned to enhance alignment in the future.

2.3.5 Making a Roadmap for Agile Implementation

Agile approaches can provide several benefits to organizations, such as enhanced flexibility, faster value delivery, and improved collaboration. Successful adoption, on the other hand, necessitates meticulous planning and a well-defined roadmap. Here are three paragraphs that outline the important components of an agile implementation roadmap:

1. *Assess Current State and Define Objectives*: Assessing the organization's current state is the first step in establishing an agile implementation roadmap. This involves evaluating extant processes, workflows, and cultural factors that may have an effect on the adoption of agile methodologies. Identify pain points, constraints, and areas where increased agility would be advantageous. Next, clearly define the implementation's objectives and align them with the organization's strategic goals. These goals must be SMART. For instance, objectives could include an X% improvement in time-to-market, an X-point increase in customer satisfaction, or an X% reduction in defects.
2. *Establish Agile Principles and Framework*: After defining the objectives, the next stage is to establish the agile principles and framework that will serve as the basis for the implementation. Determine which agile methodologies or frameworks, such as Scrum, Kanban, or Lean, best suit the organization's requirements. Ensure that the framework selected is compatible with the organization's culture, size, and industry. Develop a thorough comprehension of the duties and responsibilities within agile teams, as well as the associated processes and ceremonies. Consider providing team members with training and mentoring to promote a common understanding of agile principles and practices.
3. *Plan Iterative Implementation*: It is optimal to approach agile implementation iteratively, allowing for continuous development and adaptation. Divide the implementation into manageable phases or iterations, with each phase or iteration having its own set of objectives and deliverables. Rank initiatives according to their prospective impact and viability. Create a backlog of work

items, user stories, or duties that must be completed during each iteration. Determine the duration of each iteration, also known as a sprint, based on the capacity and complexity of the organization's work. Review and improve the backlog on a regular basis, incorporating feedback and lessons learned from each iteration. Continuously monitor and assess progress, adjusting the roadmap as necessary.

2.3.6 Creating a Framework for Change Management

Implementing a digital strategy frequently necessitates a cultural shift and the incorporation of newly developed forms of technology. Change management is essential for developing a digital strategy integrating technological advancements with organizational goals. When a business implements new technology and procedures, it is often necessary to make substantial adjustments to its operations, culture, and personnel responsibilities. If there is no effective framework for managing change, these changes may be met with resistance, which could result in the project's delay, failure, or additional expenses. Organizations should establish a comprehensive framework for change management to ensure a seamless transition and the successful execution of digital initiatives. These essential elements must be incorporated into this framework.

2.3.6.1 Leadership and vision

Vision and leadership are essential elements of effective change management. In periods of organizational transformation and change, strong leadership and a clear vision provide the necessary guidance and direction for navigating uncertainty and achieving success. This section describes the significance of leadership and vision in change management:

- *Leadership in Change Management*: Change management necessitates effective leadership at all organizational levels. Leaders play an essential role in motivating, directing, and empowering individuals and teams throughout the change process. They serve as agents of change by establishing the tone, instilling a sense of urgency, and rallying support for the change initiative. Effective leaders articulate the vision, involve stakeholders, and address opposition and concerns. They provide the necessary resources, eliminate obstacles, and foster a culture of collaboration and trust. Leadership in change management entails setting an exemplary example and exhibiting resilience, adaptability, and dedication to the change initiative.
- *Vision in Change Management*: A distinct vision is a beacon that illuminates the path of transformation. The vision conveys the desired future state and functions as a rallying point for all parties involved in the change process. Individuals are inspired and motivated by a compelling vision, which provides a sense of purpose and direction. It helps stakeholders comprehend the

value and significance of their contributions by outlining the change's potential benefits and opportunities. A well-defined vision helps to align efforts, facilitates decision-making, and enables individuals to prioritize change-supporting actions. It also serves as a benchmark for evaluating development and recognizing accomplishments along the change journey.

- *Synergistic Forces*: In change management, leadership, and vision are interdependent and mutually reinforcing components. Strong leadership is essential for articulating and communicating the change vision effectively. It ensures that the vision is adopted and comprehended by all stakeholders, instilling confidence and dedication. A clear vision, on the other hand, provides executives with a road map and a decision-making framework. It provides executives with a point of reference for aligning strategies, allocating resources, and monitoring progress. Together, leadership and vision foster a climate of trust, engagement, and accountability, propelling the change initiative forward.

2.3.6.2 Stakeholder engagement

Engagement of stakeholders is a crucial aspect of change management that involves actively involving and communicating with individuals or groups who are affected by or have a vested interest in the change initiative. By effectively involving stakeholders, organizations can foster collaboration, obtain support, and ensure the success of the change initiative. This text elaborates on the significance of stakeholder involvement in change management:

- *Understanding Stakeholder Needs*: The first step in stakeholder engagement is identifying and comprehending the various stakeholders' requirements, concerns, and expectations. This requires conducting an analysis of the stakeholders to determine who will be affected by the change, their level of influence, and their prospective attitudes toward the change. By understanding the perspectives of stakeholders, organizations can tailor their communication and engagement strategies to resolve specific concerns and build support.
- *Open and Transparent Communication*: Effective stakeholder engagement requires channels of communication that are open and transparent. Organizations should establish distinct channels of communication in order to disseminate information regarding the change initiative's objective and anticipated benefits. Regular updates, town hall meetings, workshops, and individual meetings can be utilized to provide relevant information to stakeholders and resolve their questions and concerns. It is essential to use language and channels that resonate with various stakeholder groups, ensuring that messages are clear and accessible to all.
- *Active Involvement and Collaboration*: Engaging stakeholders extends beyond the dissemination of information. It requires their active participation in the transformation process and decision-making. There must be opportunities for stakeholders to contribute their insights, ideas, and expertise. This

can be accomplished via seminars, focus groups, or the formation of specialized project teams comprised of representatives from various stakeholder groups. By involving stakeholders, organizations gain access to their expertise, foster buy-in, and increase the likelihood of successful implementation.

- *Addressing Resistance and Concerns*: The engagement of stakeholders is especially important when confronting resistance to change. It is crucial to attend to and acknowledge stakeholders' concerns, as well as provide opportunities for them to voice their reservations. By proactively addressing resistance, organizations can identify underlying issues, dispel misunderstandings, and collaborate on solutions. Participating in the change planning and decision-making process with key stakeholders can increase their sense of ownership and decrease resistance.
- *Continuous Feedback and Adaptation*: The engagement of stakeholders should be a continuous process throughout the change journey. Organizations should solicit regular feedback from stakeholders to assess the efficacy of their engagement strategies and make adjustments as necessary. Creating a culture of continuous development and demonstrating a commitment to stakeholders' input by actively soliciting feedback and involving them in the evaluation process.

2.3.6.3 Change impact assessment

Change impact assessment is a crucial stage in the change management process that entails analyzing and comprehending the potential effects and ramifications of a proposed change on various organizational aspects. It facilitates the identification of potential hazards, the evaluation of the change's scope, and the development of appropriate mitigation strategies. This section elaborates on the significance and essential components of change impact assessment:

- *Understanding the Scope of Change*: The first stage of a change impact assessment is to define the proposed change's scope precisely. This requires identifying the afflicted areas, processes, systems, and individuals. By understanding the scope, organizations can evaluate the magnitude and extent of a change, enabling them to allocate resources, plan communication strategies, and identify the key stakeholders involved.
- *Identifying the Impacted Areas*: A comprehensive analysis of the areas that will be directly or indirectly affected by the change is necessary for a change impact assessment. This entails evaluating the effect on processes, workflows, employment roles, organizational structure, systems, technologies, and culture. It is essential to identify both the positive and negative effects of the change, in addition to any potential dependencies or interdependencies between different areas. This analysis provides a thorough comprehension of the potential effects of the change and guides decision-making throughout the change management process.
- *Assessing the Impacted Stakeholders*: Understanding the effects of change on stakeholders is an essential component of change impact assessment.

This includes identifying and analyzing the individuals or groups who will be affected by the change, such as employees, customers, suppliers, and other pertinent parties. Assessing the impact on stakeholders facilitates comprehension of their requirements, concerns, and potential opposition to the change. It enables organizations to customize their communication and engagement strategies to address stakeholder expectations, reduce resistance, and ensure their participation and support throughout the change process.

- *Mitigating Risks and Developing Strategies*: The purpose of a change impact assessment is to identify potential threats and obstacles associated with the proposed change. Organizations can develop effective mitigation strategies and contingency plans if they comprehend the potential disruptions. This could entail addressing potential knowledge or skill gaps, providing training and support, or instituting change management interventions to mitigate the impact. The assessment results inform the creation of a comprehensive change management plan that includes communication, training, stakeholder engagement, and risk management strategies.

- *Monitoring and Evaluation*: Assessment of the change's impact is not a one-time activity but rather an ongoing process throughout the change journey. It is essential to monitor and assess the change's impact continuously, determining if the anticipated benefits are being realized and if any unanticipated consequences are emerging. Regular evaluation enables organizations to make adjustments, hone their change management strategies, and ensure the change's successful implementation and long-term viability.

2.3.6.4 Communication and education

Effective communication and education are crucial components of change management success. They play a crucial role in ensuring that individuals and stakeholders comprehend the initiative's purpose, benefits, and implications. Organizations can facilitate the change process and develop support among those affected by providing clear and consistent messaging, fostering two-way communication, and offering educational opportunities.

Change management depends heavily on communication. It is essential to communicate the change's vision, objectives, and rationale to all stakeholders. Clear and transparent communication helps individuals comprehend the need for change, reduces uncertainty and dread, and fosters a common understanding of the change process. Additionally, it facilitates the exchange of feedback, concerns, and ideas, enabling organizations to address potential resistance and adjust their strategies accordingly. Effective communication fosters confidence, encourages participation, and instills a sense of ownership and commitment to the change initiative.

Organizations can employ numerous strategies to ensure effective communication during change management. Create a comprehensive communication plan outlining key messages, target audiences, channels, and frequency. Second, establish two-way communication by promoting open dialogue and attentive listening, allowing individuals to pose inquiries and voice concerns. Lastly, tailor communication to various audiences by using plain language, visuals, and relevant examples to make the information engaging.

Education is crucial to change management because it equips individuals with the knowledge and skills necessary to adapt to and flourish in a new environment. It provides a deeper comprehension of the change, its purpose, and how it aligns with the organization's objectives. Education also assists individuals in acquiring the skills necessary to effectively navigate change, whether it entails new processes, technologies, or methods of operation. By investing in education, organizations enable individuals to embrace and contribute to the success of change.

Organizations can use a variety of strategies to educate individuals during change management effectively. First, identify knowledge and skill gaps by conducting a thorough assessment of learning requirements. Second, develop training programs that provide the required knowledge and skills associated with the change. Include real-world scenarios to make the training pertinent and applicable and provide a variety of learning formats to accommodate different preferences. Finally, provide ongoing support and resources to reinforce learning and assist individuals in applying newly acquired skills and knowledge to their daily work.

2.3.6.5 Change champions and training

In order for people to actively participate in developing and supporting the change effort inside an organization, change champions and training are crucial components of change management. Organizations can create a network of supporters who aid in the implementation process, create momentum, and guarantee the change's durability by identifying and supplying champions of change with the necessary tools and training. The following piece goes into detail about the value of change champions, change management training, and tactics for utilizing them:

* *The Role of Change Champions*: Change champions are individuals with influence, credibility, and a desire to drive transformation. They act as ambassadors and advocates, advocating the change initiative across the organization and encouraging others to adopt it. Champions of change play a crucial role in raising awareness, overcoming resistance, and facilitating the adoption of new behaviors and practices. They serve as a bridge between the change management team and the larger organization, assisting in aligning efforts, communicating key messages, and providing support and direction to their peers. By leveraging the passion and knowledge of change champions, organizations can increase the impact and reach of the change initiative.
* *Identifying and Engaging Change Champions*: Assessing individuals within the organization who possess the necessary qualities and are willing to assume the role is required to identify change champions. Consider individuals with influence, credibility, strong interpersonal skills, and a history of leading change successfully in the past. Engage potential change champions early in the process of change management to give them a sense of ownership and participation. Include them in the planning, decision-making, and communication processes to ensure that their opinions are considered and valued. Communicate frequently with change champions in order to keep them informed, resolve their concerns, and provide the required support and resources.

- *Training Change Champions*: Training is essential to equip change champions with the necessary knowledge, skills, and instruments to perform their duties effectively. Create training programs that emphasize the development of change management skills, including communication, stakeholder engagement, conflict resolution, and problem-solving. Provide training on the specifics of the change initiative, such as its purpose, benefits, and anticipated outcomes. Offer workshops, seminars, or online modules that combine theoretical knowledge with practical application, enabling change champions to acquire a thorough understanding of the change and the skills required to navigate obstacles and facilitate adoption.
- *Building a Change Champion Network*: By establishing a network or community where change champions can communicate, collaborate, and share their experiences, organizations can further increase the impact of change agents. Establish periodic forums or gatherings where change champions can discuss progress, share best practices, and address common obstacles. Encourage change champions to ruminate on their experiences and provide feedback on the change management strategies in order to foster a culture of continuous learning and improvement. By establishing a robust network of change champions, organizations create a system of support that facilitates knowledge sharing, collaboration, and ongoing engagement.
- *Recognizing and Celebrating Change Champions*: Recognize and honor the contributions of change champions to reinforce their dedication and inspire others. Highlight success tales, publicly acknowledge their efforts, and provide them with opportunities to showcase their accomplishments. There are a variety of celebrations and rewards, ranging from formal recognition ceremonies to tiny tokens of appreciation. By recognizing and celebrating change champions, organizations not only reinforce their significance but also motivate others to embrace the transformation and actively partake in its journey.

2.3.6.6 Agile implementation and feedback loops

Feedback loops are a fundamental aspect of agile implementation, allowing organizations to gain valuable insights, adapt quickly, and perpetually improve processes. Feedback loops provide opportunities to validate assumptions, collect user feedback, and make data-driven decisions within the context of agile methodologies. This part describes the importance of feedback loops in agile implementation.

- *Iterative Development and Delivery*: Iterative development and delivery cycles are the foundation of agile methodologies like Scrum and Kanban. Commonly known as sprints or iterations, these cycles provide natural feedback mechanisms. Teams present their work to stakeholders at the conclusion of each iteration, eliciting feedback and gaining insights that influence subsequent iterations. This iterative approach ensures that feedback is incorporated early and frequently, reducing the likelihood of creating a product or solution that does not meet the requirements of stakeholders.

- *User-Centric Feedback*: Agile methodologies prioritize end-user and stake-holder participation throughout the development process. Loops of feedback allow teams to acquire user insights and validate hypotheses. By soliciting feedback from end-users on a regular basis, organizations can better align their solutions with user requirements, preferences, and expectations. This feedback ensures that the final product or solution provides value and meets user needs.
- *Retrospectives for Process Improvement*: Continuous development is empha-sized in agile implementation, and feedback loops play a crucial role in this regard. Retrospectives, which are held at the conclusion of each iteration or project, allow teams to reflect on their work, identify areas for development, and discuss possible solutions. Teams can analyze what went well, what could be improved, and how to adjust their processes for greater efficiency and effectiveness by conducting retrospectives. This feedback-driven itera-tive procedure enables teams to make incremental changes, fostering con-tinuous improvement and learning.
- *Monitoring and Metrics*: In the agile implementation, feedback channels are not limited to qualitative user feedback and retrospectives. Additionally, agile teams utilize metrics and data to track progress and performance. Metrics and KPIs are used to assess the efficacy of iterations, monitor project veloc-ity, and identify areas for improvement. These data-driven feedback cycles allow teams to make informed decisions, identify bottlenecks, and optimize their processes for improved results.
- *Cross-Functional Collaboration*: Within agile teams, feedback channels foster cross-functional collaboration and communication. Team members can share knowledge, exchange ideas, and learn from one another if they solicit feedback frequently and engage in frank discussions. This culture of collaborative feedback strengthens team dynamics, fosters innovation, and improves problem-solving skills.
- *Adaptability and Flexibility*: Agile implementation requires flexibility and adaptability, which feedback mechanisms provide. As feedback is continu-ously incorporated into the development process, teams are able to respond to and adapt to altering requirements, emerging obstacles, and evolving market conditions. The ability to make rapid adjustments and course corrections in response to feedback enables organizations to deliver value more effectively and remain competitive.

2.3.6.7 Rewards and recognition

Organizational performance, motivation, and engagement can all benefit greatly from rewards and acknowledgment programs. Organizations can improve the work environ-ment, morale, and prospects for future success by recognizing and rewarding employees for their efforts and accomplishments. Here are some points that go into greater detail about why workplace rewards and recognition are so crucial.

- *Motivation and Engagement*: Rewards and recognition serve as powerful motivators for employees. When individuals feel recognized and appreciated for their efforts, it boosts their morale and sense of job satisfaction. Recognizing achievements and providing rewards reinforces the notion that their work is valued and contributes to the overall success of the organization. This, in turn, enhances employee engagement, productivity, and loyalty.

- *Performance and Productivity*: Rewards and recognition programs are effective tools for driving performance and productivity. By acknowledging and rewarding exceptional performance, organizations incentivize individuals and teams to go above and beyond their regular duties. When employees know that their efforts will be recognized and rewarded, they are more likely to be motivated to achieve higher levels of performance. This creates a culture of excellence, where individuals strive for continuous improvement and contribute to the overall success of the organization.

- *Employee Retention and Loyalty*: Recognizing and rewarding employees for their contributions fosters a sense of loyalty and commitment to the organization. Employees who feel appreciated and valued are more likely to stay with the company and contribute to its long-term success. Rewards and recognition programs can help organizations retain top talent by creating a positive work environment and demonstrating that their efforts are recognized and rewarded. This, in turn, reduces turnover rates and the associated costs of hiring and training new employees.

- *Fostering a Positive Work Culture*: Rewards and recognition programs contribute to building a positive work culture. When organizations celebrate and appreciate the achievements and contributions of individuals or teams, it creates a sense of camaraderie and teamwork. Recognizing both individual and collective successes fosters collaboration and a supportive work environment. It also encourages healthy competition as employees strive to achieve recognition for their efforts.

- *Driving Desired Behaviors and Values*: Rewards and recognition programs can be aligned with the organization's core values and desired behaviors. Tying rewards and recognition to specific behaviors or outcomes that align with the organization's goals reinforces the desired culture and encourages employees to exemplify those behaviors. For example, recognizing innovation and problem-solving skills can drive a culture of creativity and continuous improvement.

- *Inclusive and Personalized Approach*: Effective rewards and recognition programs consider the diversity and individual preferences of employees. It is important to tailor the rewards and recognition to suit the unique preferences and needs of individuals or teams. This can be achieved by offering a range of reward options or allowing individuals to choose rewards that are meaningful to them. Inclusive recognition programs ensure that everyone feels valued and appreciated, regardless of their role or level within the organization.

2.3.6.8 Continuous monitoring and evaluation

Continuous monitoring and evaluation are essential business practices for measuring growth, identifying opportunities for advancement, and motivating employees. Through constant monitoring and evaluation of projects, processes, and outcomes, organizations can make better decisions, respond more rapidly to changing conditions, and advance toward their goals. Here are some points that elaborate on why constant monitoring and evaluation are so important.

- *Assessing Progress and Performance*: Continuous monitoring and evaluation provide a mechanism for assessing progress toward goals and objectives. It involves tracking KPIs, milestones, and targets to gauge the effectiveness of initiatives. By regularly reviewing and analyzing data, organizations can identify areas of success and areas that require improvement. This information helps in making data-driven decisions and taking corrective actions to keep projects and processes on track.
- *Identifying Areas for Improvement*: Continuous monitoring and evaluation highlight areas that need improvement. By systematically gathering feedback, analyzing performance data, and conducting evaluations, organizations can identify bottlenecks, inefficiencies, and gaps in performance. This insight enables them to make targeted improvements, optimize processes, and enhance productivity. The regular evaluation also facilitates learning and knowledge sharing, allowing organizations to implement best practices and lessons learned across different projects and teams.
- *Adapting to Changing Circumstances*: Continuous monitoring and evaluation enable organizations to adapt to changing circumstances. In dynamic environments, conditions can shift and new challenges may arise. By closely monitoring performance indicators and evaluating the effectiveness of strategies, organizations can identify emerging risks and make timely adjustments. This flexibility and agility help organizations remain responsive and resilient in the face of change, ensuring that they stay on track toward their objectives.
- *Ensuring Accountability and Transparency*: Continuous monitoring and evaluation foster accountability and transparency within organizations. By regularly assessing performance and sharing results, organizations promote a culture of transparency and accountability among employees. This visibility creates a sense of responsibility and encourages individuals and teams to take ownership of their work. It also enables organizations to communicate progress and outcomes to stakeholders, fostering trust and confidence in their operations.
- *Driving Continuous Improvement*: Continuous monitoring and evaluation are integral to driving continuous improvement. By systematically evaluating performance, organizations can identify opportunities for innovation, process enhancement, and efficiency gains. This iterative approach to improvement helps organizations stay competitive, adapt to market demands, and deliver value to their stakeholders. Continuous improvement becomes a part

of the organizational culture, with regular feedback and evaluation leading to incremental enhancements and increased overall performance.

- *Implementing Feedback Loops*: Continuous monitoring and evaluation rely on feedback loops to gather insights and perspectives. These feedback loops involve engaging stakeholders, gathering feedback from users, and actively involving teams in the evaluation process. By incorporating diverse perspectives and soliciting input, organizations can gain a holistic understanding of their performance and make more informed decisions.

2.4 STRATEGIC ANALYSIS: ASSESSING THE IMPACT OF DIGITAL TRANSFORMATION

Incorporating digital technologies into the many parts of corporate operations has radically transformed industries, reinventing procedures, improving consumer experiences, and generating new prospects for business expansion. However, before companies can begin the digital transformation journey, they need to conduct a strategic analysis to evaluate the potential impact and ramifications of such a transition. The strategic analysis technique used to evaluate the effects of digital transformation is the primary subject of this essay.

2.4.1 Understanding the Current State

In today's swiftly changing business environment, digital transformation has emerged as a key growth and competitive advantage driver. The pervasive impact of technology has transformed traditional industries, disrupted established business models, and created new opportunities for innovation and productivity. To successfully navigate this dynamic environment, organizations must have a thorough comprehension of the current state of digital transformation and its effects on various aspects of their operations. Recognizing the ubiquitous character of digital technologies is essential to comprehending the current state. Cloud computing, AI, IoT, big data analytics, and blockchain are only a few of the technological advancements encompassed by digital transformation. These technologies have become an integral part of daily life, transforming the manner in which businesses interact with consumers, optimize processes, and make strategic decisions.

The influence of digital transformation is pervasive across all industries, affecting both established corporations and new ventures. Companies that embrace digital transformation can streamline operations, improve customer experiences, and acquire valuable data-driven insights. Those who fail to adapt, however, risk slipping behind their competitors and losing relevance in a market that is becoming increasingly digital-centric. To comprehend the current status of digital transformation in its entirety, organizations must evaluate their digital readiness. This includes assessing their current technological infrastructure, digital capabilities, and the degree to which digital technologies are incorporated into their core operations. It also necessitates knowledge of the digital skills and competencies of the workforce as well as the organization's adaptability to technological changes. In addition, organizations must assess the digital transformation initiatives of their industry colleagues and rivals. This analysis offers valuable insights regarding best practices, emerging trends, and prospective opportunities or threats. Understanding how others leverage digital technologies can help one identify digital strategy voids and inspire innovative approaches.

Beyond internal operations, the impact of digital transformation extends to the customer experience. Customers today anticipate seamless digital interactions, individualized services, and instantaneous information access. Organizations must assess their ability to meet these shifting customer expectations and identify areas for improvement. This may entail evaluating digital touchpoints, such as websites, mobile applications, and social media channels, to ensure that they are user-friendly, engaging, and in line with customer needs. Understanding the current state of digital transformation necessitates an examination of the regulatory and ethical issues surrounding digital technologies. Governments and regulatory bodies are attempting to strike a balance between innovation and data privacy, security, and ethical concerns as technological advancements continue to disrupt industries. Organizations must keep apprised of evolving regulations and ensure compliance while proactively addressing any ethical repercussions of digital initiatives.

2.4.2 Identifying Strategic Objectives

After gaining a thorough comprehension of the current state of digital transformation, the next crucial step for an organization is to establish strategic objectives. These objectives define the intended outcomes of the digital transformation journey and serve as guiding principles. By establishing distinct strategic objectives, organizations can align their efforts, allocate resources efficiently, and measure their digital transformation progress. Consider the following factors when identifying strategic objectives:

- *Alignment with Business Goals*: Strategic objectives should be closely aligned with the overall business goals and vision. Digital transformation initiatives should contribute to the organization's growth, profitability, operational efficiency, or customer satisfaction. By establishing this alignment, organizations ensure that digital initiatives have a tangible impact on the success of the business.
- *Customer-Centricity*: Customer expectations and behaviors have undergone significant changes in the digital age. Therefore, a strategic objective of digital transformation should focus on enhancing the customer experience. This can involve initiatives such as developing intuitive digital interfaces, personalizing interactions, and providing seamless omnichannel experiences. Putting the customer at the center of digital transformation efforts drives customer satisfaction, loyalty, and, ultimately, business growth.

- *Operational Excellence*: Digital transformation presents opportunities to streamline internal processes, improve operational efficiency, and reduce costs. Strategic objectives should include initiatives aimed at automating manual tasks, optimizing supply chains, and leveraging data analytics to make data-driven decisions. By achieving operational excellence through digital transformation, organizations can improve productivity, agility, and competitiveness.
- *Innovation and Agility*: In today's fast-paced business environment, organizations must be agile and adaptive to remain competitive. Strategic objectives include fostering a culture of innovation, exploring emerging technologies, and experimenting with new business models. This can involve initiatives such as setting up innovation labs, forming strategic partnerships, or investing in R&D. Embracing innovation and agility ensures that organizations can respond quickly to market changes and stay ahead of the curve.
- *Talent and Skills Development*: Digital transformation requires a skilled and capable workforce. Strategic objectives should include initiatives to attract, retain, and develop digital talent within the organization. This can involve providing training programs, upskilling employees, and fostering a culture of continuous learning. By investing in talent and skills development, organizations can build a strong foundation to support their digital transformation efforts.
- *Security and Risk Management*: Digital transformation brings with it new cybersecurity risks and challenges. Strategic objectives should include initiatives to ensure the security and integrity of digital systems and protect customer data. This can involve implementing robust cybersecurity measures, conducting regular risk assessments, and complying with relevant regulations. By addressing security and risk management as strategic objectives, organizations can safeguard their digital assets and maintain the trust of their stakeholders.
- *Measurement and Evaluation*: Finally, strategic objectives should include establishing KPIs and metrics to measure the progress and success of digital transformation initiatives. By defining measurable goals and regularly evaluating performance, organizations can track their digital transformation journey, identify areas for improvement, and make data-driven adjustments to their strategies.

2.4.3 Assessing Market and Competitive Landscape

Businesses operate in a highly dynamic and swiftly changing market environment in the digital age. As part of their digital transformation strategy, organizations must undertake a comprehensive assessment of the market and competitive landscape in order to navigate this environment successfully. Understanding market trends, customer behavior, and the actions of competitors is essential for obtaining a competitive advantage and identifying strategic opportunities. Consider the following factors when evaluating the market and competitive landscape:

(A) **Market Analysis:**
- *Identify market trends*: Analyze market dynamics, technological advancements, and changing customer preferences. Understand how digital transformation is shaping the industry and identifying emerging opportunities or potential disruptions.
- *Segment the market*: Divide the market into distinct segments based on customer needs, demographics, or behavior. This helps tailor digital strategies to specific customer segments and target niche markets effectively.
- *Analyze customer behavior*: Study customer preferences, buying patterns, and engagement with digital channels. Leverage data analytics to gain insights into customer needs and expectations and identify gaps in the market that can be addressed through digital initiatives.

(B) **Competitive Analysis:**
- *Identify key competitors*: Identify direct and indirect competitors within the industry. Understand their market position, strengths, weaknesses, and digital capabilities.
- *Assess competitive advantage*: Evaluate competitors' digital transformation efforts and assess their competitive advantages. Identify areas where competitors excel and areas where there may be opportunities to differentiate and outperform them.
- *Monitor disruptive entrants*: Keep a watchful eye on new startups or disruptive players entering the market. Assess their innovative approaches, business models, and potential impact on the industry.

(C) **Digital Maturity Assessment:**
- *Evaluate competitors' digital readiness*: Assess the digital capabilities, infrastructure, and customer-centricity of competitors. Understand how effectively they leverage digital technologies to enhance customer experiences, streamline operations, and drive innovation.
- *Benchmark against industry leaders*: Identify industry leaders or digitally mature organizations and benchmark their digital strategies and practices. Learn from their successes and challenges to inform your own digital transformation efforts.

(D) **SWOT Analysis:**
- *Conduct a SWOT analysis*: Evaluate your organization's strengths, weaknesses, opportunities, and threats in the context of the market and competitive landscape. Identify areas where digital transformation can capitalize on strengths, mitigate weaknesses, seize opportunities, and address threats.

(E) **Regulatory and Legal Considerations:**
- *Understand the regulatory landscape*: Stay informed about relevant regulations and compliance requirements related to data privacy, security, and digital practices. Ensure that digital transformation initiatives align with legal and regulatory frameworks to avoid potential risks or penalties.

2.4.4 Evaluating Technological Infrastructure

To enable the implementation and execution of digital initiatives, digital transformation primarily relies on solid and scalable technology infrastructure. A critical stage in the digital transformation path is assessing the organization's technology infrastructure. It entails assessing existing systems and capabilities and identifying areas that need improvement or investment. Here are some crucial factors to consider while analyzing technical infrastructure:

(A) **System and Application Assessment:**
- *Inventory and documentation*: Conduct a comprehensive inventory of existing systems, applications, and technologies currently in use within the organization. Document their functionalities, integration points, and dependencies.
- *Performance evaluation*: Assess the performance of systems and applications to identify any bottlenecks, latency issues, or performance gaps. Consider factors such as response times, scalability, and reliability.
- *Compatibility and integration*: Evaluate the compatibility of existing systems and applications with digital technologies. Determine if they can seamlessly integrate with new digital tools, platforms, or APIs.

(B) **Data Management and Analytics:**
- *Data quality and integrity*: Evaluate the quality, accuracy, and completeness of data across various systems and databases. Identify any data governance or data quality issues that need to be addressed.
- *Data storage and accessibility*: Assess the storage infrastructure and capabilities to handle increasing volumes of data. Consider factors such as data security, compliance with data protection regulations, and accessibility for analysis and decision-making.
- *Analytics capabilities*: Evaluate the organization's analytics capabilities, including data analytics tools, skills, and processes. Determine if the current infrastructure supports advanced analytics, ML, or AI applications.

(C) **Scalability and Flexibility:**
- *Future scalability*: Consider the organization's growth plans and whether the current infrastructure can scale accordingly. Evaluate the ability to handle increased user load, data volumes, and transactional demands as the organization expands.
- *Cloud readiness*: Assess the organization's readiness to leverage cloud technologies. Determine if there are opportunities to migrate certain systems or applications to the cloud to enhance scalability, agility, and cost-effectiveness.
- *Legacy system modernization*: Identify any legacy systems that may hinder digital transformation efforts. Evaluate the feasibility of modernizing or replacing outdated systems with more agile and digitally native solutions.

(D) **Cybersecurity and Risk Management:**
- *Security assessment*: Conduct a comprehensive cybersecurity assessment to identify vulnerabilities, potential risks, and compliance gaps. Evaluate the effectiveness of existing security controls and protocols.

- *Data privacy and protection*: Ensure compliance with data protection regulations and assess the organization's ability to safeguard customer data and sensitive information. Consider encryption, access controls, and privacy policies.
- *Incident response and business continuity*: Evaluate the organization's incident response capabilities and disaster recovery plans. Assess the readiness to mitigate and recover from cybersecurity incidents or system failures.

(E) **Technology Partnerships and Vendor Management:**
  - *Vendor assessment*: Evaluate the performance and reliability of technology vendors and service providers. Assess their ability to meet the organization's current and future technology needs.
  - *Strategic partnerships*: Identify potential strategic partnerships or collaborations with technology providers that offer complementary solutions or expertise. Consider partnerships that can enhance the organization's digital capabilities and support its transformation goals.

2.4.5 Analyzing Organizational Readiness

Across all industries, digital transformation has become a strategic priority for enterprises. The competitiveness and long-term performance of an organization can be greatly impacted by its capacity to utilize emerging technology and adapt to fast-changing digital environments. To guarantee a seamless and successful transition, it is essential to evaluate the organization's readiness before starting a digital transformation path. The goal of this procedure is to identify the organization's strengths, shortcomings, and potential obstacles that could occur during the transformation process.

To ascertain an organization's commitment to digital transformation, it is critical to evaluate its leadership and vision. Driving change and ensuring that digital projects are in line with the organization's strategic objectives require strong leadership and a clear vision. Assess the top executives' readiness to embrace digital transformation, their awareness of its possible effects, and their capacity to persuade and motivate the company to move toward a digital future. A key factor in the success of digital transformation is organizational culture. Assess the organization's readiness to adopt a digital mindset by evaluating the current culture to find any potential change resistance. Watch for indications of change resistance, compartmentalized thinking, and a lack of cooperation. The organization's preparation for digital transformation can be greatly improved by implementing change management tactics that involve the workforce, encourage an innovative culture, and offer support and training.

Analyze the organization's current technological capabilities and infrastructure to find any gaps that can obstruct efforts at digital transformation. Analyze the adaptability, security, and scalability of the current infrastructure and systems. Take into account the company's readiness to implement cutting-edge technologies, including cloud computing, big data analytics, AI, and the IoT. Determine any obstacles or restrictions that would need to be removed to support the organization's digital transformation objectives. Digital transformation depends on data to function. Examine the organization's data management skills, including processes for data collection, storage, analysis, and governance. Analyze how well data is integrated, accessible, and distributed across systems and divisions. Think about how the company can use data to gain actionable insights and make smart decisions. Determine whether the company is prepared to implement advanced analytics tools and practices that can spur innovation and a competitive edge.

A trained and flexible workforce is necessary for digital transformation. Assess the organization's present talent pool to find any skill shortages and determine how prepared people are to learn and develop the required abilities. Take into account the availability of technological know-how, digital literacy, and the capacity to accept new working methods. Find ways to reskill and upskill personnel to make sure they have the skills necessary to succeed in a digital environment. The ultimate goal of digital transformation is to enhance the customer experience. Analyze the company's current customer engagement tactics and digital channel touchpoints. To improve customer interactions, personalize experiences, and deliver value-added services, evaluate the readiness to embrace customer-centric techniques and utilize emerging technology. Take into account the company's capacity to collect and utilize client feedback and data to promote ongoing improvement.

2.4.6 Financial Analysis

Analyzing financial data is essential when evaluating how the digital transformation will affect a company. In order to evaluate the transformation's financial viability and efficacy, it requires examining the company's financial health and performance before, during, and after the transformation. Here are the important factors to take into account when performing financial analysis for a digital transformation.

- *Cost–Benefit Analysis*: Evaluate the costs associated with digital transformation initiatives, including investments in technology infrastructure, software, employee training, and implementation. Compare these costs to the expected benefits, such as increased operational efficiency, cost savings, revenue growth, and improved customer satisfaction. Conduct a comprehensive cost–benefit analysis to assess the financial viability and potential ROI of the digital transformation efforts.
- *Revenue Generation*: Assess the potential impact of digital transformation on revenue generation. Identify new revenue streams that can be unlocked through digital initiatives, such as e-commerce platforms, online services, or data monetization. Analyze market trends and customer preferences to estimate the revenue growth opportunities that can be realized through digital transformation. Consider factors like market share, pricing strategies, and the ability to reach new customer segments.
- *Cost Reduction and Efficiency*: Digital transformation can lead to cost reductions and improved operational efficiency through automation, streamlined processes, and optimized resource allocation. Analyze the potential cost savings resulting from digital initiatives, such as reduced manual labor, minimized paperwork, and improved supply chain management. Assess the

impact of digital transformation on key financial indicators like cost per unit, operating margins, and overall profitability.

- *Cash Flow Analysis*: Evaluate the impact of digital transformation on the organization's cash flow. Consider the timing of cash inflows and outflows related to the transformation initiatives. Assess the impact on working capital requirements, cash conversion cycles, and the ability to manage liquidity during the transformation process. Conduct sensitivity analysis to understand how variations in revenue, costs, or implementation delays can affect cash flow projections.
- *Risk Assessment*: Analyze the financial risks associated with digital transformation. Identify potential risks, such as budget overruns, technology failures, cybersecurity threats, or disruptions to business operations during the transition. Assess the financial impact of these risks and develop mitigation strategies to minimize their potential consequences. Consider the organization's risk appetite, insurance coverage, and contingency plans to address potential financial uncertainties.
- *ROI and Payback Period*: Calculate the expected ROI and payback period for the digital transformation initiatives. Assess the financial benefits and costs over a defined period to determine how long it will take for the organization to recoup its investment and start generating positive returns. Consider the time value of money and discount future cash flows to determine the present value of the expected benefits.

2.4.7 Creating a Roadmap

Planning and executing a successful digital transformation journey require the development of a road map. It provides a structured approach and a distinct direction to guide the organization through the process. Conducting a thorough analysis of the current state of the organization is the first stage in developing a road map. This involves analyzing the current systems, processes, and technologies, as well as the organization's strengths, vulnerabilities, opportunities, and threats (SWOT analysis). Assess the digital maturity level of the organization, including its preparedness for change, the current level of technology adoption, and the alignment of digital initiatives with strategic goals. Identify trouble spots, impediments, and improvement-required areas. This evaluation provides a foundational comprehension of the organization's current state and serves as the basis for defining the desired future state.

Define the desired future state for the organization based on the current state assessment. Align the digital transformation objectives and objectives with the organization's overall strategy. Identify the critical areas requiring transformation and determine the desired outcomes. For instance, objectives may include enhancing operational efficiency, improving customer experience, increasing revenue through digital channels, or spurring innovation through data analytics. Prioritize initiatives based on their potential impact, their feasibility, and their alignment with the organization's strategic objectives. The future state definition functions as the roadmap's guiding vision and aids in establishing the transformation journey's course.

Once the future state has been defined, create a detailed road map outlining the required actions, timelines, and resources to achieve the desired outcomes. The transformation voyage should be divided into manageable phases, each with its own objectives and milestones. Identify the essential initiatives, projects, and investments required at each phase, as well as their dependencies and interdependencies. Define the duties and responsibilities of stakeholders involved in the process of implementation and establish governance structures to ensure effective decision-making and project management. Consider budget, technology requirements, talent acquisition or upskilling, and change management strategies when developing a realistic schedule and allocating resources effectively. Throughout the transformation process, routinely monitor progress, evaluate and adjust the road map as necessary, and communicate updates and accomplishments to stakeholders.

In today's quick-paced, technologically advanced world, digital transformation has become an essential business requirement. Businesses in all sectors use digital technologies to boost productivity, improve customer service, and gain a competitive advantage. A thorough strategic study is necessary to evaluate the potential influence on various business elements before initiating and managing digital transformation efforts. This part aims to thoroughly study the strategic ramifications of digital transformation and how it will affect necessary fields, including operations, marketing, customer experience, and talent management (Table 2.2).

2.4.8 Analysis

Business operations are significantly impacted by digital transformation. Robotic process automation and AI technologies streamline operations, lower error rates, and boost productivity by automating manual tasks. Additionally, it makes it possible to collect and analyze data in real time, giving decision-makers helpful information. Organizations can improve supply chain visibility and agility through digital transformation, which results in improved inventory management and quicker responses to consumer requests. IoT and AI technology applications also provide proactive maintenance, efficient resource management, and enhanced operational performance.

Utilizing customer data analysis, digital transformation revolutionizes marketing operations. It makes it possible to create customized marketing campaigns based on demographics, behavior, and personal interests. Social media and digital platforms can be used by businesses to target specific customer segments efficiently. Integrating CRM systems allows for a more comprehensive view of all client interactions, which improves customer engagement and retention. Organizations may assess the success of marketing efforts and make data-driven decisions for improving their marketing strategy thanks to real-time analytics.

Customer Experience: Enhancing the total customer experience is made possible by digital transformation. It enables businesses to offer a seamless omnichannel experience, allowing customers to interact with the brand consistently across a range of touchpoints. Chatbots and virtual assistants powered by AI provide round-the-clock customer service, enhancing responsiveness and cutting down on customer wait times. Organizations may give personalized product and service suggestions by utilizing

TABLE 2.2   Impact of digital transformation on key business areas

BUSINESS AREA	IMPACT OF DIGITAL TRANSFORMATION
Operations	– Automation of manual processes
	– Improved data collection and analysis for decision-making
	– Enhanced supply chain visibility and agility
	– Implementation of IoT and AI technologies for predictive maintenance and optimized resource allocation
Marketing	– Personalized marketing campaigns based on customer data analysis
	– Utilization of social media and digital platforms for targeted advertising and brand promotion
	– Integration of CRM systems for improved customer engagement and retention
	– Real-time analytics for measuring marketing effectiveness and optimizing campaigns
Customer Experience	– Seamless omnichannel experience for customers
	– 24/7 customer support through AI-powered chatbots and virtual assistants
	– Customized product and service recommendations based on individual preferences and behavior
	– Integration of augmented reality and virtual reality technologies to enhance product visualization and customer interaction
Talent Management	– Upskilling and reskilling of employees to adapt to digital technologies
	– Remote work and flexible work arrangements enabled by digital tools and collaboration platforms
	– Recruitment of digital-savvy talent to drive innovation and support digital transformation initiatives
	– Adoption of data-driven performance management systems for objective evaluation and feedback

consumer data, increasing customer happiness and loyalty. Customers may view products and engage with them in novel ways thanks to integrating AR and VR technologies.

Talent management practices have changed tremendously due to the digital revolution. For businesses to adapt to new digital technologies and tools, people need to upskill and reskill. Digital tools and collaboration platforms' flexibility make working remotely and with flexible schedules possible, which promotes a healthier work–life balance. To promote innovation and support digital transformation activities within the firm, it is now crucial to recruit digitally competent employees. Additionally, using data-driven performance management systems enables objective evaluation of employee performance and prompt feedback for ongoing improvement.

2.4.9 Assessing the Impact of Digital Transformation

Strategic analysis is crucial for determining how technology-driven changes can affect different areas of an organization while evaluating the effects of digital transformation. During the strategic analysis, keep the following points in mind:

- *Business Processes*: A substantial impact of digital transformation on current business processes. It is crucial to examine present procedures and pinpoint areas where digital technology might boost effectiveness, simplify processes, and cut costs. This study assists in locating potential dependencies, bottlenecks, and opportunities for automation or digitization to provide tangible benefits.
- *Organizational Structure and Culture*: Organizational structure and culture change are frequently necessary for digital transformation. Analyzing the workforce's capacity for change in new procedures and technology is essential. Assessing organizational hierarchy, communication pathways, and cultural norms aids in spotting potential change-resistance barriers and developing management measures.
- *Customer Experience*: Digital transformation has the potential to change how businesses connect with their clients completely. Organizations can find ways to use technology to improve the overall customer experience by analyzing their customers' needs, preferences, and expectations. Understanding client touchpoints, data analytics, and the application of digital tools are all included in this analysis to personalize and maximize customer interactions.
- *Competitive Environment*: To understand how digital transformation may affect an organization's position within the industry, the strategic analysis assesses the competitive environment. Analyzing industry trends, possible disruptors, and rivals' digital capabilities aids in spotting chances for differentiation and competitive advantage. Additionally, it enables businesses to foresee changes in the industry and modify their plans accordingly.
- *Data and Analytics*: A key component of digital transformation is decision-making based on data. Analyzing a company's data assets, data management procedures, and analytics skills is part of the strategic analysis process. For companies to effectively harness data and provide actionable insights, it is important to assess the quality, accessibility, and relevance of the data that will be used to drive digital efforts.
- *Security and Risks*: Digital transformation creates new security dangers and difficulties. Assessing potential risks related to data breaches, cybersecurity threats, and compliance issues is a part of doing a strategic analysis. Throughout the process of digital transformation, this analysis aids firms in creating strong security frameworks, putting risk mitigation techniques into practice, and ensuring regulatory compliance.

To evaluate how digital transformation will affect a business, strategic analysis is an essential first step. It offers a thorough understanding of numerous aspects, including company procedures, organizational design, customer experience, market competition, data and analytics, hazards, and security. Organizations may establish effective digital strategies, make informed decisions, and successfully deal with the difficulties posed by the digital transition by undertaking a complete strategic analysis. Organizations may take advantage of new opportunities, stimulate innovation, and experience sustainable success in the digital era by embracing digital transformation with a strategic mentality.

2.5 CONCLUSION

Organizations need to embrace digital transformation to adapt and stay ahead of the competition in the fast-paced digital environment of today. Technology may be effectively used to generate value for customers, streamline internal operations, and spur innovation in the digital environment. Significant benefits of the technology include data-driven decision-making, operational efficiency, customer-centricity, and innovation and agility. Organizations have to emphasize innovation, prioritize the customer experience, adopt agile operations, invest in data analytics and insights, and create strategic partnerships if they want to exploit technology and acquire a competitive edge. Organizations need to be cognizant of the dangers and difficulties that come with technology, including security and privacy issues, talent and skill shortages, outdated systems, and change management. Organizations can prepare themselves for success in the dynamic digital age by reevaluating their business models and creating a thorough digital strategy that harmonizes technology and business objectives. The main ideas from Chapter 2 about digital transformation and its effects on organizations are summarized in Table 2.3.

TABLE 2.3   Key aspects of digital transformation for organizations

KEY ASPECTS	DESCRIPTION
Customer-Centricity	Leveraging technology to create value for customers and enhance the overall customer experience.
Operational Efficiency	Optimizing internal processes through technology adoption to improve productivity and reduce costs.
Innovation and Agility	Using technology to drive innovation, foster creativity, and adapt quickly to changing market dynamics.
Data-Driven Decision Making	Harnessing data analytics and insights to make informed and strategic business decisions.
Embracing Innovation	Encouraging a culture of innovation within the organization to explore new technologies and ideas.

(Continued)

TABLE 2.3   (Continued) Key aspects of digital transformation for organizations

KEY ASPECTS	DESCRIPTION
Prioritizing Customer Experience	Making the customer experience a top priority and tailoring digital solutions to meet their needs and preferences.
Embracing Agile Operations	Adopting agile methodologies to enable faster development cycles, iterative improvements, and efficient project management.
Strategic Partnerships	Collaborating with external partners to leverage complementary strengths, access new technologies, and drive mutual growth.
Security and Privacy Concerns	Being mindful of potential risks and challenges related to security and privacy in the digital landscape and addressing them.
Talent and Skills Gaps	Addressing the need for skilled professionals and investing in training and development to bridge any skills gaps in the workforce.
Legacy Systems	Overcoming the limitations of legacy systems by modernizing infrastructure and integrating new technologies.
Change Management	Effectively managing organizational change to ensure a smooth transition and adoption of new technologies and digital practices.
Rethinking Business Models	Evaluating and adapting existing business models to align with the opportunities and challenges presented by digital transformation.
Comprehensive Digital Strategy	Developing a well-defined strategy that integrates technology and business goals to drive success in the digital age.

REFERENCE

1. Porter, M.E., Technology and competitive advantage. *Journal of Business Strategy*, 1985. **5**(3): pp. 60–78.

Digital Organization

3

3.1 OVERCOMING CHALLENGES AND CAPITALIZING ON OPPORTUNITIES

In the realm of digital organizations, the landscape is rife with both challenges and opportunities. Overcoming these challenges and adeptly capitalizing on opportunities are paramount for success. One key challenge is the rapid pace of technological evolution, which demands constant adaptation to remain relevant and competitive. Additionally, the virtual nature of digital operations can pose hurdles in fostering effective communication and collaboration among teams. Cybersecurity threats also loom large, requiring robust measures to safeguard sensitive data. However, within these challenges lie tremendous opportunities. The digital sphere offers unparalleled reach, enabling organizations to connect with a global audience and tap into diverse markets. Data analytics empowers informed decision-making, while automation streamlines processes for enhanced efficiency. Embracing remote work capabilities can attract top talent regardless of geographical boundaries. Success in the digital realm hinges on a proactive approach—leveraging technology, embracing innovation, and cultivating a dynamic organizational culture that thrives amid change.

3.1.1 Technological Challenges

The difficulties in implementing new technology, managing data, guaranteeing cybersecurity, and dealing with old systems are the root of these difficulties. First of all, corporations may need help to incorporate new technologies. Businesses need to continually assess and deploy new tools and processes to be competitive in the face of rapid technological changes. However, integrating these technologies calls for large infrastructure, training, and change management costs. Organizations may need help to go through the numerous options available and select the technologies that are most suited to their unique requirements. The administration of data presents a serious difficulty, too. Massive volumes of data are produced by digital transformation, and companies need to be able to properly gather, store, and analyze these data. To produce actionable insights, they require reliable data governance frameworks, data storage infrastructure,

DOI: 10.1201/9781003471226-4

and data analytics technologies. Data management is further complicated by the need to protect data privacy and comply with applicable laws.

Another significant technological problem in the process of digital transformation is cybersecurity. Organizations are more susceptible to cyber dangers as they rely more on digital technologies and data. Strong cybersecurity measures are needed to safeguard sensitive data, stop data breaches, and guarantee the integrity of systems and networks. To remain ahead of possible dangers, firms need to constantly improve their security procedures and technologies as cyberattacks become more complex. Last but not least, legacy systems are a major barrier to digital transformation. Many firms still need to use updated infrastructure and technology that are compatible with more modern digital solutions. Legacy system integration can be difficult, time-consuming, and expensive. Businesses frequently have to choose between replacing entire systems or figuring out how to get them to operate together, which can slow down the speed of digital transformation.

3.1.1.1 Legacy systems

For many firms, legacy systems constitute a major roadblock to digital transformation. These systems make reference to long-established, out-of-date software, hardware, or technology. While they could have helped the company in the past, in the digital age, they can impede advancement and innovation. The incompatibility of old systems with contemporary platforms and technology is one of the key problems they present. They frequently utilize proprietary software that is difficult to integrate with more modern systems or are constructed using antiquated programming languages. The organization's capacity to make use of cutting-edge technologies, such as cloud computing, AI, and big data analytics, which are essential for digital transformation, is constrained by this need for interoperability. The inherent complexity and fragility of legacy systems is another significant problem. These systems have experienced multiple patches, modifications, and workarounds throughout time, creating a complex architecture that is challenging to comprehend and maintain. It might be difficult for new developers to browse and update the codebase in legacy systems since there is sometimes inadequate documentation. Additionally, there may be a knowledge gap since the original developers who created and maintained these systems may have left the company or retired. The implementation of new digital projects needs to be improved by this complexity and fragility, which also raises the possibility of system failures and security flaws.

When dealing with old systems, the cost is still another important aspect that makes the digital transition difficult. It can be expensive to replace or upgrade these systems, especially for large firms with substantial IT infrastructure. The cost covers data migration, training, and potential business disruptions during the change, in addition to the purchase of new gear and software licensing. Organizations are frequently discouraged from starting their digital transformation journeys by the fear of hefty upfront expenses, which drives them to continue with their current systems, even if they need to be updated and more effective. The last potential obstacle to digital transformation is culture. Long-term users of these systems will not be open to change. They are used to doing things the old way and may see the digital transformation as a threat to their expertise or job security. A thorough change management strategy is necessary to overcome this reluctance, which includes educating staff members about the advantages of the digital transition, offering training opportunities, and promoting an innovative and adaptable culture.

3.1.1.2 Change management

Change management is one of the major difficulties encountered during this transforming journey. The term "change management" describes an organized method of getting people and teams ready to embrace new procedures, and technology. Change management can frequently operate as a roadblock to effective digital transformation programs, despite its significance. First of all, resistance to change is a typical barrier to digital transformation. The advent of new technology may make workers feel intimidated and make them worry about losing their employment or areas of expertise. This opposition can impede development and delay the adoption of new digital tools and procedures if appropriate change management measures are not in place. Organizations need to spend money on programs that educate employees to comprehend the advantages of digital transformation and allay their anxieties in order to break through this barrier.

An organization's inability to be flexible and agile can hinder digital transformation initiatives. The rigid processes and traditional hierarchical structures may not be compatible with the dynamic nature of digital technologies. In order to eliminate silos, promote cooperation, and develop a culture of creativity and adaptability, change management becomes essential [1]. Teams need to be given the freedom to experiment and iterate under the direction of leaders who need to drive the transformation actively. Organizations can become more agile and responsive to the changing digital landscape by embracing change management principles. Third, a major roadblock to digital transformation can be poor planning and preparedness. Organizations may find it easier to negotiate the challenges of technology adoption, process reform, and skill development with a clear roadmap and change management strategy. A well-structured framework for managing the transition can be found in change management approaches for leading change. These techniques place a strong emphasis on the necessity of effective stakeholder participation, open communication, and ongoing evaluation. Efforts to implement digital transformation might need more leadership alignment and sponsorship. Strong leadership commitment and participation at all organizational levels are necessary for change management. Confusion, resistance, and eventual project failure can result from leaders' failure to provide clear guidance, allocate resources, and actively promote change. To effectively manage change, a business needs to identify and work with change champions who can promote efforts for digital transformation and push for necessary changes in culture and behavior.

3.1.1.3 Data and security concerns

Concerns about data and security have become important roadblocks to digital transformation attempts in a variety of businesses. Organizations are increasingly relying on digital technology to improve customer experiences and optimize operations. Therefore, it is crucial to safeguard sensitive data and implement strong cybersecurity safeguards. Concerns about data privacy, integrity, and governance are raised by the enormous amount of data that firms produce and maintain. Concerns about unauthorized access, data breaches, and potential reputational harm are also brought up by the increase in cyber threats and advanced hacking techniques. Many firms are approaching digital transformation cautiously as a result of these worries, weighing the advantages of digitization against the dangers posed by data security. The safety of employee and consumer data is one of the main issues with digital transformation. Organizations amass enormous volumes of sensitive information, including financial data, medical records, and personally identifiable information, as a result of the expansion of digital channels. Maintaining trust and abiding by privacy laws like the GDPR and the CCPA depend on protecting this data from unwanted access, misuse, or breaches. Data security is a primary consideration for firms pursuing digital transformation due to the possible negative effects of data breaches, including monetary loss, legal obligations, and reputational damage to the company.

Additionally, the interconnectedness and complexity of digital ecosystems create new risks and vulnerabilities. The attack surface increases as businesses use cloud computing, IoT devices, and third-party applications, giving attackers more access points. Strong cybersecurity measures, such as encryption, intrusion detection systems, and frequent security assessments, are needed to ensure the security and resilience of these digital infrastructures. However, putting these measures into place and keeping them up-to-date can be time- and resource-consuming, adding still another level of complexity to the process of digital transformation. Last but not least, firms looking to start digital transformation programs face a substantial hurdle due to a need for qualified cybersecurity specialists. There is a skills scarcity in the business as a result of the demand for cybersecurity expertise considerably outstripping the supply. It can take time to find qualified individuals capable of developing and executing strong security frameworks, monitoring threats, and responding to crises. Organizations may hesitate to pursue digital transformation or compromise security if they lack proper cybersecurity resources, leaving their systems and data vulnerable to assaults.

3.1.1.4 Skill gaps

Organizational initiatives for digital transformation may need to be improved by skill gaps. Digital transformation has become crucial for businesses in today's fast-paced, technologically-driven corporate environment in order to maintain competitiveness and react to shifting market dynamics. However, the development of these projects may need to be improved by a lack of the skills and knowledge needed to deploy and utilize digital technology. Organizations need to address skill shortages to successfully navigate the journey of digital transformation, regardless of whether it involves understanding emerging technologies, data analytics, or cybersecurity. The rapid growth of technology is one of the main issues with skill gaps in digital transformation. New tools and platforms are routinely released, and digital technologies are continually changing. This makes it difficult for businesses to keep up with new developments and make sure their staff members are equipped with the skills needed to use these technologies efficiently. Organizations can find it easier to embrace and integrate these technologies into their operations with a workforce that is knowledgeable about the most recent digital tools and methods, which would impede their efforts to undergo digital transformation.

Lack of specialized expertise is another facet of skill gaps as hurdles to digital transformation. Some digital efforts need specialized abilities or subject matter expertise that might not be easily accessible within the firm. For instance, putting ML or AI solutions into practice would call for data scientists or AI professionals who have a thorough understanding of these technologies. Initiatives for digital transformation may be slowed down or put on hold by the lack of such specialists since businesses find it difficult to recruit and retain the talent they need. Additionally, talent shortages are a result of the attitude and culture shift necessary for successful digital transformation. Digital transformation calls for a change in processes, methods of thinking, and technology, not just the adoption of new ones. Employees need to have a digital-first mentality and be flexible and open to learning new things. Progress can be hampered, though, by employee reluctance to change and a lack of proficiency with digital tools. To close these skill gaps and develop a workforce that is equipped for the digital age and can support ongoing digital transformation projects, organizations need to engage in training and upskilling programs.

3.1.2 Enablers of Digital Transformation

In the realm of digital transformation, "Enablers of Digital Transformation" play a pivotal role in driving organizational evolution and innovation. These enablers encompass the technological, strategic, and cultural elements that facilitate the successful integration of digital technologies into business operations. Technological enablers encompass cutting-edge tools and platforms that empower businesses to streamline processes, enhance efficiency, and expand their digital presence. Strategic enablers involve the formulation of cohesive digital strategies, including the identification of opportunities, competitive analysis, and risk assessment. Additionally, cultural enablers focus on nurturing a mindset of adaptability and continuous learning, encouraging employees to embrace change and harness digital tools to their fullest potential. Collectively, these enablers provide the foundation for businesses to navigate the digital landscape, capitalize on emerging trends, and ultimately achieve sustainable growth in an ever-evolving technological era.

3.1.2.1 Leadership and vision

Organizations can only adapt and survive in the digital age with the help of leadership and vision, which are essential enablers of digital transformation. Leaders need to have a clear strategy for utilizing technology to accomplish strategic goals in the continuously changing environment. They need to effectively convey this vision to everyone in the company in order to motivate and bring teams together around a common objective. Leaders who are aware of the potential of digital transformation and are able to explain its advantages are more likely to get stakeholders' support and commitment, which will increase the likelihood of a successful implementation.

A visionary leader understands that digital transformation involves changing corporate practices, culture, and customer experiences in addition to implementing new technologies. They are aware that in order to remain competitive, one needs to embrace innovation, take measured risks, and question conventional wisdom. Visionary leaders enable their teams to experiment with and adopt new digital tools and techniques by building a culture of continuous learning. They support agile decision-making by promoting cooperation and cross-functional integration, which breaks down silos.

To successfully navigate the complexities and uncertainties of digital transformation, leadership is essential. Leaders need to be flexible and agile in a quickly evolving digital environment, ready to seize new possibilities and change course when necessary. They need to be proactive in spotting new trends and technologies that have the potential to upend their sector and in devising plans to take advantage of them. Effective leaders also give their people the tools, training, and support they need to be prepared for digital transformation, ensuring that the company stays at the forefront of innovation.

3.1.2.2 Agile and adaptive culture

Agile and adaptive organizational cultures are essential for facilitating digital change. Agility is the capacity to react rapidly and successfully to shifting market dynamics, consumer needs, and technical breakthroughs in the context of digital transformation. Teams are better able to adapt and evolve quickly because of an agile culture that values flexibility, cooperation, and experimentation. For firms looking to use digital technologies to alter their company operations, goods, and customer experiences, this approach is crucial. Teams are empowered to make independent decisions and accept responsibility for their work in an agile culture. To enable quicker responses to market developments, hierarchies are flattened, and decision-making procedures are streamlined. Cross-functional cooperation is favored because it eliminates organizational silos and promotes seamless teamwork. With the help of this cooperative strategy, businesses may experiment quickly, learn from mistakes, and improve their digital endeavors.

An adaptive culture emphasizes ongoing learning and development, which supports an agile attitude. Organizations need to be adaptable and eager to learn from both achievements and failures in the continuously changing digital arena. A growth mentality, which pushes people to adopt new technology, pick up new skills, and investigate novel ideas, is fostered by an adaptive culture. It fosters a culture of learning that rewards risk-taking and encourages experimentation, fostering a favorable environment for digital transformation.

3.1.2.3 Customer-centricity

Customer-centricity is essential for enterprise digital changes to be effective. Organizations that prioritize the wants and preferences of their consumers are more likely to succeed in the quickly changing digital market. Companies may use digital technology to improve customer experiences, spur innovation, and achieve sustainable growth by putting the consumer at the heart of their strategy and operations. As a guiding principle, customer-centricity enables firms to adjust to shifting customer expectations, take advantage of data-driven insights, and develop individualized interactions across numerous digital platforms. The gathering and analysis of customer data is one of the major facilitators of a customer-centric digital transformation. Businesses can obtain a thorough grasp of the habits, preferences, and problems of their customers by utilizing advanced analytics and AI. Companies can customize their offerings to match the needs of specific clients thanks to this data-driven strategy. Organizations may discover patterns, predict trends, and make wise decisions that promote corporate success and customer pleasure by leveraging the power of consumer data.

The adoption of customer journey mapping is another factor that supports customer-centric digital transformation. Visualizing and comprehending the complete client experience, from the first point of contact to the last purchase and beyond, is a necessary step in this process. Businesses may pinpoint pain points, bottlenecks, and chances for development by mapping out the customer journey. This makes it possible for businesses to improve every phase of the customer experience, resulting in a smooth and customized trip across all digital touchpoints. Increased customer satisfaction and loyalty result from firms' alignment of digital transformation initiatives with consumer expectations through the use of customer journey mapping. Additionally, firms need to undergo a culture transition in order to become more customer-centric. It entails encouraging a customer-focused mindset across all organizational levels and divisions. Employees need to be given the freedom and support they need to put the needs of the customers first and actively look for ways to improve that experience. A culture that prioritizes the needs of the client should be supported through efficient training, recognition, and communication initiatives. Businesses may make sure that digital transformation activities are motivated by the objective of providing outstanding value to consumers by fostering a customer-centric mentality inside the firm.

3.1.2.4 Strategic partnerships

In today's rapidly evolving digital landscape, businesses recognize the need to leverage the expertise and resources of external partners to stay competitive and innovative. These partnerships enable companies to access new technologies, expand their reach, and enhance their capabilities, ultimately accelerating their digital transformation journey.

The capacity to access specialist knowledge and resources is one important advantage of strategic alliances in digital transformation. As technology develops at an incredible rate, it can be difficult for enterprises to stay current on their own with the newest trends and advancements. Companies can leverage the knowledge of partners who are experts in particular fields, such as AI, cloud computing, or cybersecurity, by developing strategic alliances. By working together, organizations may deploy cutting-edge technology and solutions while utilizing the expertise and resources of their partners, resulting in a smoother and more efficient digital transformation. Strategic relationships may present chances for cooperation and innovation. Organizations can build an innovation culture and share ideas that promote digital transformation by collaborating with outside partners. Co-creation of brand-new goods or services, joint R&D projects, and joint investments in emerging technology are all examples of partnerships. Companies may use the pooled brainpower and creativity of several organizations by working together, which will help them discover creative solutions to difficult digital problems.

Last but not least, strategic alliances offer access to fresh markets and clientele. Increasing client reach is essential for long-term growth in the digital era. Having a partnership with companies that serve various consumer segments or have a strong presence in emerging markets can be quite advantageous. Through these alliances, businesses can reach out to new clientele, benefit from the reputation of their partners' brands, and learn crucial information about regional markets. Organizations can establish synergies that allow them to break into new markets and expedite their digital transformation by combining complementary capabilities and resources.

3.1.2.5 Data-driven decision-making

Companies now have access to enormous volumes of data from a variety of sources, including social media, market trends, and client interactions. Organizations can gain useful insights from this data and use those insights to make wiser and more effective decisions by utilizing advanced analytics tools and approaches. Enhancing operational efficiency is one of the main benefits of data-driven decision-making. Organizations can spot patterns, trends, and anomalies that escape attention using more conventional techniques by studying massive databases. Businesses may streamline operations, identify problem areas, and enhance procedures thanks to these insights. For instance, by looking at consumer data, businesses can spot supply chain bottlenecks, change inventory levels, and speed up delivery times, all of which lower costs and boost customer happiness.

Furthermore, firms can take a proactive rather than a reactive stance thanks to data-driven decision-making. Companies can foresee trends and changes in consumer behavior, market dynamics, and competitive dynamics by keeping an eye on real-time data and applying predictive analytics. Businesses can stay ahead of the curve by timely altering their strategies, goods, and services thanks to this insight. An e-commerce business, for instance, might utilize data analytics to forecast client demand during peak holiday shopping seasons and modify its marketing initiatives, inventory levels, and pricing as necessary.

Data-driven strategies promote innovation and agility in addition to operational effectiveness and proactive decision-making. Organizations can spot new possibilities, undiscovered markets, and emerging trends by regularly collecting and evaluating data. With the use of this knowledge, businesses can create new goods and services that cater to changing consumer demands. Additionally, data-driven decision-making enables businesses to quickly adjust to shifting consumer preferences and market realities. Companies may make data-backed decisions, change their plans, and react quickly to market disruptions or changes in consumer demand by routinely monitoring and analyzing data.

3.1.3 Develop a Comprehensive Digital Strategy

A key component of achieving this shift is creating a thorough digital strategy. The vision, objectives, and action plans required to make the most of technology and promote innovation throughout the business are laid out in a digital strategy. Businesses may improve consumer experiences, optimize processes, and develop new revenue sources by embracing digitalization. However, a comprehensive strategy is required to realize the promise of digital technologies effectively. A thorough grasp of the organization's present situation and desired future is the first step in developing a comprehensive digital strategy. It entails carrying out a comprehensive analysis of the systems, procedures, and capacities already in place and determining areas in need of development. This evaluation lays the groundwork for the plan and determines the organization's level of digital maturity. Organizations can set their digital vision and goals and link them with the overarching business objectives by having a thorough awareness of the existing situation.

Finding the digital transformation enablers is the next stage in creating a comprehensive digital strategy. These enablers include the essential platforms, technologies, and functionalities that will power digitalization initiatives. Cloud computing, data analytics, AI, IoT, automation, and other technologies may be included. Organizations need to evaluate which enablers fit with their digital vision and then give those implementations the highest priority. Making a roadmap for each enabler's integration into the organization's operations entails assessing each one's viability, potential impact, and resource needs. A thorough digital strategy also comprises a workable implementation and execution plan. The precise projects, efforts, and timetables necessary to carry out the digital vision are described in this plan. To make sure the organization has the necessary skills to carry out the plan successfully, it also contains plans for change management, talent acquisition, and skill development. To keep the strategy in line with shifting market dynamics and technology improvements, regular monitoring, review, and revision are necessary.

3.1.4 Invest in Robust Digital Infrastructure

A robust digital infrastructure consists of the necessary hardware, software, networks, and data centers to support digital processes and services. Companies can unlock the full potential of digital transformation and obtain a competitive edge in the digital landscape by investing in these foundational elements. The capacity to leverage advanced technologies like cloud computing, big data analytics, and IoT is a significant advantage of investing in a robust digital infrastructure. To function optimally and deliver their maximum benefits, these technologies require a robust underlying infrastructure. Cloud computing, for example, enables businesses to remotely store and access immense quantities of data and applications, offering scalability, flexibility, and cost-effectiveness. Big data analytics enables organizations to extract valuable insights from vast datasets, thereby facilitating data-driven decision-making. The IoT enables real-time monitoring, automation, and predictive maintenance by connecting devices and systems. All of these transformative technologies rely on a dependable and secure digital infrastructure to operate.

Moreover, investing in digital infrastructure is necessary for ensuring a robust and adaptable business environment. A robust infrastructure can accommodate growing data volumes, facilitate high-speed connectivity, and preserve data integrity and security. As the pace of digital transformation quickens, organizations need to be prepared to meet the increasing demands placed on their networks, servers, and storage systems. A digital infrastructure that is well-designed and scalable can accommodate these demands and enable businesses to rapidly adapt to shifting market conditions. Additionally, it reduces the possibility of disruptions and delays, ensuring continuous operations and a seamless customer experience.

3.1.5 Foster a Culture of Innovation and Collaboration

By fostering a culture that encourages and rewards innovative thinking, organizations can motivate employees to investigate new ideas and experiment with emerging technologies. Collaboration is crucial to the success of digital transformation projects. In a swiftly evolving digital landscape, only some individuals or departments can possess all of the necessary knowledge and skills to navigate the complexities of technology-driven transformations. By fostering collaboration, organizations can bring together diverse perspectives and specialized knowledge from various departments and teams. This cross-functional collaboration facilitates a more holistic approach to problem-solving and encourages the exchange of ideas and best practices, thereby accelerating the digital transformation journey.

Developing a culture of innovation and collaboration necessitates leadership support and an openness to change. Leaders need to promote a growth mindset and encourage employees to take risks and learn from their mistakes. To facilitate the sharing of ideas and information, they should establish distinct channels for communication and collaboration, both within teams and across the organization. In addition, providing resources and tools that support innovation and collaboration, such as innovation labs, digital platforms for knowledge sharing, and agile project management methodologies, can further improve an organization's capacity to drive digital transformation effectively.

3.1.6 Prioritize Change Management and Employee Engagement

Change management is the structured process of preparing, equipping, and supporting individuals and teams to adopt and implement new technologies and processes. On the other hand, employee engagement refers to the emotional commitment and active involvement of employees in their work and the organization's objectives. When these two factors are effectively addressed and incorporated into digital transformation initiatives, organizations are able to navigate the challenges and maximize the benefits of digitalization.

Change management is essential for ensuring that employees are willing and able to embrace digital transformation. It requires evaluating the organization's readiness for change, identifying potential obstacles, and implementing strategies to surmount resistance. Organizations can cultivate a positive and supportive environment for change by involving employees early in the process, providing clear communication and training, and addressing employees' concerns and fears. Change management also assists in aligning the attitudes, behaviors, and skills of employees with the new digital initiatives, thereby enhancing the likelihood of successful implementation and adoption.

Employee engagement is a critical success factor for digital transformation. Engaged employees are more likely to embrace change, pursue opportunities to leverage digital technologies proactively, and contribute their ideas and efforts to drive innovation. Engaging employees in the digital transformation voyage requires instilling them with a sense of purpose and meaning, ensuring their voices are heard and valued, and rewarding their contributions. Organizations can increase engagement by providing opportunities for learning and development, promoting collaboration and cross-functional teamwork, and fostering a culture of trust and openness. Engaged employees become champions and advocates for digital transformation, inspiring others to adopt the change and propelling the overall success of the organization.

3.1.7 Embrace Agile and Iterative Approaches

Traditional, linear project management approaches are frequently unsuitable for the swiftly evolving digital landscape. Agile methodologies, such as Scrum and Kanban, enable organizations to rapidly adapt to changing customer demands, market conditions, and technological advances. Agile methodologies promote collaboration, flexibility, and continuous development by dividing complex projects into smaller, more manageable tasks.

One of the primary advantages of adopting agile and iterative methodologies is the ability to deliver consumer value in shorter timeframes. Instead of delivering a product or service upon completion of a protracted development cycle, agile methodologies emphasize incremental delivery. This allows organizations to collect early customer feedback and make the necessary adjustments to satisfy their needs better. By embracing iterations, businesses can continually refine and improve their digital products, ensuring their continued relevance in a fast-paced, competitive market.

An additional benefit of employing agile and iterative methodologies is improved collaboration and communication between cross-functional teams. Agile methodologies encourage stakeholders, product owners, developers, and other team members to collaborate closely. Regular meetings, such as daily stand-ups and sprint evaluations, promote open communication, transparency, and shared responsibility. This collaborative environment fosters innovation, creativity, and the capacity to respond rapidly to emerging challenges or opportunities.

3.1.8 Collaborate with External Partners and Startups

By collaborating with startups and other external partners, businesses can access an abundance of specialized knowledge, gain access to cutting-edge technologies, and gain new perspectives on tackling difficult problems. The ability of external collaborators and startups to contribute disruptive technologies and ideas is one of the primary advantages of collaborating with them. In particular, startups are frequently at the forefront of innovation, utilizing emerging technologies such as AI, blockchain, and the IoT to develop groundbreaking solutions. By partnering with these entrepreneurs, businesses can gain access to their expertise and transformative technologies, which can help streamline processes, increase efficiency, and generate new business models.

Additionally, collaboration with external partners and startups can cultivate an innovative culture within an organization. Startups are recognized for their adaptability, entrepreneurial spirit, and willingness to take calculated risks. By collaborating with them, businesses can infuse their own teams with these characteristics, fostering a mindset of continuous refinement and experimentation. This collaboration can result in the creation of new products and services, as well as the implementation of innovative strategies that promote digital transformation and keep organizations competitive in the digital age.

3.1.9 Continuously Monitor and Measure Progress

By establishing effective surveillance and measurement mechanisms, businesses can collect real-time insights, identify bottlenecks, and optimize their digital transformation journey with data-driven decisions. The capacity to track KPIs that align with the organization's digital transformation objectives is a crucial aspect of continuous monitoring. These KPIs include customer satisfaction, revenue growth, cost reduction, process efficiency, and employee productivity. By measuring these indicators on a regular basis, organizations can assess the impact of their digital initiatives and identify improvement areas. This allows them to make timely modifications, effectively allocate resources, and maintain focus on their transformation goals.

In addition, continuous monitoring and measurement provide valuable feedback loops to organizations. By capturing and analyzing data from multiple sources, such as customer feedback, operational systems, and analytics platforms, businesses can gain insight into the efficacy and impact of their digital transformation initiatives. This feedback cycle allows organizations to refine their strategies and tactics based on real-time data. It aids in the early identification of potential risks and obstacles, enabling proactive mitigation measures and reducing the likelihood of costly setbacks.

In addition, continuous monitoring and measurement foster an organizational culture of openness and accountability. By sharing progress updates and performance metrics on a regular basis, stakeholders at various levels and departments can gain visibility into the digital transformation journey. This transparency encourages collaboration and alignment because it enables teams to comprehend their contributions, share best practices, and work collaboratively toward the organization's transformation objectives. In addition, it provides leaders with the information they need to effectively support and guide their teams, ensuring that resources are allocated appropriately, and obstacles are quickly addressed.

3.1.10 Mitigating Risks and Ensuring Sustainability

This section explores the critical elements that underpin a successful digital transformation strategy. From safeguarding data integrity to ensuring adaptable scalability, these components pave the way for organizations to not only navigate the challenges but also seize the boundless opportunities presented by the digital age.

- *Addressing Data Privacy and Security*: As organizations undergo digital transformation, ensuring data privacy and security becomes paramount. Implement robust cybersecurity measures to protect sensitive data from breaches and cyber threats. Adhere to relevant data protection regulations and guidelines to maintain customer trust. Conduct regular audits, vulnerability assessments, and employee training to strengthen data privacy and security practices. By prioritizing data protection, organizations can mitigate risks associated with digital transformation.

- *Scalability and Flexibility*: Digital transformation initiatives should be scalable and flexible to accommodate future growth and changing market dynamics. Consider scalability in technology investments to support increased data volumes, user traffic, and evolving business requirements. Adopt cloud-based solutions and platforms that offer scalability and flexibility. This ensures that digital capabilities adapt to organizational needs and support long-term sustainability.

- *Continuous Innovation and Adaptation*: Digital transformation is an ongoing journey rather than a one-time project. Organizations need to foster a culture of continuous innovation and adaptation to stay ahead in the digital landscape. Encourage employees to stay updated on emerging technologies, industry trends, and customer expectations. Foster a mindset of experimentation, learning from failures, and adapting strategies accordingly. By embracing continuous innovation, organizations can sustain their digital transformation efforts and seize new opportunities.

- *Measuring ROI*: To ensure the sustainability of digital transformation initiatives, organizations need to measure and demonstrate the ROI. Establish clear metrics and KPIs aligned with the strategic objectives of digital transformation. Regularly monitor and evaluate the financial and nonfinancial impacts of digital initiatives. Assess the value created regarding increased revenue, cost savings, improved customer satisfaction, and competitive advantage. By quantifying the ROI, organizations can make informed decisions, justify investments, and secure ongoing support for digital transformation efforts.

- *Learning from Industry Best Practices and Benchmarking*: Organizations can learn from industry best practices and benchmarking against competitors and digital leaders. Stay updated on the latest trends, success stories, and case studies related to digital transformation in your industry. Analyze how other organizations have overcome similar barriers and capitalized on opportunities. This knowledge can inspire new ideas, identify potential pitfalls, and inform the development of effective strategies for sustainable digital transformation.

- *Collaboration with Ecosystem Partners*: Digital transformation often involves collaboration with various ecosystem partners. Engage with suppliers, customers, and other stakeholders to identify joint innovation and co-creation opportunities. Foster open dialogue, share knowledge, and explore partnerships that create mutual value. By leveraging the collective intelligence of the ecosystem, organizations can tap into new ideas, access additional resources, and drive collaborative digital transformation initiatives that benefit all parties involved.

Digital transformation presents both challenges and opportunities for organizations. By implementing strategies to overcome barriers such as technological challenges, legacy systems, change management, data and security concerns, and skill gaps, organizations can position themselves for success. By embracing enablers like leadership and vision, adaptive culture, customer-centricity, strategic partnerships, and data-driven decision-making, they can capitalize on the opportunities presented by digital transformation. With a comprehensive digital strategy, robust infrastructure, a culture of innovation, and effective change management, organizations can navigate the digital landscape, drive transformational change, and thrive in the digital age.

3.2 LINKING STRATEGY TO EXECUTION: MAKING DIGITAL TRANSFORMATION WORK FOR YOUR ORGANIZATION

To succeed in today's digital landscape, businesses need to align their overall strategy with their digital transformation goals. Digital transformation involves leveraging technology to drive operational efficiency, enhance customer experience, and unlock new business opportunities. By aligning business strategy with digital transformation goals, organizations can ensure that their technology investments and initiatives are strategically aligned with their long-term objectives. Here are some key points to consider when aligning business strategy with digital transformation goals:

- *Vision and Purpose*: Clearly define the vision and purpose of your digital transformation efforts. Understand how digital transformation aligns with your organization's strategic goals and objectives. This will help create a sense of purpose and direction for your digital initiatives.
- *Customer-Centric Approach*: Place customers at the center of your digital transformation efforts. Understand their needs, preferences, and behaviors. Leverage data analytics and customer insights to inform decision-making and tailor digital solutions that enhance customer experiences.
- *Technology Assessment*: Evaluate your existing technological capabilities. Understand the strengths and weaknesses of your current IT infrastructure, systems, and processes. Identify any gaps or limitations that need to be addressed to support your digital transformation goals effectively.
- *Cultural Transformation*: Foster a culture of innovation, agility, and collaboration within your organization. Encourage employees to embrace change, take risks, and drive innovation. Create an environment where learning and experimentation are valued and cross-functional teams can collaborate effectively.
- *Strategic Partnerships*: Identify strategic partners who can support your digital transformation journey. Look for technology vendors, consultants, and service providers with expertise in the areas you need assistance with. Collaborate with these partners to leverage their knowledge and experience.

- *Roadmap Development*: Develop a roadmap that outlines the sequence of digital initiatives and their priorities. Consider the organization's capacity to absorb change, resource availability, and potential risks. A well-defined roadmap will guide the implementation of your digital transformation strategy.
- *Metrics and Monitoring*: Establish metrics to measure the progress and effectiveness of your digital transformation initiatives. Define KPIs that align with your business objectives. Regularly monitor these metrics to track the impact of your digital transformation efforts and make data-driven decisions.
- *Leadership and Governance*: Establish robust and transparent governance structures for your digital transformation initiatives. Assign roles and responsibilities, empower teams, and ensure accountability. Effective leadership and governance will drive alignment and ensure that digital transformation goals are integrated into the organization's fabric.

By aligning business strategy with digital transformation goals, organizations can navigate the digital landscape effectively and realize the full potential of their digital initiatives. It requires a holistic approach considering the organization's vision, customers, technology, culture, partnerships, roadmap, metrics, and leadership. With this alignment, businesses can embrace digital transformation as a strategic enabler for long-term success.

3.2.1 Identifying Critical Success Factors and Performance Indicators

In the digital transformation journey, organizations need to identify critical success factors and performance indicators to measure the effectiveness and progress of their initiatives. These factors and indicators serve as guideposts, helping organizations stay on track and ensure that their digital transformation efforts align with their strategic goals. By defining and monitoring these metrics, organizations can gain valuable insights and make data-driven decisions to drive their digital transformation initiatives forward (Figure 3.1).

(A) **Defining Key Success Factors**:
- *Business Objectives*: Clearly define the business objectives the digital transformation initiatives aim to achieve. These objectives include improving operational efficiency, enhancing customer experience, expanding market reach, or fostering innovation.
- *Customer Focus*: Strongly emphasize customer-centricity as a critical success factor. Understand customers' evolving needs and preferences and align digital transformation efforts to deliver enhanced experiences and personalized solutions.
- *Organizational Culture*: Foster a culture of innovation, agility, and collaboration. Encourage a growth mindset, promote experimentation, and empower employees to embrace change and drive innovation.

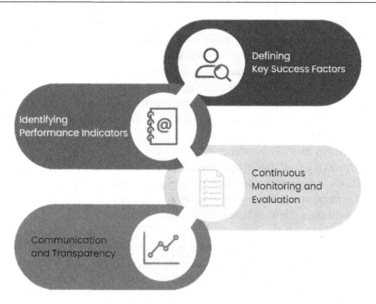

FIGURE 3.1   Steps for identifying critical success factors and performance indicators.

(B) **Identifying Performance Indicators**:
- *KPIs*: Define specific KPIs that align with the business objectives and reflect the desired outcomes of the digital transformation initiatives. These KPIs could include customer satisfaction, revenue growth, cost reduction, time-to-market, employee productivity, or market share.
- *Leading and Lagging Indicators*: Differentiate between leading and lagging indicators. Leading indicators are early predictors of success and measure activities or behaviors expected to drive desired outcomes. Lagging indicators, on the other hand, measure the actual results achieved. Both indicators are essential to provide a comprehensive view of the progress and impact of digital transformation efforts.
- *Qualitative and Quantitative Metrics*: Consider both qualitative and quantitative metrics to evaluate the effectiveness of digital transformation initiatives. Qualitative metrics may include customer feedback, employee satisfaction, or innovation culture assessments, while quantitative metrics could involve revenue growth percentages, cost savings, or conversion rates.

(C) **Continuous Monitoring and Evaluation**:
- *Regular Review*: Establish a cadence for reviewing and assessing the identified critical success factors and performance indicators. This ensures that progress is regularly tracked and adjustments can be made promptly.
- *Data-driven Decision-Making*: Use data and analytics to measure and analyze the identified performance indicators. Leverage technology solutions to collect, aggregate, and visualize data to gain actionable decision-making insights.

- *Course Correction*: Be prepared to make course corrections if performance indicators reveal areas where the digital transformation initiatives need to deliver the expected results. Flexibility and adaptability are crucial in driving successful digital transformation.

(D) **Communication and Transparency**:
- *Stakeholder Engagement*: Involve key stakeholders, such as senior leadership, employees, and customers, in the identification and understanding of critical success factors and performance indicators. Ensure a shared understanding of the measured metrics and the rationale behind their selection.
- *Transparent Reporting*: Communicate progress and results regularly through clear and concise reporting. Provide updates on the performance indicators to stakeholders, highlighting successes, challenges, and areas for improvement.

By identifying critical success factors and performance indicators, organizations can effectively monitor the progress and impact of their digital transformation initiatives. These metrics provide a framework for evaluating the alignment of digital initiatives with strategic objectives, making data-driven decisions, and fostering a culture of continuous improvement. Organizations can navigate the digital transformation journey with a robust system with clarity, agility, and confidence.

3.2.2 Establishing Governance and Accountability Mechanisms

Establishing effective governance and accountability mechanisms is crucial for driving successful digital transformation within organizations. Governance provides the structure, processes, and oversight necessary to guide and support digital initiatives, while accountability ensures that individuals and teams are responsible and answerable for their actions and outcomes. By implementing robust governance and accountability mechanisms, organizations can mitigate risks, ensure alignment with strategic objectives, and drive the desired outcomes of their digital transformation efforts.

- **Governance Framework**: A governance framework is a guiding structure for digital transformation initiatives. It encompasses the following elements:
  (a) *Clear Roles and Responsibilities*: Clearly define the roles and responsibilities of stakeholders involved in digital transformation, including senior leadership, project managers, IT teams, business units, and external partners. Each role should have well-defined objectives and accountabilities.
  (b) *Decision-Making Processes*: Establish transparent decision-making processes that outline who has the authority to make decisions at different stages of the digital transformation journey. This includes defining decision rights, escalation paths, and approval processes to ensure timely and informed decision-making.

(c) *Communication Channels*: Establish effective communication channels and mechanisms for sharing information, progress updates, and critical decisions related to digital transformation initiatives. This ensures that stakeholders are well-informed and have the necessary information to fulfill their roles effectively.

- **Oversight and Risk Management**: To ensure effective governance, organizations need to establish oversight and risk management mechanisms:
  (a) *Steering Committee*: Create a steering committee consisting of key stakeholders, including senior leaders and subject matter experts, to provide strategic direction, make critical decisions, and oversee the progress of digital transformation initiatives.
  (b) *Risk Assessment*: Conduct a thorough risk assessment to identify potential risks and challenges associated with digital transformation efforts. Establish risk mitigation strategies and monitoring mechanisms to address and manage these risks proactively.
  (c) *Compliance and Legal Considerations*: Ensure that digital transformation initiatives comply with relevant regulations, privacy laws, and industry standards. Establish mechanisms for regular compliance audits and address the necessary legal considerations.

- **Performance Measurement and Reporting**: Establish mechanisms to measure and report the performance of digital transformation initiatives:
  (a) *KPIs*: Define and track relevant KPIs that align with the organization's strategic objectives. These KPIs should reflect the desired outcomes of digital transformation, such as customer satisfaction, revenue growth, cost savings, and operational efficiency.
  (b) *Data Collection and Analysis*: Implement systems and processes to collect, aggregate, and analyze relevant data to monitor the performance of digital transformation initiatives. Leverage data analytics and reporting tools to gain insights and informed decision-making.
  (c) *Regular Reporting*: Establish a reporting cadence to communicate digital transformation initiatives' progress, challenges, and achievements to relevant stakeholders. Provide transparent and concise reports highlighting key metrics, milestones, and action plans for improvement.

- **Continuous Improvement and Learning**: Emphasize a culture of continuous improvement and learning throughout the digital transformation journey:
  (a) *Lessons Learned*: Encourage the documentation and sharing of lessons learned from each phase or project of the digital transformation. Use these insights to refine governance processes, improve decision-making, and drive future initiatives.
  (b) *Feedback Loops*: Establish feedback mechanisms to gather input and insights from stakeholders, including employees, customers, and partners. Use this feedback to identify areas for improvement, address concerns, and adapt strategies as needed.
  (c) *Training and Development*: Invest in training and development programs to enhance employees' digital skills and capabilities. This empowers individuals and teams to contribute to digital transformation initiatives effectively and fosters a continuous learning culture.

3.2.3 Building a Culture of Innovation and Agility

Building a culture of innovation and agility is essential for organizations aiming to drive successful digital transformation. In today's rapidly changing business landscape, organizations need to embrace innovation, adapt quickly to market dynamics, and foster a culture encouraging experimentation and continuous improvement. By instilling a culture of innovation and agility, organizations can effectively navigate digital transformation challenges, seize opportunities, and stay ahead of the competition.

To build such a culture, organizations need first to embrace a growth mindset that values learning and encourages employees to explore new ideas and take calculated risks. Collaboration and cross-functional teams play a vital role in fostering innovation. Breaking down silos and promoting collaboration allows employees from different departments to share knowledge and contribute diverse perspectives, enhancing creativity and problem-solving.

Allocating resources and support for innovation is crucial. Organizations should dedicate financial and human resources to support innovation initiatives and establish dedicated teams or labs. Celebrating and rewarding innovation is equally important. Organizations inspire employees to think creatively and drive successful digital transformation efforts by recognizing and rewarding innovative ideas and contributions.

Agile methodologies and iterative approaches are crucial to fostering agility within the organization. Embracing methodologies such as Scrum or Kanban enables flexibility, adaptability, and continuous improvement. It allows for quick feedback loops, faster time-to-market, and the ability to respond to changing customer needs and market trends. Fostering a customer-centric culture also ensures that innovation efforts align with customer needs and enhance the overall customer experience.

Supporting intrapreneurship, the entrepreneurial behavior within the organization, encourages employees to pitch and develop their innovative ideas. Establishing innovation challenges or internal incubation programs nurtures employees' entrepreneurial spirit. Continuous learning and adaptation are fundamental to building an innovative culture. Organizations should provide access to training programs, workshops, and conferences to foster continuous skill development and keep pace with the evolving digital landscape.

Leadership support and role modeling are paramount in driving a culture of innovation and agility. Leaders should actively support and champion innovation initiatives, provide guidance and resources, and be open to new ideas and perspectives. By role modeling the desired behaviors and demonstrating a willingness to take risks, learn from failures, and adapt to change, leaders inspire employees to embrace innovation and drive digital transformation.

3.3 DIGITAL MARKETPLACE: UNDERSTANDING THE ONLINE LANDSCAPE

The evolution of digital marketplaces has been a transformative journey, revolutionizing how people buy and sell goods and services. From the early days of online auctions to today's sophisticated platforms, digital marketplaces have reshaped industries and created new opportunities for businesses and consumers. The concept of a marketplace itself has been introduced previously. Traditional marketplaces have existed for centuries, where buyers and sellers come together to exchange goods. However, the advent of the Internet and the subsequent rise of e-commerce unlocked a new realm of possibilities.

The early days of digital marketplaces can be traced back to the emergence of online auction platforms like eBay in the late 1990s. These platforms allowed individuals to list items for sale and engage in bidding wars with potential buyers worldwide. It was a significant step forward, enabling peer-to-peer transactions on a global scale. As technology advanced and consumer behaviors shifted, digital marketplaces evolved to meet changing demands. The rise of platforms like Amazon and Alibaba in the early 2000s marked a turning point. These e-commerce giants offered various products and services, leveraging their infrastructure and logistic capabilities to create seamless shopping experiences.

Simultaneously, niche marketplaces began to emerge, catering to specific industries or target audiences. Platforms like Etsy, which focused on handmade and vintage goods, and Airbnb, enabling short-term rentals, tapped into unique market segments and disrupted traditional business models. The proliferation of smartphones and the advent of mobile applications further propelled the evolution of digital marketplaces. With the rise of on-demand services, platforms like Uber and Lyft, revolutionized the transportation industry. At the same time, food delivery apps like Uber Eats and DoorDash transformed how people order food.

The sharing economy also played a significant role in shaping digital marketplaces. Platforms like Airbnb and Uber facilitated the utilization of underutilized assets, allowing individuals to monetize their spare rooms or cars. This collaborative consumption model disrupted traditional industries and introduced new ways of accessing goods and services. More recently, blockchain technology and cryptocurrencies have started to influence digital marketplaces. Blockchain-based marketplaces provide increased transparency, security, and decentralized control, empowering users and eliminating intermediaries. These platforms enable peer-to-peer transactions with smart contracts, ensuring trust and efficiency in a trustless environment.

AI and ML have also made their mark on digital marketplaces. These technologies enable personalized recommendations, predictive analytics, and efficient matching of buyers and sellers. They enhance the overall user experience and drive business growth. Looking ahead, the evolution of digital marketplaces is set to continue. With the advent of emerging technologies like VR and AR, we can expect immersive shopping experiences and new ways of visualizing products. Additionally, integrating IoT devices and voice assistants will streamline transactions and enable seamless interactions. Digital marketplaces have played a pivotal role in the digital transformation of various industries. They have disrupted traditional business models and enabled seamless online transactions. Here are three types of digital marketplaces that have contributed significantly to this transformation:

1. *B2C Marketplaces*: B2C marketplaces are platforms where businesses sell their products or services directly to consumers. These marketplaces connect retailers or manufacturers with a large customer base, eliminating the

need for physical stores or intermediaries. Examples of B2C marketplaces include Amazon, eBay, and Alibaba. These platforms offer a wide range of products, provide customer reviews and ratings, and offer personalized recommendations, enhancing the shopping experience for consumers. B2C marketplaces have transformed retail by enabling easy access to many products and creating opportunities for small businesses to reach a global audience.

2. *C2C Marketplaces*: C2C marketplaces facilitate transactions between individual consumers. These platforms allow individuals to sell products or services directly to other consumers. Popular C2C marketplaces include eBay, Craigslist, and Facebook Marketplace. C2C marketplaces have disrupted traditional classified ads and garage sales, allowing individuals to monetize unused or secondhand items. These platforms provide a convenient and secure way to buy and sell used goods, promoting sustainability and reducing waste.

3. *B2B Marketplaces*: B2B marketplaces connect businesses with other businesses, facilitating transactions between suppliers, manufacturers, wholesalers, and retailers. These platforms streamline procurement processes, supply chain management, and business sourcing. B2B marketplaces offer features such as bulk ordering, negotiating contracts, and managing inventory. Examples of B2B marketplaces include Alibaba's B2B platform, ThomasNet, and Global Sources. B2B marketplaces have revolutionized how businesses source products and services, improving efficiency and reducing costs.

These marketplaces have accelerated digital transformation, offering increased convenience, cost savings, and access to a broader range of products and services. They have transformed industries by providing efficient channels for businesses and consumers to connect, collaborate, and conduct transactions in the digital realm. The growth of these marketplaces has been driven by advancements in technology, changing consumer preferences, and the need for businesses to adapt to the digital age.

3.3.1 Understanding the Dynamics of Digital Marketplaces

Understanding the dynamics of digital marketplaces is essential for businesses and consumers to navigate these platforms and capitalize on their opportunities effectively. Here are some fundamental dynamics that shape the functioning of digital marketplaces:

- *Network Effects*: Digital marketplaces thrive on network effects, where the platform's value increases as more participants join. For buyers, a more significant number of sellers increases product variety and competitive pricing. A larger pool of buyers expands sellers' market reach and sales potential. Network effects create a virtuous cycle, attracting more participants and reinforcing the marketplace's dominance.

- *Trust and Reputation*: Trust is crucial in digital marketplaces where buyers and sellers often interact with unknown parties. Reputation systems like user ratings and reviews are vital in establishing trust. Buyers rely on the feedback and ratings of sellers to make informed decisions, while sellers aim to maintain a positive reputation to attract more customers. Trust-building mechanisms are essential to foster a secure and reliable marketplace environment.
- *Platform Governance*: Digital marketplaces typically act as intermediaries, providing a transaction platform. These platforms set rules and policies that govern participants' behavior, ensuring fair practices and resolving disputes. Platform governance includes policies on fees, quality standards, dispute resolution mechanisms, and terms of service. Effective governance is crucial for maintaining trust, managing conflicts, and creating a level playing field.
- *Data and Personalization*: Digital marketplaces gather vast amounts of data on user behavior, preferences, and transactions. These data enable personalized recommendations, targeted advertising, and improved user experiences. Advanced analytics and ML algorithms analyze user data to provide tailored suggestions, driving engagement and increasing sales. Data-driven personalization is a critical dynamic that enhances user satisfaction and retention.
- *Competitive Dynamics*: Digital marketplaces are highly competitive, with multiple platforms vying for market share. Intense competition often leads to innovation, improved user experiences, and competitive pricing. Dominant players may leverage their scale and resources to offer additional services or expand into new market segments. On the other hand, new entrants strive to differentiate themselves through unique features, niche offerings, or improved value propositions.
- *Mobile and Omnichannel Experience*: The proliferation of smartphones and mobile apps has transformed the dynamics of digital marketplaces. Mobile access allows users to browse, buy, and sell on the go, expanding the reach and convenience of these platforms. Furthermore, digital marketplaces increasingly adopt omnichannel strategies, integrating online and offline experiences. This includes features like click-and-collect, in-store pickups, and seamless cross-channel interactions to provide a holistic shopping experience.
- *Technological Advancements*: Digital marketplaces continue to evolve with advancements in technology. Blockchain technology is being explored to enhance security, transparency, and decentralization: AI and ML algorithms power recommendation systems, fraud detection, and customer service automation. Emerging technologies like VR, AR, and voice assistants are also integrated to create immersive and intuitive user experiences.

Understanding these dynamics enables businesses and consumers to make informed decisions, adapt strategies, and leverage the opportunities presented by digital marketplaces. By recognizing and adapting to these dynamics, participants can maximize their success and drive growth in the digital marketplace ecosystem.

3.4 DIGITAL CUSTOMER EXPERIENCE: DELIVERING VALUE TO YOUR CUSTOMERS

Digital customer experience has emerged as a critical factor in today's business landscape, enabling organizations to deliver exceptional customer value. With the rapid advancement of technology and the proliferation of digital channels, customers have come to expect seamless and personalized experiences across various touchpoints. Organizations need to prioritize digital customer experience and leverage it as a strategic differentiator to stay competitive and foster customer loyalty. Digital customer experience refers to customers' overall perception and sentiment about their interactions with a brand through digital channels, including websites, mobile apps, social media platforms, and other digital touchpoints. It encompasses every customer journey stage, from initial awareness and consideration to purchase, post-purchase support, and ongoing engagement. A successful digital customer experience strategy is essential for businesses in today's digital age. It involves leveraging technology and digital channels to create meaningful and engaging customer experiences throughout their journey. Here are some critical elements of a well-rounded digital customer experience strategy:

- *Customer-Centric Approach*: A customer-centric approach is the foundation of any digital customer experience strategy. It is crucial to deeply understand your target audience's needs, preferences, and pain points. By putting the customer at the center of your strategy, you can tailor your digital experiences to meet their expectations and deliver value at every touchpoint.
- *Omnichannel Experience*: Customers interact with businesses through multiple channels, such as websites, mobile apps, social media, and more. A robust digital customer experience strategy ensures seamless integration across these channels, enabling customers to switch between them effortlessly while maintaining consistency. This approach allows customers to have a consistent and unified experience, regardless of the channel they choose to engage with.
- *Personalization*: Personalization is the key to providing unique and relevant experiences to customers. A successful digital customer experience strategy leverages customer data and analytics to understand customer behavior, preferences, and past interactions. These data can personalize content, recommendations, offers, and communications, enhancing customer experience and fostering loyalty.
- *User-Friendly Design*: The design and usability of digital interfaces play a significant role in shaping the customer experience. A well-designed user interface that is intuitive, visually appealing, and easy to navigate can significantly enhance the customer's interaction with your digital channels. Investing in user experience design and conducting usability testing is essential to ensure your digital interfaces meet customer expectations and provide a seamless experience.

- *Seamless Integration*: A successful digital customer experience strategy requires seamlessly integrating various systems, applications, and data sources. This integration enables a unified view of the customer across different touchpoints and ensures that customer information is shared seamlessly between departments and systems. It allows for efficient customer service, personalized interactions, and a holistic customer journey understanding.
- *Continuous Optimization*: Digital customer experience is an ongoing process that requires continuous optimization. It is essential to regularly collect feedback, analyze customer data, and identify areas for improvement. This feedback loop helps businesses identify pain points, optimize digital experiences, and address customer needs promptly. By continuously refining and enhancing the digital customer experience, businesses can stay relevant, competitive, and responsive to changing customer expectations.
- *Data Security and Privacy*: As businesses collect and utilize customer data, ensuring data security and privacy is paramount. A robust digital customer experience strategy incorporates measures to protect customer information, comply with data privacy regulations, and build customer trust. This includes implementing secure data storage, encryption, and transparent privacy policies that communicate how customer data are collected, used, and protected.

Digital customer experience has become essential in delivering customer value in today's business landscape. Customers now expect seamless and personalized experiences across various digital touchpoints. Organizations need to prioritize digital customer experience as a strategic differentiator to meet these expectations and foster customer loyalty. Designing and mapping the customer journey is crucial in creating a successful digital customer experience strategy. Identify customer personas representing different segments to design and map the customer journey effectively. Then, define the touchpoints where customers interact with your brand online and offline. Gather customer insights through surveys, interviews, and data collection methods to understand their behavior, preferences, and pain points. With this information, create visual representations of the customer journey, including touchpoints, emotions, pain points, and improvement opportunities at each stage.

Aligning touchpoints and channels with customer expectations and preferences is crucial. For example, optimize your mobile app or website for a seamless mobile experience if your target customers predominantly use mobile devices. Ensure that each touchpoint reflects your brand's messaging and values. However, customer journey mapping is not a one-time exercise. Continuously monitor and analyze customer feedback, engagement metrics, and market trends to refine and optimize the customer journey. Regularly update your maps to reflect any changes in customer behavior or expectations. By designing and mapping the customer journey, you gain valuable insights into your customers' needs and pain points. This enables you to create a more tailored and effective digital customer experience strategy, delivering a seamless and personalized experience across all touchpoints. Ultimately, this approach drives customer satisfaction, loyalty, and business growth. Prioritizing digital customer experience and continuously enhancing the customer journey will position your organization as a leader in delivering value to your customers in the digital age.

3.5 INNOVATION: LEVERAGING TECHNOLOGY FOR NEW OPPORTUNITIES

To effectively navigate this dynamic environment, it is crucial to understand the various facets of innovation and how they relate to digital transformation. This text will explore the types of innovation, the critical characteristics of innovative organizations, and the importance of fostering a culture of innovation focusing on digital transformation.

3.5.1 Types of Innovation

Product innovation is a crucial type of innovation that focuses on developing and introducing new or improved products to the market. It encompasses various forms, including incremental innovations, where existing products are enhanced or modified to meet evolving customer needs and preferences, as well as radical innovations that introduce entirely novel products that disrupt existing markets. Additionally, there are breakthrough innovations that push the boundaries of technological advancements, leading to significant improvements in product features and capabilities. Product innovation plays a vital role in driving competitiveness, attracting customers, and creating value for businesses by offering unique and desirable solutions that meet the ever-changing demands of consumers.

Process innovation is a key type of innovation that focuses on improving the efficiency, effectiveness, and overall quality of operational processes within an organization. It involves the development and implementation of new or improved methods, techniques, and systems that streamline and optimize various aspects of production, service delivery, and internal operations. Process innovation can range from incremental improvements to radical transformations, aiming to enhance productivity, reduce costs, minimize waste, and enhance customer satisfaction. Examples of process innovation include the adoption of new technologies, automation, reengineering workflows, lean manufacturing practices, and the implementation of quality management systems. By continually seeking process innovation, organizations can gain a competitive edge by achieving higher levels of productivity, agility, and responsiveness to meet ever-changing market demands.

Business model innovation refers to the creation or modification of an organization's underlying approach to create, deliver, and capture value. It encompasses various types of innovation that reshape the fundamental components of a business, including its target market, value proposition, revenue model, distribution channels, and cost structure. Types of business model innovations include product-service integration, platform-based models, subscription-based models, freemium models, sharing economy models, and ecosystem-based models. Business model innovation allows companies to differentiate themselves, disrupt existing markets, and capture new opportunities by reimagining how they create and deliver value to customers while generating sustainable revenue streams.

Service innovation refers to the development and implementation of new or improved services that meet customer needs in novel ways. It encompasses various types of innovations that focus on enhancing the value, efficiency, and effectiveness of service delivery. These types include process innovation, which involves redesigning service delivery methods to streamline processes and improve customer experience; technology innovation, which leverages digital tools and advancements to enhance service offerings and accessibility; business model innovation, which entails rethinking the way services are delivered and monetized; and social innovation, which addresses societal challenges by creating innovative services that promote social welfare and inclusivity. Service innovation plays a crucial role in driving customer satisfaction, competitive advantage, and long-term business growth in today's dynamic and evolving service-oriented economy.

3.5.2 Technology as an Enabler of Innovation

Technology is a potent impetus for innovation in multiple dimensions. First, it enhances product innovation by facilitating the creation of cutting-edge features, functions, and designs. Hardware, software, and engineering advancements facilitate the creation of innovative products that meet the changing needs and preferences of consumers. The incorporation of sensors and connectivities into commonplace objects, for instance, has given birth to IoT and enabled the development of smart homes, wearables, and autonomous vehicles. The second way in which technology facilitates process innovation is by automating and streamlining workflows, reducing costs, and enhancing efficiency. Automation, robotics, and AI technologies allow companies to optimize their manufacturing processes, supply chain management, and service delivery. This increases quality, shortens production cycles, and improves customer experiences.

By creating new methods of delivering value and generating revenue, technology enables business model innovation [2]. Digital platforms, e-commerce, and mobile applications have revolutionized the retail, transportation, and hospitality industries. These technologies have upended conventional business models and enabled new entrants to compete with incumbents. In addition, technology plays an essential role in social innovation, addressing societal challenges and fostering positive change. For example, digital technologies have facilitated the expansion of social enterprises, crowdfunding platforms, and online communities centered on social and environmental impact. Additionally, technology-enabled solutions in fields such as healthcare, education, and agriculture have the potential to enhance underserved populations' access, affordability, and outcomes.

In addition to the aforementioned dimensions, technology's influence as an innovation enabler extends in a number of additional ways. This includes the democratization of innovation. The barriers to entry for aspiring innovators and entrepreneurs have been substantially lowered by technology. Access to information, tools, and resources via the Internet and open-source platforms has enabled individuals and small teams to pursue and commercialize innovative ideas. This democratization has fostered a culture of innovation and entrepreneurship, resulting in a proliferation of businesses and disruptive innovations in a variety of industries. Furthermore, technological innovation has transformed the consumer experience. With the advent of digital technologies, consumers have come to expect businesses to provide them with personalized and seamless interactions. AI, big data analytics, and ML enable businesses to collect vast amounts of consumer data, analyze it, and provide individualized recommendations and experiences. This customer-centric strategy not only improves customer satisfaction but also increases customer loyalty and advocacy.

Connecting disparate stakeholders and fostering collective problem-solving, technology also facilitates collaborative innovation. Digital platforms and tools facilitate remote collaboration, allowing teams from diverse locations and origins to share knowledge and co-create innovative solutions in real time. This collaborative strategy fosters idea cross-pollination, accelerates the innovation process, and capitalizes on collective intelligence. Moreover, technology is essential to sustainability and environmental innovation. Technology offers avenues for the development of eco-friendly solutions as businesses and societies endeavor to address pressing environmental issues. From renewable energy technologies and energy-efficient systems to waste management and circular economy strategies, technology enables the development and adoption of sustainable practices, thereby reducing environmental impact and fostering a more sustainable future.

3.5.3 Implementing Innovative Solutions

Implementing innovative solutions necessitates a methodical and strategic approach to guarantee their successful incorporation into an organization or context. Identifying the issue or opportunity that the innovative solution intends to address is an essential first step. Thorough research, data collection, and stakeholder participation aid in gaining a thorough understanding of the situation. This clarity enables creativity and ideation sessions to generate a variety of innovative ideas. It is crucial at this juncture to foster a supportive environment that values diverse perspectives and outside-the-box thinking.

After concepts have been generated, they need to be evaluated and ranked. Consideration is given to criteria such as feasibility, potential impact, and alignment with organizational objectives. Prioritize the most promising concepts that align with strategic objectives and have a greater chance of success. After selecting an idea, the next stage is to develop a comprehensive implementation strategy. This plan outlines the necessary steps, timeline, resources, and responsibilities to implement the innovative solution. It also includes consideration of potential risks and obstacles along the path, as well as mitigation strategies.

To ensure successful implementation, it is essential to secure the necessary resources. This includes acquiring funding, personnel, and technology, as well as establishing the necessary infrastructure. Obtaining the buy-in and support of key stakeholders is also essential for ensuring the availability of the required support throughout the implementation process. It is essential to construct a cross-functional team composed of individuals with diverse talents and knowledge. This team collaborates across departments and disciplines to implement the solution using collective knowledge and perspectives. The collaboration and expertise of the team contribute to a more comprehensive and efficient implementation process.

Once the plan and resources are in place, the implementation of the innovative solution begins with prototyping and testing in a controlled environment. The solution is refined through a series of iterations based on user feedback and market substantiation. A pilot phase is then initiated to implement the solution on a limited scale in a real-world environment. Before scaling up to a larger audience or implementation, this phase allows for a solution's efficacy to be evaluated and any necessary adjustments to be identified. Continuous monitoring, evaluation, and data-driven enhancements guarantee that the solution continues to align with the intended results.

3.6 DATA AS AN ASSET: MAXIMIZING THE VALUE OF DATA

In the digital transformation era, organizations increasingly recognize digital transformation era, organizations increasingly recognize that data is a valuable asset. Daily data generate immense potential for businesses to gain insights, make informed decisions, and achieve a competitive edge. However, realizing the total value of data requires a strategic and proactive approach. This chapter explores the concept of data as an asset and highlights key considerations for maximizing its value in digital transformation. Data are no longer merely a byproduct of business operations; they have evolved into a valuable asset that can drive innovation and growth. Just as organizations invest in physical assets, such as infrastructure or equipment, harnessing the power of data requires recognizing their intrinsic value. Data can be monetized, leveraged for strategic decision-making, and used to create new products, services, and business models.

Several distinguishing characteristics distinguish valuable data assets from conventional data. These attributes contribute to their significance and utility in numerous domains. In the first place, valuable data assets are distinguished by their relevance. They provide information and insights that are pertinent to specific objectives or aims. This enables organizations to make well-informed decisions and take appropriate action based on the data. Oftentimes, valuable data assets are highly targeted and specific, providing precise and accurate information that can have a direct impact on business strategies. Second, valuable data assets possess superior quality and dependability. They are collected, validated, and maintained with great care to ensure their accuracy and integrity. Data assets of high quality are subjected to rigorous processes, such as data cleansing, normalization, and validation. This trustworthiness inspires confidence in the users and enables them to rely on the data when making crucial decisions. Organizations recognize the significance of investing in data quality to preserve the value of their data assets over time.

Valuable data assets have both breadth and depth. They contain extensive and specific information that addresses a vast array of variables, dimensions, and perspectives. Such data assets allow businesses to obtain a comprehensive understanding of their operations, customers, and markets. These assets enable in-depth analysis, the identification of patterns, and the discovery of valuable insights that can drive innovation and expansion. Furthermore, valuable data assets are distinguished by their timeliness. They are routinely collected and updated, granting organizations real-time or near-real-time access to the most current information. In dynamic industries and competitive markets, where remaining ahead requires swift decision-making based on the most recent insights, timely data assets are especially important. Having up-to-date data assets enables organizations to respond quickly to shifting conditions and emergent trends. Lastly, valuable data assets are often unique or exclusive. They may contain confidential or specialized information that is unavailable to competitors or the general public. Unique data assets can offer organizations a distinct competitive advantage by providing insights and perspectives that cannot be readily replicated by others. Access to exclusive data assets can improve market positioning, inform strategic planning, and facilitate innovation in a manner that distinguishes organizations from their competitors.

3.6.1 Types of Data Assets

On the basis of their structure, origin, and nature, data assets can be divided into various categories. Understanding these various categories of data assets is essential for organizations to manage and extract insights from their data effectively. Here are some frequent varieties of data assets:

- *Structured Data*: Structured data refers to data that is organized and formatted in a way that makes it simple for computer systems to interpret and process. Due to its high value and utility for businesses and organizations, it is categorized as one of the categories of data assets. Typically, structured data is stored in databases and is organized into tables, rows, and columns, making it simple to search, retrieve, and analyze. Customer information, transaction records, inventory data, and financial statements are examples of structured data. This form of data is essential for decision-making, analyzing trends, and generating insights that can drive business growth and enhance operational efficiency. By utilizing structured data, organizations can gain a competitive advantage in a variety of industries by making data-driven decisions and instituting effective strategies based on accurate and trustworthy information.
- *Unstructured Data*: Unstructured data is information that lacks a predetermined format or organization. It is a type of data asset that encompasses a variety of content types, including text documents, emails, social media posts, audio and video files, images, and sensor data. Unstructured data, in contrast to structured data, which is organized in a tabular format with clearly defined fields and relationships, needs a consistent structure, making it more difficult to process and analyze. However, unstructured data is extremely valuable because it contains a wealth of insights, consumer feedback, and valuable BI. In order to extract meaning and value from unstructured data, advanced technologies such as NLP, ML, and data mining techniques are required to uncover patterns, sentiments, and relationships concealed within the unstructured information. Organizations that effectively leverage unstructured data can obtain a competitive advantage by making informed decisions, enhancing the customer experience, and identifying new innovation opportunities.

- *Semi-structured Data*: Between structured and unstructured data, semi-structured data is a type of data asset. It refers to data that does not adhere to a rigid schema or predefined format but nonetheless demonstrates some level of organization or structure. Unlike structured data, which is organized into defined fields and tables, semi-structured data allows for greater representational flexibility. Typically, it contains categories, labels, or other identifiers that provide organization or meaning to the data elements. XML files, JSON documents, log files, and social media entries are all examples of semi-structured data. The semi-structured nature of this data type presents organizations with both challenges and opportunities, as it necessitates specialized tools and techniques to effectively extract, transform, and analyze the data.
- *Internal Data*: Internal data refers to the information produced and gathered within an organization. It includes a vast array of data assets that are unique to the organization's operations and processes. These data assets can include, among other things, customer records, sales transactions, financial statements, employee data, inventory data, and operational metrics. Internal data provides vital insights into the performance, trends, and patterns of the organization, enabling informed decision-making and strategic planning. Internal data can uncover latent opportunities, identify operational inefficiencies, and support various business functions, such as marketing, finance, human resources, and supply chain management when analyzed and interpreted appropriately. In an increasingly data-driven business environment, organizations can obtain a competitive advantage and drive growth by effectively leveraging their internal data.
- *External Data*: External data refers to any data assets obtained from sources external to an organization's internal systems. These data assets may originate from a variety of external sources, including public databases, social media platforms, market research firms, government agencies, and third-party vendors. External data can provide valuable insights and information that complement an organization's internal data, allowing businesses to gain a deeper understanding of their customers, competitors, market trends, and industry dynamics. By integrating and analyzing external data with internal data assets, organizations can reveal concealed patterns, identify new opportunities, mitigate risks, and make more holistic data-driven decisions. In today's data-driven environment, effectively leveraging external data as a valuable type of data asset can enhance business strategies, increase operational efficiency, and drive competitive advantage.
- *Big Data*: Big data refers to the vast quantity of structured and unstructured data collected and analyzed by organizations to gain insights and make informed decisions. There are numerous categories of data assets that contribute to the tremendous value of big data. These data assets include organized and readily searchable structured data, such as customer demographics or sales figures. Social media postings and email conversations are examples of unstructured data. Similar to XML or log files, semi-structured data is comprised of some organizational elements but lacks a rigid structure. In addition, big data can include real-time, continuous data, such as sensor data

or clickstream data. The diversity and volume of these data assets provide organizations with the opportunity to extract valuable insights, identify patterns, and unearth latent correlations that can drive innovation and inform strategic decision-making.

- *Meta Data*: Metadata is data about data. Metadata is an essential sort of data asset that describes other data. It functions as a descriptive layer that provides context and structure to different types of data, allowing for efficient organization and retrieval. Metadata comprises a vast array of attributes, including data source, date of creation, format, size, and data lineage. It facilitates effective data management and decision-making processes by assisting users in comprehending the content, quality, and usability of data. Metadata plays a crucial role in assuring data integrity, accessibility, and discoverability, ultimately enhancing the value and utility of the entire data ecosystem.

3.6.2 Critical Considerations for Maximizing Data Value

Maximizing data value requires a strategic approach that hinges on critical considerations. First and foremost, organizations must focus on "Data Quality," ensuring accuracy, consistency, and completeness. Without reliable data, decision-making and insights suffer. "Data Relevance" is equally crucial, directing attention toward collecting and analyzing information directly aligned with organizational goals. Effective "Data Governance" establishes accountability, security, and compliance protocols, preventing data misuse or breaches. "Integration" involves merging disparate data sources to uncover holistic insights, while "Scalability" ensures systems can handle expanding datasets. "Ethical Use" demands responsible and privacy-respecting data practices, cultivating trust among customers and stakeholders. Lastly, "Actionability" underscores the importance of turning data insights into tangible strategies and outcomes. By addressing these considerations, businesses can harness data's full potential to drive innovation, efficiency, and growth.

3.6.2.1 Data quality and governance

As organizations rely more and more on data-driven insights to make strategic decisions and enhance operational efficiency, assuring the accuracy, completeness, and dependability of data becomes essential. Data quality refers to the overall suitability of data for its intended use, whereas data governance encompasses the policies, procedures, and controls in place to administer and safeguard data assets. Data integrity and governance have become even more important in the context of digital transformation due to the increased volume, velocity, and variety of data being generated and utilized.

Initiatives for digital transformation frequently involve the integration of disparate data sources and the deployment of advanced analytics technologies. These technologies, including AI and ML, rely significantly on high-quality data to produce accurate and meaningful insights. Consistent or sufficient data can result in accurate analysis, reliable predictions, and defective decision-making. To ensure the integrity of their data assets, organizations need to establish robust data quality frameworks that include data profiling, data cleansing, and data validation procedures.

In contrast, data governance provides the structure and accountability required for managing data throughout its lifecycle. It includes establishing data stewardship roles and implementing data policies and standards. Effective data stewardship becomes essential in the context of digital transformation, where data is collected from multiple sources and shared across multiple systems and stakeholders. It guarantees that data is managed, protected, and compliant with regulations such as data privacy laws. By instituting data governance practices, organizations can increase data transparency, enhance data accessibility, and foster data collaboration, all of which are crucial for achieving successful digital transformation.

In addition, data integrity and governance enable organizations to establish a solid foundation for innovation and adaptability in the digital age. High-quality data provides a solid foundation for experimentation, allowing businesses to test new ideas and technologies confidently. Effective data governance ensures that the appropriate individuals have access to the appropriate data at the appropriate moment, thereby facilitating collaboration and empowering employees to make data-driven decisions. This agility is essential in the rapidly evolving digital landscape, where businesses need to adapt quickly to shifting customer demands and market dynamics.

3.6.2.2 Data integration and interoperability

Data integration is the process of integrating data from various sources and formats into a unified view, thereby eradicating data silos and facilitating a comprehensive understanding of the business. Interoperability, on the other hand, focuses on the capacity of disparate systems and applications to communicate, interchange data, and operate in a coordinated fashion. In the context of digital transformation, data integration is essential for maximizing an organization's data potential. It enables businesses to eliminate data silos and establish a unified data ecosystem. By incorporating data from disparate sources such as databases, cloud applications, and IoT devices, organizations can gain a deeper understanding, make more informed decisions, and foster innovation. Data integration also enables real-time synchronization of data, ensuring that all stakeholders have access to the most current information, facilitating collaboration, and accelerating business processes.

Interoperability contributes to digital transformation by facilitating the seamless transfer of data between disparate systems and applications. It ensures that data can be shared and utilized across multiple platforms, irrespective of their underlying technologies or file formats. Interoperability enables organizations to connect their existing legacy systems with contemporary digital solutions, thereby removing data bottlenecks and fostering agility. It also facilitates the incorporation of third-party services and APIs, allowing organizations to leverage external data sources and functionalities to enhance their digital capabilities.

In digital transformation, data integration and interoperability provide numerous benefits. They enable organizations to eliminate data silos and develop a comprehensive view of operations, customers, and markets. This exhaustive comprehension enables businesses to identify new opportunities, optimize processes, and provide customized customer experiences. In addition, data integration and interoperability foster innovation by facilitating the exploration and analysis of vast quantities of data from various sources. By leveraging these capabilities, organizations can unearth valuable insights, make data-driven decisions, and remain competitive in the digital era.

3.6.2.3 Data analytics and insights

In the era of rapid technological advancements, organizations generate immense quantities of data from a variety of sources, including customer interactions, social media, and IoT devices. In order for businesses to thrive in the digital era, they need to be able to harness this data and extract actionable insights. Digital transformation is the use of technology to generate substantial changes in business processes, customer experiences, and operations as a whole. Data analytics serves as the foundation for this transformation by providing organizations with valuable insights that enable data-driven decision-making. By analyzing and interpreting vast quantities of structured and unstructured data, businesses can identify trends, patterns, and correlations that provide invaluable insights into consumer behavior, market dynamics, and operational efficiencies.

With the aid of data analytics, organizations can maximize the value of their data to obtain a competitive advantage. Businesses can personalize their offerings, tailor their marketing campaigns, and optimize their product development strategies if they comprehend consumer preferences and behavior. In addition, data analytics can assist in identifying business process bottlenecks and recommending enhancements, resulting in increased operational efficiency and cost savings. Moreover, data analytics is essential for organizations to adapt and innovate in the digital landscape. By analyzing data in real-time, businesses can respond swiftly to market trends, shifting consumer demands, and emerging opportunities. Through predictive analytics and ML algorithms, businesses can anticipate future scenarios and make proactive decisions to maintain a competitive advantage.

3.6.2.4 Agile infrastructure and scalability

Agile infrastructure is an IT infrastructure management strategy that emphasizes adaptability, responsiveness, and automation—utilizing cloud computing, virtualization, and software-defined technologies to create an environment that can quickly adapt to an organization's changing requirements. Agile infrastructure enables businesses to deploy and administer applications and services more efficiently in the context of digital transformation. It enables the rapid provisioning of resources and automates scaling up or down in response to demand. By leveraging cloud services and virtualization, organizations can set up new environments, test new ideas, and iterate on their digital initiatives without being constrained by traditional hardware-based infrastructure.

In contrast, scalability is the capacity of a system or application to accommodate increased workload or increasing user demands. Scalability is essential in the context of digital transformation to accommodate the exponential growth of data, users, and transactions that frequently accompany digital initiatives. Organizations can scale their systems longitudinally by adding more resources, such as servers or virtual machines, or vertically by enhancing the capabilities of existing resources. The adoption of new technologies, such as IoT devices, big data analytics, and AI, is a common aspect of digital transformation. These technologies produce enormous quantities of data that need to be processed, analyzed, and stored. Agile infrastructure and scalability enable organizations to manage and harness this data deluge effectively, ensuring that systems can handle increased traffic and provide timely insights.

3.6.2.5 Data monetization strategies

Data monetization refers to the process of extracting value from data by transforming it into a revenue-generating asset. Organizations are increasingly recognizing the potential of leveraging their data assets to drive innovation, obtain a competitive advantage, and generate new revenue streams, given the vast amount of data generated daily. Improving consumer experiences is one of the primary data monetization strategies in the context of digital transformation. Organizations can gain insight into customer preferences, behavior patterns, and requirements by analyzing customer data. This data can then be used to personalize products and services, execute targeted marketing campaigns, and increase customer satisfaction overall. Through digital transformation initiatives, businesses are able to collect, analyze, and utilize consumer data at scale, resulting in increased customer engagement and loyalty.

In the digital transformation voyage, data-driven product development is another effective data monetization strategy. By analyzing customer data and market trends, businesses are able to identify new product opportunities, enhance existing offerings, and develop innovative solutions to resolve customer pain points. This data-driven strategy enables businesses to make informed decisions regarding product development, thereby decreasing the risk of failure and increasing the likelihood of market success. In addition, organizations can monetize their data assets by licensing or selling them to businesses in relevant industries, allowing them to derive value from their data assets without directly developing products.

In the context of digital transformation, data monetization strategies also entail leveraging data for operational efficiency and optimization. By leveraging data analytics and ML algorithms, businesses can gain insight into their internal processes, identify bottlenecks, and optimize operations for optimum efficiency. Using sensor data, predictive maintenance can assist organizations in proactively identifying and addressing impending equipment failures, thereby reducing downtime and increasing productivity. In addition, data analytics can provide valuable insights into supply chain management, inventory optimization, and resource allocation, allowing businesses to reduce expenses and streamline operations.

Organizations can investigate partnerships and collaborations to monetize their data assets. By sharing or exchanging data with reputable partners, businesses can generate new revenue streams and create opportunities that are mutually beneficial. For instance, organizations can engage in data-sharing agreements with complementary businesses in order to improve their products or services and expand their customer base. Collaborations may also involve leveraging third-party data sources or data marketplaces to augment existing data assets and provide customers with additional value. These partnerships allow organizations to broaden their influence, monetize their data assets, and foster innovation within their respective industries.

In the digital age, data has become a valuable asset that organizations need to maximize to thrive in a competitive landscape. Organizations can unlock their full potential by treating data as a strategic asset and implementing the right frameworks and technologies. From ensuring data quality and governance to leveraging analytics and exploring monetization strategies, organizations can transform data into a powerful driver of digital transformation. Those who effectively harness the value of their data will have a significant advantage in innovation, decision-making, and overall business success.

3.6.2.6 Challenges and risks in maximizing data value

In today's data-driven world, organizations' primary objective is to optimize data value. However, there are a number of obstacles and dangers associated with this endeavor. The vast quantity of available data is one of the primary obstacles. With the exponential development of digital information, it is frequently difficult for organizations to effectively process and analyze the vast quantities of data at their disposal. This can result in information excess and hinder the ability to draw meaningful conclusions. Another area for improvement is the quality and dependability of data. Data may be insufficient, inaccurate, or obsolete, which can significantly diminish its value. Processes of data cleansing and validation are indispensable for ensuring the veracity and integrity of the data. Failure to resolve data quality issues can result in flawed analysis and decision-making, which can lead to expensive errors.

Moreover, privacy and security hazards are a major concern when maximizing the value of data. Organizations need to navigate the complex landscape of data privacy regulations and ensure legal and ethical compliance. The improper management of sensitive or personally identifiable information can result in substantial reputational harm and legal repercussions. In addition, the growing sophistication of cyber threats and data breaches emphasizes the necessity of instituting stringent security measures to protect valuable data assets. Lastly, more qualified personnel and an adequate technological infrastructure are needed to ensure that the maximization of data value is maintained. Data interpretation and analysis require knowledge of data science and advanced analytics techniques. The need for qualified professionals in these fields can help an organization's ability to extract insights effectively. In addition, a technological infrastructure that is obsolete or insufficient may limit the processing power and capabilities required for comprehensive data analysis. Investing in talent development and upgrading technology infrastructure are crucial measures for mitigating these risks and maximizing data value.

3.7 CONCLUSION

This chapter has explored various key areas organizations need to focus on to embrace digital transformation and thrive in the digital era effectively. By addressing barriers and leveraging enablers, organizations can overcome challenges and create a conducive environment for digital transformation. Aligning strategy with execution, understanding the digital marketplace, delivering exceptional customer experiences, embracing innovation, and harnessing the value of data are all vital components. By prioritizing these areas and continuously adapting to technological advancements, organizations can position themselves for success in the digital age and create sustainable competitive advantages. Embracing digital transformation is no longer a choice but a necessity for organizations that seek to thrive in the ever-changing business landscape.

REFERENCES

1. Clayton, S.J., An agile approach to change management. *Harvard Business Review*, 2021. 11(January). https://hbr.org/2021/01/an-agile-approach-to-change-management
2. Vaska, S., et al., The digital transformation of business model innovation: a structured literature review. *Frontiers in Psychology*, 2021. **11**: p. 539363.

Digital Transformation Project Management

4

4.1 PROJECT PLANNING: DEFINING OBJECTIVES AND REQUIREMENTS

The process of incorporating digital technologies into an organization's operations, business processes, and customer interactions is known as a "digital transformation initiative." Utilizing technology to boost overall performance, productivity, and efficiency allows businesses to adjust to the digital age and prosper. Numerous activities, including the use of new software systems, cloud computing, data analytics optimization, automation of manual operations, improvement of the customer experience through digital channels, and rethinking business models, are frequently included in digital transformation projects. These initiatives are necessary in order to meet changing client demands and stay competitive in a digital environment that is continually changing.

Depending on the organization's size, industry, and specific objectives, the scope and magnitude of a digital transformation project can vary greatly. It frequently necessitates an integrated approach involving multiple departments or business entities, as well as cooperation with external partners or vendors. Successful digital transformation projects necessitate meticulous planning, execution, and continuous adaptation so that the organization can maximize the potential of digital technologies to achieve its goals. Planning is essential to the success of any undertaking, and digital transformation initiatives are no exception. Here are several crucial reasons why project planning is crucial:

- *Clarity of objectives*: Project planning facilitates the definition of the digital transformation project's specific aims and objectives. It enables stakeholders to align their expectations and ensure that everyone is working toward the same objective. Clearly defined objectives serve as a guide for decision-making, resource allocation, and measuring the success of a project.

- *Allocation of resources*: Appropriate project planning requires identifying and allocating the required resources, including budget, personnel, and technology infrastructure. It aids in optimizing resource utilization and ensures the project has the necessary support to proceed efficiently.
- *Risk management*: Project planning enables the identification and evaluation of potential risks and obstacles that may arise throughout the digital transformation journey. By proactively addressing risks, organizations can develop mitigation strategies to reduce their negative impact on the project's schedule, budget, and outcomes.

The planning process for the digital transformation project includes establishing realistic timelines and identifying critical milestones. This aids in tracking progress, managing dependencies, and keeping the project on schedule. Additionally, timelines allow stakeholders to anticipate and address potential bottlenecks or delays.

Effective project planning fosters effective communication and collaboration between team members, stakeholders, and external partners. It facilitates coordination, knowledge sharing, and effort alignment, fostering a collaborative and productive project environment.

During the planning stage of a digital transformation project, several objectives are pursued. It begins with defining the project's scope, goals, deliverables, and expected outcomes to give a clear understanding of what needs to be done. The planning phase also identifies and involves the appropriate stakeholders, assuring their involvement, support, and cooperation throughout the project. The planning step also necessitates the development of an extensive project plan that details tasks, dates, resource requirements, and dependencies. This plan serves as a roadmap for carrying out the project, monitoring its advancement, and making any necessary modifications. Additionally, it entails building risk response procedures, determining backup plans, and properly allocating resources.

Project planning defines channels, frequency, and methods of communication between team members, stakeholders, and project sponsors. It also establishes reporting procedures. Transparency and accountability are promoted throughout the project via clear reporting methods that guarantee that project progress, problems, and milestones are successfully reported to all pertinent parties. Organizations can lay the groundwork for a successful digital transformation journey by meeting these goals during the planning stage of a project. Creating a detailed project definition is necessary before starting a digital transformation project. It entails understanding the mission and goals of the organization, establishing the project's parameters, and identifying the principal players and their respective roles. The foundation for the entire transformation journey is laid at this phase.

Knowing the organization's mission and vision is crucial for coordinating digital transformation initiatives with strategic goals. It entails gaining an understanding of the organization's long-term vision, mission, and basic values. This comprehension makes sure that the digital transformation project directly aids in the growth and achievement of the firm as a whole. Finding the project's boundaries and goals is necessary to define the project's scope for digital transformation. It necessitates pinpointing exactly which elements of the organization's processes, practices, and systems will change. The scope must be clearly stated, practical, and achievable within the allotted spending limit and time frame. A project's success depends on identifying the key stakeholders and their respective roles. A stakeholder is a person or group that is involved with or affected by the project. Executives, department heads, employees, clients, and suppliers are examples of external partners. Each stakeholder has a unique role and an effect on the project. Establishing a collaborative and encouraging atmosphere for the digital transformation project is made easier by understanding their viewpoints, expectations, and concerns.

4.1.1 Evaluating the Current Situation

Assessing an organization's current state is a crucial phase in the digital transformation process. It involves evaluating existing systems, processes, and technologies, undertaking a SWOT analysis, and identifying pain points and improvement opportunities. Evaluating the extant systems, processes, and technologies provides a snapshot of the current digital landscape of the organization. It identifies the strengths and shortcomings of the existing systems, their compatibility with future requirements, and potential optimization opportunities. This evaluation allows organizations to make informed decisions regarding which systems need to be upgraded, replaced, or integrated to support the digital transformation objectives.

Conducting a SWOT analysis entails examining the organization's internal strengths and vulnerabilities, as well as its external opportunities and threats. It assists in identifying the internal factors that can be leveraged to drive the digital transformation, as well as the potential obstacles or hazards that need to be mitigated. The SWOT analysis provides a holistic perspective on the current condition of the organization and aids in the formulation of strategies to capitalize on its strengths and opportunities while mitigating its weaknesses and threats. Identifying pain points and areas for development requires collecting feedback from a variety of stakeholders and analyzing the organization's challenges. These pain points may be operational inefficiencies, customer dissatisfaction, data silos, a lack of automation, or any other issue impeding the development of the organization. By identifying these areas, organizations can prioritize their development and ensure that digital transformation initiatives address the most pressing pain points. Organizations obtain valuable insight into their strengths, weaknesses, opportunities, and threats as a result of a comprehensive assessment of their current state. This analysis serves as a road map for formulating the digital transformation strategy, establishing objectives, and delineating the organization's desired future state.

(A) **Internal Factors:**
   - *Strengths*: Internal strengths refer to the advantageous factors within the organization that can facilitate the digital transformation process. These may encompass existing technological infrastructure, skilled workforce, financial resources, strong brand reputation, or access to valuable data and information. Identifying and leveraging these strengths allows organizations to capitalize on their existing capabilities.

- *Weaknesses*: Internal weaknesses pertain to the limitations or challenges within the organization that may hinder the successful implementation of digital transformation projects. These weaknesses can include outdated technology systems, inadequate digital skills among employees, resistance to change, constrained budgetary resources, or an organizational structure that impedes decision-making. Recognizing these weaknesses is critical for devising appropriate mitigation strategies and implementing necessary improvements.

(B) **External Factors:**

- *Opportunities*: External opportunities encompass favorable circumstances and trends outside the organization that can be leveraged for digital transformation initiatives. These opportunities may arise from emerging technologies, shifting market demands, changing customer behaviors, regulatory changes, or potential collaborations and partnerships. Identifying these opportunities allows organizations to align their digital transformation efforts with external developments and gain a competitive advantage.

- *Threats*: External threats refer to factors outside the organization that pose risks or challenges to successful digital transformation. These threats may include competitors' innovative advancements, cybersecurity vulnerabilities, evolving regulations, economic fluctuations, or cultural resistance to digital technologies. Evaluating these threats enables organizations to develop strategies to mitigate potential risks and proactively address challenges.

By conducting a comprehensive SWOT analysis, organizations can gain valuable insights to guide their digital transformation project planning. Leveraging strengths and opportunities while addressing weaknesses and mitigating threats allows for informed decision-making and increases the likelihood of successful project outcomes.

4.1.2 Defining Digital Transformation Objectives

For the success of any digital transformation initiative, it is essential to establish measurable and specific objectives. These objectives serve as a road map, directing the organization toward its desired outcomes and ensuring that efforts are aligned with the organization's broader vision and goals. By establishing SMART objectives, businesses can effectively prioritize their initiatives and monitor their transformation progress.

Clear objectives give the digital transformation project a sense of direction and purpose. They describe the organization's objectives and foster a shared comprehension among all stakeholders. To establish precise goals, it is necessary to state them concisely and unambiguously. For instance, a goal could be to increase online sales by 20% within the next 12 months or to reduce the customer attrition rate by 15% through the implementation of a personalized customer experience platform. Measurable objectives enable organizations to monitor their progress and evaluate the success of their digital transformation initiatives. The organization can track its performance, spot areas for development, and make data-driven decisions by defining particular metrics and KPIs for each aim. For example, a business could track the average time needed to process customer orders or the drop in error rates if its goal is to boost operational efficiency.

Digital transformation objectives should be aligned with the organization's vision and goals. This connection makes sure that the transformational initiatives support the long-term performance and profitability of the company. The goals should align with the organization's strategic priorities and show how digital initiatives will make them easier to attain. A CRM system could be implemented to increase customer engagement, data analytics could be used to learn more about customer preferences, and a seamless omnichannel experience for customers could all be part of the organization's digital transformation objectives, for instance, if its vision is to become a leader in providing exceptional customer experiences.

Prioritizing Objectives Based on Their Strategic Importance: For an organization, only some goals have the same strategic importance. Prioritizing goals according to how they will likely affect the organization's overall strategy and goals is crucial. Prioritization makes certain that resources, time, and effort are directed to projects that add the most value and complement the organization's competencies. Examples of objectives, their descriptions, primary measurements and KPIs, and their strategic alignment are shown in Table 4.1. Depending on the particular business and its aims for digital transformation, the actual objectives, measurements, and alignment may change. Organizations can effectively prioritize objectives by considering multiple factors, including financial impact, customer value, competitive advantage, and feasibility. By evaluating these factors, the organization can identify high-priority objectives that address critical requirements or present significant growth opportunities. This process of prioritization helps to concentrate resources on initiatives that are most likely to produce the intended results and generate an ROI.

4.1.3 Collecting Prerequisites

Gathering requirements is a crucial stage in the software development process, which includes engaging stakeholders, determining their needs and expectations, conducting interviews, workshops, and surveys, and documenting functional and nonfunctional requirements. This process makes sure the final software solution achieves the intended aims and objectives of the stakeholders. Stakeholder involvement is crucial for requirement collection. Stakeholders are people or groups who have an interest in the software that is currently being developed. These parties could consist of CEOs, subject matter experts, administrators, end users, and other important parties. Understanding stakeholders' perspectives, goals, and software needs involves open communication and careful listening.

To efficiently acquire requirements, a variety of methodologies, including interviews, seminars, and surveys, are frequently employed. Interviews provide you the chance to speak with stakeholders directly and learn more about their needs and expectations. Individual or group interviews can be used to gather comprehensive needs and spot potential problems or possibilities. Stakeholders and development teams collaborate during workshops. They encourage brainstorming, group problem-solving, and idea development. Workshops enable the sharing of ideas and perspectives, enabling a

TABLE 4.1   Example objectives, descriptions, metrics, and strategic alignment for digital transformation initiatives

OBJECTIVES	DESCRIPTION	KEY METRICS AND KPIS	STRATEGIC ALIGNMENT
Increase online sales by 20% within the next 12 months	This objective aims to achieve a specific sales target through digital transformation initiatives.	• Total online sales revenue • Conversion rate • Average order value	Aligned with the organization's goal of driving revenue growth and expanding its online presence
Reduce customer attrition rate by 15% through the implementation of a personalized customer experience platform	The objective focuses on enhancing customer retention by leveraging a personalized customer experience platform.	• Customer churn rate • Customer satisfaction scores • Repeat purchase rate	Aligned with the organization's vision of delivering exceptional customer experiences and increasing customer loyalty
Implement a CRM system to improve customer engagement	This objective involves deploying a CRM system to enhance customer interactions and relationships.	• Customer engagement metrics (e.g., customer interactions, response time) • Customer feedback and sentiment analysis	Aligned with the organization's vision of becoming a leader in providing exceptional customer experiences
Create a seamless omnichannel experience for customers	The objective is to establish a unified and consistent customer experience across multiple channels.	• Channel integration metrics (e.g., channel switching rate, cross-channel purchase behavior) • Customer satisfaction with an omnichannel experience	Aligned with the organization's vision of delivering exceptional customer experiences and meeting customer expectations

complete understanding of the requirements. During these meetings, participants can offer feedback, clarify any ambiguities, and rate their requirements.

Surveys are another powerful tool for gathering requirements. They can be given to a bigger population, enabling the gathering of a greater range of viewpoints. Stakeholders can provide organized input on their needs and preferences through surveys. The results can be examined to find recurring trends or patterns which will have an impact on the software development process. The requirements-gathering process includes the process of documenting requirements. Requirements must be organized and well stated in order for stakeholders and development teams to communicate effectively. This documentation often includes both functional and nonfunctional requirements.

The functional requirements list the attributes, prowess, and conduct anticipated of the software. They outline how the software should interact with users, process data, and provide system outputs. Functional requirements ensure that the software fulfills stakeholders' expectations and serves the intended function. Contrarily, nonfunctional requirements specify the software's qualities and constraints. These specifications emphasize efficacy, security, dependability, usability, and scalability. Nonfunctional requirements are crucial for defining the overall user experience and ensuring that the software complies with all applicable regulations and standards.

Typically, documenting requirements requires the creation of requirement documents, use cases, user stories, and other artifacts. Throughout the software development lifecycle, these documents serve as a resource for design, implementation, and testing. In addition, they provide a benchmark for evaluating the success of the ultimate software solution. Figure 4.1 illustrates the sequential steps involved in engaging stakeholders,

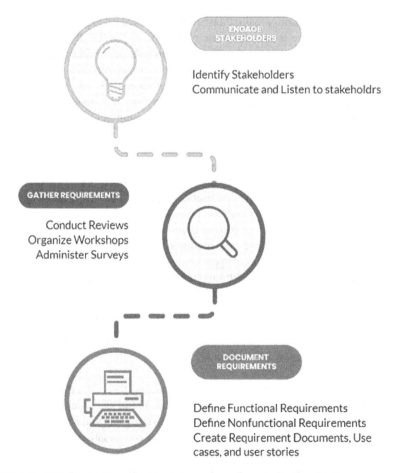

FIGURE 4.1 Requirements gathering process for software development.

gathering requirements, and documenting them for software development. Gathering requirements entails involving stakeholders, conducting interviews, seminars, and surveys, and documenting functional and nonfunctional requirements. This procedure enables a thorough comprehension of stakeholder needs and expectations, ensuring that the resulting software effectively meets their needs.

4.1.4 Documentation and Validation

In this procedure, documentation and validation are essential, especially when defining goals and requirements. Organizations may build a strong foundation for their digital transformation initiatives by clearly expressing the desired results and documenting the project goals. The goals that the company hopes to accomplish through digital transformation need to be documented early on in the project planning process. These goals act as a set of guiding principles that direct all stakeholders toward a single goal. Whether the objective is to increase operational effectiveness, enhance customer experience, or spur innovation, articulating these objectives gives the project focus and direction. It also enables the firm to compare the transformation's success to the stated goals.

The following phase is to specify the requirements for the digital transformation project once the goals have been identified. This entails determining the precise characteristics, functionalities, and capacities that the company requires to attain its goals. Technology infrastructure, software programs, data analytics, and security measures are only a few examples of requirements. Organizations can make sure they have a clear understanding of the resources and technologies required for the project's effective implementation by thoroughly documenting these needs.

In the documentation process, validation is essential because it ensures that the objectives and requirements are accurate and comprehensive. It entails a thorough examination and verification of the recorded data by pertinent parties, including company executives, IT specialists, and end users. Any discrepancies or holes in the documentation can be found and fixed early on through the validation process, reducing the possibility of misunderstandings or project failures in the future.

The alignment of the objectives and requirements with the organization's overarching strategic goals and priorities is also ensured by validation. It enables interested parties to evaluate how well the digital transformation project fits with the organization's goals, objectives, and core values. The project can be realigned with the organization's strategic direction if any misalignments are found, ensuring that the digital transformation initiatives support the organization's long-term success. When creating the goals and requirements for a digital transformation project, businesses can use a variety of strategies for documentation and validation:

- *Interviews and Workshops*: It can be beneficial to conduct interviews and workshops with important stakeholders, such as end users, department heads, and corporate executives, to gain insight into the goals and needs of the project. These interactive meetings enable candid conversations, brainstorming, and consensus-building, assisting in the gathering of various viewpoints and ensuring thorough documentation.

- *Surveys and Questionnaires*: Organizations can use surveys and questionnaires to gather feedback and input from a wider range of stakeholders. This method allows for anonymous participation, encouraging honest responses. Surveys can be distributed electronically, making it convenient for participants to provide their input. The collected data can then be analyzed to identify common themes, priorities, and requirements.
- *Documentation Templates*: Standardized documentation templates can be used to ensure uniformity and accuracy in documenting goals and requirements. These templates give stakeholders an organized format to follow as they submit the required information. They frequently have parts where the goals are stated, the success criteria are described, the functional and technical requirements are described, and any restrictions or hazards are documented.
- *Prototyping and Proof of Concepts*: Creating prototypes or proof of concepts can be an effective method for validating requirements. By building a simplified version of the digital solution or conducting small-scale experiments, organizations can validate whether the defined requirements align with the desired outcomes. Prototyping also allows for early user feedback, enabling adjustments and refinements before full-scale implementation.
- *Peer Reviews and Expert Evaluations*: Engaging subject matter experts, such as seasoned IT specialists or consultants, can offer insightful opinions and validate the stated goals and criteria. Individuals with the necessary skills thoroughly review the documentation as part of peer reviews and expert evaluations. They can spot potential holes, contradictions, or places for development, resulting in a strong and thoroughly validated set of goals and demands.

4.2 PROJECT DEVELOPMENT: IMPLEMENTING CHANGE WITH AGILITY

Implementing change requires agility above all else, particularly in the context of digital transformation. Digital transformation results in fundamental changes to how the organization operates and provides value to its consumers. Here are several crucial factors why agility is essential for implementing digital transformation (Figure 4.2):

- *Rapidly Evolving Technology Landscape*: Emerging technologies, tools, and platforms are continuously disrupting conventional business models as the digital landscape is in a constant state of evolution. To successfully implement a digital transformation, organizations need to be agile and adaptable to leverage new technologies and remain competitive.
- *Customer Expectations and Market Dynamics*: In the digital age, customer expectations are evolving swiftly. Consumers anticipate personalized interactions across multiple channels and immediate access to information and

FIGURE 4.2   Key factors for agility in implementing digital transformation.

services. To meet these requirements, organizations need to be nimble in their ability to identify and respond to shifting consumer requirements, market trends, and competitive pressures.

- *Iterative and Experimental Approach*: Frequently, digital transformation requires experimentation, iterative development, and ongoing refinement. Agile methodologies, such as agile and DevOps, enable businesses to divide complex transformations into smaller, more manageable chunks. This iterative methodology permits faster implementation, shorter feedback cycles, and the flexibility to adapt based on real-time insights and customer feedback.

- *Organizational Flexibility and Responsiveness*: Agility encourages organizational adaptability and receptivity to change. It involves fostering a culture that embraces innovation, fosters collaboration, and gives employees the authority to make decisions and assume responsibility for their work. By cultivating an agile mindset, organizations can respond swiftly to shifting market conditions, customer demands, and internal challenges, enabling them to implement digital transformation initiatives more efficiently.
- *Mitigating Risks and Managing Uncertainty*: Initiatives for digital transformation frequently entail a degree of uncertainty and risk. By employing an agile methodology, organizations can mitigate risks by implementing changes iteratively, performing frequent testing and validation, and adapting strategies based on empirical data and feedback. This iterative approach enables organizations to identify and resolve potential issues early in the process, thereby reducing the overall risk associated with large-scale transformations.
- *Accelerating Time-to-Market*: New digital products, services, and innovations can be brought to market faster by agile organizations. By dividing transformation initiatives into smaller, more manageable components, organizations can implement changes more quickly, collect customer feedback earlier, and make adjustments more quickly. This agility enables businesses to seize new opportunities, maintain a competitive advantage, and capitalize on emergent market trends.

An effective digital transformation depends on agility. It enables businesses to adapt to changing market dynamics, embrace change, and take advantage of the promise of digital technologies to spur innovation and add value. Organizations can more successfully manage the challenges of digital transformation and improve their prospects of experiencing long-term success in the digital era by cultivating an agile culture, utilizing agile practices, and placing a priority on adaptability.

4.2.1 Developing a Roadmap

Initiatives for digital transformation can be complex and challenging, requiring careful strategy and execution. A critical step in guaranteeing the success of a transformation journey is developing a road map. A roadmap is a strategy document that describes the important actions, benchmarks, and deliverables required to accomplish the desired goals of a digital transformation. This section will look at the key components of establishing a roadmap for digital transformation, such as project breakdown, prioritization of features and objectives, schedule formulation, resource allocation, and money allocation (Table 4.2).

- *Breaking down the project into smaller, manageable iterations*: If approached as a single undertaking, digital transformation initiatives can be overwhelming. It is vital to divide the project into smaller, more manageable iterations

TABLE 4.2   Elements of creating a roadmap for digital transformation

ROADMAP ELEMENTS	DESCRIPTION	IMPORTANCE	BENEFITS
Iterative Approach	Break down the project into smaller, manageable iterations or phases.	Ensures progress and focus.	• Enables incremental progress • Allows for risk management and course correction
Feature Prioritization	Rank features and initiatives based on value and impact.	Maximizes value and optimizes resource allocation.	• Maximizes value delivered • Guides decision-making based on impact and value
Timeline and Milestones	Create a clear timeline with essential milestones and deliverables.	Provides clarity and ensures project progress.	• Provides clarity and direction • Facilitates progress measurement and milestone achievement
Resource Allocation	Allocate resources and budget based on project requirements.	Ensures availability of necessary resources.	• Optimizes resource allocation for efficiency • Aligns budget with project requirements

or phases to ensure progress and maintain focus. Each iteration should have distinct goals, deliverables, and deadlines. This approach permits incremental progress and enables quick victories, thereby boosting morale and demonstrating the initiative's value. Each iteration provides an opportunity for risk management and course correction, which is made possible by the project's decomposition.

• *Prioritizing features and initiatives based on value and impact*: Not all features and initiatives in a digital transformation journey are of equal importance. It is crucial to rank them based on their importance and value. Start by identifying the most important pain points or areas with the highest investment returns. Engage stakeholders and subject matter experts to comprehend their expectations and requirements. Prioritization frameworks such as the MoSCoW method (Must-haves, Should-haves, Could-haves, and Won't-haves) and the Kano model (Basic expectations, Performance enhancements, and Excitement generators) can aid in making informed choices. By effectively prioritizing features and initiatives, it is possible to maximize the value delivered within each iteration and generate significant outcomes.

• *Creating a timeline with milestones and deliverables*: For the digital transformation initiative to remain on schedule, a well-defined timeline is essential. Start by establishing essential project milestones, which represent significant accomplishments or stages. These benchmarks provide clarity and facilitate progress measurement. Deconstruct the work associated with each milestone into actionable, measurable, and time-bound deliverables. Consider the inter-dependencies between deliverables and milestones to facilitate execution. By establishing a timeline with milestones and deliverables, you establish a road map that provides a clear path toward the ultimate objective of digital transformation.

- *Allocating resources and budget accordingly*: Digital transformation initiatives necessitate the allocation of adequate resources, such as competent personnel, technological infrastructure, and financial considerations. Assess the skills and knowledge required for each project phase and allocate resources accordingly. Determine whether internal capabilities exist or whether external support is required. Additionally, ensure that the budget required for implementing each iteration correlates with the anticipated value and impact. As the project progresses, continuously monitor and alter resource allocation to maintain efficiency and optimize results.

In conclusion, the creation of a digital transformation road map is a crucial stage in ensuring a successful and seamless journey. By dividing the project into smaller iterations, prioritizing features and initiatives, creating a timeline with milestones and deliverables, and allocating resources and budget appropriately, organizations can successfully navigate the complexities of digital transformation and achieve their desired results. Remember that a roadmap is a living document that needs to be reviewed, updated, and shared with stakeholders regularly to ensure alignment and support throughout the transformation process.

4.2.2 Execution

The successful execution of a project, particularly in the context of digital transformation, depends on several crucial factors. These elements include iterative development and implementation cycles, monitoring progress and addressing any obstacles, routinely reviewing and adapting the project plan, and ensuring effective communication and stakeholder engagement. The following parts will investigate each of these elements in depth.

- *Iterative Development and Implementation Cycles*: Frequently, digital transformation initiatives employ an iterative development and implementation methodology. This means that rather than executing the entire project in a single, linear phase, it is broken down into smaller cycles or iterations. Each iteration focuses on delivering a distinct set of features or results. By dividing a project into iterations, organizations can achieve incremental progress, collect feedback, and make modifications before proceeding to subsequent cycles. This iterative approach facilitates adaptability, encourages continuous development, and enables faster adaptation to changing requirements or emerging opportunities.
- *Monitoring Progress and Addressing Roadblocks*: It is essential to track the progress of a digital transformation project to ensure that it remains on track

and achieves its goals. This involves establishing KPIs and metrics to measure progress concerning predefined objectives. Regular monitoring enables project managers and teams to identify potential barriers and obstacles that could impede progress. When obstacles are identified, swift action needs to be taken to remove them. This may involve reevaluating project priorities, allocating additional resources, or revising the project plan to surmount obstacles and maintain the project's trajectory.

- *Regular Review and Adaptation of the Project Plan*: Digital transformation initiatives frequently operate in environments that are dynamic and swiftly changing. To effectively navigate these complexities, it is essential to review and alter the project plan regularly. Plans for a project should not be viewed as static documents but as dynamic artifacts that evolve throughout the project's lifecycle. Regular review sessions afford the chance to assess the current state of the project, evaluate its alignment with strategic objectives, and make any necessary adjustments. This adaptable strategy ensures that the project remains relevant and responsive to emerging requirements, technological advances, and changing market conditions.

- *Effective Communication and Stakeholder Engagement*: Effective communication and stakeholder engagement are crucial to the successful completion of a digital transformation project. Stakeholders consist of project sponsors, senior executives, end users, and other individuals or groups affected by the project's results. Clear and consistent communication with project stakeholders ensures that all parties are aware of the project's objectives, status, and potential impact. Engaging stakeholders throughout the lifecycle of a project fosters a sense of ownership, ensures their support, and reduces resistance to change. In addition, it enables the project team to gain valuable insights, incorporate diverse viewpoints, and make informed decisions.

In conclusion, the execution of a digital transformation project necessitates a methodical and flexible strategy. Conducting iterative development and implementation cycles, monitoring progress, resolving roadblocks, routinely reviewing and adapting the project plan, and ensuring effective communication and stakeholder engagement are crucial success factors for such initiatives. Businesses can increase their chances of implementing a successful digital transformation and benefiting from it by using these practices. Digital transformation is crucial for firms looking to stay competitive and satisfy shifting consumer needs in today's fast-paced digital economy. To overcome hurdles and ensure a smooth transition, successful digital transformation involves the application of efficient change management solutions. When implementing change management within the realm of digital transformation, there are significant considerations to take into account in this situation.

Along with outlining the exact adjustments and actions to be made, this plan should also specify the transformation's goals, scope, and timing. In order to keep stakeholders informed and involved throughout the process, it should also have a strong communication plan. By creating a thorough plan, organizations can successfully handle the challenges and uncertainties brought on by digital transformation. Second, it is critical to foresee potential opposition early on and take proactive measures to overcome it.

Employee resistance to change or skepticism of it, especially in the context of digital transformation, is common. Transparent and honest communication is the key to overcome this. By helping employees understand the reasons behind the change and the advantages it will bring, organizations may reduce resistance and foster a constructive attitude toward change. Another crucial element is offering support and training to staff. Employees frequently need to acquire new digital skills and knowledge as a result of the adoption of new technology and procedures associated with digital transformation. Businesses should spend thorough training sessions, workshops, and online resources to provide their employees with the tools they need. In addition, workers should have access to ongoing assistance as they learn how to use the new digital tools and processes. Businesses may increase their digital capabilities and guarantee a seamless transition by investing in employee training and support.

Ensuring alignment and buy-in across the organization is equally important. The vision and goals of the transformation must be successfully communicated by the leaders, who must also stress the importance of everyone's involvement. Encourage a sense of ownership and commitment among employees by involving them in the transformation process and asking for their input. The formation of cross-functional teams or task forces can facilitate collaboration and ensure that all departments are working toward the same goals. By fostering alignment and buy-in, organizations can maximize the likelihood of a successful digital transformation by leveraging the collective efforts of their workforce. Managing change in the context of digital transformation requires creating a comprehensive change management strategy, proactively addressing resistance, providing training and support to employees, and ensuring organizational alignment and buy-in. Organizations can successfully navigate the complexities of digital transformation and position themselves for success in the digital age if they manage change effectively.

4.3 AGILE MINDSET THROUGH CHANGE: BUILDING A CULTURE OF AGILITY AND ADAPTABILITY

Digital transformation is a complex endeavor that necessitates organizations to overcome numerous obstacles. The entrenched resistance to change within the organizational culture represents a significant barrier. Often, traditional practices and hierarchical structures impede the implementation of new technologies and processes. Employees may be resistant to change due to a concern of job loss or a deficiency of digital skills. Additionally, obsolete technology infrastructure and legacy systems can hinder digital transformation initiatives. To overcome these obstacles, a concerted endeavor to promote cultural change is required.

The success of digital transformation initiatives is highly dependent on the culture of the organization. A culture that fosters innovation, collaboration, and agility is more conducive to successful digital transformation because it influences how people collaborate. Leadership is essential for shaping culture and fostering change. Leaders should articulate a crystal-clear vision for transformation, inspire employees, and actively nurture a culture that encourages experimentation and continuous improvement. Breaking down departmental silos and promoting open communication and collaboration is essential.

In today's dynamic business environment, it is crucial to recognize the need for an agile and adaptable culture. Organizations need to be adaptable and responsive to technologies and market trends that undergo constant change. A culture of agility encourages workers to embrace change, take calculated risks, and learn from their mistakes. It fosters an atmosphere where continuous learning is valued, and failure is viewed as an opportunity for development. This mentality enables organizations to navigate the uncertainties and disruptions that accompany digital transformation.

In addition, fostering a culture of adaptability enables organizations to evolve and transform in response to changing consumer expectations and market conditions. Employees are encouraged to question the status quo, seek alternative methods of operation, and drive innovation. A culture of adaptability enables employees to identify opportunities for improvement, adapt to altering circumstances, and contribute to the organization's overall innovation efforts. Organizations can position themselves for success in the digital era by embracing a culture that values continuous learning, collaboration, and innovation. Table 4.3 identifies and explores five essential factors that contribute to the development of a transformational culture within organizations during digital transformation initiatives.

In conclusion, for digital transformation to be successful, a culture shift is essential. Organizations need to address resistance to change, establish a connection between

TABLE 4.3   Key factors for cultivating a transformational culture in digital initiatives

KEY POINTS	IMPORTANCE	IMPACT ON DIGITAL TRANSFORMATION INITIATIVES	EXAMPLES
Entrenched resistance to change within the organizational culture	High	Hinders implementation of new technologies	Fear of job loss, lack of digital skills
Obsolete technology infrastructure and legacy systems	High	Hampers digital transformation initiatives	Outdated software and hardware limitations
Leadership's role in shaping culture and fostering change	High	Influences adoption of new practices	Clear vision, inspiring employees
Culture of agility and adaptability	High	Enables organizations to navigate changes	Embrace change, continuous learning
Importance of collaboration, innovation, and continuous learning	High	Drives success in the digital era	Breaking down silos, questioning the status quo

culture and successful transformation, and acknowledge the significance of nurturing a culture of agility and adaptability. Leadership, effective communication, and a commitment to lifelong learning are required to overcome obstacles and difficulties. By adopting a culture that fosters innovation, collaboration, and adaptability, organizations can flourish in the constantly changing digital landscape.

4.3.1 Building an Agile Culture

An agile culture needs to be built for the digital transition project to be managed effectively. In today's rapidly changing business climate, organizations must be able to quickly adapt to new technologies, consumer needs, and market trends. Teams may create outcomes more quickly with agile approaches because they provide a structure that promotes collaboration, adaptation, and continual development. In order to foster an agile culture, organizations must encourage a mindset that values experimentation and accepts change. Giving teams decision-making power and encouraging them to take measured risks in order to experiment and learn are necessary for this. Creating a safe environment where failure is seen as an opportunity for growth rather than a setback is essential. Leadership is crucial in setting the tone for agility by creating clear goals and objectives, removing obstacles, and encouraging a culture of continuous learning and improvement.

Agile project management techniques like Scrum or Kanban are available for usage by organizations. These methods promote regular feedback loops, cross-functional collaboration, and iterative development. Project managers, development teams, and business stakeholders collaborate closely to ensure that projects adhere to strategic objectives and customer requirements. Agile rituals encourage openness and collaboration, enabling teams to adapt to changing objectives and priorities swiftly. Examples include daily stand-ups, sprint planning, and retrospectives.

4.3.2 Leadership's Role in Fostering an Agile Culture

In an agile environment, leaders must embrace and advance the values and tenets of agility while also providing the tools and assistance required for successful project execution. In order to effectively communicate the goals and objectives of the digital transformation program, leaders must first emphasize the importance of agility and the benefits it provides the firm. By articulating the team's aims and objectives in detail, the leadership creates a feeling of direction and alignment among the members, enabling them to work together toward a common target.

Leaders need to encourage a culture of creativity, risk-taking, and constant learning in order to empower their team members. They ought to foster an atmosphere of psychological safety and trust where team members are free to discuss their problems, ideas, and difficulties. People are more willing to try out novel concepts and take calculated risks as a result, which encourages innovation and creativity. Leaders should also facilitate open and transparent communication channels to enable regular feedback loops and information exchange. By actively listening to their teams and implementing their feedback, leaders can ensure that decisions are made collaboratively and that everyone's knowledge and views are recognized.

Leaders are also crucial in breaking down obstacles and providing the tools and support needed for agility. Any organizational barriers to growth, such as outdated procedures, strict hierarchies, or a lack of teamwork, must be aggressively identified and dealt with. Leaders should provide their followers the flexibility and authority to make judgments in order to promote shorter reaction times and more agility. Teams should spend appropriately on tools, technologies, and training to assist in the effective adoption of agile principles. By providing the appropriate tools and support, leaders enable their teams to navigate the complexity of digital transformation programs with agility and resilience.

4.3.3 Creating a Shared Vision and Purpose

A shared vision serves as a beacon that unites the efforts of all project participants and ensures that everyone is moving in the same direction. It establishes the organization's anticipated future state and provides direction for the process of digital transformation. It is crucial to include important stakeholders and members of the project team when creating a shared vision since their opinions and comments will help create a vision that is more inclusive and thorough. The likelihood of a project's success rises as a result of the team's sense of ownership and commitment fostered by this collaborative approach.

A distinct purpose needs to be established in addition to the agreed vision. The purpose is to communicate the importance of the digital transformation project to all stakeholders by outlining the justification for it. It makes it easier for everyone to comprehend the benefits of the journey by providing an answer to the fundamental question of "why" the organization is taking it. In the context of digital transformation, the goal is frequently to increase operational effectiveness, improve customer experiences, maintain market competitiveness, or foster innovation. Project managers can inspire and motivate the team by stating the purpose in a clear and concise manner, ensuring that everyone is on the same page and dedicated to attaining the intended results. Furthermore, a well-stated purpose offers a framework for making decisions throughout the project, ensuring that all actions and efforts support the overarching objectives of the digital transformation.

4.3.4 Promoting Collaboration and Cross-Functional Teams

Organizations increasingly depend on cross-functional teams to spearhead effective digital initiatives in the quickly changing technological landscape of today. These teams bring together people from several departments, each with their own special expertise, to work together on a similar objective. Organizations can use varied perspectives and abilities to produce creative solutions and overcome complicated challenges by encouraging teamwork among their people. The integration of many functions, including IT, marketing, operations, and finance, is made possible by the cross-functional approach, ensuring a comprehensive understanding of the project and facilitating efficient decision-making.

The success of projects involving digital transformation depends on effective cross-functional team collaboration. It allows for fluid communication and knowledge sharing, dismantling the silos that frequently impede advancement. Team members can utilize their own talents, enhance one another's abilities, and go above personal limitations by working together. As the team works together to meet project goals, this interdisciplinary approach also encourages a sense of ownership and accountability among team members. Collaboration fosters an environment where team members may exchange knowledge, best practices, and lessons gained, fostering the organization's overall growth and development.

Organizations can put a variety of tactics into practice to encourage cooperation and improve the efficiency of cross-functional teams in digital transformation project management. To ensure seamless information flow among team members, it is first important to establish clear communication channels and platforms. This can involve holding frequent team meetings, using online collaboration tools, and using project management software. In order to ensure that everyone on the team is on the same page and working toward the same aim, it is necessary to create a shared vision and develop specific goals for the project. Third, businesses need to foster an environment where team members feel free to share opinions, pose queries, and question presumptions—a culture of trust, respect, and open-mindedness. Last but not least, rewarding team accomplishments promotes a supportive and cooperative environment, inspiring team members to give their all and establishing a sense of camaraderie.

4.3.5 Empowering and Trusting Employees

Giving workers the resources, skills, and authority they need to take charge of their work and make decisions is empowering. Organizations can unlock the full potential of their workforce and promote significant digital transformation by allowing employees the freedom to experiment with new concepts, research emerging technology, and implement creative solutions.

Furthermore, the foundation of successful employee empowerment is trust. Having faith in employees involves having faith in their skills, judgment, and moral character. Employees are more likely to take risks, think creatively, and work collaboratively when they feel trusted. Employees who are trusted are more willing to embrace change and venture outside of their comfort zones, which is crucial in the context of digital transformation. Additionally, it promotes an environment in which staff members take ownership of their activities and pursue continual improvement. Organizations may unleash their employees' full potential, encourage a sense of ownership, and propel successful digital transformation programs by creating a culture of trust.

4.3.6 Encouraging Experimentation and Learning from Failure

Project managers may enable their teams to think creatively and try out novel ways of problem-solving by creating an environment that values experimentation. This kind of thinking makes it possible to find innovative answers that would have yet to be found via more conventional means. As team members feel encouraged to try and refine their ideas, it also fosters a sense of ownership and creativity among them.

Project management for the digital transition needs to include learning from mistakes. Projects will inevitably run into difficulties and setbacks in a digital environment that is evolving quickly. Project managers should encourage their employees to consider failure as an opportunity for growth and learning rather than as a negative conclusion. Project teams can pinpoint the main reasons why things went wrong, glean important lessons, and use those lessons to inform their future work by performing extensive postmortem studies. Project managers can continuously improve by using this process to hone their plans and methods for making decisions. Accepting setbacks as a learning opportunity promotes resilience, adaptability, and a readiness to make changes, which, in turn, results in more successful digital transformation initiatives.

4.3.7 Developing Agile Mindset in Individuals

Agile project management approaches, like Scrum or Kanban, give teams the flexibility and iterative approach they need to adapt fast to changes and produce value in small doses. Success is influenced by the development of an agile mindset among those working on the project, not only the adoption of agile procedures. An agile attitude entails welcoming change, appreciating teamwork and communication, and being receptive to ongoing learning and development. People with an agile mindset are aware that requirements can change, and they are prepared to modify their plans as necessary. They appreciate criticism and make use of it to guide decisions and advance the project. Additionally, they value cross-functional teams, which promote cooperation and draw on a variety of viewpoints to address complicated issues. Additionally, people with an agile mentality are inspired to experiment and learn from setbacks because they feel at ease with uncertainty, and this ultimately fosters innovation and creativity inside the digital transformation project.

4.3.8 Emphasizing Continuous Learning and Professional Development

It is vital to emphasize the significance of these behaviors for both individuals and businesses. Building an agile and adaptable culture, in particular, requires adopting an agile mentality via transformation. People with an agile mindset are urged to view change as a chance for creativity and growth rather than as a danger or disruption. As a result, learning and growth are viewed as continuing processes rather than one-time events, fostering a culture of continuous progress.

Organizations may provide their employees with the information and skills they need to successfully navigate change by placing a strong emphasis on professional development and continual learning. Access to pertinent training courses, seminars, and other materials that encourage flexibility and adaptability is one aspect of this. The development of an agile mentality is further aided by fostering a welcoming workplace that promotes experimentation, cooperation, and feedback. Organizations can also make use of tools and platforms, such as online courses, virtual communities of practice, and knowledge-sharing platforms, that promote continual learning. Through these programs, people are given the power to accept change, pick up new skills, and keep on top of trends in a work environment that is becoming more and more dynamic.

4.3.9 Nurturing Growth Mindset and Resilience

A growth mindset comprises having faith in one's ability to advance both personally and professionally and in the idea that skills can be acquired via hard work, perseverance, and ongoing education. It encourages people to view obstacles as chances for improvement and to accept failures as instructive experiences. Organizations can develop a culture that emphasizes learning, creativity, and adaptability by encouraging a growth mindset.

Another essential component of an agile mentality is resilience. It is the capacity to overcome obstacles, overcome problems, and overcome adversity. Developing a strong sense of self-belief, optimism, and the capacity to adjust to changing circumstances are all part of the process of building resilience. Effectively navigating through uncertainty, setbacks, and interruptions is more likely for resilient people and teams. They are able to accept change, grow from mistakes, and swiftly modify their methods and strategies. Individuals are encouraged to take risks, learn from mistakes, and constantly improve through developing resilience within the organizational culture, which enables the organization to adapt and flourish in a constantly changing environment.

4.3.10 Encouraging Proactive Problem-Solving and Decision-Making

A key component of creating such a culture is to promote proactive problem-solving and decision-making. Adopting an agile mentality equips people and teams to foresee problems, deal with change skillfully, and promote creativity. Organizations should highlight the value of learning and continual improvement in order to foster proactive problem-solving. Employees should be urged to spot possible problems and take the initiative to solve them. This can be accomplished through encouraging a sense of ownership and autonomy, where people are free to take charge of their own lives and try out novel ideas. Leaders may set the tone by creating an atmosphere that encourages initiative and taking risks while also offering resources and support for experimentation. Organizations can foster a culture that prioritizes proactive problem-solving by developing a growth mindset and highlighting the importance of learning from mistakes as important chances for improvement.

Similar to this, agility and adaptability require proactive decision-making. Organizations should empower people at all levels to make decisions based on their knowledge and the information at hand rather than waiting for them to be handed down from above. To do this, it is vital to create clear frameworks for decision-making and to offer the required instruction and direction. Organizations may adjust swiftly to developments and make use of the group intelligence of their teams by decentralizing decision-making authority. Employee collaboration and informed decision-making are also made possible by encouraging open and transparent communication channels. A sense of ownership and accountability that is fostered by proactive decision-making enables quicker problem-solving and more flexibility in changing circumstances.

4.3.11 Fostering Adaptability and Embracing Change

Companies need to be able to react rapidly to changes in the market, improvements in technology, and client needs. This calls for cultivating an agile attitude that pushes workers to be flexible, to continuously learn and improve, and to modify their methods and tactics as necessary. The first step in creating an agile and adaptable culture is leadership. Leaders need to set an example by being open to changing themselves and motivating others to follow suit. They ought to foster an atmosphere where trying new things, taking risks, and failing should be viewed as a chance to learn rather than a mistake. Employees who adopt this approach are more adaptive and flexible, giving them the assurance they need to face uncertainty and ambiguity.

Organizations should also spend money on training and development initiatives that improve workers' agility. Workshops on agile techniques, design thinking, and other pertinent frameworks may be included in these programs. Organizations may empower people to become change agents who can spot opportunities, put forth creative ideas, and adjust to changing conditions by providing them with the skills and information necessary to manage change successfully. Through these initiatives, encouraging adaptation and accepting change is engrained in the corporate culture, helping the organization to flourish in a quickly changing business environment.

4.3.12 Cultivating Effective Communication and Collaboration Skills

A clear and simple message that guarantees everyone is aware of the objectives, aims, and expectations is essential for effective communication. Encourage open and honest communication so that team members feel free to share their thoughts, worries, and suggestions. Equally important is active listening, which fosters empathy and understanding and improves communication and problem-solving. Organizations that value active communication are better able to adapt to change because information can flow freely and decisions can be taken as a group.

Effective communication and cooperation go hand in hand. It entails cooperating to achieve a common objective while utilizing the various talents, viewpoints, and experiences of team members. When people work together to create answers, it encourages creativity, innovation, and a sense of ownership among the participants. Additionally, it promotes building trust among team members and encouraging mutual learning. Teams that work well together may navigate change more easily because they are better able to manage ambiguity, adjust to changing conditions, and reach consensus on decisions that result in desirable outcomes.

4.4 SCRUM PROJECT MANAGEMENT: BEST PRACTICES FOR AGILE DEVELOPMENT

Scrum is a widely utilized agile framework for software development initiatives. It emphasizes iterative and incremental development, allowing teams to deliver high-quality products. There are three essential responsibilities in Scrum: Product Owner, Scrum Master, and Development Team. Each role has distinct responsibilities and works closely together to accomplish the project's objectives. Let us examine the specifics of each role and its associated responsibilities (Figure 4.3).

(A) **Product Owner**: The Product Owner represents all stakeholders and consumers. Their primary responsibility is to maximize the product's value by managing the Product Backlog efficiently. Key Product Owner activities include:
- *Defining and Prioritizing the Product Backlog*: The Product Owner works closely with stakeholders to gather requirements, create user stories, and prioritize them based on value and customer needs.
- *Communicating the Product Vision*: The Product Owner ensures that the development team understands the overall product vision and goals, providing clarity and direction.

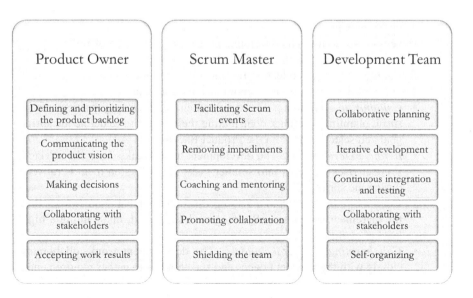

FIGURE 4.3 Analyzing each function's tasks and qualities.

- *Making Decisions*: The Product Owner has the final say on the Product Backlog and makes critical decisions regarding scope, priorities, and release planning.
- *Collaborating with Stakeholders*: The Product Owner engages with stakeholders, gathers feedback, and ensures that the product is aligned with their expectations.
- *Accepting Work Results*: The Product Owner reviews and accepts completed work items, ensuring they meet the agreed-upon criteria and align with the product vision.

(B) **Scrum Master**: The Scrum Master functions as the Scrum Team's facilitator and coach. They are accountable for ensuring that the Scrum methodology is understood and adhered to. Among the most important responsibilities of the Scrum Master are the following:

- *Facilitating Scrum Events*: The Scrum Master schedules and facilitates the various Scrum events, such as sprint planning, daily stand-ups, sprint reviews, and retrospectives.
- *Removing Impediments*: The Scrum Master identifies and helps to remove any obstacles that might hinder the team's progress. They ensure that the team has a conducive working environment.
- *Coaching and Mentoring*: The Scrum Master guides the team on agile principles, values, and practices. They support the team's continuous improvement efforts and encourage self-organization.
- *Promoting Collaboration*: The Scrum Master fosters effective collaboration within the team and with stakeholders. They facilitate communication and promote a culture of transparency and trust.
- *Shielding the Team*: The Scrum Master protects the team from external distractions and influences, enabling them to focus on delivering the product increment.

(C) **Development Team**: The development team is comprised of professionals tasked with delivering the product increment. Self-organizing and cross-functional, they take collective responsibility for the work. The principal activities of the development team include the following:

- *Collaborative Planning*: The development team actively participates in sprint planning meetings, contributing their expertise to define the sprint goal and select items from the Product Backlog.
- *Iterative Development*: The development team breaks down the selected Product Backlog items into smaller tasks and works on them iteratively during the sprint.
- *Continuous Integration and Testing*: The development team ensures that the increment is continuously integrated and tested, maintaining a high level of quality.
- *Collaborating with Stakeholders*: The development team collaborates closely with the Product Owner and stakeholders to gather requirements, seek clarifications, and receive feedback.
- *Self-organizing*: The development team decides how to accomplish the work, organizes itself, and divides tasks among team members. They collaborate to optimize productivity and deliver value.

A Scrum team's ability to work together and communicate effectively is essential. To promote transparency, cooperation, and understanding among team members, the Product Owner, Scrum Master, and development team work closely together. To coordinate their activities and remove any hurdles, they communicate frequently using methods like daily stand-ups. The Product Owner gives the development team the information and feedback they require, while the Scrum Master makes sure the Scrum process runs smoothly and encourages productive teamwork. Scrum enables organizations to embrace agility, adapt to changing requirements, and successfully deliver valuable products by clearly defining roles and encouraging collaborative teamwork.

Agile product management is an approach for managing and developing products that place a focus on flexibility, teamwork, and incremental improvement. It is extensively utilized in the IT sector and beyond and was developed on the concepts of agile software development. The creation of a clear product vision and strategy is a crucial component of agile product management. This entails coordinating the needs and goals of the intended users or clients with the overarching corporate goals. The product vision serves as a guide, offering clear instructions to the development team and stakeholders. It guarantees that the product is focused and in line with market demands.

User stories and backlog management are essential components of agile product management. User stories are succinct narrative summaries of a feature or functionality as seen from the user's perspective. The development team uses them to convey user requirements and expectations by identifying the "who," "what," and "why" of a requirement. The process of keeping a prioritized list of user stories, often known as the Product Backlog, is called backlog management. The Product Backlog evolves over time as fresh requirements are introduced, old requirements are improved, and finished requirements are dropped. Agile product management establishes the order in which user stories should be worked on using prioritizing approaches. Methods including value versus effort analysis, Kano model analysis, and MoSCoW prioritizing are included. The goal is to determine the most important characteristics and communicate them as effectively as possible.

Another essential aspect of agile product management is release planning. It entails the creation of a road map outlining the releases and their corresponding features. The release planning process takes into consideration business objectives, customer feedback, and market conditions. It assists the team in setting realistic expectations, managing communication with stakeholders, and ensuring a constant flow of value delivery. In agile product management, frequent collaboration, continuous feedback, and flexibility are emphasized. Agile's iterative nature enables regular inspection and modification, ensuring that the product evolves in response to real-world utilization and shifting market dynamics. By employing agile principles and practices, product managers can maximize value delivery, minimize waste, and create products that truly satisfy their users' requirements.

4.4.1 Scrum Events

Scrum, an agile framework for managing complex projects, is comprised of a series of events that provide structure and foster effective collaboration within the development team. These occasions, also known as ceremonies, promote transparency, inspection, and adaptation throughout the lifecycle of a project. Let us examine each of the Scrum events in detail.

- *Sprint Planning*: Sprint planning is a collaborative session held at the start of every sprint. During this event, the Scrum team, consisting of the Product Owner and the Development Team, determines which items from the Product Backlog will be addressed in the subsequent iteration. The team evaluates the requirements, discusses the necessary work, and determines how to complete it. The result of sprint planning is the construction of a Sprint Backlog, which consists of a list of user stories, tasks, and their estimated sprint effort.
- *Daily Scrum*: The Daily Scrum, also known as the daily stand-up, is a brief meeting that occurs daily during the sprint. Its purpose is to improve team members' communication, coordination, and transparency. The Development Team assembles to address three fundamental questions: What progress have I made since the last Daily Scrum? What am I going to focus on until the next Daily Scrum? Are there any obstacles impeding my progress? The Daily Scrum facilitates problem identification and resolution, promotes collaboration, and keeps the team focused on sprint objectives.
- *Sprint Review*: Each sprint concludes with the Scrum team conducting a sprint review. This event allows the Product Owner, customers, and other interested parties to view the completed work. The Development Team presents the product increment built during the sprint, emphasizing any new features or modifications. Stakeholders provide feedback, pose queries, and collaborate on possible Product Backlog modifications. The sprint review enables adaptive planning and ensures that the product is aligned with stakeholders' expectations.
- *Sprint Retrospective*: After the sprint review, the Scrum team conducts a retrospective. This event emphasizes continuous development and learning from the prior sprint. The team evaluates its processes, interactions, and practices to determine what went well, what could be improved, and any prospective next-sprint action items. The sprint retrospective enables the team to make adjustments, optimize their performance, and increase their overall output by fostering open communication and providing a secure environment for feedback.

Effective execution of these Scrum events fosters collaboration, transparency, and adaptation within the Scrum framework. By emphasizing continuous improvement, they contribute to the iterative and incremental development process, enabling teams to deliver high-quality products that satisfy the changing requirements of stakeholders.

4.4.2 Agile Estimation and Planning

Agile planning and estimation are essential to the successful implementation of agile methodologies. Agile teams rely on these techniques to estimate effort and complexity, plan their work, and adapt to shifting priorities and requirements. Let us examine each of these facets in greater depth.

(A) **Techniques for Estimating Effort and Complexity**: Agile teams estimate the effort and complexity of their work items using a variety of techniques. Commonly employed techniques include:

- *Story Points*: Agile teams often use story points to estimate the relative effort required to complete a user story or a work item. Story points are a measure of complexity, effort, and risk involved in delivering a particular requirement. The Fibonacci sequence (1, 2, 3, 5, 8, 13, etc.) is commonly used to assign story points, representing increasing levels of complexity.
- *Planning Poker*: Planning poker is a collaborative estimation technique where team members assign story points to user stories or work items. Each team member privately selects a story point value, and then all the values are revealed simultaneously. This technique encourages discussion and alignment among team members.
- *T-Shirt Sizing*: T-shirt sizing is a simplified estimation technique where work items are classified into sizes such as XS, S, M, L, and XL, representing increasing effort or complexity. This technique provides a rough estimate of the relative size of work items without assigning specific numeric values.

(B) **Agile Planning Approaches**: Agile planning requires the creation of a road map or plan to direct the team's efforts. Velocity planning and capacity planning are two common approaches to agile planning:

- *Velocity Planning*: Velocity is a metric that measures the amount of work a team can complete in a given iteration or sprint. Agile teams calculate their velocity based on the number of story points or work items they successfully deliver in each iteration. By analyzing past velocities, teams can forecast how much work they can complete in future iterations, aiding in release planning and project scheduling.
- *Capacity Planning*: Capacity planning involves determining the team's available capacity for each iteration. It takes into account factors such as team size, individual availability, and any non-project-related commitments. By understanding the team's capacity, agile teams can plan and allocate work items effectively for each iteration, avoiding overloading or underutilizing team members.

(C) **Adapting Plans in Response to Changing Requirements and Priorities**: One of the fundamental principles of agile is adaptability. Agile teams continuously reevaluate and modify their plans in response to shifting priorities and requirements. They embrace the concept of incremental and iterative development. Teams collaborate with stakeholders to reprioritize, reevaluate, and modify the plan in response to new information or changes. This adaptability enables teams to deliver value frequently and quickly while maximizing customer satisfaction.

Agile estimation and planning techniques are crucial for agile teams to estimate effort and complexity, plan their work, and adapt to shifting priorities and requirements. These practices enable teams to achieve transparency, predictability, and flexibility in their

TABLE 4.4   Essential facets of agile planning and estimation

FACETS	TECHNIQUES	DESCRIPTION	EXAMPLE
Techniques for Estimating Effort and Complexity	Story points	Measures complexity and effort of user stories or work items	Assigning story points using the Fibonacci sequence
	Planning poker	Collaborative estimation technique that encourages discussion	Team members reveal story point values simultaneously
	T-Shirt sizing	Simplified estimation based on the relative size of work items	Classifying work items into XS, S, M, L, and XL
Agile Planning Approaches	Velocity planning	Measures team's work completed in each iteration	Analyzing past velocities for future release planning
	Capacity planning	Determines the team's available capacity for each iteration	Considering team size and individual availability
Adapting Plans in Response to Changing Requirements	Incremental and iterative development	Reevaluating and modifying plans based on shifting priorities	Collaborating with stakeholders for plan adjustments

project execution, resulting in iteratively successful product development. Table 4.4 summarizes five essential facets of agile planning and estimation techniques used in agile methodologies.

4.4.3 Agile Development Practices

A collection of guiding ideas and procedures known as agile development practices are intended to increase the efficiency, adaptability, and caliber of software development initiatives. These procedures place a strong emphasis on close team cooperation, incremental and iterative development, and continuous code integration. Three fundamental agile development approaches are pair programming, test-driven development, and continuous integration (CI).

The practice of writing tests prior to writing actual code is known as test-driven development. In test-driven development, developers specify the desired behavior of a feature or capability using automated tests. These tests guide the development process and act as a code definition. The developers then create code to fulfill the test requirements, passing the tests as a result. Test-driven development makes refactoring and maintenance easier and guarantees that the code performs as intended. Writing tests first in test-driven development helps developers to think about desired outcomes and extreme scenarios, resulting in more robust and reliable code.

Developers who use the CI method commonly incorporate changes to their code into a public repository. Early in the development process, CI's main goal is to spot and fix integration issues. Developers make many daily contributions to a central repository. An automatic build process is started every time a change is made, compiling the code, running automated tests, and looking for errors and conflicts. CI guarantees that the codebase is always current, lowers the chance of integration problems, and gives developers quick feedback. Software development teams can work more productively and create software of a higher caliber because of the atmosphere it creates.

Agile development approaches are fundamentally based on collaboration. Direct communication between all team members, including developers, testers, designers, and product owners, is prioritized in agile teams. Individuals with various skills and viewpoints are encouraged to work together, share knowledge, and contribute to the project's success through collaborative growth. Two developers work together on the same code in pair programming, a technique for collaborative software development. While the other observes, checks, and gives immediate feedback, one programmer develops the code. The duties may alternate from time to time. Pair programming enhances the quality of the code, makes it easier to share knowledge, and encourages lifelong learning. Additionally, it lowers mistakes and increases the group's productivity as a whole.

4.4.4 Scaling Agile for Large Projects

As organizations increasingly adopt agile methodologies for software development projects, they are frequently faced with the need to scale agile practices to accommodate larger and more complex initiatives. Scaling agile requires coordinating and synchronizing the efforts of multiple teams, ensuring alignment with organizational objectives, and addressing the unique challenges that arise when implementing agile at a larger scale. This section examines various scaling frameworks, including Scrum of Scrums, Large-Scale Scrum (LeSS), and Scaled Agile Framework (SAFe) [1], and discusses how they facilitate the scalability of agile for large projects.

(A) **Scaling Frameworks**
  - *Scrum of Scrums*: A straightforward and lightweight method for synchronizing the actions of various agile teams is the Scrum of Scrums framework. It entails designating representatives from each team to establish a Scrum of Scrums, where they convene on a regular basis to talk about interteam interdependence, share project updates, and handle any obstacles. This structure promotes cross-team cooperation, information sharing, and issue-solving.
  - *LeSS*: LeSS is a framework that applies Scrum's tenets and methods to significant projects. It encourages openness, empirical process control, self-managing teams, and simplicity and minimalism. LeSS offers scalability through the use of many Scrum teams centered around a single Product Backlog and a single Product Owner and Scrum Master to oversee and coordinate everything. LeSS encourages teamwork and collaborative ownership to produce a cohesive output.
  - *SAFe*: SAFe is a thorough framework that directs the scaled adoption of agile throughout a whole organization. It provides a methodical way to

synchronize and coordinate agile efforts among several teams, programs, and portfolios. SAFe offers a set of roles, events, artifacts, and practices to promote alignment, cooperation, and value delivery. It also combines agile and Lean ideas. SAFe adds more levels of planning and governance to enable widespread agile adoption.

(B) **Coordination and Synchronization**: When many agile teams work on inter-dependent features or components, coordination and synchronization problems can appear. These problems must be resolved in order to scale agile. Regular cross-team communication, such as daily stand-ups or Scrum of Scrums meetings, aids in the identification and resolution of dependencies, the alignment of priorities, and the maintenance of a unified strategy for product delivery. Tools like shared backlogs, visual management boards, and integrated tooling can keep teams visible and transparent.

(C) **Addressing Challenges in Scaling Agile**: Agile scaling in large enterprises brings special difficulties that should be carefully considered. A few typical difficulties include (a). Organizational culture: Adopting agile at scale calls for a change in the organization's culture. It requires fostering a collaborative, adaptive, and learning-oriented culture that supports agile principles and practices. (b). Communication and knowledge sharing: Large projects often involve geographically dispersed teams, making effective communication and knowledge sharing vital. Leveraging collaboration tools, conducting virtual meetings, and establishing communities of practice can facilitate information exchange and cross-team learning. (c). Dependencies and integration: As project complexity increases, dependencies between teams become more intricate. It is crucial to identify and manage dependencies proactively, establish clear interfaces, and coordinate integration activities to ensure seamless product delivery. (d). Scaling roles and responsibilities: Scaling agile may require redefining roles and responsibilities to distribute work across teams while maintaining clear accountabilities effectively. This includes adapting the Product Owner role, establishing agile coaches, and defining governance mechanisms.

Emerging agile and digital transformation trends and technologies continue to shape how organizations operate and adapt to the ever-changing business landscape. Several key trends are anticipated to drive the evolution of agile project management and digital transformation practices in the future.

- *Agile at Scale*: The emphasis is shifting from individual teams to enterprise-wide agile transformations as organizations increasingly adopt agile methodologies. Scaling agile practices across multiple teams and departments has emerged as a crucial aspect of digital transformation. SAFe and LeSS are gaining popularity as they guide scaling agile principles, fostering collaboration, and aligning organizational objectives.

- *DevOps Integration*: In agile and digital transformation initiatives, the integration of development and operations (DevOps) is gathering importance [2]. DevOps emphasizes collaboration between the development, operations, and quality assurance teams to deliver software more quickly and reliably. By incorporating DevOps practices into agile methodologies, organizations can streamline the software delivery process, eliminate bottlenecks, and improve overall productivity.

- *AI and Machine Learning*: The application of AI and ML technologies will transform agile and digital transformation practices. Automating repetitive duties, providing real-time insights, and optimizing resource allocation are all capabilities of AI-powered tools. Massive quantities of data can be analyzed by ML algorithms to identify patterns, predict outcomes, and facilitate data-driven decision-making. AI and ML will play a crucial role in augmenting agile project management by boosting productivity, quality, and delivery speed.

- *Agile Marketing*: Agile methodologies are being applied to other business functions, including marketing. Agile marketing embraces iterative planning, cross-functional collaboration, and data-driven decision-making to adapt to fluctuating market conditions rapidly. Agile practices are adopted by marketers to enhance campaign execution, consumer engagement, and ROI. Agile marketing enables businesses to respond quickly to customer feedback, initiate campaigns more quickly, and optimize marketing strategies based on real-time data.

- *Agile Leadership*: Leadership is transforming in agile and digital transformation endeavors. Within their organizations, agile leaders need to cultivate a culture of collaboration, innovation, and continuous learning. They need to provide agile teams with support and authority, eliminate organizational barriers, and drive change from the top down. Agile leaders need to also embody agility by being flexible, receptive to feedback, and willing to experiment.

4.4.5 Scrum Artifacts

Artifacts are observable, visible components in the Scrum framework that give crucial information and direct the development process. Collaboration, openness, and efficient communication within the Scrum Team and with stakeholders are made possible by these artifacts. They are essential in ensuring that everyone involved is aware of the tasks at hand, the progress being made, and the project's overall objective.

- *Product Backlog*: A dynamic, prioritized list of all the requested features, functionality, upgrades, bug fixes, and other requirements for the product is known as the Product Backlog. For the Scrum team to comprehend what has to be built and the potential value each item offers to the project, it acts as the only reliable source of information. Curating and maintaining the Product Backlog is the responsibility of the Product Owner, who continually adjusts and reprioritizes the items depending on customer wants, market trends, and corporate objectives. The items on the Product Backlog are typically expressed as user stories, which outline the required functionality from the viewpoint of the user. Acceptance criteria are provided with each item, outlining the particular requirements that need to be satisfied before the item may be deemed complete.

- *Sprint Backlog*: The items chosen for a specific sprint are contained in the Sprint Backlog, which is a subset of the Product Backlog. It shows the strategy the Scrum Team will use to turn the chosen items into a possibly releasable increment over the sprint. The items on the Sprint Backlog are chosen by the Scrum Team as a whole, taking into account their capabilities and the anticipated amount of work they can finish within the sprint timebox. The Sprint Backlog is a dynamic document that changes during the course of the sprint. It provides a visual depiction of the Development Team's commitments and aids in their understanding of the tasks they need to do. Items in the Sprint Backlog may be added, removed, or reordered as the team works to address new information or events that arise.

- *Increment*: The Product Backlog items that have been finished during a sprint are added along with all of the preceding increments to create the increment. It should be in a usable and release-worthy form and represent the current functional version of the product. Delivering a useful and shippable increment is the aim of each sprint. In Scrum, the increment serves as the main barometer of development. It offers the Product Owner and stakeholders a concrete result to assess and offer input on. With each sprint, the increment expands, adding new features and enhancements that eventually result in the completion of the full product.

4.4.6 Challenges and Solutions

The implementation of the Scrum project management methodology within the context of digital transformation is beset with numerous obstacles. However, if the necessary precautions are followed, it can resolve these problems effectively. The constantly shifting character of the criteria and scope is a recurring issue. To address this issue, it is necessary to adopt the agile philosophy of being open to change and maintaining a malleable mindset. Engage with the various stakeholders frequently to ensure that everyone has the same understanding of the evolving requirements. Techniques such as user story mapping and backlog refinement sessions can assist with establishing priorities and adapting to changing requirements.

Integration with existing computer networks and reliance on third-party services are two typical types of integration required by digital transformation initiatives. This could lead to bottlenecks. Early identification and documentation of dependencies is one of the mitigation strategies. Other strategies include working with key teams or stakeholders and holding regular meetings or sync-ups to resolve any potential integration issues. CI and automated testing can help identify and resolve integration issues earlier in the software development life cycle. Another area for improvement is effectively managing team members' availability and talents. By avoiding singular points of failure, maintaining cross-functional teams with diverse skill sets is one way to reduce the likelihood of this happening. Ensure that, in addition to proper resource planning and capacity management, knowledge sharing and ongoing learning are actively encouraged. It is essential to implement proper onboarding procedures for new team members in order to ensure a seamless transition and eliminate any skill deficiencies.

When working on digital transformation initiatives with distributed teams, time zone differences can hinder communication and collaboration. To surmount this challenge, you should utilize collaboration tools and technology, establish overlapping work hours, and utilize video conferencing and real-time collaboration tools for productive meetings and conversations. Define communication channels in a clear and precise manner and work to foster a culture of inclusiveness and mutual understanding among geographically separated teams. Due to Scrum's emphasis on short-term iterations, achieving a balance between short-term and long-term planning is one of its unique challenges. Strategic thinking and long-term planning are essential components of successful digital transformation programs. Regular Product Backlog refinement sessions are held as part of the mitigation strategies in order to examine and rank the importance of long-term objectives. In addition, time is allocated for strategic planning and visioning exercises, and techniques such as Product Roadmap and Release Planning are employed to align short-term iterations with long-term project objectives. In order to reach a consensus on the long-term vision and priorities, it is essential for the Product Owner and the stakeholders to work collaboratively together.

Scrum teams have a greater chance of successfully navigating the complexities of digital transformation projects if they are aware of and able to address the challenges they face. By maintaining effective communication, collaboration, and adaptation in the face of evolving needs, integration complexity, team dynamics, distributed team configurations, and long-term planning, the implementation of the aforementioned mitigation techniques can increase the likelihood that the project will be successful.

4.4.7 Predictions for the Future of Agile Project Management

Predicting the future of agile project management is always challenging, as it is influenced by various factors such as technological advancements, market trends, and evolving business needs. However, based on current trends and observations, here are some potential predictions for the future of agile project management.

4.4.7.1 Continuous delivery

Continuous delivery will continue to evolve and shape the agile landscape as organizations seek to accelerate software delivery and meet ever-increasing customer demands. Here is a summary of continuous delivery, a future prediction for agile project management: Continuous delivery enables frequent and dependable software releases by automating the complete deployment procedure. It focuses on constructing a robust and streamlined pipeline that enables organizations to deliver software modifications rapidly, effectively, and with minimal risk. Continuous delivery will become even more ingrained in agile practices in the future, enabling organizations to accomplish faster time-to-market and seamless customer value delivery.

Technology and tooling advancements will further improve continuous delivery capabilities. Automation will continue to play a crucial role in the software delivery process, eradicating manual and error-prone steps. This will result in quicker, more consistent deployments and a reduction in testing and validation time and effort. In addition, organizations will employ containerization technologies, such as Docker, to produce portable and reproducible deployment artifacts, thereby enhancing the consistency and scalability of the continuous delivery pipeline. Additionally, continuous delivery will be incorporated closely with other agile practices and methodologies. It will align with continuous integration, where frequent code integration and testing ensure that software is always in a state suitable for release. Continuous delivery will also complement agile collaboration and feedback principles by facilitating rapid iterations and the capacity to collect user feedback on released software. This integration of continuous delivery with other agile practices will cultivate a culture of continuous improvement and innovation, enabling organizations to respond quickly to changes in market dynamics and customer requirements.

4.4.7.2 Hybrid agile approaches

The future of agile project management may involve the development of hybrid approaches that combine agile and conventional project management methodologies. Organizations may employ a flexible approach, leveraging agile principles and practices where they provide the most value while incorporating elements of traditional project management for specific project aspects such as budgeting and regulatory compliance. Hybrid agile approaches acknowledge that not all projects and organizations are able to completely adopt agile methodologies due to various constraints or specific requirements. In such cases, organizations can choose to combine agile and conventional project management practices to construct a solution that meets their specific requirements. This hybrid approach enables organizations to take advantage of agile's adaptability, iterative development, and customer-centricity while incorporating traditional project management elements to resolve particular project aspects.

Organizations can use standard project management methods for scheduling and budgeting while incorporating agile concepts for iterative development and frequent feedback. Organizations can successfully manage projects needing a mix of flexibility and structure by striking a balance between agile and traditional project management. Agile concepts may also be incorporated into current project management frameworks and methodologies using hybrid agile approaches. Teams and stakeholders who are more accustomed to traditional project management practices can transfer and adopt this integration more easily. Organizations may maximize the advantages of agile while reducing disruption and reluctance to change by using agile practices that meet their unique requirements.

4.4.7.3 Agile in non-IT domains

Agile project management, which was first used in the IT industry, is currently advancing significantly outside of the software industry. The understanding that agile concepts and practices can contribute value and innovation to a range of sectors led to this expansion. Numerous industries, including marketing, human resources, finance, and operations, have adopted agile approaches because of their adaptability, flexibility, and customer-centric orientation. Organizations in these industries are implementing agile project management to improve project management and promote innovation. Non-IT teams may work more efficiently together, adjust to shifting requirements, and provide more value to customers thanks to agile.

Agile principles, including iterative development, frequent feedback loops, and continuous refinement, are well-suited to the requirements of non-IT domains. Agile allows teams to respond quickly to market dynamics, experiment with various strategies, and optimize campaigns based on customer feedback, for instance, in marketing. Agile can facilitate agile talent management processes in HR, such as iterative performance reviews and continuous employee development, fostering a culture of growth and learning. Agile's implementation in non-IT fields extends beyond project management. It involves an organization-wide mentality transformation that emphasizes agility, adaptability, and customer focus. Agile practices, such as Kanban boards, daily stand-up meetings, and retrospectives, can be implemented in a variety of non-IT contexts to improve workflow, enhance communication, and increase productivity. By adopting agile principles, non-IT organizations can improve their ability to deliver value, adapt to change, and remain competitive in an ever-changing business environment.

As agile continues to penetrate non-IT domains, it is anticipated that more organizations will recognize its value and adopt agile methodologies to foster innovation and enhance project outcomes. Agile's adaptability and customer-centricity enable marketing, HR, finance, and operations departments to navigate uncertainty, adapt to evolving trends, and deliver solutions that exceed customer expectations. Agile's expansion into non-IT domains signifies a fundamental shift in project management practices and creates new opportunities for collaboration, efficiency, and growth.

4.4.7.4 Remote and distributed agile

Organizations are beginning to recognize the possibilities and advantages of agile techniques in dispersed contexts as a result of the COVID-19 epidemic, which has expedited the adoption of remote work. As a result, agile project management will keep developing to support distributed and remote teams.

Agile teams that work remotely and across a distributed environment use a variety of tools and technology to promote collaboration and uphold clear communication. Teams may stay in touch and work together on projects regardless of where they are physically located, thanks to remote collaboration solutions like video conferencing platforms and project management software. Teams can coordinate their work and monitor the status of deliverables thanks to the insight into project progress provided by virtual Kanban boards and digital communication systems.

Agile teams place a high emphasis on creating vibrant remote work cultures in distributed and remote contexts. To ensure openness and responsibility, they establish procedures, clear communication routes, and working agreements. Agile rituals, such as daily stand-ups and sprint planning, are carried out online to keep team members in sync and informed about the status of the project and forthcoming tasks.

Tools and approaches created to support agile principles in remote situations will continue to advance in the future of distributed and remote agile. Businesses will spend money on tools that promote engagement, enable real-time teamwork, and streamline communication between team members. To maximize productivity, guarantee work–life balance, and advance the well-being of remote team members, remote work policies and practices will also be improved. Remote and distributed agile will no longer be the exception in agile project management but rather the rule due to the rapid developments in technology and the rising acceptability of remote labor.

4.4.7.5 Agile mindset

Agile project management will keep extending beyond IT departments and ingraining itself into corporate culture. All company functions will value cooperation, continuous improvement, and customer-centricity as business executives, managers, and stakeholders adopt the agile attitude. Organizational agility and strategic decision-making will be guided by agile concepts. The agile mindset places a strong emphasis on flexibility, adaptability, and change-responsiveness. It encourages people and teams to adopt a growth mentality, where mistakes are seen as opportunities for learning and criticism is welcomed as a way to get better. With regular feedback loops and iterative development, this mentality promotes a culture of experimentation that helps firms stay ahead of the curve.

Organizations may eliminate silos and foster cross-functional cooperation by embracing the agile attitude. Teams are given the freedom to self-organize, decide together, and own their work. As it is acknowledged that good communication, collaboration, and trust are the cornerstones of successful agile project management, this attitude prioritizes people and interactions over processes and tools. The agile attitude will influence project teams in the future, as well as leaders and managers. Agile leaders will promote autonomy and empowerment while offering the support and tools needed for teams to succeed. They will promote a climate of ongoing learning and development, fostering a setting where people feel secure enough to try new things, share their ideas, and question the status quo.

4.5 CONCLUSION

Project management for digital transformations includes a number of crucial elements that are necessary for success. It begins with project planning, which entails identifying precise criteria and objectives to lay a strong foundation. This guarantees that teams and stakeholders are in sync and making progress toward a common goal. Project development is the subsequent phase, where change is applied quickly. Agile approaches let firms respond fast to changing requirements, produce value gradually, and adapt to new situations. Organizations can continue to be sensitive to market trends and consumer needs by adopting an iterative and gradual approach.

Although project execution is only one aspect of agility, a cultural shift is also necessary. It is essential to cultivate an agile mentality and an adaptable culture across the entire firm. This entails encouraging teamwork, welcoming experimentation, and

TABLE 4.5   Important elements and best practices for managing digital transformation projects

KEY COMPONENTS	IMPORTANCE	BEST PRACTICES
Project Planning	Establishes foundation and alignment	Define clear objectives and requirements
		Ensure teams and stakeholders share a common vision
Project Development	Enables adaptability and value delivery	Embrace agile methodologies for flexibility and responsiveness
		Implement an iterative and incremental approach.
Building an Agile Culture	Drives organizational adaptability	Promote collaboration and teamwork
		Embrace experimentation and risk-taking.
		Empower individuals to make decisions and take ownership
Scrum Project Management	Framework for effective project management	Organize and manage projects using Scrum
		Emphasize iterative and time-boxed approaches.
		Foster frequent feedback and transparency.
		Enhance collaboration and value delivery.

giving people the freedom to choose their own paths. Organizations may successfully manage the challenges of the digital transition by fostering an agile culture. Scrum project management is among the greatest methods for agile development. Scrum offers a framework for planning and overseeing initiatives related to digital transformation. Collaboration and effective value delivery are encouraged by its iterative and time-boxed methodology, which is coupled with frequent feedback and transparency. Implementing Scrum methods can promote team productivity, project management procedures, and client satisfaction. Organizations can build a solid foundation, adjust to changing requirements, promote an agile culture, and improve project management procedures by adhering to the elements and techniques listed in Table 4.5 in order to shift to the digital age successfully.

REFERENCES

1. Ozkan, N. and A. Tarhan, A review of scaling approaches to agile software development models. *Software Quality Professional*, 2019. **21**(4): pp. 11–20.
2. Azad, N. and S. Hyrynsalmi, DevOps critical success factors—A systematic literature review. *Information and Software Technology*, 2023. **157**: p. 107150.

5 Emerging Technologies

5.1 3D PRINTING

Digital technology integration has had a significant impact on every aspect of the lifespan of 3D printing, from design through production and supply chain management. This paradigm shift has sped up innovation in the area, boosted efficiency, and opened up new opportunities. The adoption and integration of digital tools, processes, and technologies to improve and optimize the entire 3D printing workflow is at the heart of what is meant by "digital transformation" in the context of 3D printing. It includes the application of sophisticated Computer-Aided Design (CAD) software, modeling applications, digital material repositories, and real-time monitoring systems. These technological developments have enabled additive manufacturing to achieve previously unheard-of levels of precision, customization, and scalability.

Digital design and modeling are important components of digital transformation in 3D printing. Designers can now easily generate detailed, complex shapes because of the change from manual drafting to sophisticated CAD software in traditional design procedures. Additionally, the combination of VR and AR technology has improved the design process by allowing designers to envision and refine their concepts in immersive environments. A further essential element of the change is digital material science. Designers and engineers can now examine a wide range of material possibilities and attributes thanks to the development of digital material development and simulation tools. To get the required outcomes, they can simulate material behavior, forecast structural integrity, and optimize print parameters. This has opened the door for the development of novel materials and composites, broadening the uses for 3D printing.

The entire production process is included in the digital revolution, which goes beyond design and materials. Digital manufacturing workflows automate and streamline a number of processes, including file preparation, slicing, and real-time monitoring. With the seamless integration of additive manufacturing with other digital technologies like automation and robots, productivity and precision have increased. Furthermore, the supply chain and logistical components of 3D printing have been significantly impacted by digital transformation. Traditional manufacturing and distribution practices have been impacted by the capacity to produce locally and on demand. Faster response times and lower inventory costs have been made possible through the digitization of inventory

DOI: 10.1201/9781003471226-6

management, order fulfillment, and logistics. Looking ahead, there is much promise for digital change in 3D printing. Big data analytics, ML, and AI will all be combined to automate better and improve many components of the 3D printing process. This will make it possible to use materials more effectively, monitor quality better, and produce goods more quickly.

5.1.1 Digital Material Science

An important component of the digital shift in 3D printing is digital material science. It alludes to the creation, modeling, and optimization of materials specifically for additive manufacturing processes using digital tools and methods. Researchers, designers, and engineers can investigate a variety of material alternatives, tailor material properties, and forecast material behavior by utilizing digital material science to produce desired results in 3D printing. Consider the following important elements when talking about digital material science in relation to 3D printing:

- *Material Development*: New materials that are suited for 3D printing can be created thanks to digital material science. Researchers can enhance material characteristics like strength, flexibility, thermal conductivity, or biocompatibility by blending conventional materials with additives and modifiers or even by developing completely new compositions. Digital technologies aid in understanding how various materials interact and forecasting how they will behave in particular printing processes.
- *Material Simulation*: In the field of digital materials science, simulation tools are crucial. The behavior of materials under various conditions, such as mechanical stresses, temperature changes, or fluid interactions, can be realistically tested by designers and engineers. In order to guarantee the quality and dependability of 3D printed parts, it is possible to predict material deformations, failures, or other features using simulations. To achieve desired performance results, simulation helps optimize the material composition, printing parameters, and postprocessing procedures.
- *Digital Material Libraries*: Comprehensive databases of material qualities, performance information, and printing settings are available through digital material libraries. Designers and engineers can use these libraries as helpful resources to help them choose the best materials for particular applications. Information on a material's composition, mechanical qualities, thermal behavior, chemical compatibility, and other pertinent factors are frequently included in material libraries. The availability of digital material catalogs makes the process of choosing materials simpler and contributes to good 3D printing results.
- *Tailored Material Properties*: With the aid of digital material science, material properties can be altered to suit particular needs. Materials can be designed to have desirable features, such as increased strength in particular directions (anisotropy), greater elasticity, or even conductive properties, by using additive processes. The spectrum of applications for 3D printing is

expanded by the ability to modify material properties digitally, allowing the creation of functioning prototypes, end-use parts, and specialty components.

- *Multimaterial Printing*: The investigation and use of multimaterial printing capabilities is made easier by digital material science. Designers can create intricate geometries, functional gradients, or multicomponent assemblies by combining various materials in a single print. Optimizing the compatibility of various materials, their adherence, and the transitions between various material regions requires the use of digital design and simulation tools. New uses for 3D printing are made possible by multimaterial printing, particularly in the production of complex technical components, electronics, and biomedical devices.

- *Iterative Design and Material Optimization*: Rapid prototyping and iterative material optimization cycles are made possible by digital material science, which enables an iterative design methodology. On digital models, designers can iterate, changing material compositions and structures to improve utility, lighten weight, or improve performance. Design defects or performance constraints can be found and fixed early in the development cycle thanks to this iterative approach, simulations, and analysis, which speeds up the innovation process.

5.1.2 Digital Manufacturing Processes

The digital transformation of 3D printing depends heavily on digital manufacturing processes. These procedures cover a variety of tasks, devices, and technological advancements that optimize and simplify the entire additive manufacturing process. Manufacturers may increase production, improve accuracy, and produce 3D-printed goods of superior quality by combining digital tools and automation. Here are some crucial elements of 3D printing's digital production procedures (Figure 5.1):

(A) *Digital File Preparation and Slicing*: Digital manufacturing starts with the preparation of a digital file that represents the 3D model to be printed. This file can be created using CAD software or obtained through 3D scanning techniques. Once the digital file is ready, it undergoes a slicing process, where specialized software divides the 3D model into a series of thin layers. Each layer represents a specific height in the final printed object. The slicing software also generates instructions for the 3D printer, including parameters such as layer thickness, printing speed, and support structures. These instructions ensure that the printer accurately reproduces the digital model in the physical world.

(B) *Real-Time Monitoring and Control*: Digital manufacturing processes often involve real-time monitoring and control systems to ensure quality and consistency throughout the printing process. Sensors placed within the 3D printer can monitor various parameters such as temperature, humidity, and print progress. This data is fed back to the control system, allowing for adjustments and optimizations to be made in real time. Monitoring systems can also detect and flag potential errors or anomalies during printing, enabling operators to

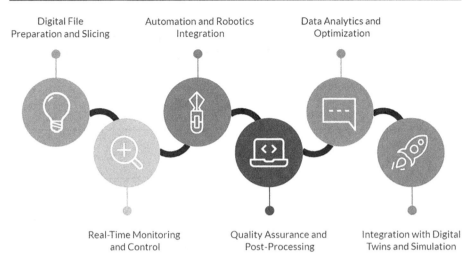

Digital File Preparation and Slicing

Automation and Robotics Integration

Data Analytics and Optimization

Real-Time Monitoring and Control

Quality Assurance and Post-Processing

Integration with Digital Twins and Simulation

FIGURE 5.1   Process of digital manufacturing.

take corrective actions promptly. This helps in reducing material waste and avoiding defective prints.

(C) *Automation and Robotics Integration*: Automation plays a significant role in digital manufacturing processes, particularly in industrial-scale 3D printing. Robotic arms and automated systems can handle various tasks, such as part handling, material loading, and postprocessing. Robotic systems can perform repetitive and complex tasks with high precision, improving the overall efficiency and accuracy of the manufacturing process. Automated material handling systems ensure the smooth flow of materials to the printer, reducing the need for manual intervention and optimizing production time.

(D) *Quality Assurance and Postprocessing*: Digital manufacturing processes enable advanced quality assurance techniques to ensure the integrity and reliability of 3D printed parts. Nondestructive testing methods, such as optical inspection, CT scanning, and ultrasonic testing, can be integrated into the workflow to detect defects, measure dimensional accuracy, and assess structural integrity. Postprocessing steps, such as removing support structures, surface finishing, and painting, can also be automated or digitally guided, resulting in consistent and high-quality final products.

(E) *Data Analytics and Optimization*: Digital manufacturing generates a vast amount of data throughout the 3D printing process. This data can be analyzed using data analytics and ML techniques to gain insights, identify patterns, and optimize the manufacturing process. By analyzing data related to printer performance, material properties, and environmental conditions, manufacturers can identify areas for improvement, optimize print parameters, and enhance overall efficiency.

(F) *Integration with Digital Twins and Simulation*: Digital twins, virtual replicas of physical objects or processes, can be integrated into the digital manufacturing process. These digital representations enable manufacturers to simulate and predict the behavior of 3D-printed objects in a virtual environment. Simulation tools allow manufacturers to optimize print settings, evaluate material performance, and predict structural behavior before the physical printing process begins. This reduces material waste, speeds up development cycles, and ensures higher success rates.

5.2 5G

With improved capabilities that support digital transformation, 5G, the fifth generation of wireless communication technology, provides a considerable improvement over earlier generations like 4G and 3G. 5G offers new opportunities for both individuals and businesses, thanks to its better data rates, reduced latency, enhanced device connectivity, and support for massive machine-type communication (MTC).

5G offers up to 10 gigabits per second (Gbps), which is a major improvement over its forerunners in terms of data transfer rates. Real-time data processing, fast cloud-based applications, and flawless streaming of ultra-high-definition videos are all made possible by this high-speed access. Additionally, the near-instantaneous connectivity made possible by 5G's reduced latency, which is as low as 1 millisecond (ms), is essential for applications like driverless vehicles, remote surgery, and immersive AR experiences.

The ability of 5G to link a huge number of devices in a condensed space is one of its main features. The expansion of the IoT ecosystem is facilitated by 5G, which supports up to 1 million devices per square kilometer. For applications like smart cities, where many sensors and devices must simultaneously interact to optimize urban infrastructure and enhance resource management, this feature is essential.

Additionally, 5G improves network capacity, enabling more people to connect at once without performance being affected. With this increased capacity, even in densely populated locations, users will enjoy a smooth user experience as a result of the expanding data demands of our digital age. With its sophisticated features, 5G supports cutting-edge technologies like AR, driverless vehicles, and smart infrastructure, accelerating digital transformation across industries.

5.2.1 Enabling Digital Transformation

The process of integrating digital technology into various corporate operations in order to spur innovation, increase productivity, improve customer experiences, and create new value is known as "digital transformation." By providing the required infrastructure and capabilities to enable a variety of digital projects, 5G is essential in driving this transformation.

- *Enhanced Connectivity*: 5G's higher data rates, lower latency, and increased device connectivity create a foundation for enhanced connectivity, enabling businesses to connect and communicate with customers, partners, and employees more effectively. This connectivity allows for seamless collaboration, real-time data exchange, and remote work capabilities, enabling businesses to operate more efficiently and serve customers in new and innovative ways.

- *IoT Enablement*: The proliferation of connected devices and sensors is a key aspect of digital transformation. 5G's support for massive MTC and the ability to connect a large number of IoT devices per unit area facilitate the growth of IoT applications. With 5G, businesses can leverage IoT to collect and analyze data in real time, optimize processes, automate tasks, and gain valuable insights to improve decision-making and drive operational efficiency.
- *Advanced Technologies*: 5G unlocks the potential of advanced technologies such as AR, VR, edge computing, and AI. These technologies are instrumental in transforming industries such as healthcare, manufacturing, retail, and entertainment. With 5G's high bandwidth and low latency, businesses can deliver immersive AR/VR experiences, leverage edge computing for faster processing and response times, and harness AI algorithms to automate tasks, personalize experiences, and optimize operations.
- *Innovation and New Business Models*: 5G acts as a catalyst for innovation, empowering businesses to develop new products, services, and business models. The high-speed, low-latency connectivity of 5G opens doors to innovative applications such as autonomous vehicles, smart cities, remote monitoring, and real-time analytics. It enables businesses to reimagine customer experiences, create new revenue streams, and stay ahead in a rapidly evolving digital landscape.
- *Data-driven Insights*: Data is at the core of digital transformation. With 5G, businesses can collect, transmit, and analyze vast amounts of data in real time. This data-driven approach provides valuable insights into customer behavior, market trends, operational efficiency, and predictive analytics. By leveraging these insights, businesses can make informed decisions, optimize processes, personalize offerings, and deliver superior customer experiences.
- The importance of 5G in facilitating digital transformation across various corporate functions is shown in Table 5.1.

5.2.2 Industrial Applications

The adoption of 5G technology opens up significant potential for businesses to make use of its capabilities and promote digital innovation. The adoption of 5G technology has opened up a slew of game-changing prospects across numerous industries, allowing businesses to make use of its capabilities and promote digital innovation. Table 5.1 outlines the substantial effects of 5G on several sectors, including healthcare services, manufacturing processes, transportation and logistics operations, agricultural practices, the development of smart cities, and the media and entertainment industry. Here are some examples of business sectors where 5G has a big influence:

- *Healthcare*: 5G has the potential to revolutionize healthcare delivery. It enables real-time sharing of medical data, remote patient monitoring, and telemedicine services with high-quality video and audio. With 5G's low latency, healthcare professionals can perform remote surgeries and collaborate with experts in real

TABLE 5.1   Transformative applications of 5G technology across industries

INDUSTRY	5G APPLICATIONS	BENEFITS	EXAMPLES
Healthcare	Real-time sharing of medical data, remote patient monitoring, telemedicine	Improved healthcare delivery, remote surgeries, collaboration with experts, IoT for patient monitoring	Remote surgeries, telemedicine services, connected medical devices
Manufacturing	Smart factories, real-time monitoring, and predictive maintenance	Efficient production, quality control, robotics, autonomous vehicles, and real-time supply chain	Real-time monitoring of production, asset tracking, and predictive maintenance
Transportation	Connected and autonomous vehicles and real-time tracking and monitoring	Enhanced road safety, optimized logistics, last-mile delivery, and surveillance	Connected and autonomous vehicles and real-time tracking of goods and assets
Agriculture	Precision agriculture and smart farming	Increased crop yields, reduced resource consumption, and autonomous farming machinery	5G-connected sensors and drones for real-time data collection, autonomous farming machinery
Smart Cities	Real-time monitoring and control systems	Improved livability, sustainability, intelligent traffic management, and optimized energy distribution	Real-time monitoring of utilities, transportation, public safety, waste management
Entertainment and Media	High-quality video streaming and AR/VR experiences	Immersive entertainment experiences, interactive gaming, and personalized content delivery	High-quality video streaming and AR/VR experiences for gaming and live events

time. Additionally, 5G facilitates the use of IoT devices for patient monitoring, smart ambulances, and connected medical devices, improving efficiency and patient outcomes.

- *Manufacturing and Industry 4.0*: In manufacturing, 5G enables the deployment of smart factories and supports the vision of Industry 4.0. It enables real-time monitoring of production processes, asset tracking, and predictive mainte-nance through IoT sensors. 5G's high bandwidth and low latency facilitate the use of robotics, autonomous vehicles, and AR for efficient production and quality control. It also enables seamless connectivity among machines, enabling real-time data exchange and optimization of the entire supply chain.

- *Transportation and Logistics*: 5G has significant implications for the transportation and logistics industries. It enables connected and autonomous vehicles to communicate with each other and with smart infrastructure, enhancing road safety and traffic management. 5G also enables real-time tracking and monitoring of goods and assets, optimizing logistics operations. Additionally, 5G-powered drones can be used for last-mile delivery and surveillance in transportation and logistics.
- *Agriculture*: In agriculture, 5G can revolutionize farming practices by enabling precision agriculture and smart farming. With 5G-connected sensors and drones, farmers can collect data on soil moisture, temperature, and crop health in real time. This data can be analyzed to optimize irrigation, fertilization, and pest control, leading to increased crop yields and reduced resource consumption. 5G also facilitates the use of autonomous farming machinery, improving productivity and efficiency in agriculture.
- *Smart Cities*: 5G plays a crucial role in the development of smart cities, where various systems and infrastructure are connected to improve livability and sustainability. With 5G, smart cities can deploy real-time monitoring and control systems for utilities, transportation, public safety, and waste management. It enables the implementation of intelligent traffic management, smart lighting, environmental monitoring, and optimized energy distribution, resulting in enhanced quality of life for residents.
- *Entertainment and Media*: The media and entertainment industry can leverage 5G to deliver immersive experiences to consumers. 5G enables high-quality video streaming, AR, and VR experiences with low latency and high bandwidth. This opens up opportunities for interactive gaming, live events streaming, and personalized content delivery, transforming the way people consume and engage with entertainment media.

5.2.3 Infrastructure and Network Deployment

To fulfill the rising demand for high-speed, low-latency connection, the successful implementation of 5G networks requires a solid infrastructure and careful planning. The following are crucial factors and considerations for the deployment of 5G's network and infrastructure:

- *Stations and Small Cells*: Base stations are critical components of 5G networks, responsible for transmitting and receiving wireless signals. These stations, equipped with advanced antennas and radios, provide coverage and capacity to users. To ensure seamless connectivity, base stations need to be strategically deployed to cover a wide area. In addition to traditional macro base stations, 5G networks also rely on small cells, which are compact and can be deployed in dense urban areas to enhance coverage and capacity.

- *Fiber Optic Connectivity*: To support the high data rates and low latency of 5G, robust backhaul infrastructure is essential. Fiber optic cables play a vital role in providing high-capacity, low-latency connectivity between base stations and core network infrastructure. The deployment of fiber optic networks needs to be prioritized to ensure that sufficient bandwidth is available to handle the increased data traffic associated with 5G.
- *Densification and Network Capacity*: To meet the demand for increased data capacity, 5G networks require denser deployment of base stations and small cells. This densification helps in improving coverage, capacity, and overall network performance. However, densification also presents challenges related to site acquisition, power supply, and coordination with local authorities to ensure compliance with regulations and esthetics.
- *Spectrum Allocation*: The successful deployment of 5G networks depends on the availability and allocation of suitable frequency bands. Different frequency bands, such as sub-6 GHz and millimeter wave (mmWave), are utilized in 5G networks. Sub-6 GHz frequencies provide broader coverage, while mmWave frequencies offer higher data rates but with more limited coverage. Regulatory bodies play a crucial role in allocating and managing spectrum resources to ensure efficient and interference-free operations of 5G networks.
- *Network Slicing*: Network slicing is a key concept in 5G that allows the creation of virtualized, customizable networks to meet specific industry requirements. It enables network operators to allocate resources and tailor network services based on specific use cases, such as enhanced mobile broadband, massive MTC, and ultra-reliable low-latency communication. Network slicing facilitates efficient resource utilization, optimized service delivery, and flexibility in meeting diverse industry needs.
- *Integration with Existing Infrastructure*: The deployment of 5G networks requires integration with existing infrastructure, including legacy networks and systems. Network operators need to ensure compatibility, seamless handovers, and interoperability between different network generations (4G and 3G) and technologies to provide uninterrupted connectivity and a smooth transition to 5G.
- *Security and Privacy*: As 5G networks connect more devices and handle increasing volumes of sensitive data, ensuring robust security measures and protecting user privacy become paramount. Network operators and service providers must implement strong encryption, authentication mechanisms, and advanced security protocols to safeguard data and mitigate potential cyber threats.

5.3 6G

A new era of connectedness and digital creativity has arrived as a result of the unrelenting march of technological development. With the introduction of 6G, wireless communication networks are prepared to advance yet further as we continue to push the envelope of what is possible. 6G is poised to change the digital world and enable a fundamental transition across numerous sectors by building on the foundation built by its forerunners. Fundamentally, 6G refers to wireless technology's sixth generation, which replaces the present 5G standard. However, it goes beyond merely being a speed and capacity improvement. With the help of 6G, civilization will be propelled into a hyperconnected future where technology will be seamlessly integrated into every area of our lives. 6G promises to unlock new levels of performance, dependability, and intelligence by utilizing cutting-edge technologies and novel methodologies, opening doors to possibilities we can only now imagine.

The strategic necessity for organizations, governments, and people alike is digital transformation. It includes the use of digital technologies to promote growth, innovation, and efficiency. Digital transformation is changing how we live, work, and interact in a variety of ways, including industry automation, smart cities, healthcare, and transportation. The underlying infrastructure and capabilities required to drive the digital revolution will be provided by 6G, which is positioned to be a crucial enabler of this transition. The potential effects of 6G on digital transformation are extensive and varied. 6G will enable companies to reach new levels of automation, efficiency, and production because of its ultrafast and dependable connectivity, ultralow latency, and high dependability. A wide range of revolutionary applications will be made possible by 6G, including remote surgery, driverless vehicles, and immersive entertainment. 6G will also enable real-time monitoring of crucial infrastructure. However, there are several difficulties with this transformation, including issues with security and privacy, as well as infrastructure deployment and standardization. For 6G to reach its full potential and to guarantee a seamless and inclusive digital future, these issues must be resolved.

6G provides lightning-fast and dependable connectivity, far beyond those of its forerunners. Real-time communication, quick information interchange, and frictionless transmission of enormous volumes of data are all made possible by this high-speed networking. As the foundation for digital transformation, this, in turn, supports the use of cutting-edge technologies like AI, IoT, and big data analytics. Businesses can make use of these technologies with 6G to improve operational effectiveness, streamline procedures, and obtain insightful information through data-driven decision-making. Additionally, the exceptional reliability and ultra-low latency of 6G networks are essential for realizing the full promise of disruptive technologies. Critical applications like driverless vehicles, telemedicine, and remote surgery can be implemented with the least amount of data transmission latency possible. For operations to be seamless and effective across a variety of areas, real-time responsiveness and dependability are crucial. The capabilities of 6G in this area allow for the creation and use of sophisticated automation, remote collaboration, and immersive experiences, all of which are crucial to efforts at digital transformation.

The improved spectrum capacity and efficiency of 6G are also essential for the digital transition. The dynamic spectrum sharing and intelligent resource allocation techniques of 6G ensure the effective use of the scarce spectrum resources as the demand for data-intensive applications rises. This enhances network capacity, improves network performance, and supports the simultaneous connecting of many devices. These features are especially important for sectors like manufacturing, logistics, and smart cities, where a large number of interconnected systems and devices must effortlessly communicate and exchange data. The combination of 6G with AI increases the connection between 6G and digital transformation. Intelligent decision-making, network self-healing, and predictive maintenance are all made possible by AI-powered network management and optimization algorithms. This enhances network performance, guarantees effective resource allocation, and prevents problems before they arise. Edge devices and the IoT can now evaluate data in real time, get contextual insights, and make autonomous decisions thanks to AI integration. These AI-driven developments promote creativity, effectiveness, and agility, three crucial characteristics of successful digital transformation projects.

The impact of 6G on digital transformation is poised to be significant, revolutionizing various sectors and unlocking new possibilities for innovation, efficiency, and connectivity. Here are some key areas where 6G is expected to have a transformative impact:

- *Industry 4.0 and Smart Manufacturing*: 6G's ultrafast and reliable connectivity, coupled with its low latency and high reliability, will facilitate real-time monitoring, control, and optimization of manufacturing processes. This will enable the widespread adoption of automation, robotics, and AI-powered systems in factories, leading to increased productivity, streamlined operations, and improved resource utilization. Smart factories leveraging 6G technology will achieve seamless communication and coordination across machines, supply chains, and production lines, transforming the manufacturing landscape.
- *Healthcare and Telemedicine*: With its ultralow latency and high bandwidth capabilities, 6G will revolutionize healthcare delivery. Real-time telemedicine consultations, remote surgeries, and patient monitoring will become commonplace, enabling access to high-quality healthcare regardless of geographical location. The integration of AI and IoT with 6G will enhance the capabilities of wearable health devices, enabling personalized medicine and preventive healthcare. The combination of 6G and healthcare applications will lead to improved patient outcomes, reduced costs, and greater accessibility to healthcare services.
- *Transportation and Autonomous Vehicles*: 6G will play a vital role in enabling connected and autonomous vehicles (CAVs) and transforming transportation systems. The ultra-low latency and high reliability of 6G networks will allow for real-time communication among vehicles, infrastructure, and pedestrians, facilitating safer and more efficient transportation. 6G's capabilities will enable advanced features like cooperative perception, platooning, and intersection management, leading to enhanced traffic flow, reduced congestion, and increased road safety. CAVs will benefit from uninterrupted connectivity, enabling seamless navigation, over-the-air updates, and enhanced passenger experiences.
- *Immersive Experiences and Entertainment*: 6G's ultrafast speeds and high capacity will revolutionize immersive experiences, including AR, VR, and holographic communication. With 6G, users will enjoy seamless,

high-quality streaming of ultra-high-definition content, immersive gaming experiences, and real-time collaboration in virtual environments. 6G's low latency will minimize motion sickness and enable near-instantaneous interactions, opening up new avenues for entertainment, communication, and creative expression.

5.4 ADVANCED MATERIAL

Advanced materials, which are distinguished by their exceptional properties and performance, play a vital role in numerous industries, including aerospace, automotive, electronics, healthcare, and others. These materials offer distinct benefits, such as increased strength, durability, conductivity, and flexibility, which facilitate the development of novel applications and solutions. However, in order to maximize the potential of advanced materials, digital transformation must be embraced. Digital transformation is the integration of digital technologies and processes to radically alter how industries operate, deliver value, and interact with consumers. It has emerged as a potent catalyst for development and innovation across multiple industries. Digital transformation offers unprecedented opportunities to revolutionize the entire material development lifecycle, from design and simulation to production, supply chain management, and application, in the context of advanced materials.

Digital transformation has a significant impact on the field of advanced materials. Researchers and engineers can now accelerate material discovery, optimize material properties, and design new materials with greater precision due to the advent of advanced computational power, complex algorithms, and data-driven analytics. Digital technologies, including CAD software, virtual testing, and simulation tools, enable rapid prototyping and iteration, thereby shortening the time-to-market for advanced material products. The digitalization of material processes also encompasses the supply chain and logistics. Real-time inventory monitoring, integration of IoT devices, and predictive maintenance enabled by sensor data enable efficient management of material resources, thereby reducing costs and minimizing disruptions. The integration of digital technologies into additive manufacturing and 3D printing has revolutionized the production of advanced materials, enabling complex geometries, customization, and on-demand manufacturing.

5.4.1 Digitalization of Advanced Material Processes

In the realm of advanced materials, digital design and simulation tools have become indispensable. CAD software allows engineers and designers to create complex 3D models, facilitating the exploration of innovative material structures and properties. These virtual models can be subjected to simulations and analysis, providing insights into material behavior under different conditions and aiding in the optimization of material properties. Simulation techniques, such as finite element analysis (FEA) and computational fluid dynamics (CFD), enable the evaluation of structural integrity, performance, and durability of advanced materials before physical prototypes are manufactured, saving time and resources.

The digital transformation of advanced materials is strongly supported by data-driven approaches. Large-scale material data can be collected, curated, and analyzed to uncover patterns, correlations, and predictive models. ML and AI algorithms can then be applied to extract meaningful insights from this data, accelerating material discovery and optimization. Data-driven approaches enable researchers to identify new material compositions, predict material behavior, and develop customized solutions tailored to specific applications. Furthermore, the integration of digital platforms and databases facilitates the sharing of material data and knowledge among researchers and industries, fostering collaboration and innovation.

Additive manufacturing, commonly known as 3D printing, has transformed the landscape of advanced material production. Digital technologies are at the heart of additive manufacturing processes, allowing the translation of digital designs into physical objects layer by layer. Complex geometries and intricate structures that were once difficult or impossible to achieve with traditional manufacturing methods can now be realized using 3D printing. The digitalization of additive manufacturing enables precise control over material deposition, optimized material usage, and rapid prototyping capabilities. It also paves the way for on-demand manufacturing, where products can be produced in a decentralized manner, reducing lead times and inventory costs.

Digital transformation has revolutionized material characterization and testing processes. Advanced imaging techniques, such as scanning electron microscopy (SEM) and atomic force microscopy (AFM), allow researchers to visualize and analyze material structures at nanoscale resolutions. These imaging methods provide valuable insights into material morphology, composition, and defects, aiding in the understanding of material properties and performance. Digital sensors and IoT devices can be integrated into material testing setups, enabling real-time monitoring of material behavior, stress, and environmental conditions. This digitalization of material testing not only improves the accuracy and efficiency of characterization but also enables continuous monitoring and predictive maintenance of advanced materials in real-world applications.

5.4.2 Digital Transformation in Advanced Material Applications

Digital transformation has had a substantial effect on the application of advanced materials in a variety of industries. The incorporation of advanced materials, such as conductive polymers, carbon nanotubes, and graphene, has enhanced device performance, miniaturization, and energy efficiency in the electronics industry. The design, simulation, and optimization of these materials for specific electronic applications rely heavily on digital technologies. Moreover, the digitalization of the electronics supply chain ensures the seamless incorporation of advanced materials into electronic devices.

Digital transformation has revolutionized the application of advanced materials in the healthcare industry. From drug delivery systems to prosthetics and medical implants, advanced materials improve patient outcomes. Digital technologies enable the precise customization and individualization of medical devices made from sophisticated materials, thereby enhancing patient comfort. In addition, digital platforms and data analytics enable monitoring and analysis of material performance, which contributes to the ongoing development of healthcare technologies.

Additionally, the digitalization of advanced materials has applications in the sustainability and environmental fields. In eco-friendly building construction, advanced materials with increased strength and durability are used to create energy-efficient structures. Digitalization enables the monitoring and optimization of material utilization, waste reduction, and recycling processes, thereby promoting the sustainable development of materials. Additionally, digital technologies facilitate the creation of advanced materials for the production of renewable energy, such as solar panels and energy storage systems.

Digital transformation has had a significant impact on lightweight materials in the automotive industry. Advanced composites, such as carbon-fiber-reinforced polymers (CFRPs) and aluminum alloys, enhance fuel economy and decrease emissions. Digital technologies, such as simulation tools and virtual prototyping, facilitate the design and optimization of advanced materials-based lightweight structures. The digitalization of manufacturing processes, including additive manufacturing and robotic automation, allows for the efficient production of lightweight components and the incorporation of advanced materials in electric vehicles.

In conclusion, despite the fact that the digital transformation of sophisticated materials presents its own set of challenges, it also offers substantial opportunities. The key obstacles include addressing security concerns, cultivating a competent workforce, and fostering a digital-first culture. However, the opportunities for accelerated innovation, optimized production processes, and improved supply chain management are enormous. Adopting the digital transformation in advanced materials has the potential to open up new frontiers in materials science and revolutionize all industries.

5.5 ARTIFICIAL INTELLIGENCE

AI refers to the simulation of human intelligence in machines that are programmed to reason and learn similarly to humans. It comprises a vast array of technologies and techniques that enable machines to carry out tasks that ordinarily require human intelligence. AI has become a transformative force in many disciplines, driving innovation, efficiency, and decision-making. In the era of digital transformation, where businesses and organizations are leveraging technology to adapt and thrive in the fast-paced digital landscape, AI has acquired immense importance. By leveraging AI, businesses can automate processes, obtain insights from vast amounts of data, and provide customers with personalized experiences. AI has the potential to transform numerous industries, including healthcare, finance, retail, manufacturing, and transportation.

The essence of AI is its ability to learn and develop over time. ML is a crucial component of AI, in which algorithms are designed to recognize patterns and make predictions or decisions based on data. Deep learning, a subset of ML, employs neural networks to analyze complex data and derive insightful conclusions. NLP facilitates communication between humans and machines by allowing machines to comprehend and process human language. Computer vision is an important aspect of AI that enables machines to interpret and analyze visual data from images and videos. Applications of this technology include autonomous vehicles, surveillance systems, and medical diagnostics. The combination of robotics, automation, and AI has led to the creation of intelligent machines that can perform tasks with precision and efficiency, thereby reducing human labor and increasing productivity.

AI drives digital transformation by revolutionizing customer experiences, optimizing operational efficiency, and facilitating data-driven decision-making. AI improves consumer interactions and satisfaction through personalized recommendations, chatbots, and sentiment analysis. Through predictive maintenance, supply chain optimization, and intelligent process automation, it assists businesses in streamlining their operations. Moreover, AI enables organizations to effectively leverage data, enabling accurate predictions, the detection of deception, and the acquisition of real-time insights for strategic decision-making. AI offers enormous potential, but it also presents obstacles and considerations. Concerns about ethics and privacy arise as the use of AI technologies grows. To ensure fairness and transparency, data integrity and bias concerns must be addressed. It is necessary to close skill gaps and cultivate a workforce with AI expertise. In addition, the regulatory and legal implications of AI must be navigated carefully to ensure compliance and responsible use.

AI plays a crucial role in promoting digital transformation across all industries. AI offers transformative capabilities to enhance customer experiences, optimize operational efficiency, and enable data-driven decision-making as businesses seek to adapt and flourish in the digital era.

Transformation of the customer experience is a crucial area where AI excels in digital transformation. Through AI-powered personalization and recommendation systems, businesses can provide customized customer experiences, thereby boosting customer engagement and satisfaction. AI-powered chatbots and virtual assistants facilitate seamless and effective consumer interactions, delivering instant support and resolving inquiries. In addition, AI enables sentiment analysis and customer feedback analysis, allowing businesses to comprehend better consumer preferences, sentiments, and needs in order to make more informed decisions.

AI plays an important role in enhancing operational efficacy as part of digital transformation. AI technologies, such as predictive maintenance and asset optimization, enable businesses to proactively identify maintenance requirements, reduce downtime, and optimize asset performance. AI-powered supply chain optimization enables businesses to streamline inventory management, demand forecasting, and logistics, resulting in cost reductions and enhanced operational agility. In addition, AI-powered intelligent process automation automates repetitive tasks, freeing up human resources for more strategic endeavors.

AI significantly facilitates data-driven decision-making during the digital transformation journey. AI-based analytics and forecasting models utilize historical data to make accurate predictions, allowing businesses to anticipate customer behavior, demand patterns, and market trends. By analyzing massive amounts of data and identifying anomalies or suspicious activities in real time, AI also contributes to fraud detection and risk management. AI-provided real-time data analysis and insights enable organizations to make informed decisions swiftly and adapt to ever-changing market conditions.

Integration of AI into digital transformation initiatives is only possible with obstacles. The extensive acquisition and utilization of customer data raises ethical and privacy issues. It is imperative that organizations handle data responsibly and adhere to regulations. To assure fairness and precision in AI-driven decision-making, we must address data quality and bias issues. AI expertise skill deficits and talent shortages present a challenge, necessitating organizations to invest in upskilling and reskilling programs. Additionally, successfully navigating the regulatory landscape encircling AI usage and addressing legal implications are essential for implementation success.

Successful implementation of AI in digital transformation requires careful planning, strategic execution, and continuous learning (See Figure 5.2). Here are key considerations for organizations to ensure the successful integration of AI into their digital transformation initiatives:

- *Strategy and Planning*: Begin by defining clear goals and objectives for AI implementation. Identify specific areas of the business where AI can drive the most significant impact. Develop a roadmap that outlines the steps, resources, and timeline required for successful implementation. Align the AI strategy with overall business objectives to ensure coherence and maximize value.
- *Data Management and Infrastructure*: AI relies on high-quality data for training and decision-making. Ensure data governance practices are in place to maintain data quality, integrity, and security. Establish robust data infrastructure and storage systems that can handle large volumes of data and enable efficient data processing. Consider leveraging cloud computing and scalable solutions to manage data effectively.

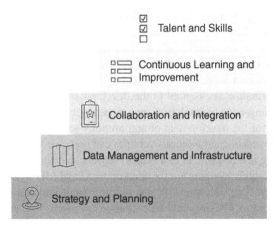

FIGURE 5.2   Consideration for successful integration of AI in a company.

- *Collaboration and Integration*: AI implementation should involve collaboration across teams and departments. Foster a culture of cross-functional collaboration to encourage knowledge sharing and ensure the successful integration of AI technologies. Facilitate seamless integration of AI systems with existing IT infrastructure and applications to maximize efficiency and minimize disruptions.
- *Continuous Learning and Improvement*: AI models require continuous learning and improvement to deliver optimal results. Develop mechanisms to collect feedback, monitor performance, and refine AI models over time. Implement robust evaluation frameworks to assess the effectiveness of AI systems and make necessary adjustments. Encourage a culture of experimentation and innovation to explore new AI applications and technologies.
- *Talent and Skills*: Invest in acquiring and developing AI talent within the organization. Identify skill gaps and provide training opportunities to upskill existing employees. Recruit AI experts, data scientists, and ML engineers who can drive successful AI implementation. Foster a learning environment that encourages employees to embrace AI technologies and adapt to new ways of working.

5.6 AUTONOMOUS VEHICLES

Self-driving automobiles, also known as autonomous vehicles, represent a revolutionary advancement in transportation technology. Using a combination of sophisticated sensors, AI, and connectivity, these vehicles have the ability to navigate and operate on roads without human intervention. In recent years, the concept of autonomous vehicles has garnered considerable attention, with the potential to revolutionize various aspects of transportation and society as a whole.

The development of autonomous vehicles is motivated by the pursuit of improved road safety, efficiency, and comfort. By eliminating human error from the equation, autonomous vehicles have the potential to reduce accidents and fatalities caused by human factors such as distraction, fatigue, and impaired driving. In addition, autonomous vehicles can optimize traffic flow, reduce congestion, and improve the overall efficacy of transportation networks.

Digital transformation is essential to the development of autonomous vehicles. The convergence of cutting-edge technologies such as sensor technology, AI, and connectivity has paved the way for the development of autonomous vehicles. Using lidar, radar, cameras, and ultrasonic sensors, autonomous vehicles can perceive and comprehend their surroundings, detecting and reacting in real time to objects, pedestrians, and other vehicles.

Autonomous vehicle systems are founded upon AI and ML algorithms. These algorithms assess sensor data, interpret the surrounding environment, and make informed navigation, acceleration, braking, and lane-change decisions. ML enables autonomous vehicles to continually enhance their performance based on real-world driving data, thereby enhancing their capabilities over time.

Connectivity is an additional important aspect of autonomous vehicles. Vehicle-to-Vehicle (V2V), Vehicle-to-Infrastructure (V2I), and Vehicle-to-Everything (V2X) communication systems enable autonomous vehicles to exchange data with other vehicles, traffic signals, and diverse elements of the transportation infrastructure. This connectivity enables coordinated and intelligent decision-making, which improves road safety and productivity.

5.6.1 Key Technologies Enabling Autonomous Vehicles

Autonomous vehicles rely on several key technologies to operate safely and efficiently. These technologies work together to enable perception, decision-making, and control, allowing the vehicle to navigate its environment autonomously. Here are the key technologies that make autonomous vehicles possible:

(A) **Sensor Technology**: Sensors are crucial for perceiving the surrounding environment. Autonomous vehicles use various types of sensors, including:
  - *Lidar (Light Detection and Ranging)*: Lidar sensors emit laser pulses and measure the time it takes for the pulses to bounce back, creating a detailed 3D map of the vehicle's surroundings.
  - *Radar (Radio Detection and Ranging)*: Radar sensors use radio waves to detect objects and measure their distance, speed, and direction of movement. They are particularly useful in detecting objects in poor weather conditions.
  - *Cameras*: Vision-based cameras capture images and videos to identify objects, pedestrians, road signs, and lane markings. Computer vision algorithms analyze the camera data to interpret the environment.
  - *Ultrasonic Sensors*: Ultrasonic sensors use sound waves to detect objects at close range, helping with parking and maneuvering in tight spaces.
(B) **AI and Machine Learning**: Autonomous vehicles rely on advanced AI algorithms and ML models to process sensor data, make real-time decisions, and adapt to different driving scenarios. These technologies enable the vehicle to understand its environment, predict the behavior of other road users, and plan safe and efficient routes.
  - *Perception Algorithms*: AI algorithms analyze sensor data to identify and classify objects, recognize traffic signs and signals, and track the movement of vehicles and pedestrians.
  - *Decision-Making Algorithms*: AI algorithms evaluate sensor data, traffic conditions, and navigation goals to make decisions about acceleration, braking, lane changes, and interactions with other vehicles.
  - *Deep Learning Models*: Deep neural networks are used to train models on large datasets to improve perception, decision-making, and behavior prediction. These models can learn from vast amounts of real-world driving data, allowing the vehicle to improve its performance continuously.

(C) **Connectivity and Communication**: Autonomous vehicles need to communicate with each other and the surrounding infrastructure to enhance safety and coordination. This communication is achieved through various technologies, including:

- *Vehicle-to-Vehicle (V2V) Communication*: V2V communication allows vehicles to exchange information, such as position, speed, and intentions, to coordinate movements and avoid collisions.
- *Vehicle-to-Infrastructure (V2I) Communication*: V2I communication enables vehicles to communicate with traffic signals, road infrastructure, and centralized systems. This interaction provides real-time information on traffic conditions, road hazards, and optimized routing.
- *Vehicle-to-Everything (V2X) Communication*: V2X communication encompasses both V2V and V2I communication, as well as communication with pedestrians, cyclists, and other elements of the transportation ecosystem. It enables comprehensive situational awareness and collaboration.

(D) **Mapping and Localization**: Accurate mapping and precise localization are crucial for autonomous vehicles to navigate and understand their position on the road. These technologies include:

- *HD (High-Definition) Maps*: HD maps provide detailed information about road geometry, lane markings, traffic signs, and other relevant features. Autonomous vehicles use these maps to plan routes and compare real-time sensor data with the map for localization.
- *GPS (Global Positioning System)*: GPS technology allows vehicles to determine their global position, which is used as a reference for localization. However, GPS alone may not provide the required accuracy for precise autonomous vehicle positioning, so additional sensors and localization techniques are employed.
- *Inertial Measurement Units (IMUs)*: IMUs combine accelerometers and gyroscopes to measure the vehicle's acceleration, rotation, and orientation. IMUs are used to augment GPS data and provide accurate vehicle localization, especially in areas with limited GPS signals or when GPS accuracy is compromised.

5.6.2 Digital Transformation in Autonomous Vehicles

Digital transformation plays a pivotal role in the development and advancement of autonomous vehicles. It encompasses the integration of various digital technologies, data-driven processes, and connectivity solutions to enhance the capabilities and functionality of self-driving cars. Here are the key aspects of digital transformation in autonomous vehicles:

- *Data Collection and Analysis*: Autonomous vehicles generate an enormous amount of data through their sensors, cameras, and communication systems. Digital transformation involves the collection, storage, and analysis of this data to extract valuable insights. Advanced data analytics techniques, including ML and AI, are applied to understand patterns, improve performance, and enhance decision-making in autonomous vehicles.

- *Connectivity and IoT Integration*: Autonomous vehicles are part of the larger IoT ecosystem. They are equipped with connectivity technologies that enable real-time communication with other vehicles, infrastructure elements, and cloud-based services. This connectivity facilitates the exchange of critical information such as traffic conditions, road hazards, and updates on navigation routes. Integration with IoT platforms enhances the capabilities and responsiveness of autonomous vehicles in dynamic traffic scenarios.
- *Cybersecurity and Safety*: As autonomous vehicles become more reliant on digital technologies and connectivity, ensuring cybersecurity and safety becomes paramount. Digital transformation involves implementing robust cybersecurity measures to protect the vehicle's systems from cyber threats and unauthorized access. Encryption mechanisms, authentication protocols, and intrusion detection systems are employed to safeguard the vehicle's data and functionality.
- *User Experience and Human–Machine Interaction*: Digital transformation focuses on enhancing the user experience and improving human–machine interaction in autonomous vehicles. User interfaces, displays, and controls are designed to be intuitive and user-friendly. Voice recognition and NLP technologies enable seamless communication between passengers and the vehicle's AI system. Human-centered design principles guide the development of interfaces that keep passengers informed, engaged, and comfortable during their autonomous journeys.
- *Simulation and Testing*: Digital transformation enables the use of advanced simulation and testing techniques to accelerate the development and validation of autonomous vehicle technologies. Virtual simulations replicate real-world driving scenarios, allowing engineers to assess the performance of self-driving systems under various conditions. This approach helps identify and address potential challenges, refine algorithms, and enhance the overall safety and reliability of autonomous vehicles.

5.7 BIG DATA

In the swiftly evolving digital landscape of the present day, organizations are generating data at an unprecedented rate. This inundation of data, also known as big data, presents both opportunities and obstacles for businesses seeking to remain competitive and foster innovation. Big data refers to the massive volumes of structured and unstructured data collected by organizations from various sources, such as social media, consumer interactions, sensors, and other digital touchpoints. This information is distinguished by its volume, velocity, variety, veracity, and importance.

Concurrently, digital transformation has become a strategic necessity for businesses across all industries. Digital transformation is the utilization of digital technologies to alter how businesses operate profoundly, provide value to customers, and achieve a competitive advantage. It involves the incorporation of digital tools, processes, and capabilities into all aspects of an organization's operations, from customer engagement to supply chain management.

Big data is instrumental in advancing digital transformation initiatives. The abundance of data provides organizations with valuable insights and intelligence that can enlighten decision-making, facilitate personalized customer experiences, optimize business processes, and stimulate innovation. By leveraging the power of big data, organizations can gain a deeper understanding of their customers, predict market trends, and unearth latent patterns that can lead to innovative breakthroughs and new business models. However, the road to utilizing big data for digital transformation is challenging. Organizations must contend with issues such as data integrity, privacy, security, governance, and a need for more professionals capable of analyzing and interpreting data effectively. In addition, integrating and harmonizing data from disparate sources, systems, and formats can be a difficult task.

5.7.1 Characterization

Big data refers to the vast and complex sets of data that organizations collect from a variety of sources, both structured and unstructured. It is characterized by its volume, velocity, variety, veracity, and value. To fully comprehend big data, it is important to explore each of these aspects:

- *Volume*: Big data is characterized by its sheer volume. Traditional data storage and processing systems may need more capacity to handle the massive amounts of data generated daily. This includes data from social media, customer interactions, sensors, logs, and more. The ability to store, manage, and analyze such large volumes of data is a defining characteristic of big data.
- *Velocity*: Big data is generated and processed at a remarkable speed. The data flows in real-time or near real-time, demanding rapid processing and analysis. Technologies and tools that can handle high-velocity data streams, such as stream processing and real-time analytics, are crucial in managing big data effectively.
- *Variety*: Big data comes in various formats and types. It includes structured data (e.g., databases and spreadsheets) and unstructured data (e.g., emails, social media posts, and videos). The variety of data sources and formats adds complexity to data management and analysis. Organizations need to employ diverse techniques to extract insights from different data types.
- *Veracity*: Veracity refers to the reliability and accuracy of the data. Big data often includes noisy, incomplete, or inconsistent data. Ensuring data quality and veracity is crucial for making informed decisions and drawing reliable insights from the data. Data cleansing, validation, and quality assurance processes play a vital role in addressing veracity challenges.

- *Value*: The ultimate objective of big data is to derive value and actionable insights from the data. By analyzing large and diverse datasets, organizations can gain valuable insights that drive business decisions, enhance customer experiences, optimize operations, and fuel innovation. The value of big data lies in its potential to uncover patterns, correlations, and trends that were previously unseen.

5.7.2 Role of Big Data in Digital Transformation

Big data plays a crucial role in driving digital transformation initiatives across organizations. By harnessing the power of big data, organizations can transform their operations, customer experiences, and overall business strategies. Here are some key roles that big data plays in the process of digital transformation:

- *Data-driven Decision-making*: Big data provides organizations with a wealth of information and insights that can drive data-driven decision-making. By analyzing large and diverse datasets, organizations can identify patterns, correlations, and trends that help them make informed decisions. Big data analytics enables organizations to move away from traditional intuition-based decision-making toward evidence-based approaches.
- *Customer Insights and Personalization*: Big data allows organizations to gain a deeper understanding of their customers. By analyzing customer data from various sources, such as purchase history, browsing behavior, social media interactions, and feedback, organizations can develop detailed customer profiles and segmentations. This enables personalized marketing campaigns, tailored product recommendations, and improved customer experiences.
- *Process Optimization and Efficiency*: Big data analytics can identify inefficiencies and bottlenecks in business processes. By analyzing operational data, organizations can uncover areas of improvement, optimize workflows, and streamline operations. This can lead to cost savings, increased productivity, and enhanced overall efficiency.
- *Predictive Analytics and Forecasting*: Big data enables organizations to leverage predictive analytics to anticipate future trends, behaviors, and outcomes. By analyzing historical and real-time data, organizations can develop models and algorithms that forecast demand, market trends, customer preferences, and more. This allows organizations to plan and strategize for the future proactively.
- *Innovation and New Business Models*: Big data fuels innovation by providing organizations with valuable insights and intelligence. By analyzing market trends, customer preferences, and competitive landscapes, organizations can identify new opportunities and develop innovative products, services, and business models. Big data allows organizations to experiment, iterate, and adapt their strategies based on data-driven insights.

5.7.3 Challenges

Utilizing big data for digital transformation presents organizations with numerous opportunities, along with a number of obstacles. The first obstacle is assuring the data's quality and reliability. The volume, variety, and velocity of big data can result in issues of accuracy and completeness, necessitating the implementation of stringent data purification and validation procedures. Due to the vast volume of data collected, data privacy and security are also vital considerations. Organizations must adhere to data protection regulations and implement stringent security measures to secure sensitive data.

The second set of difficulties concerns data governance and compliance. To maintain data integrity, privacy, and compliance across all big data initiatives, it is essential to establish appropriate data governance frameworks. In addition, there is frequently a need for more professionals with expertise in data analytics, ML, and data engineering, making it difficult to leverage big data effectively. Integration and interoperability issues are also prevalent, as data originates from a variety of sources and formats, necessitating the investment of technologies and tools to facilitate seamless data integration.

In order to surmount these obstacles, businesses must prioritize data quality, security, and governance. They must invest in talent acquisition and upskilling programs to close the skills gap and guarantee effective big data utilization. In addition, it is essential to implement integration solutions that facilitate the harmonization of data across systems and platforms. By addressing these challenges head-on, organizations can maximize the value of big data and drive digital transformation initiatives with success. Table 5.2 provides a summary of some of the challenges organizations face when utilizing big data for digital transformation, as well as suggestions for overcoming these obstacles.

5.8 BLOCKCHAIN COMPUTING

Computing on the blockchain is a revolutionary technology that has garnered considerable attention in recent years due to its potential to transform various industries and facilitate digital transformation. At its core, blockchain is a decentralized and distributed ledger system that enables multiple parties to record and verify transactions without the need for intermediaries in a secure and transparent manner. Blockchain technology plays a significant role in this transformation by providing a secure, efficient, and reliable framework for managing and validating digital transactions and data.

Decentralization, transparency, security, and immutability are the guiding principles of blockchain technology. By eliminating the need for a central authority or intermediary, blockchain decentralizes control and decision-making across a network of nodes. This feature improves security and removes single points of failure, making it more difficult for malicious actors to manipulate the system.

All network participants can view and verify the transactions recorded on the blockchain, making transparency another fundamental aspect of blockchain technology. This transparency increases participant confidence and allows for greater accountability and audibility in business processes.

TABLE 5.2 Challenges and solutions in leveraging big data for digital transformation

CHALLENGES	SOLUTIONS
Data Quality	Implementing rigorous data cleansing and validation processes
	Utilizing automated tools for data quality assessment and improvement
	Establishing data quality metrics and monitoring mechanisms
	Conducting regular data audits and maintenance activities
Data Privacy and Security	Complying with data protection regulations (e.g., GDPR and CCPA)
	Implementing robust security measures (encryption and access controls)
	Conducting regular vulnerability assessments and penetration testing
	Educating employees on data privacy and security best practices
Data Governance and Compliance	Establishing data governance frameworks and policies
	Defining roles and responsibilities for data management
	Implementing data classification and access controls
	Monitoring and enforcing compliance with regulations
	Conducting periodic audits and reviews of data governance practices
Skills Gap	Investing in talent acquisition for data analytics, machine learning, and data engineering
	Providing training and upskilling programs for existing employees
	Collaborating with universities and research institutions for the talent pipeline
	Fostering a data-driven culture to attract and retain skilled professionals
Integration and Interoperability	Deploying integration solutions for seamless data harmonization
	Utilizing standardized data formats and protocols
	Adopting data integration tools and middleware
	Establishing data exchange agreements with external partners
	Ensuring compatibility and interoperability across systems and platforms

Using cryptographic techniques that safeguard the integrity and confidentiality of data, blockchain is secured. The use of cryptographic algorithms to secure transactions ensures that they cannot be altered or tampered with after being added to the blockchain. Moreover, the use of consensus mechanisms, such as proof-of-work or proof-of-stake, ensures that the majority of participants concur on the validity of transactions, thereby adding an additional layer of security.

A key characteristic of blockchain is immutability, which means that once data is recorded on the blockchain, it cannot be altered or deleted. This immutability feature provides a secure and tamper-proof record of transactions, making it ideally suited for applications where data integrity is of the utmost importance.

Utilizing blockchain technology in digital transformation yields numerous benefits. First, it increases trust and security by removing the need for intermediaries and providing a transparent, verifiable ledger of transactions. This trust factor is especially valuable in industries where secure and auditable transactions are crucial, such as finance, supply chain management, and healthcare.

By streamlining processes and automating workflows, blockchain technology can substantially enhance efficiency and reduce costs. Complex transactions can be simplified and accelerated through the elimination of manual reconciliation and the use of smart contracts, which are self-executing contracts with predefined rules inscribed on the blockchain.

In addition, blockchain has the potential to revolutionize industries by facilitating new business models and peer-to-peer interactions. Decentralized finance (DeFi) applications, which provide financial services without the need for intermediaries, are one example.

Despite its potential, there are obstacles associated with blockchain adoption for digital transformation. Scalability remains a significant obstacle, as blockchain networks must efficiently manage a large volume of transactions. To ensure the seamless integration of blockchain into existing frameworks, regulatory and legal considerations, such as data privacy and compliance, must also be addressed. Interoperability between diverse blockchain platforms and legacy systems is an additional obstacle that must be surmounted for widespread adoption.

5.8.1 Blockchain and Digital Transformation

Blockchain technology is a significant catalyst for digital transformation across industries. By eliminating intermediaries and providing transparent, verifiable transactions, it increases trust and security. Blockchain's decentralized character instills confidence in its participants, especially in the finance, supply chain management, and healthcare industries. Transparency and audibility are essential characteristics, allowing all network participants to securely view and validate transactions. This transparency increases accountability and allows businesses to ensure regulatory compliance. Moreover, through automation, blockchain streamlines processes and reduces costs. When certain conditions are met, smart contracts automatically execute predefined actions. Blockchain improves efficiency and accelerates transactions by eliminating manual intervention and intermediaries. Additionally, it enables the tokenization of assets, revolutionizing industries such as real estate and intellectual property rights.

Blockchain facilitates collaboration and data sharing by providing a secure platform for multiple parties to access and contribute to shared ledgers. In supply chains, where real-time information sharing increases efficiency and reduces delays, this feature is indispensable. In addition, the impact of blockchain extends to DeFi applications, which offer financial services without the use of traditional intermediaries. DeFi promotes financial inclusion by democratizing access to lending, borrowing, and trading. In addition, blockchain integrates with the IoT, augmenting the connected devices' security, privacy, and interoperability. It empowers IoT networks by enabling secure communication, data exchange, and autonomous transactions.

While blockchain offers tremendous opportunities for digital transformation, it also presents obstacles. As blockchain networks must efficiently manage high transaction volumes, scalability remains a concern. For compliance, regulatory frameworks and legal considerations such as data privacy must be addressed. Integration with existing systems and interoperability between blockchain platforms present additional obstacles. Despite these obstacles, blockchain's potential impact on digital transformation is substantial. As businesses adopt blockchain technology and investigate novel use cases, they unleash new digital efficiencies, transparency, and value creation.

5.8.2 Implementation

As part of digital transformation, implementing blockchain requires a strategic approach. Identify specific use cases where blockchain can add value, taking into account areas where trust, transparency, and security are required. Next, conduct a technical feasibility analysis to determine whether blockchain is the appropriate solution. Evaluate various platforms and consensus mechanisms with scalability, performance, and data security in mind. Establish a governance structure and choose a suitable consensus model.

Integration with extant systems is essential for implementation success. Consider data collaboration and exchange mechanisms when planning interoperability between blockchain and legacy systems. Collect and evaluate requirements with the participation of stakeholders and subject matter experts. Define data structures, smart contracts, and transaction flow when designing the blockchain's architecture. Collaborate with blockchain developers to assure robustness and scalability.

In the development phase, smart contracts and components are constructed and rigorously tested. Functional and security testing should be conducted to guarantee the dependability and integrity of the system. Deploy the blockchain solution in a production setting and closely monitor its efficacy. Consider collaborating with partners, industry consortiums, and blockchain communities in order to leverage shared knowledge and resources. Keep abreast of blockchain developments and emergent trends in order to maximize blockchain's benefits in driving innovation and transforming business processes.

Organizations can effectively implement blockchain technology as part of their digital transformation strategy by adhering to these steps. To ensure a smooth and effective adoption of blockchain for driving innovation and efficiency, meticulous planning, technical evaluation, integration with existing systems, and continuous monitoring are required. The stages involved in implementing blockchain as part of a digital transformation strategy are outlined in Table 5.3.

TABLE 5.3 Implementing blockchain as part of digital transformation: Key steps

IMPLEMENTATION STEPS	DESCRIPTION	CONSIDERATIONS	EXAMPLES/TASKS
Identify Use Cases	Identify specific areas where blockchain can bring value, such as supply chain management, financial transactions, or healthcare records.	• Areas requiring trust, transparency, and security • Potential cost savings or efficiency improvements • Impact on existing processes and stakeholders	• Supply chain traceability • Digital identity management • Tokenization of assets
Conduct Technical Feasibility	Assess the technical feasibility of implementing blockchain, including platform and consensus mechanism evaluation.	• Scalability and performance requirements • Data privacy and security needs • Compatibility with existing systems and infrastructure	• Ethereum vs. Hyperledger Fabric comparison • Proof-of-Work vs. Proof-of-Stake evaluation
Establish Governance and Consensus	Define a governance structure and select an appropriate consensus model for decision-making within the blockchain network.	• Decision-making authority and processes • Participation and incentives for network participants • Scalability and throughput considerations	• Consortium-based governance model • Delegated Proof-of-Stake (DPoS) consensus mechanism
Integrate with Existing Systems	Plan for interoperability between blockchain and legacy systems, considering data sharing and exchange mechanisms with other systems.	• Data compatibility and standardization • Integration methods (APIs, oracles, etc.) • Impact on data privacy and regulatory compliance	• Designing APIs for data exchange • Establishing secure communication channels with external systems

5.8.3 Future Trends

The future of blockchain computing and digital transformation will be characterized by a number of intriguing trends. First, it is anticipated that the combination of AI and blockchain will unleash potent synergies. AI can analyze blockchain data for valuable insights, while blockchain can improve AI systems' credibility and safety. This integration has substantial repercussions for industries such as healthcare, finance, and cybersecurity. The tokenization and digitization of assets is another trend. By representing assets as tokens, the blockchain enables fractional ownership and liquidity. This creates new investment opportunities and permits the efficient transfer of assets. We can anticipate the tokenization of diverse assets, including real estate, intellectual property, and commodities, which will facilitate the development of new trading platforms and markets.

Interoperability between distributed ledger networks is also acquiring importance. Efforts are being made to establish communication and data exchange protocols and standards. This interoperability will facilitate collaboration, scalability, and the creation of blockchain solutions across industries. In addition, private and hybrid blockchains are gaining popularity because they offer enhanced privacy, control, and scalability for enterprise applications. The evolution of regulatory frameworks will likely influence the future of blockchain technology. Governments and regulatory agencies are developing guidelines to resolve data privacy, identity management, and the legality of smart contracts. Clear and supportive regulatory environments will encourage the wider adoption of blockchain solutions, particularly in industries that are highly regulated.

5.9 CLOUD COMPUTING

Cloud computing is a model for delivering services over the Internet, eliminating the need for local infrastructure and enabling users to access resources and applications remotely. It provides a shared pool of rapidly provisional and releasable configurable computational resources, such as servers, storage, and software. The advantages of cloud computing are substantial. It provides scalability, enabling businesses to manage fluctuating workloads efficiently. Pay-as-you-go pricing models attain cost efficiency by reducing capital expenditures. The adaptability and responsiveness of cloud platforms facilitate the rapid deployment of applications and encourage experimentation and innovation. In addition to enhancing collaboration and enabling remote access, cloud services empower teams to work together seamlessly from any location. In addition, cloud providers' reliability, security, and disaster recovery capabilities assure data protection and availability.

The evolution of cloud computing closely parallels the era of digital transformation. It plays a crucial function in assisting businesses to adopt modern technologies, such as AI, big data analytics, and IoT. Cloud services accelerate innovation by providing a scalable and adaptable infrastructure and enable businesses to adapt to market shifts rapidly. As a result of the cloud's accessibility and global reach, organizations can expand their operations and reach consumers across geographic boundaries without making substantial infrastructure investments. In addition, cloud computing democratizes the adoption of technology by making enterprise-level computing power and resources accessible to small and medium-sized businesses (SMEs), thereby leveling the playing field in the business landscape.

Cloud computing transforms the manner in which businesses approach IT infrastructure and services, thereby spurring digital transformation. It provides a more agile, scalable, and cost-effective method for adopting technology. Cloud computing enables businesses to remain competitive in a swiftly changing digital landscape by fostering innovation, facilitating collaboration, and providing the necessary adaptability to meet market demands. As organizations continue to adopt the cloud, its influence on digital transformation will only increase, paving the way for a more connected and technologically advanced future.

5.9.1 Components

Cloud computing encompasses several key components that work together to deliver infrastructure and services. These components can be grouped into three main models: Infrastructure as a Service (IaaS), Platform as a Service (PaaS), and Software as a Service (SaaS).

- *IaaS*: IaaS provides virtualized computing resources over the Internet. It offers a scalable and flexible infrastructure, including virtual machines, storage, and networking capabilities. Leading IaaS providers like AWS, Azure, and Google Cloud Platform offer organizations the ability to host websites, run virtual servers, manage databases, and store large amounts of data. With IaaS, businesses can easily scale their infrastructure as needed, paying only for the resources they consume.
- *PaaS*: PaaS provides a platform that developers can leverage to build, deploy, and manage applications without dealing with underlying infrastructure concerns. It typically includes development tools, runtime environments, and database management systems. Platforms like Azure App Service, Google App Engine, and Heroku empower developers to focus on coding while abstracting away infrastructure complexities. PaaS streamlines application development, automates deployment, and enables rapid iteration and scalability.
- *SaaS*: SaaS delivers software applications over the Internet on a subscription basis, eliminating the need for local installation and maintenance. Users can access these applications through a web browser. Popular SaaS offerings such as Salesforce, Office 365, and Dropbox enable organizations to leverage CRM systems, collaborative tools, and document management platforms without managing infrastructure or software updates. SaaS provides convenience, accessibility, and seamless updates, enhancing user experience and productivity.
- *Function as a Service (FaaS)*: FaaS, also known as serverless computing, allows developers to write and execute code in the cloud without managing the underlying infrastructure. Cloud providers handle scaling and resource allocation based on demand. AWS Lambda, Google Cloud Functions, and Azure Functions are prominent FaaS platforms. FaaS is ideal for event-driven and microservices architectures, where functions are triggered by specific events or requests. It enables developers to focus on writing code and rapidly responding to events without worrying about infrastructure management.

- *Desktop as a Service (DaaS)*: DaaS delivers virtual desktop environments to users over the Internet. It allows users to access their desktops and applications from any device with an Internet connection, facilitating remote work and centralized management. DaaS solutions like Citrix Virtual Apps and Desktops, VMware Horizon, and Amazon WorkSpaces offer businesses flexibility, security, and simplified desktop management. DaaS is particularly valuable for remote workers, bring your own device (BYOD) environments, and organizations seeking streamlined desktop provisioning and maintenance.

These cloud computing components collectively provide organizations with the flexibility, scalability, and convenience to meet their computing needs. By leveraging IaaS, PaaS, SaaS, FaaS, and DaaS, businesses can optimize their operations, improve productivity, and drive digital transformation. Each model offers distinct advantages, enabling organizations to choose the most suitable approach based on their specific requirements and use cases. The cloud computing ecosystem continues to evolve, presenting businesses with a range of options to effectively leverage cloud services for their success.

5.9.2 Role of Cloud Computing in Digital Transformation

Cloud computing plays a pivotal role in driving digital transformation across industries. It provides organizations with the necessary tools and capabilities to embrace technological advancements and reshape their business processes. The role of cloud computing in digital transformation can be summarized as follows:

- *Scalability and Elasticity*: Cloud computing enables organizations to scale their resources up or down based on demand. This scalability allows businesses to handle fluctuating workloads and adjust resources as needed efficiently. It eliminates the need for up-front investment in hardware and infrastructure, providing cost-effective solutions that align with business requirements.
- *Cost Efficiency*: Cloud computing significantly reduces capital expenditure by eliminating the need for on-premises infrastructure and maintenance. It offers pay-as-you-go pricing models, enabling organizations to optimize costs by only paying for the resources they use. This cost-efficiency allows businesses to allocate their budgets to other areas of innovation and growth.
- *Agility and Flexibility*: Cloud platforms provide rapid provisioning and deployment of resources, allowing organizations to quickly adapt to changing market conditions. It enables businesses to experiment, innovate, and launch new products and services more efficiently. The flexibility of cloud computing also allows for seamless collaboration among teams and remote access to applications and data, supporting the modern work environment.
- *Data-Driven Decision-Making*: Cloud computing empowers organizations to harness the power of data through advanced analytics and processing

capabilities. It facilitates the collection, storage, analysis, and visualization of large volumes of data, enabling businesses to derive valuable insights and make data-driven decisions. Cloud-based analytics tools and ML services further enhance the capabilities of organizations in leveraging data for competitive advantage.

- *Enhanced Security and Compliance*: Cloud providers offer robust security measures and compliance frameworks to protect data and applications. They invest heavily in security technologies, expertise, and certifications, often surpassing the security capabilities of individual organizations. Cloud computing enables businesses to leverage these advanced security features and ensure data protection, privacy, and regulatory compliance.
- *Innovation and Collaboration*: Cloud computing fosters innovation by providing access to cutting-edge technologies such as AI, ML, and IoT. It offers platforms and services that simplify the development and deployment of innovative applications. Cloud-based collaboration tools and workflows enable seamless communication and collaboration among teams, promoting creativity and productivity.
- *Scalable Infrastructure for Growth*: Cloud computing provides organizations with the infrastructure needed to scale their operations rapidly. It allows businesses to expand their reach globally, serving customers across geographical boundaries without the need for significant infrastructure investments. The cloud enables startups and small businesses to access enterprise-level computing power, leveling the playing field and fostering growth.

5.10 CROWDFUNDING

With the advent of digital technologies, crowdfunding, a method for raising funds from a large number of individuals, has witnessed a significant transformation. Digital transformation, the incorporation of digital tools and strategies into business operations, has transformed the operation of crowdfunding. Historically, crowdfunding relied on offline methods and face-to-face interactions, limiting its accessibility and reach. The emergence of online platforms and the adoption of digital tools have, however, made the transition to digital crowdfunding seamless.

Crowdfunding has benefited greatly from the digital transformation of the sector. It allows project creators to interact with a global audience of potential backers. The transition to online platforms has eradicated geographical barriers and widened the scope of opportunities for collaboration and assistance. Second, digital transformation has decreased the entry barriers for both project creators and backers. It has democratized the fundraising process, allowing individuals and organizations with innovative ideas to gain access to capital and initiate projects. In conclusion, the digital transformation of crowdfunding has greatly improved the user experience. Online platforms offer user-friendly interfaces, streamlined procedures, and real-time interaction, making it simpler for patrons to discover projects, contribute funds, and monitor the progress of campaigns.

The integration of social media and networking has been a crucial aspect of the digital transformation of crowdfunding. Social media platforms have evolved into potent instruments for project creators to promote their campaigns, interact with their audience, and create a community around their projects. The ability to share campaign updates, stories, and milestones on social media platforms has substantially increased the visibility and impact of crowdfunding campaigns. In addition, the application of data analytics and AI has enabled project creators and crowdfunding platforms to gain valuable insights into user behavior, optimize campaign strategies, and personalize the crowdfunding experience. By utilizing these digital tools, crowdfunding has become more effective, targeted, and data-driven, resulting in increased campaign success rates.

5.10.1 Traditional Crowdfunding

In the predigital era, traditional crowdfunding relied on offline interactions and personal networks to support initiatives or ventures. It involved soliciting donations, pursuing investments, or offering incentives for participation, such as rewards. However, traditional crowdfunding had reach, scalability, and efficiency limitations. It relied largely on personal connections and local communities, which limited its geographic reach. Manual processes for collecting funds and managing contributions were time-consuming, and the need for centralized online platforms hampered monitoring and marketing efforts.

Traditional crowdfunding platforms included community-driven initiatives in which local communities supported projects, donation boxes, collection jars placed in public spaces, fundraising events and campaigns such as charity auctions or telethons, and investor networks that linked entrepreneurs with potential investors for equity-based funding.

Although these traditional methods were somewhat effective, expanding their reach and optimizing the fundraising process presented obstacles. Significant changes in crowdfunding have resulted from the advent of digital transformation, which has shifted the emphasis to online platforms and digital tools. In the following sections, we will examine the impact of digital transformation on crowdfunding, the benefits it provides, and the various models and players in the landscape of digital crowdfunding.

5.10.2 Digital Transformation in Crowdfunding

By leveraging online platforms and cutting-edge technologies, the digital transformation of crowdfunding has significantly reshaped the fundraising landscape. This transformation has resulted in numerous benefits, including improved accessibility, user experience, and overall efficacy of crowdfunding campaigns. The emergence of online crowdfunding platforms has been a significant driver of digital transformation. These platforms function as centralized centers where project creators can present their initiatives and connect with potential backers. By relocating the crowdfunding process online, geographical barriers are eliminated, allowing creators of projects to reach an international audience. This increased accessibility has democratized fundraising, allowing individuals and organizations from diverse backgrounds to gain access to capital and support for their initiatives.

Additionally, digital transformation has reduced entry barriers for both project creators and supporters. In the past, successful crowdfunding campaigns frequently required extensive personal networks or substantial financial resources. With online platforms, project creators can easily establish campaigns with minimal up-front costs, making it easier for enterprises, entrepreneurs, and individuals with innovative ideas to seek funding. Similarly, backers can contribute any quantity that fits their budget, allowing even modest contributions to have a significant impact on campaigns.

Through digital transformation, the user experience has been drastically improved. For project creators and contributors, online platforms with user-friendly interfaces, streamlined procedures, and secure payment gateways facilitate the campaign setup and contribution process. These platforms' communication tools and real-time updates foster a sense of community and transparency, allowing project creators to interact with their patrons. In addition, the incorporation of social media and networking into crowdfunding campaigns expand their reach and influence. Using social media platforms, project creators can promote their campaigns, post updates, and interact with potential backers, thereby increasing campaign visibility and gaining more support.

Additionally, digital transformation has introduced the use of data analytics and AI in crowdfunding. Platforms can collect and analyze information regarding user behavior, campaign effectiveness, and market trends. These insights enable project creators to optimize their campaigns, identify their target demographics, and refine their messaging for greater success. By automating duties such as fraud detection and risk assessment, AI technologies bolster the crowdfunding process's security and credibility.

5.10.3 Types of Digital Crowdfunding Models

Not only has digital transformation revolutionized how crowdfunding is conducted, but it has also spawned numerous models within the crowdfunding ecosystem. These models represent various fundraising strategies, each with its own characteristics and benefits. Table 5.4 presents a comparison of various digital crowdfunding models. Listed below are some of the most prominent digital crowdfunding models (Figure 5.3).

5.10.4 Benefits and Challenges

Digital crowdfunding offers several benefits that have transformed the fundraising landscape:

- First, it increases access to capital by connecting project creators with a worldwide pool of potential supporters. This democratization of funding enables individuals, entrepreneurs, and small businesses to obtain financial assistance without relying solely on traditional sources. It encourages innovation

TABLE 5.4   Digital crowdfunding models: A comparative overview

CROWDFUNDING MODEL	DESCRIPTION	FINANCIAL RETURN	REWARDS	INVESTOR REGULATION
Donation-based	Individuals or organizations seek donations without expecting financial returns.	No financial return is expected.	No specific rewards; backers contribute out of goodwill.	Generally no specific investor regulation.
Reward-based	Backers receive tangible or intangible rewards based on their contribution level.	No financial return is expected; backers receive rewards.	Backers receive rewards based on contribution level.	Generally no specific investor regulation.
Equity-based	Backers invest in early-stage businesses or startups in exchange for equity or shares.	Potential financial returns if the company succeeds.	With no specific rewards, backers become shareholders.	Subject to regulatory requirements.
Debt-based	Individuals or businesses seek loans from a pool of lenders and repay with interest.	Lenders receive repayment with interest over a specified period.	No specific rewards; lenders earn interest on loans.	Subject to regulatory requirements.

and entrepreneurship by providing funding opportunities for a variety of initiatives. Second, digital crowdfunding functions as a platform for market validation. Before launching their offerings on the market, project creators can gauge market demand and collect feedback from potential sponsors, allowing them to refine their offerings. This procedure reduces the possibility of investing in products or services that may not resonate with the intended audience. Additionally, digital crowdfunding encourages participation and community development. It enables project creators to cultivate a community of ardent supporters emotionally invested in the project's success. Potentially resulting in long-term relationships and support for the initiative, backers feel a sense of participation and connection. In addition, crowdfunding campaigns generate publicity and marketing opportunities, attracting media attention and boosting brand visibility.

• However, the landscape is extremely competitive, with thousands of initiatives vying for attention and funding. To distinguish from the crowd, project creators must develop compelling pitches and differentiate themselves.

1 Donation-based
crowdfunding

**2 Reward-based
crowdfunding**

3 Equity-based
crowdfunding

4 Debt-based
crowdfunding

1

In this model, individuals or organizations seek donations from backers who contribute funds without expecting any financial return. Donation-based crowdfunding is often used for charitable causes, personal emergencies, community projects, or social initiatives. Backers contribute out of goodwill and to support a particular cause or campaign without the expectation of financial gain.

2

This model involves offering tangible or intangible rewards to backers who contribute funds. Project creators set up reward tiers, specifying different levels of contribution and corresponding rewards. These rewards can range from exclusive merchandise, early access to products or services, personalized experiences, or recognition. Reward-based crowdfunding is commonly used by startups, creative projects, and product launches to incentivize backers and build a loyal customer

3

Equity-based crowdfunding allows individuals to invest in early-stage businesses or startups in exchange for equity or shares in the company. Backers become shareholders and have the potential to gain financial returns if the company succeeds. This model provides an opportunity for individuals to invest in promising ventures and participate in the growth of the business. Equity-based crowdfunding is subject to regulatory requirements and often takes place on specialized platforms.

4

Also known as peer-to-peer lending or crowdlending, debt-based crowdfunding involves individuals or businesses seeking loans from a pool of lenders. Backers provide loans to borrowers and receive repayment with interest over a specified period. Debt-based crowdfunding provides an alternative to traditional lending institutions, allowing borrowers to access capital and lenders to earn interest on their investments. This model is commonly used for personal loans, small business financing, or real estate projects.

FIGURE 5.3 Digital crowdfunding models.

Establishing trust and credibility is also essential. To gain supporters' trust, project creators must demonstrate transparency, provide regular updates, and fulfill their commitments. The inability to execute rewards or deliver products/services on time can result in backer dissatisfaction. As potential supporters are exposed to multiple crowdfunding campaigns, there is also a risk of campaign fatigue. This saturation may dampen enthusiasm and make it more difficult for project creators to attract interest and obtain funding. Despite these obstacles, digital crowdfunding continues to prosper due to its accessibility, opportunities for market validation, engagement potential, and ability to connect project creators with backers from around the globe.

5.11 DEEP LEARNING

Deep learning is a subset of ML that concentrates on training artificial neural networks with multiple layers to extract meaningful representations from massive amounts of data. It is inspired by the structure and function of the neural networks of the human brain. Deep learning algorithms can autonomously discover hierarchical data representations, allowing them to solve complex problems without explicit programming. Deep learning plays a vital role in this transformation by providing potent tools for analyzing and extracting insights from vast and diverse datasets. It enables organizations to automate processes, enhance decision-making, improve customer experiences, and discover valuable patterns and trends that can fuel innovation and competitive advantage.

Deep learning algorithms excel at processing complex and unstructured data types, such as images, text, audio, and video. They are able to process and analyze these data sources at scale, allowing businesses to obtain deeper insights and make decisions based on data. Deep learning has the potential to revolutionize multiple industries and fuel digital transformation initiatives, whether it is NLP, computer vision, recommendation systems, or predictive analytics.

Deep learning is a subfield of ML that extracts meaningful representations from large datasets using artificial neural networks with multiple layers. Neural networks composed of interconnected nodes that replicate the structure and function of the human brain are the foundation of deep learning. These networks are trained utilizing techniques such as backpropagation and gradient descent in order to optimize the model's parameters and minimize the loss function. Deep learning algorithms, including convolutional neural networks (CNNs) for computer vision and Recurrent Neutral Networks (RNNs) for sequential data, have revolutionized disciplines such as NLP, computer vision, and predictive analytics.

The fundamentals of deep learning include numerous components. Neural networks consist of perceptrons that receive inputs, apply weights, and pass the outputs through activation functions. The architecture of deep learning models consists of multiple layers of nodes, with input layers receiving raw data, hidden layers conducting computations, and output layers producing predictions. Backpropagation calculates gradients to modify parameters, while gradient descent optimizes the model by updating parameters in the opposite direction of gradients. Loss functions quantify the difference between predicted and actual outputs, directing the optimization process of the model.

Different algorithms for deep learning serve specific functions. CNNs excel at visual data analysis, utilizing convolutional and pooling layers to learn and extract image features. RNNs are efficient at processing sequential data by capturing dependencies and patterns over time using memory elements. Generative Adversarial Networks (GANs) are comprised of competing generator and discriminator networks that enable the generation of synthetic data that resembles actual data. Reinforcement learning uses deep neural networks to train agents in decision-making processes, enabling them to maximize rewards in their environments.

5.11.1 Applications of Deep Learning in Digital Transformation

- *NLP*: Deep learning has transformed duties in NLP. By analyzing text data such as customer reviews and social media posts, sentiment analysis enables companies to assess public opinion. Deep learning-powered neural machine translation models have substantially improved language translation, allowing businesses to overcome language barriers and expand their global reach. Moreover, deep learning algorithms have enabled the creation of intelligent chatbots and virtual assistants able to comprehend and respond to NLP, thereby providing personalized customer service and enhancing user experiences.
- *Computer Vision*: Computer vision applications have been significantly advanced by deep learning algorithms. Object detection and recognition models, especially CNNs, accurately identify and classify objects within images or videos, which is beneficial for autonomous vehicles, surveillance systems, and inventory management. Deep learning-based image and video classification models can classify visual content, automating duties like content moderation, visual search, and personalized recommendations. Deep learning enables facial recognition applications such as access control, identity verification, and personalized marketing experiences.
- *Speech Recognition and Synthesis*: Speech recognition systems have been revolutionized by techniques of deep learning, enabling accurate transcription of spoken words and facilitating voice-controlled interfaces. Voice assistants, voice-controlled devices, and other speech-enabled services have incorporated these developments. In addition to generating human-like speech, deep learning models can enhance applications such as audiobooks, voice-over services, and interactive voice response systems.
- *Recommendation Systems, Fraud Detection, and Predictive Analytics*: Deep learning algorithms excel at extracting preferences and patterns from massive datasets. These capabilities are utilized by recommendation systems to provide personalized suggestions for products, services, content, and advertisements, thereby increasing consumer engagement and revenue growth. In the realms of fraud detection and cybersecurity, deep learning models can recognize patterns and anomalies in data, allowing for the detection of fraudulent activities and the bolstering of security measures. Deep learning also plays a significant role in predictive analytics and forecasting by analyzing historical

data, identifying concealed patterns, and making accurate predictions, which can contribute to operational efficiency and well-informed decisions.

5.11.2 Benefits and Challenges of Deep Learning in Digital Transformation

Deep learning has numerous advantages for digital transformation initiatives. Initially, it facilitates improved data analysis and insights by revealing intricate patterns and valuable insights from vast and diverse datasets. This results in improved decision-making, process optimization, and the identification of opportunities for innovation. Second, deep learning enables automation and efficiency gains by automating tasks such as data classification, image recognition, and language translation, thereby freeing up resources for more strategic endeavors. Moreover, deep learning enables businesses to provide personalized customer experiences by means of customized recommendations, targeted marketing campaigns, and responsive chatbots or virtual assistants, thereby enhancing customer satisfaction and loyalty.

Nonetheless, there are obstacles to consider. Due to the reliance on large datasets, data privacy and ethical concerns arise, requiring organizations to guarantee proper data governance and compliance with privacy regulations. In addition, the quality and biases of training data can affect the performance and impartiality of deep learning models, necessitating meticulous data curation and evaluation. The interpretability of deep learning models continues to be a challenge, as their complexity makes it challenging to explain their decisions and predictions. To completely leverage the benefits of deep learning in digital transformation, it is crucial to address these challenges with robust data management, bias mitigation techniques, and efforts to improve interpretability.

5.12 DISTRIBUTED COMPUTING

Distributed computing is crucial to the current digital transformation of enterprises. Digital transformation has become a key driver for growth, innovation, and competitive advantage as organizations seek to adapt to the rapidly evolving technological landscape. At the center of this transformation is the concept of distributed computing, which refers to the collaborative use of multiple interconnected computers or nodes to solve complex problems, process data, and provide services.

In the traditional centralized computing model, all duties and operations are handled by a single computer or server. As the volume and complexity of data have increased exponentially, centralized systems still need to be improved to satisfy the requirements of contemporary applications. Distributed computing is a scalable and flexible alternative that utilizes the power of multiple computers to distribute workloads and process data in parallel, resulting in enhanced performance, dependability, and efficiency.

Infrastructure modernization, data analytics, IoT, and microservices are all aspects of digital transformation that heavily rely on distributed computing principles. By leveraging distributed systems, organizations can realize the full potential of contemporary technologies, allowing them to innovate, make data-driven decisions, and provide seamless consumer experiences.

5.12.1 Key Distributed Computing Concepts

Distributed computing relies on a number of fundamental concepts to facilitate the efficient operation of interconnected systems. Distributed systems are fundamentally composed of multiple computers or nodes collaborating to accomplish a common goal. These systems are intended to distribute duties and data across multiple nodes, enabling parallel processing and distributed storage. The client–server model, in which a central server provides services to multiple consumers, and the peer-to-peer model, in which nodes collaborate as both clients and servers, are two prevalent models in distributed systems.

In distributed computing, scalability and resource management are essential considerations. Horizontal scaling entails adding more nodes to handle increased workloads and accommodate more users, whereas vertical scaling entails increasing the resources of individual nodes to enhance performance. Load balancing guarantees an even distribution of duties across nodes in order to maximize resource utilization and prevent bottlenecks. The implementation of fault tolerance mechanisms allows for the handling of defects and the continued operation of the system, even if some nodes or components fail.

Distributed systems require communication protocols and middleware technologies that are efficient. Message passing enables communication between nodes through the transmission and receiving of information-containing messages. Remote Procedure Calls (RPC) abstract network communication complexities by allowing programs on one node to invoke functions on another node. Middleware technologies, such as CORBA, RMI, and gRPC, serve as an intermediary layer between the operating system and applications, facilitating communication and integration between distributed components.

5.12.2 Role of Distributed Computing in Digital Transformation

Distributed computing plays a crucial role in driving digital transformation across multiple business operations, enabling organizations to modernize their infrastructure, process and analyze large volumes of data, leverage IoT, and adopt microservices architectures. Infrastructure modernization is a crucial area in which distributed computing contributes to digital transformation. By migrating to cloud computing, organizations can take advantage of distributed computing's scalability, flexibility, and cost-effectiveness. Hybrid and multicloud architectures improve resource allocation and reduce risks of vendor lock-in.

Another important aspect is the processing and analysis of massive amounts of data. Distributed file systems, including Hadoop and Apache HDFS, distribute data storage and processing across multiple nodes, thereby enhancing performance, fault tolerance, and scalability. On enormous datasets, distributed data processing frameworks such as Apache Spark and Apache Flink permit real-time analytics, ML, and data transformations. Distributed computation is also crucial to the IoT ecosystem. By leveraging distributed computing capabilities, real-time data processing at the periphery decreases latency and improves responsiveness. Moreover, distributed intelligence and decision-making enable IoT devices to conduct localized analytics and make autonomous decisions, thereby enhancing efficiency and real-time decision-making capabilities.

In addition, distributed computing enables organizations to employ service-oriented architectures and container orchestration platforms such as Kubernetes and Docker Swarm by supporting microservices and containerization. This method improves adaptability, scalability, and maintenance simplicity, making it a fundamental aspect of modern application development and deployment. Adopting distributed computing in digital transformation offers numerous advantages, such as enhanced performance, scalability, defect tolerance, cost optimization, and effective resource utilization. Nevertheless, issues such as system complexity, data consistency, synchronization, and security must be addressed. Organizations can drive innovation, transform their operations, and remain competitive in today's digital landscape by leveraging the potential of distributed computing.

5.13 INTERACTIVE COMPUTING

Interactive computing refers to the application of computational technologies that facilitate real-time, dynamic, and interactive human–machine interactions. It involves the seamless exchange of information, commands, and responses, allowing users to interact naturally and intuitively with computers and digital systems. As a result of the rapid development of technology and the increasing digitization of various industries, interactive computing has become an integral part of our daily existence. From smartphones and smart devices to virtual assistants and web applications, interactive computing has revolutionized how we access information, communicate, and complete tasks. Interactive computing incorporates a variety of technologies, including user interfaces, real-time data processing and analytics, AI, ML, and hardware device and sensor integration. Users are able to interact with digital systems in a manner that is intuitive, efficient, and tailored to their requirements because these elements work together to create engaging and personalized experiences.

The rise of digital transformation has highlighted the significance of interactive computing even further. Across industries, organizations are leveraging interactive computing technologies to improve consumer experiences, streamline business processes, and make decisions based on data. It enables companies to deliver personalized services, automate repetitive tasks, and obtain real-time insights that fuel innovation and competitive advantage. Nevertheless, interactive computing presents challenges, such as assuring security and privacy, addressing accessibility and inclusivity concerns, and managing scalability and infrastructure needs. It is essential to overcome these obstacles in order to realize the complete potential of interactive computing and reap its benefits.

5.13.1 Key Components of Interactive Computing

- *User Interface (UI) and User Experience (UX) Design*: User interface design focuses on creating interfaces that are visually appealing, intuitive, and easy to navigate. User experience design encompasses the overall experience a user has while interacting with a system, ensuring it is engaging, efficient, and satisfying.
- *Real-time Data Processing and Analytics*: Interactive computing relies on real-time data processing and analytics to enable dynamic and personalized interactions. It involves collecting, analyzing, and interpreting data in real time, allowing for immediate responses and customized experiences based on user inputs and preferences.
- *AI and Machine Learning*: AI and ML technologies are integral to interactive computing. They enable systems to understand and interpret user inputs, learn from user behavior, and make intelligent decisions or recommendations. AI and ML algorithms enhance the interactivity and responsiveness of interactive systems.
- *Integration with Hardware Devices and Sensors*: Interactive computing often involves integration with various hardware devices and sensors. This includes devices such as smartphones, tablets, wearables, and IoT devices. Sensors, such as touchscreens, motion sensors, and biometric sensors, enable users to interact with systems in more natural and immersive ways.

5.13.2 Digital Transformation and Interactive Computing

Digital transformation and interactive computing are closely intertwined, with interactive computing playing a significant role in driving and enabling digital transformation efforts. Here are some key aspects of their relationship:

- *Enhanced Customer Experience and Engagement*: Interactive computing technologies allow organizations to deliver highly personalized and engaging experiences to their customers. By leveraging real-time data processing, AI, and intuitive interfaces, businesses can provide tailored recommendations, personalized content, and seamless interactions across multiple touchpoints. This leads to improved customer satisfaction, loyalty, and, ultimately, business growth.
- *Streamlined Business Processes and Efficiency*: Interactive computing can automate and streamline various business processes, reducing manual efforts

and improving efficiency. Tasks that were once time-consuming and repetitive can be automated, allowing employees to focus on higher-value activities. For example, interactive chatbots and virtual assistants can handle customer inquiries, freeing up human agents for more complex and strategic tasks. This leads to increased productivity, cost savings, and improved operational efficiency.

- *Data-Driven Decision-Making*: Digital transformation relies heavily on data-driven decision-making, and interactive computing enables organizations to leverage real-time analytics and insights. By processing and analyzing vast amounts of data in real time, businesses can make informed decisions and respond swiftly to changing market dynamics. Interactive dashboards, visualizations, and predictive analytics provide actionable insights, empowering organizations to optimize operations, identify opportunities, and mitigate risks.

- *Collaboration and Communication*: Interactive computing tools facilitate collaboration and communication among teams, stakeholders, and customers. Cloud-based collaboration platforms, virtual meeting tools, and project management systems enable seamless remote work and virtual collaboration. These technologies foster real-time communication, knowledge sharing, and collaboration, regardless of geographical boundaries. This is especially relevant in the context of distributed teams and remote work arrangements.

5.14 INTERNET OF THINGS

IoT is the network of physical devices, vehicles, appliances, and other objects equipped with sensors, software, and connectivity capabilities that allow them to collect and exchange data. These devices can communicate with each other and with humans, forming a vast ecosystem of intelligent, automated systems. Internet-connected or local-area network-connected IoT devices are designed to communicate and interact with one another. They can range from basic sensors and actuators to sophisticated appliances, wearable devices, industrial machinery, and even autonomous vehicles. These devices capture and share data, allowing them to respond and adapt to their environment, thereby constituting an integral part of the digital transformation landscape.

The expansion of IoT has considerably contributed to the ongoing digital transformation in numerous industries. IoT facilitates automation, optimization, and enhanced decision-making by connecting physical objects and enabling data exchange. It enables businesses to gain valuable insights, improve operational efficiency, and provide innovative products and services. In addition, IoT has the potential to revolutionize industries such as healthcare, manufacturing, transportation, and energy, resulting in enhanced quality of life and economic expansion. As organizations adopt IoT technologies, they can unlock new opportunities, enhance consumer experiences, and remain competitive in a world that is becoming increasingly digital.

5.14.1 Key Components of IoT

IoT consists of three essential components that are responsible for its functionality and enable digital transformation. The first component consists of devices and sensors, which include a variety of physical objects embedded with sensors and software. These devices consist of intelligent thermostats, wearable fitness monitors, and sensors for industrial machinery. They play a crucial role in the collection of real-time data from the physical world, measuring parameters including temperature, motion, and location. This information enables IoT systems to function and make informed decisions.

Connectivity is the second component, which enables IoT devices to communicate and exchange data. IoT employs numerous wireless communication protocols, including Wi-Fi, Bluetooth, Zigbee, cellular networks, and LoRaWAN. For uninterrupted data transmission, dependable connectivity is essential, allowing devices to remain connected to the Internet or local networks. It ensures monitoring, supervision, and analysis of IoT data in real time.

Cloud computing provides a scalable and cost-effective solution for storing and processing vast quantities of IoT data. The infrastructure of the cloud provides storage capabilities, data analytics instruments, and computing resources. It enables centralized storage and management of IoT data, scalability to handle growing data volumes, and real-time processing for deriving actionable insights. Cloud computing is essential for realizing the full potential of the IoT because it enables organizations to access and analyze IoT data efficiently.

These essential elements of devices and sensors, connectivity, and cloud computing form the basis of IoT systems. They are indispensable for digital transformation because they allow organizations to collect and analyze data, optimize operations, and make decisions based on data. IoT enables industries and sectors to discover new opportunities, increase productivity, and deliver innovative products and services, thereby accelerating the digital transformation voyage.

5.14.2 Applications of IoT in Digital Transformation

IoT has numerous applications across a variety of industries and is a key driver of digital transformation. IoT benefits smart homes and buildings by facilitating the automation and remote control of appliances and systems. Through smart devices and mobile applications, homeowners can control the illumination, temperature, security, and entertainment devices in their homes. IoT also contributes to energy efficiency and cost reductions via real-time monitoring and optimization of energy consumption.

Industrial IoT (IIoT) revolutionizes operations in industrial contexts through predictive maintenance and equipment optimization. Continuously monitoring the health and performance of machinery with IoT sensors enables predictive maintenance to mitigate downtime and maximize equipment efficiency. Moreover, IIoT improves supply chain management and logistics by providing real-time visibility into the location and condition of products, optimizing inventory management, and streamlining logistics operations.

IoT offers transformative applications in the healthcare industry, such as remote patient monitoring and telemedicine. Using IoT devices and wearables, healthcare providers can remotely monitor patients' vital signs, medication adherence, and overall health. This facilitates personalized and proactive care, decreases hospitalizations, and enhances patient outcomes. In addition, IoT-enabled medical devices and systems enhance patient care and treatment outcomes, ensuring patient safety and accurate diagnoses with features such as intelligent infusion pumps and RFID-enabled asset tracking.

Smart cities use IoT to enhance urban living conditions. Intelligent transportation systems and traffic management leverage the IoT for real-time traffic monitoring, intelligent parking solutions, and optimized traffic signal control. This improves traffic flow, reduces congestion, and increases the overall efficacy of transportation. For effective urban planning, IoT also contributes to waste management and environmental monitoring by monitoring waste levels, optimizing collection routes, and measuring air quality and decibel levels.

5.14.3 Benefits and Challenges of IoT in Digital Transformation

IoT offers numerous advantages that facilitate digital transformation. First, it improves productivity and efficiency by automating processes, enabling real-time monitoring, and facilitating data-driven decision-making. Organizations are capable of streamlining operations, optimizing resource allocation, and enhancing overall productivity. The IoT enables enhanced decision-making through data analytics. The vast quantity of data generated by IoT devices can be analyzed to extract valuable insights, resulting in a greater comprehension of customer behavior, market trends, and operational patterns. This enables organizations to make educated decisions and formulate effective strategies. By facilitating predictive maintenance, optimizing energy consumption, and streamlining supply chain management and procedures, IoT contributes to cost savings and resource optimization.

However, a number of obstacles must be overcome in order to implement IoT for digital transformation. Due to the interconnected nature of IoT systems, security and privacy issues are prevalent. To mitigate the risks of cyberattacks and unauthorized access, robust security measures and data privacy protocols are required. The diversity of devices, protocols, and platforms can impede the integration and scalability of IoT systems due to interoperability and standardization concerns. Managing large-scale IoT deployments, handling massive amounts of data, and ensuring reliable connectivity also requires meticulous planning, infrastructure investment, and effective device management strategies. By addressing these obstacles, organizations can maximize the benefits of IoT to drive digital transformation.

5.15 MACHINE LEARNING

Machine learning is a subfield of AI concerned with the development of algorithms and models that allow computers to learn from data and make predictions or decisions without being explicitly programmed. It involves the development of techniques that enable machines to learn and progress automatically through experience. ML is crucial to digital transformation because it enables organizations to extract valuable insights from vast quantities of data and make decisions based on that data. It enables organizations to automate processes, improve customer experiences, optimize operations, and obtain a competitive edge in the digital age.

5.15.1 Basic Principles and Concepts of Machine Learning

ML algorithms can be broadly classified into three categories: Supervised learning, unsupervised learning, and reinforcement learning. Each category addresses different types of problems and learning scenarios. Table 5.5 provides a breakdown of ML

TABLE 5.5   Machine learning algorithm categories

CATEGORY	DEFINITION	INPUT DATA	OUTPUT DATA	EXAMPLE ALGORITHMS
Supervised Learning	Learned from labeled data with known outputs or target variables.	Labeled data	Predicted output for unseen data	Linear Regression, Decision Trees, and Support Vector Machines
Unsupervised Learning	Learned from unlabeled data to identify patterns, structures, and relationships.	Unlabeled data	Clusters, patterns, or relationships within the data	K-means Clustering, Hierarchical Clustering, and Principal Component Analysis
Reinforcement Learning	It involves an agent learning to interact with an environment to maximize rewards.	Observations, rewards, and penalties	Optimal actions to maximize rewards	Q-Learning, Deep Q-Networks, and Policy Gradient Methods

algorithm categories: Supervised learning, unsupervised learning, and reinforcement learning.

- *Supervised Learning*: In supervised learning, the algorithm learns from labeled data, where each data point is associated with a known output or target variable. It aims to predict the output for unseen data based on the learned patterns and relationships from the labeled data.
- *Unsupervised Learning*: Unsupervised learning deals with unlabeled data, where the algorithm learns to identify patterns, structures, and relationships within the data without any predefined output labels. It helps in clustering similar data points or identifying hidden patterns in the data.
- *Reinforcement Learning*: Reinforcement learning involves an agent that learns to interact with an environment and take actions to maximize a reward signal. The agent receives feedback in the form of rewards or penalties based on its actions, enabling it to learn through trial and error.

ML techniques, such as deep learning, neural networks, decision trees, support vector machines, and many others, provide powerful tools to solve complex problems and unlock the potential of data in various domains.

5.15.2 Applications of Machine Learning in Digital Transformation

Across multiple domains, ML has revolutionized digital transformation. By analyzing consumer data, ML algorithms enable personalized marketing and recommendations in CRM. It also facilitates the segmentation and targeting of customers, enabling businesses to customize their strategies. Moreover, ML aids in predicting customer attrition and implementing retention strategies. ML facilitates demand forecasting, inventory management, predictive maintenance, and route optimization in supply chain optimization, thereby augmenting operational efficiency and reducing costs.

ML is crucial for fraud detection and cybersecurity. It uses techniques for anomaly detection and pattern recognition to identify fraudulent transactions, network intrusions, and suspicious activities in real time. ML models evaluate transaction risks and automate fraud prevention measures, thereby protecting businesses from financial losses. In addition, ML improves network security by identifying aberrant network patterns and facilitating a timely response to threats.

In digital transformation, ML also has a significant impact on process automation. Robotic Process Automation uses ML-enabled programs to automate repetitive tasks, thereby reducing errors and enhancing productivity. Intelligent document processing eliminates manual data entry and accelerates document workflows by extracting information from documents using ML models. Workflow optimization and decision-support systems propelled by ML analyze historical data to provide recommendations and automate decision-making processes, thereby increasing overall productivity and enabling data-driven decision-making.

5.15.3 Challenges and Considerations in Implementing Machine Learning for Digital Transformation

Implementing ML in the context of digital transformation brings numerous opportunities, but it also comes with its own set of challenges and considerations. It is essential for organizations to be aware of these factors to ensure successful adoption and implementation. Here are some key challenges and considerations:

- *Data Quality and Availability*: ML models heavily rely on high-quality, relevant, and representative data for training and accurate predictions. Ensuring data quality, addressing data biases, and maintaining data integrity can be challenging. Organizations need to establish robust data collection processes, perform data cleaning and preprocessing, and address any issues related to data quality and availability.
- *Privacy and Ethical Concerns*: ML involves processing vast amounts of data, including personal and sensitive information. Protecting data privacy, complying with regulations, and maintaining ethical practices are critical considerations. Organizations must implement robust data governance frameworks, establish privacy policies, and prioritize the ethical use of data to build trust with customers and stakeholders.
- *Model Interpretability and Transparency*: ML models, particularly complex ones like deep learning neural networks, can be considered black boxes. Understanding the reasoning behind model predictions and decisions is crucial for transparency, accountability, and regulatory compliance. Developing techniques for model interpretability and explainability is a challenge that organizations need to address.
- *Skills and Expertise Requirements*: Implementing ML for digital transformation requires a multidisciplinary team with expertise in data science, ML, programming, and domain knowledge. Organizations may need help finding and retaining skilled professionals in this rapidly evolving field. Investing in talent development and training initiatives is vital to overcome this challenge.
- *Integration with Existing Systems and Processes*: Integrating ML capabilities into existing systems, infrastructure, and processes can be complex. Legacy systems may need to be compatible or may need more resources for ML implementation. Organizations need to consider architectural considerations, scalability, and compatibility to ensure seamless integration and avoid disruptions.
- *Deployment and Maintenance*: Deploying and maintaining ML models in production environments require careful planning and continuous monitoring. Organizations need to ensure model scalability, performance optimization, and update mechanisms to adapt to changing data patterns and evolving business requirements.

- *Cost and Resource Considerations*: ML implementation can involve significant costs, including data storage, computing resources, infrastructure, and skilled personnel. Organizations need to assess the cost–benefit ratio and allocate resources effectively to ensure the sustainability of ML initiatives.

By recognizing and addressing these challenges and considerations, organizations can mitigate risks and maximize the benefits of ML in their digital transformation journey. Proactive planning, robust governance frameworks, and continuous monitoring and adaptation are key to the successful implementation and utilization of ML technologies.

5.16 NATURAL LANGUAGE PROCESSING

AI subfield is concerned with the interaction between computers and human language. It entails the creation of algorithms and models that enable computers to comprehend, interpret, and generate meaningful human language. NLP is essential to digital transformation because it bridges the gap between human communication and machine comprehension. It enables organizations to extract valuable insights from large volumes of textual data, automate mundane tasks, improve client experiences via chatbots and virtual assistants, enhance information retrieval, and enable more natural human–computer interactions. NLP has the potential to revolutionize industries such as healthcare, finance, customer service, and marketing in the digital age, spurring innovation and efficiency.

NLP comprises a number of essential components that allow computers to comprehend and process human language. Text preprocessing consists of tasks such as tokenization, the separation of text into individual words or tokens; stop word removal, the elimination of common and less informative words; stemming and lemmatization, the reduction of words to their root forms; and spell checking and correction to ensure accurate input. These preprocessing processes serve as a foundation for subsequent analysis.

Part-of-speech tagging allocates grammatical labels to words, and parsing analyzes the structure of sentences to comprehend word relationships. These elements illuminate the grammatical structure of the text and enhance comprehension. Semantics and comprehension are other essential aspects of NLP, including named entity recognition to identify and classify entities, word sense disambiguation to resolve word meanings based on context, sentiment analysis to determine the emotional tone of text, and topic modeling to uncover hidden themes in a collection of documents. These elements allow machines to comprehend the meaning and emotion of human language.

In conclusion, machine translation is the process of converting text from one language to another. This component consists of rule-based machine translation, which employs predefined linguistic principles, statistical machine translation, which employs statistical models trained on bilingual data, and neural machine translation, which employs neural networks to produce more accurate and fluent translations. These translation methods facilitate interlingual communication and facilitate the use of multilingual applications.

5.16.1 Applications of NLP in Digital Transformation

NLP has a variety of applications that contribute to the digital transformation of diverse domains. NLP facilitates NLP, intent recognition, and dialogue management in chatbots and virtual assistants, enhancing communication between humans and machines. In addition, NLP facilitates sentiment analysis, enabling chatbots to analyze consumer feedback and provide personalized, empathetic responses.

Text analytics and information extraction are other essential applications of NLP. It enables text classification, categorization, and entity extraction, facilitating the retrieval and organization of information. In addition to supporting text summarization and document clustering, NLP techniques enhance both data management and knowledge discovery. Voice assistants and voice recognition rely heavily on NLP for speech-to-text conversion, which enables seamless voice interactions and device control. The interpretation of voice commands by NLP algorithms enables hands-free operation. In addition, NLP-powered voice biometrics enable secure user authentication.

NLP enables organizations to monitor social media sentiment, analyze customer reviews, and acquire valuable market insights through sentiment analysis and opinion mining. NLP aids in the management of brand reputation, improvement of consumer satisfaction, and market research. Language generation and content creation use NLP to automate content generation, thereby enabling personalized recommendations and automatic report/document creation. By leveraging NLP, businesses can provide engaging content, personalize user experiences, and increase productivity through automated content generation.

These applications demonstrate the significant role of NLP in digital transformation, redefining consumer interactions, information management, voice-enabled technologies, market insights, and content creation. The influence of NLP extends across industries, fostering innovation and efficacy in the digital age.

5.16.2 Challenges and Limitations of NLP in Digital Transformation

While NLP offers immense potential for digital transformation, it also faces several challenges and limitations that need to be addressed. These include:

- *Ambiguity and Contextual Understanding*: NLP struggles with the ambiguity inherent in human language. Understanding the context and nuances of words and phrases can be challenging, leading to misinterpretations and errors in analysis. Resolving ambiguity requires advanced techniques such as contextual embeddings and deep learning approaches.
- *Multilingual and Cross-cultural Considerations*: NLP models often perform better in the language they are trained in, and their performance may vary across different languages. Cross-lingual understanding and handling of cultural nuances pose challenges for accurate language processing. Developing

robust multilingual models and accounting for cultural variations are ongoing research areas.

* *Privacy and Ethical Concerns*: NLP involves processing and analyzing vast amounts of personal data. Ensuring privacy, data protection, and ethical considerations, such as consent and transparency, are critical. NLP systems must adhere to legal and ethical guidelines to safeguard user information and mitigate potential biases in data and algorithms.
* *Handling Noisy and Unstructured Text Data*: Real-world text data are often noisy, with grammatical errors, abbreviations, slang, and informal language. NLP models may struggle to process and extract meaningful information from such data accurately. Preprocessing techniques and robust algorithms are required to handle noise and effectively utilize unstructured text data.

Overcoming these challenges is crucial to maximizing the benefits of NLP in digital transformation. Continued R&D, along with advancements in ML and deep learning, is essential to address these limitations and enhance the capabilities of NLP systems in handling complex language understanding and processing tasks.

5.17 QUANTUM COMPUTING

Quantum computing is an intriguing field that employs the principles of quantum mechanics to construct a new computing paradigm. Quantum computers use qubits, which can exist in a superposition of states, to process multiple possibilities simultaneously. This unique property creates intriguing opportunities for solving complex problems more efficiently than traditional computers.

The fundamental framework of quantum computing, quantum mechanics, introduces concepts such as superposition and entanglement. Superposition enables qubits to exist simultaneously in multiple states, which exponentially increases their computational capacity. Entanglement enables the instantaneous exchange of information between qubits, even when they are physically separated. These principles distinguish quantum computing from classical computing because they have the potential to solve computational challenges that are inaccessible to classical algorithms.

Quantum computing has a broad range of applications. It has the potential to revolutionize cryptography by breaching existing encryption algorithms and facilitating the creation of more secure systems. Quantum algorithms can provide faster and more efficient solutions in disciplines such as optimization, benefiting industries such as finance, logistics, and supply chain management. Quantum simulations have the potential to expedite drug discovery and advance disciplines such as materials science. In addition, the combination of quantum computation, ML, and AI can result in improved pattern recognition and data analysis capabilities. Quantum computing is poised to generate significant advances in digital transformation across multiple industries as a result of these potential applications.

5.17.1 Quantum Computing Technologies

Quantum computing technologies consist of a number of essential components for harnessing the computational potential of quantum mechanics. At the core of quantum computing are qubits, which differ from conventional bits in that they can reside in a superposition of states. Superconducting qubits, ion-trapped qubits, and topological qubits are among the various varieties being investigated, each with its own advantages and difficulties. These qubits serve as the fundamental building blocks of quantum computing, allowing for parallel processing and exponential computing capacity.

Quantum gates and circuits are employed to manipulate qubits and execute computations. Quantum gates, which are represented by unitary transformations, make it possible to manipulate qubit states. Instances include the Hadamard gate for generating superposition, the CNOT gate for entangling qubits, and the Toffoli gate for more complicated computations. In conjunction with classical operations, these gates form quantum circuits that execute particular algorithms. Quantum algorithms, such as Grover's algorithm and Shor's algorithm, take advantage of the unique properties of qubits, such as superposition and entanglement, to solve problems more effectively than classical algorithms. In certain domains, such as optimization and cryptography, these algorithms have the potential for exponential speedups.

While quantum computing technologies have made remarkable advancements, many obstacles remain. Assuring qubit coherence, which refers to preserving the fragile quantum states, continues to be a formidable challenge. Error correction techniques are also indispensable for mitigating the effects of noise and environmental interference on qubits. In addition, scalability is a crucial factor because quantum computers must manage an increasing number of qubits to solve increasingly complex problems. Despite these obstacles, quantum computing technologies continue to drive innovation and stretch the limits of what is possible in computation, paving the way for transformative applications in a variety of fields.

5.17.2 Digital Transformation and Quantum Computing

By revolutionizing problem-solving capabilities, quantum computing has the potential to fuel digital transformation across multiple industries. Quantum algorithms can provide solutions to optimization problems in finance, such as portfolio optimization, risk analysis, and option pricing, that are quicker and more accurate. Quantum simulations can speed up the process of drug discovery by predicting molecular interactions, identifying potential drug candidates, and optimizing molecular structures. This has the potential to revolutionize the pharmaceutical industry and spur the creation of novel treatments. In addition, quantum computing can optimize supply chain management and logistics by allowing businesses to make data-driven decisions based on complex variables and constraints, resulting in increased efficiency, decreased costs, and improved customer satisfaction.

Nonetheless, as with any emergent technology, the digital transformation process must address the risks and difficulties associated with quantum computing. Quantum security and cryptography represent one of the major dangers. Quantum computers are capable of breaking current encryption algorithms, posing a risk to data security. New quantum-resistant cryptographic techniques must be devised to mitigate this risk. Quantum error correction and noise reduction present an additional difficulty. Quantum systems are susceptible to errors and noise due to decoherence and environmental interference. Quantum computations require robust error correction techniques and noise reduction strategies to maintain their dependability and precision.

Scalability is another important obstacle in quantum computation. It is essential to increase the number of qubits and construct larger, more stable quantum systems in order to solve increasingly complex problems. In order to realize the full potential of quantum computing in digital transformation initiatives, it is vital to overcome hardware limitations and develop scalable quantum architectures.

Several methods exist for integrating quantum computing into digital transformation strategies effectively. Collaboration between quantum computing startups and established corporations can facilitate the exchange of knowledge, the formation of research partnerships, and the creation of quantum-powered solutions tailored to the requirements of specific industries. Quantum-inspired algorithms that utilize the principles of quantum computing can improve and optimize classical algorithms. Using the strengths of both paradigms, hybrid classical-quantum approaches can integrate classical and quantum computations to solve complex problems more efficiently. Furthermore, it is essential to invest in employee training and talent development. Education of the workforce on quantum principles, quantum algorithms, and potential applications pertinent to their positions will enable organizations to leverage quantum computing effectively.

5.18 RECYCLING

Recycling is the process of converting refuse materials into new products, with the goal of preventing their disposal as waste and reducing raw material consumption. It is essential for sustainable waste management and environmental preservation. Recycling helps conserve resources, reduce energy consumption, reduce pollution, and mitigate climate change by accumulating, sorting, processing, and transforming materials such as paper, plastic, glass, metal, and electronics.

Significant environmental challenges, such as land and water pollution, greenhouse gas emissions, and habitat devastation, are posed by waste production. The improper disposal of waste, particularly nonbiodegradable materials such as plastics, has become a global issue. Recycling addresses these problems by diverting waste from landfills, conserving energy, lowering greenhouse gas emissions, and conserving natural resources. It incorporates the concept of a circular economy, in which materials are reused and recycled, thereby minimizing the extraction of virgin resources and reducing waste.

Despite their significance, traditional recycling techniques encounter obstacles. These include inefficient waste collection systems, contamination of recyclables, low consumer awareness and participation, inadequate infrastructure for recycling particular materials, and high costs and energy needs. The recycling industry is embracing digital transformation in order to surmount these limitations and increase recycling efficiency.

Digital transformation in recycling aims to optimize waste management, improve trace-ability and transparency, engage consumers, and drive cost savings and resource optimization via innovative technologies such as IoT, big data analytics, blockchain, and AI.

5.18.1 Digital Transformation in Recycling

Diverse industries have been greatly impacted by digital transformation, allowing them to adapt to the evolving technological landscape. Several industries, including manufacturing, logistics, healthcare, and finance, have effectively incorporated digital technologies to improve efficiency, optimize processes, and deliver enhanced services. In a similar fashion, the recycling industry is undergoing a digital transformation in order to overcome traditional obstacles and unleash new opportunities.

In numerous ways, digital technologies are being applied to recycling. IoT and intelligent waste management systems are deployed initially. These systems employ networked sensors and devices to monitor waste levels, optimize collection routes, and effectively manage recycling receptacles. The collection and analysis of real-time data facilitates efficient waste management, reduces costs, and enhances resource allocation.

Second, big data analytics is indispensable for monitoring and optimizing waste management processes. Companies that recycle can analyze immense quantities of data concerning waste generation patterns, recycling rates, and supply chain dynamics. This data-driven strategy assists in optimizing collection, sorting, and processing processes, identifying areas for refinement, and making well-informed decisions to maximize recycling efficacy. In addition, blockchain technology is being utilized to ensure transparency and traceability in the recycling supply chain. Utilizing a decentralized and transparent platform, blockchain permits the monitoring and verification of the movement of recycled materials. This instills consumer and business confidence in the provenance and authenticity of recycled products.

Additionally, AI is used to automate the classification and processing of recyclable materials. Powered by AI, technologies such as ML and computer vision can precisely identify and separate various recyclables. This streamlines recycling facility operations, reduces the need for manual labor, and improves overall efficiency.

Mobile applications and online platforms are being developed to provide consumers with recycling information and opportunities for engagement. These digital platforms provide easily navigable and intuitive interfaces that enable users to access recycling information, locate recycling facilities, and partake in recycling initiatives. These platforms enable individuals to make sustainable decisions and contribute to the recycling ecosystem by fostering awareness, education, and participation. Table 5.6 illustrates how digital technologies are revolutionizing the recycling industry.

5.18.2 Benefits of Digital Transformation in Recycling

The digital transformation of recycling offers numerous advantages to both the industry and society. First, it improves waste management's efficacy and precision by refining

TABLE 5.6   Digital transformation in the recycling industry: Key applications and benefits

DIGITAL TECHNOLOGY	APPLICATION	BENEFITS	EXAMPLES
IoT	Smart waste management systems	• Efficient waste management	– Connected sensors monitoring waste levels
		• Optimize collection routes	– Real-time data analysis for resource allocation
		• Cost reduction	– Effective recycling bin management
Big Data Analytics	Tracking and optimizing waste management processes	• Data-driven decision-making	– Analyzing waste generation patterns
		• Identifying areas for improvement	– Optimizing collection, sorting, and processing
		• Maximizing recycling efficiency	– Understanding supply chain dynamics
Blockchain Technology	Ensuring traceability and transparency in the supply chain	• Tracking and verifying recycled materials' movement	– Decentralized and transparent platforms
		• Boosting consumer and business confidence	– Authenticating recycled products
AI	Automated sorting and processing of recyclable materials	• Streamlining recycling operations	– Machine learning for accurate identification
		• Reducing manual labor	– Computer vision for material separation
Mobile Applications	Providing recycling information and engagement	• Accessible and user-friendly interfaces	– Recycling information and facility locators
	opportunities to consumers	• Increasing awareness and education	– Participation in recycling initiatives
		• Empowering individuals to make sustainable choices	

processes, minimizing human error, and optimizing resource allocation. Real-time data and automation facilitate timely decision-making, which results in cost savings and enhanced waste management outcomes. Second, digital technologies enable the monitoring and optimization of recycling processes in real time. Through the use of sensor-enabled devices and data analytics, recycling operations can be closely monitored, yielding insights into equipment performance, material flows, and quality control. This data-driven strategy allows for preventative maintenance, process optimization, and continuous refinement, resulting in increased productivity and recycling rates.

Third, digital transformation enhances the recycling supply chain's traceability and transparency. Using blockchain technology, every transaction and material movement can be recorded, creating an immutable audit trail. This transparency fosters confidence among stakeholders, verifies the authenticity of recycled products, and increases recycling industry accountability. In addition, digital platforms and mobile applications increase consumer participation and awareness. These platforms provide users with information about recycling practices, recycling tips, participation incentives, and the ability to monitor their environmental impact. By promoting awareness and encouraging behavior modification, digital platforms increase consumer engagement and foster a recycling culture.

Through data-driven insights, digital transformation in recycling yields cost savings and resource optimization. Recycling companies can make informed decisions about resource allocation, pricing strategies, and investments by analyzing data on waste generation, recycling rates, and market trends. This results in more efficient resource utilization and cost-effective operations.

5.18.3 Challenges and Considerations

The digital transformation of the recycling industry presents its own unique set of obstacles and factors to consider. Priority should be given to data privacy and security concerns in order to safeguard sensitive information and maintain consumer trust. Risks must be mitigated with robust cybersecurity measures, explicit data governance policies, and regulatory compliance.

Equal access to affordable digital technologies in the recycling industry is a further obstacle. Due to cost constraints, smaller or less resource-rich recycling facilities may need help to implement digital solutions. The implementation of these technologies should be supported by efforts to provide affordable access to them. In addition, integrating and guaranteeing interoperability between various digital solutions is essential for developing a cohesive ecosystem that facilitates the exchange of data and communication between stakeholders. Training and upskilling programs are necessary to empower the workforce with the skills necessary to utilize digital tools effectively. Moreover, social and behavioral factors must be addressed to achieve the desired effect. To leverage the efficacy of digital transformation in the recycling industry, it is crucial to increase recycling participation through education, incentives, and awareness campaigns.

By addressing these challenges and factors through collaboration, investment, and the development of supportive policies and regulations, the recycling industry can successfully navigate digital transformation and realize the full potential of digital technologies for sustainable waste management and a circular economy.

5.19 SOFT COMPUTING

Soft computing is a subfield of AI that concentrates on creating computational models inspired by human intelligence in order to solve complex real-world issues. It incorporates a variety of methodologies and techniques for dealing with ambiguity, imprecision, and uncertainty. Soft computing approaches are designed to manage and process incomplete, uncertain, or noisy data, as opposed to traditional computing methods, which rely on precise mathematical models and algorithms.

Fuzzy logic, neural networks, evolutionary computation, probabilistic reasoning, and ML are all components of soft computing that are complementary to one another. Together, these components simulate human-like decision-making, learning, and adaptability.

Soft computing's primary objective is to provide robust and adaptable solutions for complex problems that need more well-defined mathematical models or strict principles. It acknowledges the uncertainty and imprecision inherent to many real-world domains and employs computational models that approximate human cognitive processes. By employing soft computing techniques, challenging tasks involving pattern recognition, optimization, prediction, classification, and decision-making in uncertain or complex environments can be accomplished.

Soft computing has become increasingly significant in the age of digital transformation. As organizations and industries adopt digital technologies and process immense amounts of data, there is a growing demand for intelligent systems capable of coping with uncertainty, adapting to changing conditions, and gleaning meaningful insights from data. Soft computing techniques play a vital role in addressing the challenges of digital transformation by facilitating adaptive and flexible decision-making, data-driven learning, the management of complex and nonlinear problems, and process optimization.

5.19.1 Role of Soft Computing in Digital Transformation

Soft computing plays a significant role in driving digital transformation by providing powerful tools and techniques to tackle the challenges posed by complex and uncertain environments. Here are some key roles of soft computing in the context of digital transformation:

- *Handling Uncertainty and Vagueness*: In digital transformation initiatives, there is often a high degree of uncertainty and vagueness in data and decision-making processes. Soft computing techniques, such as fuzzy logic, enable the representation and processing of uncertain and imprecise information.

This allows systems to handle incomplete or ambiguous data and make intelligent decisions in uncertain situations.

- *Learning from Data*: Data is at the core of digital transformation. Soft computing approaches, such as neural networks and ML, excel at extracting patterns, relationships, and insights from large and complex datasets. These techniques enable systems to learn from data, identify trends, and make data-driven decisions for optimization, prediction, and recommendation tasks.
- *Adaptive and Flexible Decision-Making*: Digital transformation often involves dynamic and changing environments. Soft computing techniques, including neural networks and evolutionary computation, support adaptive and flexible decision-making processes. These approaches can continuously learn and evolve based on feedback, enabling systems to adapt to new conditions, optimize performance, and improve decision accuracy over time.
- *Handling Complex and Nonlinear Problems*: Many real-world problems encountered in digital transformation initiatives are inherently complex and nonlinear, making them challenging for traditional computing approaches. Soft computing methods, such as neural networks and evolutionary computation, excel at handling complexity and nonlinearity. These techniques can model and solve intricate problems, such as optimization, pattern recognition, and prediction tasks, that are common in digital transformation scenarios.
- *Optimization and Pattern Recognition*: Digital transformation often aims to optimize processes, improve efficiency, and identify patterns for actionable insights. Soft computing techniques provide powerful optimization algorithms, evolutionary algorithms, and pattern recognition tools to achieve these goals. These methods can optimize complex systems, identify hidden patterns in data, and enable data-driven decision-making for enhanced efficiency and productivity.

5.19.2 Challenges and Future Directions

In the context of digital transformation, soft computing confronts a number of challenges and has promising future prospects. When developing and deploying soft computing models, addressing ethical considerations and ensuring transparency, fairness, accountability, and privacy are significant obstacles. Data privacy and security also present obstacles, necessitating robust mechanisms for protecting sensitive data and warding off cyber threats. Collaboration across disciplines is essential for the advancement of soft computing as it fosters the integration of knowledge and expertise from various domains. In addition, the integration of soft computing with emerging technologies like IoT and blockchain can result in the development of new applications and enhanced capabilities.

Explainability and interpretability of soft computing models are crucial for obtaining user confidence and comprehension of decision-making processes. The focus of research is on devising methods to interpret and explain the reasoning behind intricate models. Significant concerns include scalability and efficiency, necessitating the development of algorithms and architectures capable of handling large-scale datasets and real-time processing requirements. Another prospective direction is human–machine collaboration, which aims to augment human capabilities with soft computing techniques for enhanced decision-making and user experiences.

5.20 CONCLUSION

The enumerated emerging technologies represent a vast array of innovations that are reshaping numerous industries and sectors. These technologies have the potential to revolutionize our lives and redefine our interactions with the global community. Each technology offers unique opportunities, from 3D printing and advanced materials that enable customization and sustainable manufacturing to the transformative potential of AI, ML, and big data in automating processes and generating valuable insights. The introduction of 5G and 6G wireless communication paves the way for enhanced connectivity and the complete manifestation of the IoT. Cloud computing provides the infrastructure for processing vast amounts of data, while blockchain computing assures the safety of transactions. Distributed computing and interactive computing improve collaboration and scalability, whereas quantum computing and deep learning stretch the boundaries of computational power and intelligent systems. Together with recycling initiatives and soft computing techniques, these technologies have the potential to drive innovation, solve complex problems, and improve the quality of life for individuals and communities around the globe. As we embrace these technologies and chart a course toward a better future, it is crucial to consider their ethical, legal, and societal implications.

6 Organizational Culture/Change Management

6.1 THE ROLE OF PEOPLE IN DIGITAL TRANSFORMATION: EMPOWERING EMPLOYEES FOR SUCCESS

In the present era, digital transformation has become a crucial process that organizations need to go through since it gives them the ability to adapt and survive in a constantly changing digital world. It includes integrating digital technologies, redesigning corporate processes, and producing new value for stakeholders and customers. However, despite the focus on digital strategy and technology improvements, businesses frequently need to pay more attention to a critical element that can make or break their efforts to undergo a digital transformation: Their workforce. These are the people in charge of carrying out the digital transformation. The importance of employees in the process of digital transformation cannot be overstated. They are active participants and change agents on this route to transformation rather than passive observers. People need to be empowered and given the means to embrace and lead digital change if we are to succeed in the long run in the digital world in which we live.

In order for a digital transformation to be effective within an organization, people are essential. Although they are crucial enablers, technological advancements, and digital tools, an organization's people are ultimately in charge of leading and putting forth new projects. The workforce drives the demand for digital transformation and promotes it; they also act as change agents. They are able to overcome change opposition and organize the organization toward digital transformation because of their enthusiasm, vision, and capacity for inspiring others. To successfully implement a digital transformation, it is critical to consider the level of employee involvement and buy-in. Advocates for organizational change are employees who are actively involved in the process and dedicated to seeing it through to completion. Their excitement, creativity, and dedication have a big impact on the effectiveness of the implementation, and you

DOI: 10.1201/9781003471226-7

can instill in them a feeling of ownership and encourage them to share their ideas and expertise by incorporating them in the decision-making and planning processes.

Due to their significant subject matter expertise and abilities, employees are a priceless resource during the digital transformation process. They have a thorough awareness of market dynamics, consumer needs, and company practices. When employees are involved, firms can take advantage of their ideas, allowing them to pinpoint areas that need development, create solutions that are user-friendly, and guarantee alignment with company goals. Their involvement encourages creativity and helps to get better results.

Employees have a vital role in successful digital transformation since flexibility and adaptation are essential. Employees who feel empowered may quickly adopt new technology, test out radical concepts, and refine solutions in response to client feedback. Organizations need people who are open to change and have a growth mentality in order to effectively respond to digital disruption and sustain a competitive advantage in a constantly changing and increasing digital ecosystem. Employees contribute a customer-centric viewpoint to digital transformation, to sum up. They can better understand the wants, preferences, and trouble spots of the clients because they interact with them directly as frontline agents. Employers may gain priceless customer insights and make sure the digital transformation is in line with customer expectations by involving their staff in the design and implementation of digital initiatives. Employee involvement in the planning and execution of digital initiatives helps to achieve this. The drive driving the development of solutions that enhance the customer experience is the workers' customer-centric viewpoint.

6.1.1 The Role of Employees in Digital Transformation

Initiatives for digital transformation are driven and shaped in large part by employees. By recognizing the need for transformation and promoting its adoption inside the organization, they serve as change agents. They need to be actively involved and empowered if successful outcomes are to be attained.

6.1.1.1 Employees as agents of change in digital transformation

When it comes to accelerating and guiding digital transformation within firms, employees are essential change agents. They have special knowledge and skills that can significantly boost the success of digital projects. Here are some essential ways that staff members can contribute to and accelerate digital transformation (Figure 6.1):

Identifying Opportunities and Challenges: Employees are well-positioned to recognize possibilities and obstacles for digital transformation because they are at the center of everyday operations and consumer interactions. Their firsthand knowledge and observations might reveal problems, inadequacies, and new patterns that suggest possible areas for development. Encouragement of employee insight and idea sharing

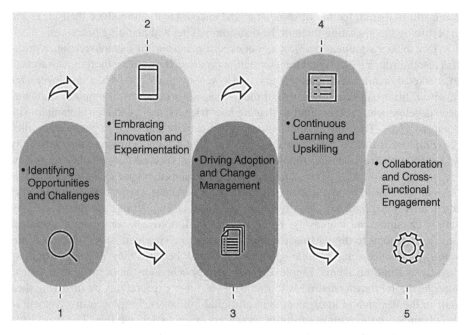

FIGURE 6.1   Employees in the digital transformation as change agents.

equips workers to offer their knowledge and aids businesses in identifying areas where digital technology can bring about good change.

- *Embracing Innovation and Experimentation*: Employees who have a sense of empowerment are more likely to embrace innovation and try out novel concepts and technology. They provide new viewpoints, question accepted standards, and put forth creative ideas. Companies may tap into their employees' creativity and passion for development by fostering an innovative culture and giving them platforms to test and experiment with new technology. Organizations may speed up the process of digital transformation by allowing staff to experiment with and apply novel ideas.
- *Driving Adoption and Change Management*: The adoption of digital tools, procedures, and cultural shifts is mostly driven by employees. They can act as advocates for digital transformation efforts, reducing resistance and serving as role models for their colleagues. Employee participation in the development and execution of digital transformation programs ensures their support and allows a more seamless transition. Employees can also assist their coworkers through the transformation process by sharing their knowledge, best practices, and lessons learned with them.
- *Continuous Learning and Upskilling*: New skills and abilities are frequently needed to adapt to the digital age. Employees can actively contribute to their own development by adopting upskilling and continual learning.

Organizations enable people to develop the skills necessary to thrive in the digital world by offering training opportunities and fostering a learning culture. Employees who possess the requisite skills and knowledge can become change agents within their teams and departments, promoting the adoption of cutting-edge procedures and digital technology.

* *Collaboration and Cross-Functional Engagement*: Successful digital transformation depends on cross-departmental and cross-functional collaboration. Employees can encourage cooperation by actively interacting with coworkers, exchanging best practices and knowledge, and looking for cross-functional alliances. Employees can develop integrated solutions that span several organizational domains by dismantling silos and fostering collaboration. By working together, they increase the effect of digital transformation and ensure a comprehensive and coordinated approach to organizational change.

6.1.1.2 Importance of employee engagement and buy-in

Employee engagement and buy-in have a strong correlation with the success of digital transformation initiatives. When employees participate in the process and receive support from their colleagues, they demonstrate commitment to the organization's digital transformation journey and a sense of ownership. Due to this commitment, output has increased, collaboration has improved, and there is a greater willingness to go above and beyond. Engaged employees are more likely to propose original ideas and participate in the creative process of digital transformation, both of which are advantageous to the organization. Engaged employees are more adaptable and flexible in the face of change, which are crucial characteristics in the context of digital transformation. They adopt new technologies, processes, and working methods with enthusiasm and a positive attitude. Employee engagement also fosters an environment conducive to collaboration and information exchange. Actively participate in cross-team and cross-hierarchy collaboration, sharing their knowledge, perceptions, and lessons learned. This collaboration expedites the adoption of digital tools and processes, thereby enhancing the efficacy and efficiency of the digital transformation process.

In addition, motivated employees place a significant emphasis on the customer. They are cognizant of the impact digital transformation has on their ability to provide exceptional consumer experiences. Engaged employees are more likely to seek out innovative digital solutions to increase customer satisfaction actively. Due to their commitment to placing the customer first, they have been able to successfully integrate digital technology into their business operations, which include direct client interaction, thereby increasing customer satisfaction and loyalty.

6.1.1.3 Leveraging employees' domain expertise

The domain expertise of employees needs to be utilized for a successful digital transformation. Employees with specific knowledge and experience relevant to digital efforts should be identified by organizations, and they should be included in decision-making processes. Organizations may develop successful digital transformation strategies and make informed decisions by utilizing their insightful perspectives and valuable insights. Leveraging employees' subject expertise requires collaboration and cross-functional teams to be effective. Organizations can use their combined knowledge to create novel solutions by bringing together people from various departments and fields of expertise. These teams are capable of handling difficulties, spotting opportunities, and designing and putting into action digital activities that support the goals of the company.

It is crucial to establish a culture of information sharing and ongoing education. Organizations should set up forums or communities of practice where staff members can exchange information about digital transformation-related expertise, experiences, and best practices. Organizations may improve employees' domain expertise and give them the skills they need to effectively drive digital transformation by promoting knowledge exchange and offering training and upskilling opportunities. Organizations may make informed decisions, encourage cooperation, and develop a culture of continuous learning by utilizing their employees' domain expertise. As a result, staff members are given more freedom to contribute their specialized knowledge and take an active role in determining the organization's digital destiny.

6.1.1.4 Employee empowerment and autonomy

Autonomy and employee empowerment are essential for a successful digital transition. Employees are encouraged to participate actively by being given ownership and accountability, which develops a sense of duty. Employees who are empowered take the initiative and work hard, which is what makes digital efforts successful. Employee empowerment also fosters an innovative and creative culture. Employees who are given autonomy are free to experiment with novel concepts and question accepted practices, which results in new insights and creative solutions that catalyze substantive change.

Employee empowerment also makes it possible for firms to be flexible and nimble. Employees who feel empowered can respond quickly to changing conditions and seize new possibilities by making decisions and taking actions. Their independence encourages adaptability and flexibility, which helps the company successfully manage the challenges of the digital revolution. Employee empowerment also promotes lifelong learning and personal development. Employees are encouraged to look for educational opportunities, develop their skills, and support their own professional growth. The organization's attempts to undergo digital transformation are benefited by the employees' increased capacity to adopt new technology and adjust to shifting market conditions.

Employee retention and happiness are also impacted by employee empowerment. Employees are more content in their work when they feel valued, trusted, and empowered. Employees who feel empowered at work are more loyal, engaged, and productive, all of which contribute to the long-term success of projects for digital transformation. Talented personnel retention guarantees continuity, knowledge retention, and a solid framework for future expansion. Organizations may unleash the full potential of their employees, foster a vibrant environment for digital transformation, and achieve effective results by embracing employee empowerment and offering autonomy.

6.1.2 Strategies for Empowering Employees in Digital Transformation

Initiatives for digital transformation success need to include employee empowerment. Organizations can unlock the potential of their workforce and create significant change by putting effective initiatives into place. Key tactics for empowering staff members during the digital transformation process are listed below.

6.1.2.1 Effective communication and change management

A successful digital transformation requires the ability to communicate and manage change effectively. Transparent communication is a need if you want to ensure that your staff is aware of the transition's purpose, objectives, and advantages. It aids in creating a shared understanding of the procedure, fosters trust, and lessens resistance. By actively considering their opinions and taking part in decision-making processes, stakeholders, including employees, can develop a sense of ownership and commitment. Using change management techniques, including providing clear communication of the change plan, training programs, and ongoing support, employees are helped in adapting to the change and managing the transition. When there are channels of communication that are open in both directions, employees may express their ideas, ask questions, and make comments, which promote collaboration and innovation. Periodically highlighting and praising progress accomplished along the way is necessary for boosting morale and maintaining momentum.

When organizations place a high priority on effective communication and change management, they create an environment where employees are informed, engaged, and inspired to embrace the digital revolution. Establishing a foundation of trust, openness, and cooperation makes sure that employees comprehend the change's purpose and are given the necessary training and support. Additionally, it builds a foundation of openness, collaboration, and trust. As a result, transitions are made more smoothly, employee engagement is increased, and the possibility that the digital transformation will provide positive results is increased.

6.1.2.2 Continuous learning and skill development

Continuous education and the expansion of one's skill set are crucial components of a successful digital transition. Continuous learning provides employees with the skills necessary to effectively accept new digital technologies, which is essential for organizations that wish to keep pace with the rapid pace of technological innovation. Organizations may empower their employees to take control of their professional development and drive innovation and creativity by cultivating a culture of learning and giving employees the tools they need to do so. Continuous education helps employees future-proof their careers by educating them about changing job responsibilities and assisting them in maintaining relevance in the digital world. This, in turn, future-proofs the workforce.

Increasing employee engagement and retention is a benefit of investing in initiatives that promote continuous learning. The importance that an employer has on the personal and professional development of their workforce can be inferred from the availability of training and advancement opportunities. Employees who are engaged in their work are more likely to make active contributions to the digital transformation journey, which ultimately leads to greater results. Additionally, continual learning raises levels of employee satisfaction while simultaneously lowering turnover rates. This results in the creation of a workforce that is devoted to the organization and enthusiastic about its digital transformation efforts.

6.1.2.3 Creating a supportive and inclusive culture

It is essential to have a supportive and inclusive culture for a digital transition to be effective. This kind of culture fosters psychological safety, allowing staff members to take risks and freely express their ideas without being concerned about being scrutinized. It capitalizes on the advantages of diversity by encouraging collaboration and teamwork across a variety of departments and professional backgrounds to enhance cooperative problem-solving. A supportive culture also emphasizes learning and development opportunities, giving staff members the digital skills they require and demonstrating the company's dedication to their ongoing professional growth.

An inclusive culture also values diversity and acknowledges the value of the contributions made by people from different backgrounds, which fosters innovation and adaptability. It ensures that digital transformation initiatives are inclusive of all parties and reflect the needs of several consumer bases. By creating cultures that are encouraging and inclusive of all employees, organizations may create an environment where workers are motivated to innovate, collaborate, and contribute to the digital transformation process to the best of their abilities, ultimately driving the success of the company.

6.1.3 Case Studies and Examples

To better illustrate why it is crucial to provide employees agency during the digital transformation process, let us look at a few case studies and examples from the real world. These case studies illustrate the benefits of employee empowerment in digital transformation. By nurturing a culture of innovation, providing resources for experimentation, and promoting continuous learning, organizations can unlock the potential of their employees and facilitate successful digital transformations. When employees are empowered and given the autonomy to contribute their ideas and talents, they become catalysts for innovation and change, ultimately driving the digital success of the organization. Table 6.1 presents case studies and their corresponding benefits that highlight the importance of employee empowerment during the digital transformation process.

TABLE 6.1 Case studies and benefits of employee empowerment in digital transformation

CASE STUDY	DESCRIPTION	BENEFITS	KEY TAKEAWAY
Microsoft's Cultural Transformation	Nurtured a growth mindset and encouraged experimentation. Hackathons led to profitable products like Microsoft Teams. Established Microsoft as a market leader in cloud computing.	Creation of profitable products	Empowering employees drives digital success.
Adobe's Employee-Led Innovation	Kickbox program empowers employees with tools, resources, and funding for innovative ideas. Fostered an innovative culture and led to successful initiatives.	Fostered an innovative culture	Providing resources and autonomy fuels innovation.
General Electric's Digital Learning Platform	The BrilliantYOU platform provides individualized learning opportunities for new digital skills. Equipped workforce for digital transformation.	Empowered employees with new skills	Continuous learning supports digital proficiency.
DBS Bank's Digital Culture	Encouraged entrepreneurial mindset and led digital initiatives. Innovation centers and labs fostered collaboration and developed customer solutions.	Fostered entrepreneurial mindset	Embracing digital culture drives innovation.

6.1.4 Overcoming Challenges and Mitigating Risks in Employee Empowerment for Digital Transformation

Empowering people can provide a number of challenges and hazards when it comes to digital transformation. However, by employing effective strategies, businesses are able to overcome these obstacles. Some of the most serious issues and potential solutions are listed here:

- *Resistance to Change*: Some employees may resist digital transformation due to fear or unfamiliarity. To mitigate this, organizations should communicate the benefits of transformation, address concerns, and provide training and support to build employees' digital literacy. Involving employees in decision-making and sharing success stories of digital adopters can also alleviate resistance.

- *Skill Gaps and Training Needs*: Employees may need more skills for digital transformation. Identifying skill gaps and providing targeted training programs are crucial. Organizations should offer a mix of internal and external training, encourage continuous learning, and provide opportunities for upskilling and reskilling to ensure employees acquire the necessary competencies.
- *Organizational Silos and Lack of Collaboration*: Silos and a lack of collaboration hinder digital transformation. To mitigate this, organizations should foster a culture of collaboration through cross-functional teams, knowledge sharing, and communication platforms. Breaking down silos, encouraging open channels, and recognizing collaborative efforts will promote teamwork and collective success.
- *Limited Resources and Budget Constraints*: Limited resources and budget constraints pose challenges. Organizations should prioritize and allocate resources effectively by identifying areas with the most significant impact. Seeking creative solutions, such as leveraging internal expertise or exploring low-cost training options, can help overcome budget limitations. Demonstrating the value and ROI of employee empowerment initiatives will also secure additional resources.
- *Leadership Support and Alignment*: Lack of leadership support or misalignment can impede employee empowerment efforts. Mitigation strategies involve gaining leadership buy-in through clear communication of benefits, engaging leaders in decision-making, and regularly updating them on progress. Ensuring leaders exhibit desired behaviors and actively support and promote empowerment initiatives strengthens alignment.

6.2 ORGANIZATIONAL CULTURE: CREATING A CULTURE OF INNOVATION AND CHANGE

In today's rapidly changing business environment, firms need to constantly innovate and adapt in order to maintain their market leadership positions. A company's culture is an essential factor that has the potential to foster innovation and facilitate successful change. The organizational culture is comprised of the values, beliefs, behaviors, and standards that determine how individuals within an organization think and conduct. Organizations need to establish a culture of innovation and change in order to embrace new ideas, experiment with different techniques, and successfully navigate the complexity of a rapidly changing digital landscape. Within the context of this discussion, digital transformation is a crucial element in the function of innovation and change catalyst. The proliferation of digital technology affords these advantages: New opportunities, disruption of existing business models, and the ability to enhance products, services, and processes.

6.2.1 Importance of Organizational Culture in Driving Innovation and Change

When it comes to generating innovation and facilitating successful transformation inside an organization, organizational culture plays a significant and critical role. In this context, it is crucial to have a strong organizational culture for a number of reasons, which are listed below:

- *Encourages Risk-Taking and Experimentation*: A strong culture that values innovation creates an environment where employees feel empowered to take risks and explore new ideas. It encourages experimentation and provides a safety net for failure, fostering a mindset that sees failures as learning opportunities rather than setbacks. This willingness to take risks is crucial for driving innovation and embracing change.
- *Fosters Open Communication and Collaboration*: A culture that promotes open communication and collaboration enables the free flow of ideas and knowledge sharing. When employees feel comfortable expressing their opinions and perspectives, it leads to diverse insights and creative problem-solving. Collaboration across different teams and departments facilitates cross-pollination of ideas and sparks innovation through interdisciplinary approaches.
- *Supports Continuous Learning and Adaptability*: A culture of innovation values continuous learning and encourages employees to expand their knowledge and skills. This emphasis on personal and professional development helps individuals stay up-to-date with emerging trends and technologies, making them more adaptable to change. When employees are continuously learning, they can identify opportunities for improvement and drive innovation within their roles.
- *Aligns with Vision and Strategy*: Organizational culture acts as a unifying force that aligns employees with the organization's vision and strategic objectives. When innovation and change are embedded in the culture, employees understand their role in driving these initiatives. They actively contribute to achieving the organization's goals by embracing new technologies, processes, and ideas that support the strategic direction.
- *Attracts and Retains Top Talent*: A culture of innovation and change appeals to top talent who are seeking dynamic and forward-thinking organizations. When companies prioritize innovation in their culture, they become magnets for creative and ambitious individuals who are eager to contribute and make a difference. Moreover, such a culture helps retain employees by fostering a sense of purpose and engagement.
- *Enhances Customer Focus*: A culture of innovation and change encourages organizations to be customer-centric. By continuously seeking ways to improve products, services, and experiences, organizations can better meet the evolving needs and expectations of their customers. This customer focus is instrumental in driving innovation and ensuring that change efforts are aimed at delivering value and maintaining a competitive edge.

6.2.2 Focus on Digital Transformation as a Catalyst for Innovation and Change

The digital transformation of a business serves as a catalyst for new concepts and methods of operation within that business. It causes existing business models, industries, and marketplaces to become unstable, thereby creating new opportunities for value creation. The adoption of digital technologies permits businesses to reinvent their products, services, and procedures, thereby accelerating the rate of innovation. Agile methods, rapid prototyping, and collaborative platforms allow for the rapid testing and improvement of ideas, which reduces the time required to bring innovative products to market.

Moreover, digital transformation enhances the overall quality of the client experience through the use of various technologies, such as mobile apps, individualized websites, and AI-driven analytics. Organizations gain profound insights into the preferences and behaviors of their consumers, enabling them to create personalized customer experiences that exceed their expectations. The collection and analysis of vast quantities of data opens the door to another possibility: Data-driven decision-making. The insights provided by advanced analytics, ML, and AI guide efforts toward innovation and make it simpler to make decisions based on accurate data.

In addition to these advantages, digital transformation enables businesses to become more adaptive and flexible. The combination of flexible infrastructure, cloud computing, and virtual collaboration tools enables businesses to respond quickly to altering market conditions, evolving client expectations, and emerging trends. This contributes to the development of a culture of continuous development and innovation within an organization, one in which people view change as an opportunity for advancement. A further essential aspect of digital transformation is granting employees greater autonomy. By providing their employees with the knowledge, tools, and resources necessary for innovation, organizations can unlock the complete potential of their workforce. Digital platforms and automation contribute to the optimization of workflows and the improvement of communication, which in turn encourage cross-functional collaboration and the sharing of knowledge. Table 6.2 serves as a useful reference to understand and communicate the various ways in which digital transformation can bring about positive changes and value creation within a business across different areas.

6.2.3 Organizational Culture

The values, beliefs, attitudes, behaviors, and standards that are held consistently throughout an organization are referred to as its organizational culture. This culture plays a significant role in determining the collective identity and personality of an organization. It takes into account the unspoken norms and social dynamics that govern how individuals interact with one another and cooperate with one another within the company. Some of the elements that make up an organization's culture are as follows (Figure 6.2):

- *Values*: Core principles and beliefs that guide decision-making and behaviors. They reflect what the organization deems important and serve as a compass for actions.

TABLE 6.2   Benefits of digital transformation in business

ASPECT	BENEFITS	EXAMPLES
Impact on Business	– New opportunities – Reinvention – Accelerated innovation	Disruptive business models, new revenue streams, and digital marketplaces
Customer Experience	– Improved experience – Personalization – Informed decision-making	Mobile apps with personalized recommendations, AI-driven chatbots, and customized websites
Adaptability and Flexibility	– Adaptability – Empowered employees – Continuous development	Cloud-based infrastructure, virtual collaboration tools, and employee empowerment programs
Workflow Optimization	– Streamlined workflows – Enhanced communication – Knowledge sharing	Project management software, workflow automation tools, collaborative knowledge-sharing platforms

- *Beliefs*: Assumptions and convictions held by individuals within the organization influence their perceptions and actions.
- *Norms*: Established patterns of behavior and unwritten rules that govern how things are done within the organization.
- *Rituals and Symbols*: Formal and informal practices, ceremonies, and symbols that reinforce the organization's values and traditions.
- *Language and Communication*: The way people communicate and the shared vocabulary within the organization, including jargon and common expressions.

6.2.4 The Role of Values, Beliefs, and Norms in Shaping Culture

The organizational culture of an organization is formed in large part by the values, beliefs, and standards held by its members. To act as a set of guiding principles that establish expectations for conduct and decision-making, values are extremely important. They create a sense of purpose and direction, which contributes to the formation of the organization's overall identity as a whole. On the other side, individuals' beliefs influence how they see and interpret events, which in turn affects their attitudes and behaviors within the organization. Beliefs can be influenced by both conscious and unconscious processes. A culture that welcomes change and actively seeks out opportunities for experimenting is fostered by the cultivation of positive beliefs, such as firm faith in the value of innovation and ongoing progress. The interactions that take place within an organization are governed by the norms, which are the recognized patterns of behavior and the unwritten laws that regulate them. They shape the culture of the organization as a whole and determine what is deemed to be acceptable. Organizations can foster an environment that is receptive to innovation and change if they encourage open communication and collaboration among their employees, among other desired practices [1].

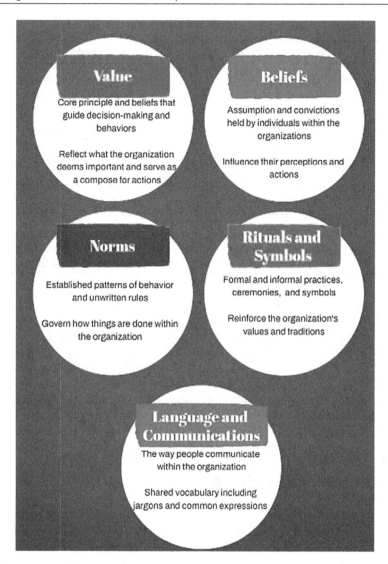

FIGURE 6.2   Elements of organizational culture.

When the aims and strategic objectives of an organization are linked with the values, beliefs, and norms of the organization, this shapes a culture that is supportive of innovation, adaptability, and effective change. Culture can be actively shaped by organizations by defining and reinforcing desired values, encouraging the adoption of good attitudes, and developing norms that support behaviors that organizations want to see more of in their employees. Leaders are able to establish a culture that encourages cooperation, is open to change, and stimulates creativity if they consciously bring these aspects into alignment with the vision of the firm. Because of this culture, employees are encouraged to take risks, offer their ideas, and work toward the general growth and success of the firm. In the end, it is necessary to drive innovation and change to have a robust organizational culture that is founded on the foundation of values, beliefs, and norms. This is especially true in the context of digital transformation.

6.2.5 Types of Organizational Cultures

The culture of an organization can take on many different manifestations, each of which has its own set of features as well as its own influence on innovation and change. The following are the four most typical forms of corporate culture. Table 6.3 provides a concise overview of different corporate cultures and their impact on innovation and change within an organization.

(A) **Hierarchical Culture**
   - *Characteristics*: In a hierarchical culture, there is a strong emphasis on structure, rules, and formal authority. Decision-making authority is centralized, typically resting with top-level management. Communication flows predominantly from the top to the bottom.

TABLE 6.3 Corporate culture and its impact on innovation and change

CORPORATE CULTURE	CHARACTERISTICS	IMPACT ON INNOVATION AND CHANGE
Hierarchical Culture	Emphasizes structure, rules, and formal authority: Centralized decision-making and top-down communication.	Less conducive to innovation and change. Rigid and resistant to deviations. Slow decision-making inhibits agility and adaptation.
Collaborative Culture	Values teamwork, cooperation, and open communication. Encourages inclusivity and shared decision-making.	Promotes innovation and change. Fosters a collaborative environment where diverse perspectives are valued. Enables knowledge sharing and creative problem-solving. Facilitates the adoption of new approaches.
Agile Culture	Prioritizes flexibility, adaptability, and quick decision-making. Embraces experimentation, risk-taking, and continuous improvement.	Thrives on innovation and change. Encourages employees to experiment, learn from failures, and adapt quickly. Agile methodologies enable rapid iteration and adjustment. It helps organizations respond to emerging opportunities and challenges.
Innovative Culture	Values creativity, exploration, and challenging the status quo. Fosters curiosity and continuous learning. Embraces calculated risks and new ideas.	Highly conducive to innovation and change. Empowers employees to think creatively and experiment. Encourages a growth mindset that embraces change as an opportunity for improvement and progress.

- *Impact on Innovation and Change*: This culture may be less conducive to innovation and change as it can be rigid and resistant to deviations from established protocols. Decision-making can be slow and bureaucratic, inhibiting agility and adaptation.

(B) **Collaborative Culture**
- *Characteristics*: A collaborative culture values teamwork, cooperation, and open communication. There is a strong emphasis on inclusivity and shared decision-making. Collaboration across teams and departments is encouraged.
- *Impact on Innovation and Change*: This culture promotes innovation and change by fostering a collaborative environment where diverse perspectives are valued. It enables knowledge sharing, creative problem-solving, and cross-pollination of ideas, facilitating the adoption of new approaches and initiatives.

(C) **Agile Culture**
- *Characteristics*: An agile culture places a premium on flexibility, adaptability, and quick decision-making. It embraces experimentation, risk-taking, and continuous improvement. Feedback loops and iterative processes are common.
- *Impact on Innovation and Change*: This culture thrives on innovation and change. It encourages employees to experiment with new ideas and approaches, learn from failures, and adapt quickly. Agile methodologies facilitate rapid iteration and adjustment, enabling organizations to respond to emerging opportunities and challenges.

(D) **Innovative Culture**
- *Characteristics*: An innovative culture values creativity, exploration, and a willingness to challenge the status quo. It encourages a mindset that fosters curiosity and continuous learning. Taking calculated risks and embracing new ideas are celebrated.
- *Impact on Innovation and Change*: This culture is highly conducive to innovation and change. It cultivates an environment where employees feel empowered to think creatively, experiment with new concepts, and push boundaries. It encourages a growth mindset that embraces change as an opportunity for improvement and progress.

6.2.6 Creating a Culture of Innovation

Developing a culture of innovation requires a commitment from leadership, fostering collaboration and cross-functional communication, recognizing and rewarding innovation, encouraging curiosity and exploration, cultivating an entrepreneurial mindset, cultivating external partnerships, measuring and monitoring innovation progress, and providing resources and support. Organizations may develop a culture that encourages and fosters innovation by integrating these aspects into their organizational structures. This gives them the ability to adapt to changing circumstances, discover new possibilities, and generate sustainable growth in this era of digital transformation.

6.2.6.1 Leadership's role in fostering innovation

When it comes to encouraging innovation inside a business, leadership is one of the most important factors. Leaders who are effective articulate a coherent vision for their organizations, one that places emphasis on the significance of innovation and is in line with the long-term objectives of the business. They cultivate an atmosphere of trust and encouragement for workers, giving them the confidence to contribute ideas, try new things, and take risks. Leaders make it possible for innovation to thrive by removing obstacles and making available the resources that are necessary. They also encourage collaboration by fostering teamwork and exchange of knowledge, as well as by stimulating the intersection of a variety of perspectives and igniting fresh ideas.

In addition, leaders inspire their followers to take risks and regard setbacks as opportunities to gain vital insight. They develop a culture that is open to trying new things and improving upon existing ones. One further essential part of leadership is making sure that innovation is acknowledged and rewarded. Innovative efforts are recognized and celebrated by leaders, who also build recognition and incentive systems to encourage innovative thinking and behavior among their followers. The best way for leaders to demonstrate their dedication to innovation, risk-taking, accepting new ideas, and advocating change is to set an example for others to follow.

Additionally, leaders are responsible for providing individuals and teams working on innovation initiatives with coaching, mentoring, and support services. They encourage professional development, skill-building, and being informed about emerging trends, all of which contribute to the culture of continuous learning that they cultivate. Employees are inspired to think creatively, take chances, and generate significant change as a direct result of their actions because they build an environment that promotes and nurtures innovation. In the end, strong leadership creates the conditions for a flourishing culture of innovation, which positions the company for success in the rapidly changing terrain of digital transformation.

6.2.6.2 Establishing a supportive infrastructure

The establishment of an infrastructure that fosters innovation and change necessitates the incorporation of a number of crucial elements. Initially, businesses and other organizations should reserve certain resources, such as financial and human capital, for innovation-related endeavors only. This ensures that inventive endeavors receive the necessary support to flourish. Second, the implementation of distinct procedures and frameworks for innovation streamlines the innovation process and enables the execution of activities in a methodical and efficient manner. Innovation management systems or platforms enable the tracking of progress, evaluation of ideas, and accumulation of insights. In addition, fostering a culture of cross-functional collaboration helps break down divisions, encourages information sharing, and brings together a variety of perspectives, which are all essential to the innovation process.

It is crucial to make the workplace as flexible as feasible. Employees have the opportunity to investigate and test out new concepts when they have the discretion and autonomy to determine their work procedures and schedules. The adoption of digital collaboration tools and remote work expands the boundaries of innovation beyond their previous physical limitations. Additionally, open communication channels play an essential role in fostering an open and inclusive dialogue throughout the organization. By encouraging employees at all levels to express their ideas and by creating forums for the sharing of ideas and for receiving feedback on those ideas, organizations can gain access to a vast array of perspectives and insights.

There should be a strong emphasis on ongoing learning and development within the organization. When training programs, seminars, and other learning materials are made available to employees, they have the opportunity to develop their skills and stay abreast of evolving trends and technology. Through these investments in education, individuals are able to contribute novel concepts and strategies to ongoing innovation initiatives. In addition, businesses need to develop metrics for measuring performance and evaluation criteria that align with their innovation objectives. When innovation initiatives are routinely reviewed and evaluated, they pave the way for feedback and modifications, both of which contribute to continuous development. In conclusion, the implementation of recognition and incentive programs acknowledges and celebrates innovative contributions, thereby fostering a culture that respects and values innovative thought and accomplishments.

6.2.6.3 Nurturing a growth mindset

An organization needs to foster a learning culture that values resilience and continual improvement in order to foster a growth mentality. This can be accomplished by creating a friendly environment that motivates staff to take on new tasks, perceive failures as teaching moments, and ask for feedback. It is important to highlight effort and perseverance and to reward and recognize those who show commitment and a readiness to take on new challenges. Employees who are encouraged to take calculated risks and be innovative are more likely to adopt a growth mindset because they are more accepting of the learning process and understand that setbacks are stepping stones to success.

Fostering a growth mentality also requires encouraging collaboration, offering mentorship, and setting an excellent example. Employees work in collaborative settings where they are exposed to various viewpoints and where mentorship and support networks offer direction and inspiration. Leaders are essential in promoting a growth mindset and sharing their own personal stories of development and learning. A growth attitude is important, and recognizing and rewarding individual and team growth encourages others to embrace lifelong learning and personal development. Organizations may enable their staff to adapt, innovate, and succeed in the dynamic world of digital transformation by encouraging a growth mindset.

6.2.7 Driving Change through Digital Transformation

The digital transformation of businesses is essential to the acceleration of innovation and transformation within those businesses. It is necessary to maximize the power of digital technologies in order to profoundly transform business processes, company operations, and consumer experiences. Businesses need to first articulate the need for digital transformation by describing its benefits and competitive advantages while addressing any concerns and resistance to change. Only then can businesses anticipate driving change successfully through digital transformation. It is essential to develop digital capabilities, which requires determining the organization's current level of digital maturity, investing in the appropriate infrastructure and technology, and cultivating the necessary digital skills and competencies. In addition, effective change management techniques should be implemented, with active stakeholder participation and transformation process management. The adoption of digital transformation by businesses paves the way for innovation and flexibility in an ever-changing business environment.

6.2.7.1 Understanding the role of digital transformation

The use of digital technologies to alter numerous aspects of an organization's operations and strategies is one of the most crucial roles that digital transformation performs in contemporary businesses. It entails adopting and integrating digital technologies, processes, and perspectives throughout the entire organization in order to promote innovation, enhance efficiency, and create exceptional customer experiences. Implementing digital transformation within an organization facilitates the simplification of workflows, the automation of tasks, and the optimization of operations, which all contribute to increased productivity and cost reductions. In addition, it facilitates data-driven decision-making by providing users with access to real-time insights and analytics. In addition to increasing consumer engagement and satisfaction, digital transformation increases consumer engagement by providing customized experiences, consistent interactions across multiple channels, and innovative digital products and services. In conclusion, digital transformation enables businesses to remain competitive, adaptable, and responsive in an ever-changing digital landscape.

6.2.7.2 Communicating the need for digital transformation

To successfully effect organizational change, it is essential to communicate the imperative of digital transformation in an effective manner. The initial step for businesses is to identify the advantages of digital transformation for their operations, such as enhanced operational efficiency, enhanced consumer experiences, data-driven decision-making, and increased competitiveness. If these benefits are enumerated in a clear and concise manner, stakeholders will be able to understand the value of embracing digital transformation and how it aligns with business objectives. Second, addressing concerns and difficulties is one of the most crucial things you can do to reduce resistance to change. Organizations should identify potential concerns, such as job security or disruption of established processes, and provide reassurance by describing how digital transformation can create new opportunities, enhance operations, and enhance employee skills. In addition, organizations should elucidate the impact of digital transformation on job security. Organizations are able to cultivate a supportive environment and build stakeholder trust if they manage problems with transparency and candor.

The most effective method for organizations to engage stakeholders is to include them in their digital transformation voyage. This includes not only CEOs and administrators but also employees and external partners or clients. Firms can gain the support of stakeholders and ensure a more seamless transition by soliciting their feedback, responding to the questions they pose, and incorporating their insights into their digital transformation strategy. Sharing success stories of digital transformation initiatives, both from within the organization and from industries comparable to the target industry, can inspire stakeholders and demonstrate the positive outcomes that are possible.

6.2.7.3 Building digital capabilities

Successful digital transformation within enterprises depends on the development of digital competencies. To start, it is critical to evaluate the organization's present degree of digital maturity in order to pinpoint its strengths, flaws, and potential improvement areas. This evaluation serves as a basis for establishing reasonable objectives and tracking development over the course of the transformation process. Investments in digital infrastructure and technologies are also essential. This entails refining cybersecurity protocols, implementing cloud-based solutions, upgrading hardware and software systems, and investigating cutting-edge technologies like AI and IoT. Organizations can set the stage for successful digital transformation by strategically investing in the appropriate digital tools and infrastructure.

Second, businesses need to concentrate on enhancing staff members' digital competencies and skills. This can be done through partnering with educational institutions or industry professionals or by using training programs, workshops, certifications, or other methods. Organizations may guarantee that their employees have the skills and knowledge necessary to successfully traverse the digital world by upskilling their staff in fields like data analytics, digital marketing, user experience design, and agile project management. It is also essential to promote a digital-first mindset. This entails encouraging an eagerness to accept new technology, fostering experimentation, and rewarding digital endeavors. Organizations can promote continual development and a readiness to accept change by fostering a culture that values digital innovation.

To improve their digital capabilities, organizations should look for partnerships and collaborations. They can have access to specialist information, keep up with market trends, and promote innovation by working with outside organizations, startups, or digital professionals. The sharing of ideas, best practices, and access to cutting-edge technologies are all made possible via partnerships. They make it possible for businesses to maintain their competitiveness, agility, and leadership in digital innovation. Building collaborative networks enables firms to utilize outside expertise to supplement internal capabilities and quicken the process of digital transformation.

6.2.7.4 Managing change during digital transformation

For a digital transformation to be successful, change management is crucial. Organizations should first create a thorough change management strategy and plan that defines goals, deadlines, and routes for communication. This plan provides a structured approach and acts as a roadmap for the transformation process. It is essential to involve stakeholders at all levels since their support and engagement are essential for overcoming change resistance. Organizations may increase commitment and promote a feeling of ownership among employees by addressing the concerns of stakeholders and clearly communicating the justification and advantages of digital transformation.

Companies should offer employees the assistance and training they need to prepare for the changes brought about by digital technology. This involves technical training on new platforms and tools as well as soft skill development to encourage collaboration and a digital mentality. To aid staff members through the shift, ongoing support through helplines, user manuals, and mentoring programs is essential. It is critical to track the transformation's progress to find areas that need corrections or enhancements. Organizations are able to make educated judgments and modify the transformation process as necessary by collecting input from stakeholders, including employees, customers, and clients. Finally, acknowledging accomplishments and contributions is essential to managing change. To foster an environment that is encouraging and uplifting, milestones and accomplishments should be recognized and appreciated. Employee commitment is strengthened and motivated to keep embracing the shift when they are recognized for their contributions, original ideas, and efforts. Organizations may sustain engagement and passion throughout the digital transformation journey by developing a culture of appreciation and acknowledgment.

6.2.8 Sustaining the Culture of Innovation and Change

For a business to be successful in the long run, it is essential to maintain a culture of innovation and change. A culture of continuous improvement and adaptation, learning from successful initiatives, employee empowerment, and the promotion of diversity and inclusion are all necessary for leaders to achieve this. Innovation needs to be ingrained in the company's DNA. Performance management and awards need also to be aligned with innovation. Organizations can create an environment that welcomes change and fosters innovation by embedding innovation as a core value, recognizing and rewarding innovative contributions, encouraging continuous learning and improvement, documenting best practices, empowering employees to take ownership, and fostering a diverse and inclusive environment. Organizations are able to maintain their competitiveness, grasp opportunities, and successfully manage the changing digital landscape because of this persistent culture of innovation and transformation.

6.2.8.1 Embedding innovation and change in the organization's DNA

A culture of continual development and adaptability can only exist with innovation and change being ingrained in the very fabric of the organization. It starts out by making innovation a core value and strategic goal. Leaders are required to convey its importance and incorporate it into the company's purpose, vision, and values. Innovation's relevance is further emphasized by integrating performance management and rewards with it. This results in clear expectations, performance evaluation, and recognition of innovative efforts. Organizations may tap into their employees' collective intellect and establish a secure environment for innovation by encouraging collaboration, idea sharing, and employee ownership.

In order to integrate innovation and change, it is essential to promote a culture of lifelong learning and professional growth. By giving staff members chances to learn and develop through workshops, mentorship, and training, you can keep them informed about new trends and create a culture that welcomes change. Sharing the organization's dedication to innovation, success stories, and the effects of creative efforts all depend heavily on effective communication channels. Transparent communication channels make it easier for ideas and information to circulate throughout the company, fostering a culture of change and innovation.

Innovation and change can be a driving force for growth, competitiveness, and long-term success when they are ingrained in an organization's DNA [2]. It takes teamwork, with leadership setting the tone and offering assistance and staff members embracing an innovative and adaptable approach. Innovation becomes the standard when it is established in an organization's culture, enabling continual development and adaptation in a constantly changing digital environment. Organizations provide the groundwork for long-term success in a world that is changing quickly by creating an atmosphere where innovation is recognized and fostered.

6.2.8.2 Continuous improvement and adaptation

Particularly in the context of digital transformation, continuous improvement and adaptability are essential components in establishing and maintaining an organizational culture of innovation and change. Continued improvement-focused organizations are aware that the path to innovation is a continual process rather than a single event. They are aware that in order to stay competitive in a corporate environment that is constantly changing, they need to adapt, hone, and evolve their strategies, processes, and technology.

A component of continuous improvement is reviewing and revising digital tactics and technology on a regular basis. New platforms, tools, and approaches are constantly emerging in the digital era. Organizations need to proactively evaluate their current digital infrastructure, applications, and systems to find opportunities for innovation and improvement if they want to stay competitive. This can entail utilizing cutting-edge technologies like AI, ML, or blockchain to streamline processes, improve consumer experiences, or inspire the development of new business models.

Organizations need also to promote a culture of learning and feedback both internally and externally. All staff should be encouraged to offer feedback and suggestions for improvement. Regular polls, feedback sessions, or designated methods for idea submission could help with this. Frontline workers frequently have insightful knowledge of client demands, problems, and potential for innovation. Organizations can tap into a multitude of ideas and effect significant change by fostering an environment that values and encourages their contribution.

Customer feedback is equally crucial to the process of ongoing improvement. Organizations can match their offers to market demands by listening to customers, comprehending their shifting preferences, and implementing their feedback into product and service development. Organizations can gather insights that spark innovation and direct iterative changes by using methods like user testing, customer interviews, and data analysis. By focusing on the needs of the client, businesses may remain competitive and relevant.

Organizations need to set up systems for tracking and evaluating progress in order to undertake continuous improvement and adaptation efficiently. The performance of innovation projects can be measured quantitatively using KPIs that are in line with strategic goals. Organizations can use regular review sessions and data-driven research to pinpoint areas that require alterations, allowing them to decide where to concentrate resources and spur further advancements.

6.2.8.3 Learning from successful innovation and change initiatives

When it comes to developing and maintaining a culture of innovation inside a company, one of the most important aspects is learning from previous innovation and change projects that have been successful. Organizations are able to duplicate previous accomplishments, build upon those successes, and continuously enhance their innovation and change processes if they have a solid grasp of what worked effectively in previous initiatives. When drawing lessons from instances of successful innovation and change initiatives, the following are some important considerations to keep in mind:

(A) *Documenting and Sharing Best Practices*: When a successful innovation or change initiative takes place, it is essential to document the process, strategies, and key factors that contributed to its success. This documentation serves as a valuable resource for future initiatives and helps avoid reinventing the wheel. Best practices should be clearly articulated, including the specific steps, methods, and approaches that led to successful outcomes.

(B) *Lessons Learned Analysis*: Conducting a thorough analysis of successful initiatives can provide valuable insights into what worked, what did not, and what could be improved in future endeavors. This analysis involves identifying both the positive aspects and any challenges faced during the initiative. It is essential to assess the impact on the organization, the stakeholders involved, and the overall outcomes achieved. By examining the lessons learned, organizations can extract valuable knowledge and make informed decisions for future innovation and change efforts.

(C) *Continuous Improvement and Adaptation*: Successful initiatives should not be seen as endpoints but as stepping stones for ongoing improvement. Organizations should adopt a mindset of continuous improvement, constantly looking for ways to refine and enhance their innovation and change processes. This involves soliciting feedback from employees, customers, and stakeholders and actively seeking opportunities for optimization and adaptation. By continuously learning and iterating, organizations can stay ahead of the curve and maintain their competitive edge.

(D) *Creating a Culture of Learning*: To truly benefit from successful initiatives, organizations need to foster a culture of learning and knowledge sharing. This entails creating platforms and mechanisms for employees to share their experiences, insights, and lessons learned. Encouraging open dialogue and collaboration across teams and departments allows for the transfer of knowledge and ideas, promoting a culture of continuous improvement and innovation.

(E) *Embracing Experimentation and Risk-Taking*: Learning from successful initiatives requires embracing experimentation and encouraging a willingness to take calculated risks. Not all innovation and change initiatives will be successful, but failures can provide valuable insights and learning opportunities. By creating an environment that supports risk-taking and encourages learning from failures, organizations can foster a culture of innovation that embraces continuous learning and improvement.

6.2.9 Overcoming Challenges and Resistance

Organizations can cultivate an atmosphere that encourages and welcomes innovation and change if they address and overcome resistance to change and any cultural barriers. It calls for efficient communication, the participation of important players, and a dedication to altering cultural norms that may impede progress.

6.2.9.1 Addressing resistance to change

Taking measures to reduce people's resistance to change is one of the most crucial steps for successful innovation implementation and organizational transformation. For resistance to be effectively addressed, straightforward communication is required. It is essential to communicate the need for change plainly and concisely, including the benefits and drawbacks of continuing business as usual. Participation in the transformation process can also give workers agency and a sense of ownership. Facilitating participant buy-in and commitment can be accomplished by actively soliciting their thoughts and ideas and incorporating them into the planning and decision-making processes.

Another essential component of overcoming resistance is confronting one's concerns and anxieties head-on. Taking the time to listen to employees' concerns, demonstrating empathy for them, and providing knowledge and resources to alleviate the uncertainty they are experiencing are all ways to reduce resistance. In addition, it is necessary to offer training and support programs. Through training, mentoring, and counseling programs, it is possible to increase employees' confidence and decrease their resistance to change. These programs provide the necessary competencies and abilities. Consistent communication and status updates are essential for maintaining transparency and confidence. To increase employee engagement and decrease resistance to change, it is necessary to keep workers apprised of the change's progression, promptly address questions and concerns, and provide transparent updates on milestones, accomplishments, and obstacles.

Leadership is an essential element in the process of overcoming resistance to change. The most effective method for leaders to inspire followers is to participate actively in whatever changes occur and demonstrate that they are adaptable. Their commitment inspires others to embrace the change and continue. Acknowledging and celebrating one's progress and accomplishments along the way is essential. A culture that recognizes and promotes change can be developed by recognizing and rewarding individuals and teams for their contributions to the success of a change initiative and for embracing the change itself. When these methods are implemented, organizations can effectively resolve resistance to change and create an environment receptive to innovation and organizational transformation.

6.2.9.2 Overcoming cultural barriers

Businesses should implement two primary strategies if they wish to surmount cultural barriers and foster innovation- and change-friendly culture. Existing cultural norms need to be examined and modified as a first step. This requires conducting a cultural analysis in order to identify the aspects of the culture that impede innovation and transformation. Organizations can adapt and cultivate a culture that fosters creativity, risk-taking, and continuous development if they are aware of and acknowledge the existence of these barriers. Second, one of the most crucial responsibilities is to promote diversity and inclusiveness. It is crucial to demonstrate a commitment to diversity in all of its manifestations and to cultivate an inclusive environment where all voices can be heard. In order to foster creativity, this involves recognizing and valuing the distinct perspectives and experiences that people from diverse backgrounds bring to the table. The elimination of cultural barriers is aided by the implementation of strategies that reduce prejudices and provide equal participation opportunities. Moreover, by cultivating open and transparent channels of communication, employers can encourage their employees to share their thoughts, concerns, and suggestions without fear of retaliation. Due to the establishment of feedback systems, the organization is able to address and surmount cultural barriers effectively. Using the aforementioned methods to address cultural barriers allows organizations to foster an environment that encourages and welcomes innovation and change. Changing current norms, emphasizing diversity and inclusion, and cultivating open communication channels enable businesses to capitalize on the diverse perspectives and ideas of their workforce, which in turn increases their innovative capacity and adaptability in the face of change. Table 6.4 provides a concise overview of the strategies, benefits, and examples for addressing resistance to change and overcoming cultural barriers.

6.3 CHANGE MANAGEMENT: MANAGING CHANGE EFFECTIVELY FOR DIGITAL TRANSFORMATION SUCCESS

In this era of digital revolution, change is becoming an unavoidable aspect of the business landscape. The rapid advancement of technology has drastically altered the way in which businesses operate, requiring them to adjust or risk becoming irrelevant. The implementation of digital transformation initiatives, on the other hand, presents its own set of challenges and complications. At this point in the process of ensuring the success

TABLE 6.4   Strategies for cultivating an innovation-friendly culture by addressing resistance to change and overcoming cultural barriers

STRATEGIES TO ADDRESS RESISTANCE TO CHANGE	STRATEGIES TO OVERCOME CULTURAL BARRIERS	BENEFITS	EXAMPLES
Clear communication about the need for change and its benefits and drawbacks.	Conduct a cultural analysis to identify barriers to innovation and transformation.	Encourages open dialogue and understanding. Provides clarity and transparency.	Communicate the need for new technology systems.
Encourage participation and ownership by involving employees in the transformation process.	Promote diversity and inclusiveness, valuing distinct perspectives.	Increases employee engagement and harnesses diverse perspectives.	Brainstorm process improvements with employees from different departments.
Address concerns and anxieties with empathy, knowledge, and resources.	Implement strategies to reduce prejudices and provide equal opportunities.	Builds trust and fosters a supportive environment.	Conduct workshops on the benefits of diversity and inclusion.
Offer training, mentoring, and counseling programs to increase employees' confidence.	Cultivate open and transparent communication channels.	Enhances employees' skills and facilitates information flow.	Provide training on new software for improved technical skills.
Recognize and reward contributions to change, fostering a culture that promotes change.	Establish feedback systems to address and overcome cultural barriers.	Motivates employees and enables continuous improvement.	Implement an employee recognition program for innovative ideas.

of digital transformation initiatives, change management becomes a crucial element. The term "change management" refers to the systematic strategy and collection of processes that help businesses transition from their current state to their desired future state. It requires planning, implementing changes, and then reinforcing those changes in order to achieve the intended results effectively and efficiently. Change management assumes a greater level of importance in the context of digital transformation due to its function in assisting businesses to navigate the complexities of technological advancements, business model shifts, and organizational culture shifts.

Change management is of the uttermost importance in the context of digital transformation for a number of reasons. To begin with, it helps reduce resistance from employees, some of whom may be resistant to change because they are comfortable with the current processes and systems. Change management helps eradicate employee resistance, addresses their concerns, and fosters a receptive environment, which increases the likelihood of successful adoption of digital transformation initiatives. Second, effective change management is essential for attaining the highest level of success possible in the adoption of new processes and technologies. It ensures that employees comprehend the need for change, receive the necessary training and support, and have access to the necessary resources to implement new tools and procedures. This comprehensive strategy increases the likelihood of widespread adoption of digital transformation and maximizes ROI in digital transformation.

With the assistance of change management, the complexity of digital transformation can be more readily managed. These types of initiatives frequently involve a large number of stakeholders, interdependencies, and changes in a number of company-wide areas. This complexity can be navigated using a methodical and organized strategy provided by change management. It reduces the likelihood of disruptions and reduces the negative effects of change by establishing clear objectives, facilitating effective communication, coordinating efforts, and ensuring seamless transitions. Change management can increase employee engagement by involving employees in the change process, empowering them to partake in the process, and soliciting their feedback. This helps to foster a sense of ownership and commitment to the transformational efforts being made. Change management also aligns the extant organizational culture with the desired culture, which is essential for the successful completion of digital transformation. By increasing awareness, encouraging the formulation of a common vision, and reinforcing desirable behaviors, change management facilitates the establishment of a change-ready culture within an organization that embraces ongoing transformation.

In addition, risk assessment and strategy development are incorporated into the change management process, which assists in mitigating the risks associated with digital transformation. It ensures that potential risks are identified, evaluated, and addressed in a proactive manner, thereby decreasing the likelihood that the organization will suffer negative consequences. Ultimately, the objective of change management is to increase the sustainability of an organization by integrating new attitudes, technologies, and processes throughout it. Change management ensures that new behaviors become ingrained in the organization's culture by implementing actions such as monitoring, evaluating, continuously refining, and reinforcing. This ultimately increases the probability of long-term success.

6.3.1 The Change Management Process

Change management is a crucial component that needs to be implemented in order to navigate the complexities of digital transformation successfully. It requires a systematic approach to planning, implementing, and maintaining change within an organization. Change management is a process constituted of several essential elements that assist businesses in managing change effectively and increasing the likelihood of successful digital transformation. Figure 6.3 represents the sequential steps involved in managing change during the digital transformation process.

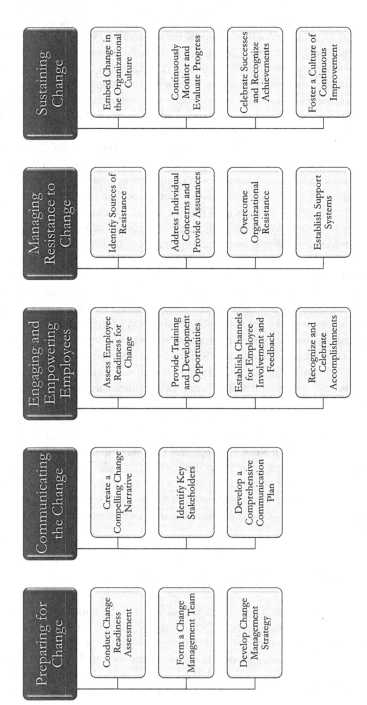

FIGURE 6.3   Change management process for successful digital transformation.

6.3.1.1 Preparing for change

An essential step in the change management process that lays the groundwork for a successful digital transformation is becoming ready for change. Building a change management team, creating a thorough change management plan, and evaluating the organization's readiness for change are all part of this phase. Organizations can proactively address potential barriers to change and provide a strong framework to direct the transformation effort by properly preparing for change.

The initial stage in preparing for change is to carry out a change readiness assessment. Organizations can use this assessment to understand their current situation better, spot prospective problems, and gauge their adaptability. Organizations can learn important information about how prepared they are for the digital transition by evaluating their organizational culture, competencies, and stakeholder engagement. This evaluation assists in subsequent planning and guarantees that the change activities are in line with the particular context of the organization.

To manage change throughout the transformation process successfully, it is imperative to create a change management team. People with knowledge of business procedures, technology, and change management should be on the team. The change project is driven and supported in large part by the change management team. They help with communication, deal with resistance, and make sure the transformation is in line with the goals of the organization. The complexity of the digital transformation journey can be navigated by enterprises by forming a committed team and utilizing their knowledge and experience.

To create a roadmap for implementing digital transformation, it is crucial to develop a change management strategy. This strategy provides a communication plan, identifies training and development needs, establishes change milestones and timetables, and incorporates risk management techniques in addition to outlining the initiative's vision and goals. A clearly defined strategy directs the organization through the transformation process, communicates the significance of the change, and aids in building a common understanding among stakeholders. It offers direction, structure, and clarity to make sure the change effort is well-intentioned and carried out.

6.3.1.2 Communicating the change

The management of change during the digital transformation process depends on effective communication. A shared understanding of the change is facilitated through clear and consistent communication, which also increases employee involvement. Making a compelling change narrative, identifying the important stakeholders, and creating a thorough communication plan are all necessary for communicating the change.

To effectively communicate the goal, advantages, and vision of the digital transformation program, a compelling change narrative needs to be created. The story should explain why the change is essential, how it fits with the organization's objectives, and how it will benefit both the employees and the business as a whole. The narrative should be modified to appeal to various stakeholder groups and speak to their particular needs and interests. Employees should be motivated and inspired by it as it will assist them in understanding the importance and value of the change.

Effective communication depends on identifying important stakeholders and their responsibilities in the change process. Stakeholders can include staff members at all levels, clients, vendors, and any pertinent outside parties. Organizations can create customized communication strategies to engage and involve each stakeholder group by understanding their interests, viewpoints, and influence. A sense of ownership and a collaborative atmosphere are fostered throughout the transformation process by involving important stakeholders early on and asking for their views.

For the right messages to reach the right people at the right time, a thorough communication plan needs to be created. The main messages, communication routes, frequency of communication, and accountable individuals or teams for delivering the messages should all be specified in the strategy. It should cover both formal and informal modes of communication, including one-on-one conversations, intranet platforms, email updates, and town hall gatherings. To improve comprehension and engagement, the strategy should also take into account the usage of visual tools like infographics and films. The efficacy of the communication plan can be ensured by routinely reviewing it and making changes in response to feedback and changing demands.

Being receptive to answering queries and addressing employee issues is crucial during the communication process. Employees will feel heard and valued if two-way communication is encouraged and opportunities for input are provided, which helps to develop a culture of conversation. Through focus groups, feedback surveys, Q&A sessions, or other channels made specifically for employee input, this can be accomplished. Honest, timely communication fosters a culture of support for digital transformation by fostering trust and reducing opposition.

6.3.1.3 Engaging and empowering employees

One of the most important aspects of change management during digital transformation is engaging and empowering people. Employers may build ownership, dedication, and passion for the change endeavor by actively involving employees and giving them the support and tools they need. Assessing an employee's preparedness for change, offering chances for training and growth, and setting up feedback systems for ongoing improvement are all part of engaging and empowering people during the transformation process. Understanding an employee's readiness, worries, and expectations requires first determining how prepared they are for change. This evaluation assists in identifying any knowledge or skill gaps that need to be filled in order to get workers ready for the digital transition. It also aids in foreseeing future opposition or obstacles that can appear throughout the transition process. Surveys, interviews, or focus groups can be used to conduct employee readiness assessments, and the results should guide the creation of change interventions.

Offering staff opportunities for training and development is essential to ensuring that they have the skills and knowledge required to traverse the digital revolution successfully. Training events, workshops, or online learning modules that concentrate on technology proficiency, fresh procedures or workflows, and other pertinent topics can be a part of this. Different staff groups should receive training that is specifically suited to them, taking into account their organizational roles and responsibilities. Giving employees continual assistance and resources—such as job aids or access to subject matter experts—encourages them to accept change and use their newly acquired abilities in productive ways.

To foster a culture of collaboration and continual improvement, it is crucial to set up channels for employee involvement and feedback. Surveys, suggestion boxes, and routine check-ins with staff are a few examples of feedback techniques. Employee engagement is increased when their opinions are actively sought after and addressed, which shows that they are valued contributors to the transformation process. Employee participation in decision-making and process improvement initiatives also enables people to offer their knowledge and viewpoints, promoting a sense of empowerment and engagement.

Another crucial component of involving and empowering employees is acknowledging and celebrating their accomplishments and milestones throughout the transformation process. Employee loyalty and motivation are strengthened when their efforts and accomplishments are recognized and rewarded. This can be accomplished through open praise, incentives, and prizes or team-building exercises that highlight group successes. In order to keep the transformation process moving forward and create a pleasant and encouraging environment, it is important to celebrate accomplishments.

6.3.1.4 Managing resistance to change

During the digital transformation process, resistance to change is a typical and natural reaction. A smooth and successful shift depends on successfully managing resistance. Organizations may address issues, reduce resistance, and boost employee buy-in by comprehending the causes of resistance and putting in place sensible methods. The first step in handling resistance to change is identifying the sources of opposition. To discover the precise worries and perceptions causing resistance, this entails conducting surveys, interviews, or focus groups. Sources of resistance can include a lack of knowledge about the advantages of digital transformation, fear of the unknown, a sense of control loss, worry about job security, and others. Organizations can modify their strategy to successfully address the underlying challenges by locating these sources.

Addressing both human and organizational factors is necessary for managing resistance. Clarity in communication is crucial for overcoming personal reluctance. Employees need to comprehend the rationale for the change, its advantages, and how it fits with the objectives of the company. Resistance can be reduced by addressing individual worries and giving assurances about job stability and future potential. Giving employees the tools they need to succeed and integrating them into decision-making processes also empowers them to contribute and lowers resistance. Organizational resistance may be brought on by ingrained procedures, competing priorities, or a need for leadership backing. Creating a sense of urgency is essential for solving this. Organizational resistance can be overcome by stating the case for change and the effects of inactivity clearly. The advantages and viability of the transformation can be shown by putting change interventions, such as pilot projects or proof-of-concept efforts, into practice. Organizational support for the change is further strengthened by matching incentives and rewards with desired behaviors and results.

To assist employees in navigating the transition process, support systems need to be put in place. Champions of change or change agents can encourage and mentor their colleagues while they undergo the shift by acting as advocates and role models. A sense of community and collaboration is fostered via support groups or communities of practice, which offer forums for exchanging experiences, difficulties, and best practices. It is ensured through ongoing feedback and improvement processes that issues are handled, and the change process is modified as necessary.

6.3.1.5 Sustaining change

The phase of managing change, known as "sustaining change," is an essential part of the process that focuses on ensuring that digital transformation will be successful over the long term and will be successfully integrated. Incorporating the changes into the culture of the organization, regularly reviewing progress, and adapting to ever-changing requirements are all required steps. For companies to effectively maintain change, they need to concentrate their efforts on the following critical areas. Organizations can successfully traverse the issues that are connected with digital transformation and boost their chances of being successful if they follow the change management method that is explained below. Each phase plays an important part in ensuring that employees are prepared, engaged, and given the authority necessary to accept the changes that are brought about by digital transformation.

- *Embedding Change in the Organizational Culture*: Successful change goes beyond the initial implementation phase. It requires integrating new ways of working and mindsets into the organizational culture. This involves aligning values, norms, and behaviors with the desired change. Leaders and managers play a crucial role in modeling and promoting the desired behaviors, creating a culture that embraces innovation, adaptability, and continuous learning.
- *Continuous Monitoring and Evaluation*: Regular monitoring and evaluation are essential to track the progress of digital transformation and identify areas that require further attention. This can involve setting KPIs to measure the impact of the change, conducting regular assessments, and seeking feedback from employees and stakeholders. Monitoring allows organizations to identify any gaps, address emerging challenges, and make necessary adjustments to sustain the change effort.
- *Celebrating Successes and Recognizing Achievements*: Celebrating successes and recognizing achievements along the way helps to maintain momentum and motivate employees. This can be done through formal recognition programs, rewards, or public acknowledgment of teams or individuals who have contributed to the success of the digital transformation. Celebrating milestones and highlighting positive outcomes reinforces the importance of the change and encourages continued commitment from employees.
- *Fostering a Culture of Continuous Improvement*: Sustaining change requires an ongoing commitment to improvement. Organizations should encourage and support employees to continuously seek ways to enhance digital transformation. This can involve promoting a culture of experimentation, providing opportunities for innovation, and actively soliciting ideas and feedback from employees. Regularly assessing and adapting processes, technologies, and strategies ensures that the change remains relevant and effective in the face of evolving challenges and opportunities.

6.3.2 Tools and Techniques for Change Management

The successful navigation of the process of change is dependent on change management, which uses a variety of tools and strategies. These tools include change impact assessments, which help organizations understand the potential effects of change on different aspects of the business; stakeholder analysis, which identifies and analyzes the individuals or groups affected by the change; change readiness surveys, which assess the organization's preparedness; training and development programs, which equip employees with the necessary skills; communication channels and platforms, which facilitate the effective sharing of information; and so on. Throughout the process of change management, these tools and strategies provide structure, insights, and support, which ensures a smoother transition and increases the likelihood of success.

6.3.2.1 Change impact assessment

A change impact assessment is a tool that is used in change management to examine and understand the potential effects and repercussions of a proposed change on various elements of an organization. This is done so that the change may be managed more effectively. It assists in identifying and assessing the breadth, scale, and consequences of the change, which in turn enable companies to establish appropriate strategies and plans to handle the impact of the change. As part of the change impact assessment, you will evaluate how the change will have an effect on a variety of factors, including people, processes, and resources, among other things. It seeks to provide responses to questions such as:

- What processes and workflows will be impacted by the change?
- How will the change affect the organization's systems, technologies, and infrastructure?
- What resources, such as personnel, budget, and equipment, will be required for the change?
- How will the change affect different departments, teams, and individuals within the organization?
- What potential risks and challenges may arise due to the change?

The results of a thorough change impact assessment can provide businesses with valuable insights into the potential risks, opportunities, and problems that are related to the change that is being proposed. This assessment contributes to the process of making informed decisions and devising appropriate strategies for minimizing disruptions, mitigating risks, and maximizing the benefits of the change. In most cases, the change impact assessment is carried out by employing a variety of methods, such as interviews, surveys, data analysis, and meetings with key stakeholders. It entails collecting information, analyzing the existing situation, projecting the future state, finding the gaps and ramifications of the change, and projecting the future state.

6.3.2.2 Stakeholder analysis

A key component of change management and stakeholder analysis identifies and evaluates the individuals or groups who will be affected by a change project. The procedure involves identifying the various stakeholders, determining their level of importance and influence, obtaining an understanding of their concerns and interests, and developing individualized engagement strategies. By conducting a comprehensive analysis of their stakeholders, businesses can proactively address the potential risks, obstacles, and resistance associated with the change, while concurrently cultivating support and collaboration among those who will be affected by it.

Identifying all internal and external stakeholders who have a stake in the change is the first step in conducting a stakeholder analysis. Once stakeholders have been identified, they are evaluated according to their significance and influence, allowing organizations to prioritize their engagement efforts. The subsequent crucial step is to comprehend the interests and concerns of the stakeholders. This will facilitate a deeper understanding of their needs, expectations, and potential obstacles. This information is a guide for the development of specific methods to engage stakeholders effectively, such as communication plans, participation in decision-making, and addressing their concerns.

Managing relationships with a large number of stakeholders is a crucial aspect of any transformation process. This involves maintaining all lines of communication open, delivering consistent information, and resolving any issues or complaints as quickly as possible. By actively involving them in the process, organizations can ensure that their stakeholders feel heard, valued, and a part of the change journey. This method of collaboration aids in generating support, gaining buy-in, and fostering an environment conducive to the successful implementation of change.

6.3.2.3 Change readiness surveys

Change readiness surveys are a valuable change management instrument for evaluating the readiness and preparedness of individuals and organizations for a proposed change. These surveys require the development and administration of targeted questionnaires in order to collect feedback from employees and constituents. The collected data is subsequently analyzed to determine readiness gaps and specific areas of concern or strength. Change readiness surveys help increase the likelihood of successful change adoption and reduce resistance by informing decision-making processes and guiding the development of tailored interventions.

Creating survey questions that address various aspects of preparedness, such as awareness, perceived impact, adaptability, and support or opposition, is part of the survey design process. The surveys can be administered using a variety of methods that ensure anonymity and confidentiality in order to elicit sincere responses. After the surveys are completed, the data are collected and analyzed to determine the patterns and trends. This analysis provides insight into the organization's overall level of preparedness and identifies specific areas requiring attention.

The results of change readiness surveys inform decision-making by highlighting deficits in preparedness. These gaps guide the development of targeted interventions and strategies to address concerns and enhance change readiness. The insights obtained from the surveys assist in the development of communication plans, training programs, strategies for stakeholder engagement, and change management interventions. By proactively resolving identified gaps and concerns, organizations can improve readiness and create a conducive environment for successful change implementation.

6.3.2.4 Training and development programs

Training and development programs are essential change management tools because they equip employees with the necessary skills, knowledge, and competencies to acclimate to a change initiative. This allows workers to be more adaptable in the face of change. The first stage of the procedure entails evaluating the training needs by identifying specific knowledge and skill gaps associated with the change. On the basis of the results of this evaluation, businesses devise customized training programs that align with the objectives of the change initiative. These programs may utilize workshops, e-learning modules, and on-the-job training, among other instructional formats. These courses are taught in an environment that encourages active participation, cooperation, and collaboration.

Throughout the duration of the training process, organizations monitor and evaluate the effectiveness of the programs to ensure that they meet the established training requirements. It is necessary to conduct feedback surveys, assessments, and performance evaluations in order to gain insight and determine what types of adjustments are required for progress. In addition, businesses provide their employees with regular training and education opportunities to help them adapt to new circumstances. This may include access to remedial classes, seminars on skill development, and other resources designed to encourage ongoing education and skill development.

Training and development programs play an essential role in change management because they equip employees with the skills necessary to accept and adapt to proposed changes. When companies resolve skills and knowledge gaps, they can increase the likelihood of successful change implementation, improve employee engagement and satisfaction, and foster an organizational culture that encourages continuous learning and professional development.

6.3.2.5 Communication channels and platforms

Change management heavily relies on communication channels and platforms because they enable employees at all organizational levels to share information quickly and effectively. These tools are essential for informing employees, stakeholders, and other relevant parties about the change, addressing concerns, and increasing employee and stakeholder engagement. Within organizations, communication takes place through a variety of channels and platforms.

Large-scale events, such as town hall or all-hands meetings, provide executives with the opportunity to interact directly with employees and share updates, goals, and the reasoning behind any upcoming changes. Email is widely used for communication and is frequently employed for formal announcements, progress reports, and the exchange of vital documents. By providing resources, frequently asked questions, project updates, and interactive forums, intranets and internal websites serve as the primary information hubs for change. The utilization of team meetings and departmental briefings enables managers to exchange information and address concerns in more intimate settings. The use of collaboration tools and platforms facilitates real-time communication and coordination among teams, whereas the use of social media and online communities engages a larger audience and enables debates and feedback.

Before deciding on the communication channels and platforms to use, it is essential to consider the preferences of the audience and the nature of the change initiative. It is essential to utilize a variety of communication channels in order to provide extensive coverage and meet a wide range of communication needs. By fostering openness, participation, and alignment through the use of efficient communication channels and platforms, businesses can increase the likelihood of successfully implementing change and decrease the amount of resistance encountered. These technologies establish a collaborative environment that facilitates the sharing of information, addresses issues, and supports the entire change management process.

6.3.2.6 Resistance management strategies

To address and lessen opposition during the implementation of a change initiative, change management requires the creation of solutions for handling resistance—any successful plan needs to have open and honest communication as a key element. Regular updates on the change-causing causes, as well as the expected benefits and outcomes, are necessary for this component. Building trust and a sense of ownership over the change is facilitated by including stakeholders in the decision-making process and giving them opportunities for debate. The need for more understanding related to the shift and the fear related to it should also be addressed by implementing programs of education and training. To decrease the resistance that ambiguity causes, these programs need to make expectations clear and provide support.

Individuals' concerns should be addressed after making an attempt to understand the issues and worries they are experiencing. Customized support and communication can help calm fears and show how a change will advance the person's goals and values. Another effective tactic is to put together a coalition of supporters made up of influential individuals or groups that can speak out in favor of the change project and influence others. By acknowledging and applauding their active participation and positive behaviors, which may be done through the use of incentives and awards, people can be motivated and encouraged to embrace the change.

One should keep an open mind, be flexible, and be prepared to modify one's approach to change as necessary when one recognizes the likelihood of resistance at any stage of the process. Iterative feedback loops and a willingness to modify the implementation strategy in response to individual comments and concerns facilitate ongoing improvement and better alignment with organizational needs. Utilizing dispute resolution techniques is also necessary. These include offering a platform for people to voice their complaints and promoting a collaborative problem-solving methodology, such as discussion facilitation or mediation.

6.3.2.7 *Continuous improvement and feedback loops*

Continuously improving as well as incorporating feedback loops are crucial aspects of efficient change management. Throughout the process of change, organizations can get useful insights into the effectiveness of their initiatives by gathering feedback from employees, stakeholders, and other relevant parties. This input may be acquired through a variety of techniques, including questionnaires, interviews, and suggestion boxes, among others. The analysis of the data obtained helps discover patterns and areas that require improvement, which enables organizations to make decisions and modifications based on accurate information.

Specific areas within the change project have been highlighted as needing improvement based on the analysis of the comments received. These domains could consist of communication strategies, training programs, objectives, or processes. With the identified areas in mind, businesses put into action the necessary adjustments to improve the overall effectiveness of the change and to increase the level of acceptance of the change. A transparent and understandable environment may be maintained through effective communication of the adjustments to all parties involved.

It is vital to maintain continuous monitoring and evaluation in order to measure the impact and efficacy of the adjustments that have been performed. Continuous evaluation provides companies with the opportunity to collect additional data, monitor outcomes, and evaluate the extent to which the changes have been successful. This information is then utilized to make additional adjustments, with the end goal of ensuring that the change endeavor continues to be aligned with the outcomes that are sought. It is through the use of this iterative methodology that businesses cultivate a culture of learning and adaptation, thus proving their dedication to overcoming problems and maximizing the effectiveness of the change process. Table 6.5 provides a more condensed description of each tool or strategy, highlighting examples and key considerations.

6.3.3 Overcoming Common Challenges

One of the most frequent challenges to be solved during the change management process for digital transformation is winning the support and buy-in of the leadership. Companies should involve their highest-level leaders as early in the process as feasible to address this issue, convince them of the benefits of digital transformation, and win their support for implementing change. The development of a culture of cooperation and shared responsibility between the leadership and the workforce is of the highest importance for ensuring the active engagement of leaders to both inspire and guide the change process.

The opposition that needs to be met from employees and stakeholders is another challenge that needs to be overcome. The identification of potential sources of resistance needs to be done proactively. By clearly explaining the justification for the change and the advantages it will bring, as well as including employees and stakeholders in the process, it is feasible to reduce the level of resistance experienced. When people receive assistance in the form of coaching, training, and attention to their concerns, they are

TABLE 6.5   Tools and strategies for change management

TOOL/STRATEGY	EXAMPLES/USE CASES	KEY CONSIDERATIONS/ CHALLENGES
Change Impact Assessment	Assessing the impact of implementing new software systems on different departments and workflows.	Ensuring comprehensive data collection, addressing biases, and effective communication of assessment results.
Stakeholder Analysis	Analyzing stakeholders impacted by a company merger and developing strategies to address their concerns and gain their support.	Ensuring inclusivity, managing conflicts, and balancing stakeholder needs.
Change Readiness Surveys	Conducting a survey to assess employees' preparedness for a shift in company culture and tailoring change management interventions based on results.	Designing relevant surveys, ensuring confidentiality, and effectively analyzing results for actionable insights.
Training and Development Programs	Providing training programs to develop necessary skills for adopting new sales methodology.	Identifying knowledge gaps, evaluating effectiveness, and providing ongoing training opportunities.
Communication Channels and Platforms	Using internal social media platforms to communicate updates, address questions, and encourage discussion during company-wide reorganization.	Choosing appropriate channels, ensuring consistency, and managing information overload.
Resistance Management Strategies	Holding town hall meetings to allow employees to voice concerns and provide opportunities for dialogue and collaboration.	Identifying underlying causes, handling conflicts, and adapting strategies based on resistance.
Continuous Improvement and Feedback Loops	Conducting regular feedback sessions and incorporating suggestions to refine and enhance the change management process.	Establishing a structured feedback mechanism, prioritizing and acting on feedback, and overcoming resistance to change in implementing improvements.

more inclined to embrace change. When positive actions and results are recognized and rewarded along the way, they are more likely to be repeated. This contributes to fostering an atmosphere that is more open to novel concepts.

For change to be successfully managed, communication needs to be open and effective. The best method to keep everyone informed and involved in the dialogue is to develop a comprehensive communication plan that identifies key themes, platforms, and target audiences. Transparency and regular updates on the performance of digital transformation programs help to foster trust and lessen uncertainty. Clarity and comprehension are aided by two-way communication, routes for feedback, and the resolution of specific problems and queries brought up by workers and other stakeholders. Resistance and uncertainty are lessened as a result.

When there are insufficient resources and support, change management initiatives may be hindered. It is imperative to do a thorough analysis of the required resource allocations and obtain the required budget allocations. By deploying dedicated teams and individuals to drive and support change, as well as by offering training and development programs, one can improve their skills and capacities. Getting assistance or collaboration from outside parties can help close the resource gap when internal resources are scarce and increase the likelihood that a digital transformation will be successful.

If organizations can successfully handle the common hurdles they encounter and identify answers to those problems, they may navigate the complexities of change management and increase the chances of a successful digital transformation. It's crucial to foster an environment that values change, encourages open dialogue, and adapts one's tactics to the situation. Businesses will be able to overcome obstacles, seize opportunities, and accomplish their goals for digital transformation by operating in this way.

6.4 CONCLUSION

This chapter focuses on and emphasizes the crucial part that individuals play in the process of digital transformation. It highlights how crucial it is for the business to establish an inventive and adaptive culture in order to give its employees the resources they require to succeed in their positions. If businesses foster a culture of continuous development and technological adaptability within their organizations, they will have a better chance of managing the opportunities and challenges posed by digital transformation. Effective change management strategies need to be used in order to guarantee the successful implementation of digital transformation activities. Organizations may overcome their employees' resistance to change and produce outstanding results by including their staff in the change process, paying attention to their concerns, and offering the right resources. Success in this new era of business will be easier for organizations that prioritize their people, corporate culture, and capacity to adapt to changing conditions.

REFERENCES

1. Zhang, W., et al., Understanding how organizational culture affects innovation performance: a management context perspective. *Sustainability*, 2023. **15**(8): p. 6644.
2. Yadav, O.P., et al., Lean implementation and organizational transformation: a literature review. *Engineering Management Journal*, 2017. **29**(1): pp. 2–16.

7 Digital Transformation Cybersecurity Roadmap

7.1 CYBERSECURITY IN INDUSTRY 4.0

The Fourth Industrial Revolution—also referred to as "Industry 4.0"—is characterized by the integration of cutting-edge digital technologies with more traditional manufacturing processes. This revolution has led to an increase in automation, data interchange, and connectivity between digital and physical systems. Industry 4.0 has many benefits, like improved production, efficiency, and creativity, but it also creates new cybersecurity challenges that need to be resolved. Due to the many benefits that Industry 4.0 offers, these challenges must be overcome. Cybersecurity is crucial in the Fourth Industrial Revolution because of the interconnectedness of the systems and the possible repercussions of hacks. The attack surface available to hostile actors has considerably increased as a result of the integration of cyber-physical systems, IoT-connected devices, cloud computing, and large-scale data analytics. Cybercriminals are now able to steal private information, infringe on intellectual property, disrupt business operations, and even physically harm manufacturing facilities.

Due to its distinctive features, Industry 4.0 brings new cybersecurity risks that must be properly addressed. One of the most urgent problems at the moment is the integration of OT (operational technology) and IT networks. Systems for OT and IT have traditionally been kept apart. However, as part of Industry 4.0, these systems are interconnected, increasing the attack surface and the potential for cross-contamination by cyber threats. Additionally, businesses are exposed to the hazards of illegal access, data breaches, and the manipulation of crucial information due to the increased interconnectedness and reliance on data-driven decision-making. Data is significant in the context of Industry 4.0 not only for the businesses that gather it but also for

DOI: 10.1201/9781003471226-8

cybercriminals who want to take advantage of the flaws and manage industrial equipment without authorization.

Cybersecurity in Industry 4.0 needs a comprehensive and proactive approach to address these problems appropriately. In order to lessen the effects of cyberattacks, it is necessary to put in place strict security controls to protect network infrastructure, industrial systems, and personnel, as well as to implement strict access controls and train staff on cybersecurity best practices. Cybersecurity now performs more than just protecting individual enterprises in the era of Industry 4.0. To stay ahead of developing threats and jointly defend crucial infrastructure and supply chains, it is imperative that various industry participants, governmental organizations, and cybersecurity professionals work together and exchange information.

7.1.1 Roadmap

The Digital Transformation Cybersecurity Roadmap is a strategic plan designed to assist organizations in effectively addressing cybersecurity issues within the context of Industry 4.0. The objective of the plan is to prepare businesses for the arrival of Industry 4.0. It provides a methodical strategy for the implementation of cybersecurity measures and ensures the security of digital assets, systems, and processes throughout the digital transformation process. One of the primary functions of a business' cybersecurity roadmap is to serve as a guide for managing and minimizing cyber threats efficiently. It facilitates the integration of cybersecurity initiatives with business objectives, streamlines resource allocation, and provides a structure for ongoing development. Defining a roadmap enables organizations to prioritize cybersecurity initiatives, identify voids in their current security practices, and establish a plan for moving forward, allowing them to develop a plan for implementing the necessary controls and procedures.

7.1.2 Risk Assessment and Threat Analysis

The Digital Transformation Cybersecurity Roadmap includes essential elements such as risk assessment and threat analysis. These components offer businesses a methodical strategy for detecting and mitigating potential cybersecurity hazards in Industry 4.0. During the initial phase of the digital transformation process, organizations must identify the critical assets and systems involved in the transition. This comprises the network's infrastructure, equipment, software, and data storage facilities. In order to conduct an appropriate risk assessment, it is utterly essential to have a firm grasp on both the value and significance of these assets.

The next step is to identify potential attacks that could exploit vulnerabilities to compromise the security of the assets. These threats may come from the outside in the form of hackers and other cybercriminals or from the inside in the form of accidental data breaches or disgruntled employees. Organizations can conduct a comprehensive risk assessment for the preservation of their confidentiality, integrity, and availability when both intentional and unintentional threats are considered. Conducting a vulnerability assessment after identifying threats helps identify exploitable flaws in hardware, software, configurations, or procedures. Malicious parties could exploit these vulnerabilities. Utilizing vulnerability assessment probes, penetration testing, and security audits can facilitate the quantification and comprehension of the nature and scope of vulnerabilities.

By conducting a risk analysis and assigning risk ratings or scores to each hazard, businesses can prioritize their efforts to improve their cybersecurity in accordance with the assessed risks. It is essential to consider multiple factors, such as the probability of an event occurring, its potential impact on business operations, regulatory compliance, reputation, and financial repercussions. Due to this prioritization, organizations are able to allocate resources effectively and employ risk mitigation techniques that are tailored to the areas with the greatest importance and impact.

By adopting this methodical approach to risk assessment and threat analysis, organizations can gain valuable insights regarding their cybersecurity posture. As a result, they can make decisions based on accurate information, prioritize investments, and implement appropriate risk reduction measures. Regular monitoring and reevaluation of the risk landscape ensure that cybersecurity solutions continue to be effective in addressing new threats and changes in the digital environment. This preventive strategy strengthens the overall cybersecurity framework for Industry 4.0, thereby enhancing the security of vital assets and ensuring the successful execution of digital transformation programs. Figure 7.1 shows the secure digital transformation cybersecurity pathway.

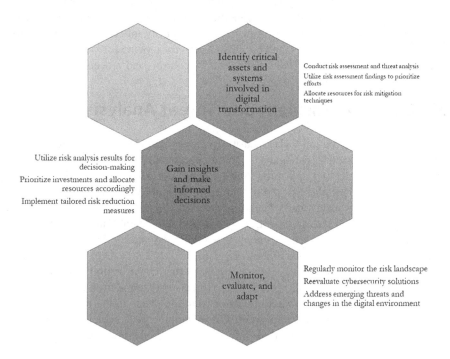

FIGURE 7.1   Strategic cybersecurity roadmap for secure digital transformation.

Risk assessments, threat analysis, vulnerability assessments, prioritization, resource allocation, informed decisions, and monitoring and responding to emerging threats protect and strengthen digital assets and systems.

7.1.3 Security Policies and Governance Framework

Security policies and a governance framework are essential elements of a comprehensive Industry 4.0 cybersecurity strategy. These components provide guidelines, rules, and procedures for the protection of digital assets, the management of risks, and the fulfillment of regulatory requirements. The formulation of security policies is an essential initial step. Organizations should establish a comprehensive set of policies outlining the expectations, standards, and procedures for safeguarding digital assets and systems. These policies should address access control, data classification and management, incident response, acceptable use of technology resources, and employee cybersecurity responsibilities.

Similarly, the governance framework should incorporate risk management practices in order to identify, evaluate, and mitigate cybersecurity risks. This includes performing regular risk assessments, implementing controls to resolve identified risks, and continuously reviewing and updating risk management strategies to accommodate evolving threats and technologies. Compliance with applicable laws, regulations, and industry standards is of the utmost importance. The governance framework should include monitoring and compliance assurance procedures. This includes adhering to regulations such as GDPR, the NIST Cybersecurity Framework, and industry-specific regulations such as the Health Insurance Portability and Accountability Act (HIPAA) for the healthcare industry.

To ensure effective implementation, roles and responsibilities must be defined precisely. The governance framework must assign individuals or teams with oversight responsibilities for cybersecurity initiatives, incident response, and compliance. Assigning specific responsibilities promotes accountability and enhances coordination and communication within an organization. In addition, a well-defined incident response plan is essential for effectively managing cybersecurity incidents. The governance framework should define the steps to be taken in the event of a security incident or breach, including incident reporting, assessment, containment, investigation, and recovery. In addition, the governance framework should incorporate continuous cybersecurity training and awareness programs for employees. These programs educate employees on cybersecurity threats, best practices, and their role in sustaining a secure computing environment. Regular evaluations and audits are required to guarantee the efficacy of security policies and the governance framework. Periodic audits, vulnerability assessments, penetration testing, and compliance reviews enable the identification of gaps, weaknesses, and improvement opportunities. This enables organizations to continually strengthen their cybersecurity posture and adapt to new threats. The components for establishing a comprehensive security policies and governance framework are summarized in Table 7.1.

TABLE 7.1 Components of a security policies and governance framework

COMPONENT	IMPORTANCE	BENEFITS	EXAMPLES OF IMPLEMENTATION
Security Policies	High	Provides a clear framework for protecting digital assets	Developing an acceptable use policy for technology resources
Access Control	High	Prevents unauthorized access to sensitive information	Implementing multifactor authentication for system logins
Data Classification	Medium	Facilitates effective data management and protection	Implementing a data classification policy that categorizes data as public, internal, and confidential
Incident Response	High	Enables swift and effective response to minimize damage	Developing an incident response plan with defined escalation procedures
Acceptable Use Policy	Medium	Ensures responsible and secure use of technology resources	Creating an acceptable use policy that outlines guidelines for using company-provided devices and networks
Employee Responsibilities	High	Creates awareness and accountability among employees	Conducting regular cybersecurity training sessions for employees
Governance Framework	High	Establishes a structured approach to cybersecurity governance	Implementing a cybersecurity governance committee to oversee security initiatives
Risk Management	High	Proactively identifies and addresses potential vulnerabilities and threats	Conducting regular risk assessments to identify security gaps and prioritize remediation actions
Compliance Assurance	High	Helps avoid legal and regulatory penalties	Conducting periodic audits to ensure compliance with GDPR requirements
Roles and Responsibilities	Medium	Enhances coordination and communication within the organization	Designating a Chief Information Security Officer (CISO) responsible for overseeing cybersecurity efforts
Incident Response Plan	High	Minimizes the impact of security incidents and enables efficient recovery	Testing and practicing the incident response plan through simulated exercises
Training and Awareness	Medium	Empowers employees to identify and respond to security threats	Conducting regular cybersecurity awareness campaigns and providing training modules to employees
Evaluations and Audits	Medium	Identifies areas of improvement and strengthens the overall security posture	Engaging external security firms to perform penetration testing on critical systems
Continuous Improvement	High	Ensures ongoing protection against evolving threats	Establishing a security governance board to review and update security policies and procedures on a regular basis

7.1.4 Securing the Network Infrastructure

As businesses embrace digital transformation and interconnect various systems and devices, they must implement stringent security measures to protect their network infrastructure. This is particularly crucial as an increasing number of businesses embrace digital transformation. Network segmentation is an integral part of the network infrastructure protection procedure as a whole. The division of a network into segments or zones enables organizations to restrict and monitor access across systems while also reducing the impact of potential security vulnerabilities. In addition, the installation of firewalls and intrusion detection and prevention systems (IDS/IPS) permits network traffic monitoring, the identification of attempts to gain unauthorized access, and the prevention of malicious activity. Utilizing secure remote access techniques, such as secure VPN connections and multifactor authentication (MFA), is absolutely necessary for protecting against unauthorized access and data interception.

If stringent network access controls are implemented, only authorized users and devices will be able to access the network infrastructure. These controls assure the existence of strong password restrictions, user authentication procedures, and privilege management. Monitoring and recording network activity in real time is an essential component of identifying and responding to potential network security breaches. The elimination of known vulnerabilities in network devices can be achieved by applying security patches and enhancements on a regular basis. Using encryption methods for network communications can enhance the confidentiality and integrity of data that is transmitted across a network.

To increase network security, organizations should design and implement comprehensive network security policies, conduct regular network security audits and assessments, and deploy network monitoring technologies such as IDS and SIEM solutions. These are some of the most effective methods for ensuring network security. If businesses implement the aforementioned network infrastructure security measures, they can significantly improve the resistance and protection of their networks within the context of Industry 4.0. Maintaining network security is an ongoing process requiring consistent maintenance, close monitoring, and adjustments in response to newly identified vulnerabilities and threats.

7.1.5 Identity and Access Management

Identity and Access Management, or IAM, is the process of identifying and authorizing people or things in accordance with their obligations and privileges. IAM is crucial for maintaining the safety, availability, and integrity of an organization's resources while also lowering the risk of unauthorized access or data breaches. MFA is employed to achieve this. IAM is composed of a few crucial components that function together. Giving unique identities to users, systems, or applications that are part of an organization is the first step in identifying. The process of authenticating someone's claimed identity involves employing a number of different tools, including biometrics, passwords, and MFA. Roles and responsibilities establish the level of access rights and permissions that are granted to authenticated users; this level is known as authorization. The process of automating the creation of user accounts, as well as the alteration and revocation of access credentials, is known as user provisioning.

In addition, IAM offers Single Sign-On (SSO) for quicker authentication across numerous systems, Privileged Access Management (PAM) for managing and keeping an eye on privileged accounts, and User Lifecycle Management (ULM) for quick user onboarding and offboarding. Increased safety is one of the benefits of IAM because it reduces the likelihood of unauthorized access and data compromise. Additionally, it enhances adherence to legal requirements and automates user management, saving IT organizations time and resources. Higher productivity inside the organization is a result of elements like centralized administration and efficient access management.

7.1.6 Security Awareness and Training Programs

The purpose of security awareness and training programs is to educate and empower personnel at all levels of an organization so that they can recognize potential cyber hazards and respond appropriately. Adopting a methodical strategy may result in both the fortification of a company's cybersecurity defenses and the reduction of associated risks. To get started, businesses should establish a comprehensive security awareness and training program that can be tailored to their specific needs and is consistent with the industry's standards, guidelines, and best practices. This training must cover a variety of topics, such as secure passwords, social engineering, phishing attacks, data protection, secure remote access, and incident reporting.

Education is essential for cultivating a strong perspective toward cybersecurity among employees. It is essential to conduct training sessions on a regular basis in order to increase awareness of cybersecurity risks, emergent threats, and risk mitigation best practices. Important topics include educating employees on proper password maintenance, recognizing suspicious emails and attachments, secure web browsing, and responsible use of company resources. Employees gain a deeper understanding of their position in the protection of the organization's digital assets when they are made aware of the potential consequences of cyberattacks. By utilizing engaging and interactive training materials, the program's effectiveness can be significantly enhanced. Through the use of gamified learning platforms, assessments, online courses, and videos, cybersecurity training can be done in a manner that is both more engaging and accessible. In addition, conducting simulated phishing exercises allows employees to test their knowledge in real-world scenarios and teaches them how to identify the telltale signs of phishing scams. When they receive regular feedback and direction, employees can improve their ability to recognize and report potential hazards.

The training must be reinforced consistently, and reporting procedures must be established. These are both essential. Things such as newsletters, posters, and periodic reminders can serve as constant reminders of good cybersecurity practices. Establishing transparent reporting protocols for security issues contributes to the development of a culture that values open communication. Employees should not be afraid to report incidents for fear of retaliation, and incident response teams should promptly investigate and address reported incidents. Utilizing metrics and conducting evaluations enables businesses to evaluate the program's effectiveness and identify areas for improvement.

7.1.7 Incident Response and Recovery Plan

With the aim of reducing the impact and allowing a speedy recovery, an incident response and recovery plan offers an organized method for resolving security occurrences, such as cyberattacks or data breaches. Several important components are usually included in the design. The plan first provides criteria and indicators for event reporting and identification. The proper identification and early reporting of potential occurrences require clear instructions for employees. Second, it describes the makeup and duties of an incident response team, which could include representatives from management, IT, security, legal, and human resources. All incident-response-related activities must be coordinated by this team.

The plan directs the assessment and containment procedure in the event of an occurrence. It aids in determining the extent, seriousness, and impact of the incident and offers instructions on what actions to take right away to stop it and limit the harm. The methods for notification and communication are also described, including the internal and external channels to be used for coordination and incident reporting. The plan also stresses the significance of gathering and preserving evidence. It emphasizes the importance of keeping thorough logs, records, and paperwork throughout the incident response process in case they are needed for future legal or investigative needs. The next step in the plan is incident analysis and mitigation; when the root cause is found, the scope of the compromise is established and a plan is created to close vulnerabilities and prevent further occurrences.

The recovery and restoration phase is also covered in the plan, along with instructions on how to return affected systems, data, and services to their regular operating state. In order to make data restoration easier, it highlights the significance of backups, their frequent execution, and testing. Lessons learned from the incident are recorded, and any security control gaps or potential improvement areas are noted for future improvements. The incident response and recovery plan should be periodically evaluated, updated, and tested to keep up with new threats and technological advancements. Organizations can successfully respond to security issues, reduce possible harm, and rapidly resume operations by adhering to an incident response and recovery plan. This proactive strategy strengthens overall cybersecurity resilience and protects sensitive data and important assets.

7.1.8 Continuous Monitoring and Improvement

Continuous monitoring and development involve ongoing systems and practices that enable businesses to identify, evaluate, and respond to evolving cybersecurity threats. Establishing channels for obtaining real time threat intelligence from reputable sources is something that businesses should do to ensure that they are current on the most recent vulnerabilities, attack vectors, and threats. They are, therefore, able to take preventative measures to enhance their defenses against newly emerging threats. Businesses must implement security event monitoring solutions in order to collect and analyze data from multiple sources, such as log files and network traffic. Continuous monitoring of security events enables businesses to detect suspicious behavior and potential security breaches quickly. This allows businesses to respond quickly and limit the problem's impact.

It is essential to execute regular vulnerability assessments and scans in order to detect flaws in systems and infrastructure. In these assessments, the rectification of vulnerabilities is prioritized based on the severity of the vulnerabilities. In addition, regular penetration testing serves as a simulation of real-world cyberattacks, which helps evaluate the effectiveness of the existing security controls and exposes vulnerabilities that may not be apparent using other methods. By emphasizing security awareness and training programs, employers can ensure that their employees are aware of the most recent threats, attack methods, and recommended procedures. This enables employees to identify and report security violations, which contributes to the development of a security-conscious culture within the organization. Drills and exercises focusing on incident response should also be conducted to evaluate the effectiveness of response plans and identify areas for improvement.

In addition, businesses are obligated to stay abreast of ever-changing regulatory standards and compliance requirements. Compliance with applicable cybersecurity standards, regulations, and privacy laws can only be ensured via ongoing assessments and audits, which also ensure continued adherence to industry standards. To cultivate a culture of continuous improvement within an organization, the security policies, processes, and controls should be regularly reviewed and updated. It is essential to conduct risk assessments so that new hazards can be identified and the effectiveness of existing controls can be assessed. The processes for handling incidents should be enhanced by implementing the lessons learned from past incidents and exercises.

7.1.9 Importance of Cybersecurity in Industry 4.0

With the introduction of Industry 4.0, cybersecurity has assumed a position of utmost importance. In this era of digital transformation, the interconnected character of industrial systems makes them vulnerable to a variety of potential threats. These threats include conventional assaults such as malware infections and data breaches, as well as more complex risks such as ransomware, supply chain attacks, and industrial espionage. Successful cyber assaults against industrial systems can have devastating consequences, including operational disruptions, financial losses, compromised safety, and reputational harm. Inadequate Industry 4.0 cybersecurity measures, expose organizations to risks such as unauthorized data access, intellectual property theft, regulatory noncompliance, and erosion of consumer trust. Organizations must prioritize comprehensive cybersecurity measures, such as risk assessment, security policies, secure network infrastructure, access management, training programs, incident response plans, and continuous monitoring, to mitigate these risks and ensure the resilience of industrial systems. Industry 4.0's digital ecosystem requires a proactive and comprehensive approach to cybersecurity to secure critical infrastructure, maintain operational continuity, and safeguard sensitive data.

7.1.10 Potential Cybersecurity Threats in the Context of Industry 4.0

Malware and ransomware attacks, in which malicious software can infiltrate industrial systems via multiple channels and disrupt operations, steal sensitive data, or hold systems captive, are a major concern. Cyberextortion is another term for these attacks. Another form of risk involves attacks against the supply chain. These attacks involve the insertion of a compromised component at any position along the supply chain. This component could then either enable unauthorized access to software or hardware or inject malicious code into software or hardware. In the context of Industry 4.0, insiders with access to vital systems can willfully abuse their privileges, take sensitive information, or sabotage systems, posing a substantial risk. The potential for distributed denial of service, or DDoS, attacks to disrupt industrial systems by flooding them with an excessive quantity of network data is another cause for concern. Weak access controls and compromised credentials can result in unauthorized data modifications and breaches. Additionally, unauthorized access and identity theft may result from these vulnerabilities.

Physical attacks, specifically those that target the intersection of digital and physical systems in Industry 4.0, pose an additional form of cybersecurity threat. When sensors are tampered with, when unauthorized personnel obtain physical access, or when infrastructure is intentionally damaged, both the availability and the integrity of industrial systems can be compromised. In addition, outdated software or firmware that does not include patching or vulnerability management leaves systems vulnerable to previously discovered exploits. In order to effectively address the challenges that exist today, organizations should employ a multilayered approach to cybersecurity. This includes the implementation of stringent network security measures, consistent vulnerability assessments, employee training, awareness initiatives, incident response planning, as well as industry standards and best practices.

7.1.11 Impact of Cyberattacks on Industrial Systems

In the era of Industry 4.0, cyberattacks on industrial systems have significant and far-reaching effects. These assaults can disrupt operations, result in financial losses, lead to the theft of intellectual property, pose safety risks, create environmental risks, and harm the reputation of an organization. Cyber assaults on industrial systems frequently result in operational disruptions, leading to production downtime and inefficiency. Manipulation or disabling of critical components hinders productivity, profitability, and customer satisfaction, thereby disrupting operational continuity as a whole.

Cyberattacks result in substantial financial losses due to system downtime, recovery efforts, investigations, and potential legal liabilities. Such financial burdens can have lasting effects on a company's development and stability. When industrial systems are compromised, intellectual property theft poses a grave threat. Attackers who obtain access to a company's proprietary designs, sensitive data, and trade secrets can undermine its competitive advantage, market position, and research efforts. Financial and reputational harm can be substantial when intellectual property is taken.

Cyberattacks on industrial control systems (ICSs) pose threats to public safety and the environment. Attackers can cause physical damage to equipment, compromise safety mechanisms, and disrupt critical infrastructure by manipulating control systems. This could contribute to accidents, injuries, or even environmental disasters, endangering worker safety. Organizations must prioritize robust cybersecurity measures to mitigate these hazards. Important components include proactive risk management, regular security assessments, employee training, and incident response planning. By investing in cybersecurity, businesses can defend industrial systems, lessen the impact of cyberattacks, and maintain operational continuity while protecting their financial stability, intellectual property, and reputation.

In the context of Industry 4.0, the absence of adequate cybersecurity protections exposes businesses to significant risks that could have been avoided. One of these hazards is the possibility of a data breach and subsequent information theft, which can lead to the loss of sensitive and valuable data, such as customer and intellectual property information. In addition to financial losses and reputational harm, these types of breaches have legal repercussions for the company. Operational interruptions and outages represent yet another significant threat. If insufficient cybersecurity measures are in place, vulnerabilities can be exploited, leading to unauthorized access to control systems, data modification, and the introduction of malware. These detrimental behaviors have the potential to severely disrupt industrial processes, which may lead to substantial monetary losses.

Inadequate cybersecurity increases the possibility of intellectual property theft as well as industrial espionage. If an organization does not prioritize cybersecurity, it leaves itself vulnerable to the prospect of unauthorized access, which makes it easier for confidential information, trade secrets, and R&D data to be stolen. Because of this, a company's ability to remain competitive and its future expansion potential are both hampered. In addition, the prevalence of malware infections and ransomware attacks cannot be disregarded and must be taken into account. Industrial systems with inadequate cybersecurity protections are susceptible to malware that can rapidly propagate throughout a network, resulting in disruptions to operations and the encryption of vital data. Typically, a company incurs financial losses and reputational harm as a result of such assaults.

Vulnerabilities in the supply chain are an additional risk associated with inadequate cybersecurity safeguards. Within the interconnected ecosystem of Industry 4.0, weak supply chain connections can be exploited to grant unauthorized access to attackers or enable the injection of malicious code into products and components. This can occur when an attacker effectively exploits a supply chain vulnerability. This places the supply chain's security and integrity at risk, which could lead to disruptions and compromised systems. In addition, there is a significant risk associated with failing to adhere to the sector-specific regulations and the laws that protect personal information. If an organization fails to take adequate cybersecurity precautions, it risks incurring legal consequences, such as fines, and suffering a reputational blow.

Companies must make cybersecurity a top priority within the context of Industry 4.0 if they wish to mitigate these threats effectively. When it comes to safeguarding digital infrastructure, systems, and data, the implementation of stringent safeguards becomes a must. These steps include the installation of robust security controls, the execution of frequent vulnerability assessments, and the development of a cybersecurity-focused culture through the implementation of awareness and training programs. Investing in cybersecurity enables businesses to defend against the risk of data breaches, limit the impact of operational disruptions, protect intellectual property, bolster the resilience of supply chains, and comply with applicable regulations. Moreover, adopting a proactive cybersecurity strategy contributes to the enhancement of brand reputation, the development of consumer trust, and the positioning of businesses for success within the digital ecosystem of Industry 4.0.

7.1.12 Implementing the Digital Transformation Cybersecurity Roadmap

An organized method is needed to implement the Digital Transformation Cybersecurity Roadmap. Organizations should first evaluate their present cybersecurity posture to find any gaps and weaknesses. It is necessary to identify specific goals and objectives that are in line with the organization's digital transformation strategy. To enable implementation, a phased approach with resource allocation and responsibility distribution should be designed. Firewalls and encryption tools should be installed and security policies and technology should also be regularly tested and validated. The roadmap can be modified and updated as needed by ongoing monitoring, ensuring that it is still effective against new threats. Following this roadmap will help businesses improve their security posture and protect vital processes and assets in the Industry 4.0 environment (Figure 7.2).

- *Assessing the Current Cybersecurity Posture*: Before embarking on the implementation of a cybersecurity roadmap, it is crucial to assess the current state of cybersecurity within the organization. This assessment helps identify existing vulnerabilities, gaps in security controls, and potential risks. It involves evaluating the effectiveness of current security measures, reviewing incident response capabilities, and assessing the level of employee awareness and training regarding cybersecurity.
- *Defining Goals and Objectives*: Once the assessment is complete, clear goals and objectives should be defined for the cybersecurity roadmap. These goals should align with the overall digital transformation strategy of the organization and address the specific cybersecurity challenges of Industry 4.0. Examples of goals include reducing the risk of cyberattacks, enhancing incident response capabilities, and ensuring compliance with relevant regulations and standards.
- *Developing a Phased Approach for Implementation*: Implementing the cybersecurity roadmap should be done in a structured and phased manner. Breaking down the implementation process into manageable phases allows for better resource allocation, risk management, and measurement of progress. Each phase should have specific tasks, timelines, and milestones to track the implementation progress effectively.

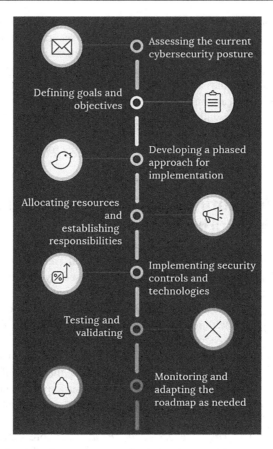

FIGURE 7.2   Roadmap for improving security posture.

- *Allocating Resources and Establishing Responsibilities*: Adequate resources, both financial and human, must be allocated to support the implementation of the cybersecurity roadmap. This includes budgetary considerations for acquiring security technologies, conducting training programs, and hiring skilled cybersecurity personnel if necessary. Clear responsibilities should be assigned to individuals or teams involved in the implementation process to ensure accountability and effective coordination.
- *Implementing Security Controls and Technologies*: The cybersecurity road-map should outline specific security controls and technologies that need to be implemented. This may include deploying firewalls, IDS, security infor-mation and event management (SIEM) systems, and encryption mechanisms. Additionally, access controls, secure coding practices, and secure network con-figurations should be implemented to strengthen the overall security posture.
- *Testing and Validating the Effectiveness of Implemented Measures*: It is essential to regularly test and validate the effectiveness of the implemented security measures. This can involve conducting vulnerability assessments,

penetration testing, and security audits to identify any weaknesses or gaps in the security controls. Testing should be done under both simulated and real-world scenarios to evaluate the resilience of the cybersecurity infrastructure against potential threats.

* *Monitoring and Adapting the Roadmap as Needed*: Cybersecurity is an ongoing process that requires continuous monitoring and adaptation. Regular monitoring of security logs, incident reports, and threat intelligence sources can help identify emerging threats and vulnerabilities. The cybersecurity roadmap should be flexible and adaptable, allowing for adjustments and updates as new risks and technologies emerge. It is important to stay updated with the evolving threat landscape and industry best practices to maintain a robust cybersecurity posture.

7.1.13 Best Practices and Considerations for Cybersecurity in Industry 4.0

To implement effective cybersecurity measures within Industry 4.0, it is necessary to adhere to a number of essential best practices and factors. Industry participants, government entities, and cybersecurity specialists must collaborate and share information to combat cybersecurity threats. This allows for the sharing of information, the dissemination of best practices, and the maintenance of heightened awareness of new threats. Increasing the number of sector-specific Information Sharing and Analysis Centers (ISACs) strengthens the community's defenses against intrusions.

It is imperative that the principles of security by design are incorporated into the industrial system lifecycle throughout the entire process. This requires incorporating cybersecurity considerations from the onset of the project, employing secure coding techniques, and undertaking thorough security evaluations as the system is being developed. A defense-in-depth strategy increases overall security by implementing multiple layers of security controls, such as firewalls, IDS, encryption, and authentication procedures. This strategy can be executed by instituting multiple layers of security controls. When it comes to identifying vulnerabilities in industrial systems, networks, and applications, vulnerability assessments and penetration testing must be performed on a regular basis. These assessments help prioritize the deployment of security updates and upgrades, whereas penetration testing simulates actual cyberattacks to identify potential vulnerabilities. Taking action to resolve these findings will enhance the overall security posture of the systems and ensure their effectiveness.

Moreover, ensuring the security of the supply chain is an absolute requirement. The establishment of stringent supplier screening criteria ensures that third-party partners and vendors adhere to the most effective cybersecurity practices. Routinely auditing and evaluating the security procedures of suppliers enables both the identification of potential threats and the maintenance of compliance with security standards. Compliance with all applicable cybersecurity legislation and standards is of the uttermost importance. Organizations are obligated to maintain an up-to-date understanding of the regulatory landscape and to comply with the requirements of regulations such as GDPR and industry-specific standards such as the NIST Cybersecurity Framework. Implementing a methodical strategy to analyze and maintain compliance guarantees the conformity of cybersecurity measures with industry standards and laws.

7.2 RISK ASSESSMENT AND PLAN

In this era of rapid digital transformation, businesses are constantly adopting new technologies and methods to remain competitive and meet the ever-changing needs of their consumers. Despite having a number of advantages, digital transformation poses a number of risks, particularly in terms of cybersecurity. To ensure the success of digital transformation programs and their long-term viability, it is necessary to comprehend these risks and implement countermeasures. In the context of digital transformation, the purpose of conducting a risk assessment is to identify, analyze, and evaluate the various potential threats that could compromise the availability, integrity, and confidentiality of sensitive data and systems. A company can develop an effective cybersecurity roadmap by methodically examining the risks it encounters. This enables the company to protect itself from potential threats while achieving its strategic objectives.

The Digital Transformation Cybersecurity Roadmap is a comprehensive roadmap designed to guide businesses in managing the cybersecurity risks associated with their digital transformation endeavors. It provides a structured method for identifying vulnerabilities, assessing the potential impact of threats, and implementing appropriate controls and safeguards to manage risks. The road map takes into consideration numerous factors, including technologies, processes, and people, in order to construct a comprehensive cybersecurity architecture. It entails identifying vital assets and systems that are part of digital transformation, undertaking an evaluation of potential threats and opportunities, and developing a strategic plan for mitigating risks.

By implementing the Digital Transformation Cybersecurity Roadmap, businesses can enhance their cybersecurity posture, reduce the likelihood of security events and the damage they cause, and cultivate a secure digital environment for their operations and the stakeholders they serve. The following sections will discuss the process of risk assessment, the development of a cybersecurity roadmap, risk reduction strategies, plan implementation and monitoring, stakeholder communication and reporting, and the ongoing nature of cybersecurity initiatives.

7.2.1 Process

The process of risk assessment is an essential component in providing digital transformation efforts with the necessary level of cyber protection. It entails using a methodical approach for detecting and analyzing the potential dangers and weak spots in digital assets and systems, which could lead to a breach of confidentiality, integrity, and availability of those assets and systems. An organization can obtain useful insights into the possible dangers they face and establish an effective plan to minimize those risks if they

TABLE 7.2 The risk assessment process for digital transformation

STEPS	OUTPUT	ACTION	RESULT
Identification of assets and systems involved in digital transformation	Documented digital assets, systems, and technologies involved in the initiative	Identify and document digital assets, systems, and technologies involved in the initiative	List of identified digital assets, systems, and technologies
Determination of potential threats and vulnerabilities	Identified potential threats and vulnerabilities in the identified assets and systems	Analyze and identify potential threats and vulnerabilities in the identified assets and systems	List of identified potential threats and vulnerabilities
Assessment of likelihood and impact of risks	Evaluation of the likelihood and potential impact of each identified risk	Assess the likelihood and potential impact of each identified risk	Evaluation of the likelihood and potential impact of identified risks
Prioritization of risks based on severity and criticality	Prioritized risks based on severity and criticality	Prioritize risks based on their severity and criticality	List of prioritized risks based on severity and criticality
Documentation of risk assessment findings	Documented risk assessment findings, including identified risks, their likelihood, and impact	Document the findings of the risk assessment process, including identified risks, their likelihood, potential impact, and prioritization.	Comprehensive documentation of risk assessment findings and their associated details

undertake a thorough risk assessment and follow it up with regular risk management reviews. Table 7.2 outlines the different steps involved in conducting a risk assessment to ensure cyber protection for digital transformation efforts. The process of carrying out a risk assessment can be broken down into the following steps:

(A) *Identification of Assets and Systems Involved in Digital Transformation*: The first step is to identify and document the digital assets, systems, and technologies that are part of the digital transformation initiative. This includes identifying databases, networks, cloud services, software applications, and IoT devices.

(B) *Determination of Potential Threats and Vulnerabilities*: Next, a careful analysis is performed to identify potential threats that could exploit vulnerabilities in the identified assets and systems. Threats may include cyberattacks, data breaches, insider threats, or natural disasters. Vulnerabilities such as weak passwords, outdated software, misconfigurations, or lack of security controls are also assessed.

(C) *Assessment of Likelihood and Impact of Risks*: Each identified risk is evaluated to determine its likelihood of occurrence and potential impact on the organization. Factors such as the capabilities of threat actors, the value of the asset, potential consequences of an attack, and historical data on similar incidents are considered during this assessment.

(D) *Prioritization of Risks based on Severity and Criticality*: Risks are prioritized based on their severity and criticality. The focus is placed on risks with high potential impact and likelihood. This prioritization helps allocate resources effectively and enables the organization to address the most significant risks first.

(E) *Documentation of Risk Assessment Findings*: The findings of the risk assessment process, including identified risks, their likelihood, potential impact, and prioritization, are documented. This documentation serves as a reference for developing risk mitigation strategies and for monitoring progress over time.

7.2.2 Cybersecurity Roadmap Development

Developing a cybersecurity roadmap as part of the process of digital transformation is an essential step that must be taken to manage risks and guarantee the safety of essential assets properly. The process of developing a cybersecurity roadmap requires several important actions to be taken. To begin, it is absolutely necessary to identify the aims and objectives of cybersecurity in a way that is compatible with the entire company's objectives. Among these objectives may be the protection of client data, the continuation of corporate operations, and the fulfillment of regulatory requirements. The next step in the successful management of cybersecurity is to create a governance structure and divide up the tasks among the various members of the organization. This involves identifying important stakeholders within the organization, such as executive management, IT teams, and legal and compliance departments, and outlining the roles that they play as well as the decision-making authority that they have inside the cybersecurity governance framework.

Once the goals and governance have been established, the next step is to determine the controls and mechanisms required for adequate cybersecurity. Assessing the risks that are involved with digital transformation and choosing controls that are suitable on a technological, administrative, and physical level are components of this process. Firewalls on networks, IDSs, access controls, and encryption protocols are a few examples of the types of controls that fall under this category. Establishing a comprehensive implementation timeline with milestones is recommended in order to increase the likelihood of a successful implementation. This timeframe makes it possible to track progress and guarantees that cybersecurity actions will be put into place at the appropriate moment. In addition, the process of budgeting and allocating resources plays an essential part in providing support for the cybersecurity plan. For the purpose of supporting the implementation of cybersecurity measures, sufficient resources, which should include finance, qualified employees, and the requisite technology, should be allocated.

7.2.3 Risk Mitigation Strategies

Implementing suitable measures for risk mitigation is an absolute must if one is serious about effectively addressing the dangers posed by cybersecurity in the context of digital transformation. These tactics are intended to reduce the possibility of potential threats and vulnerabilities as well as the impact of those threats and vulnerabilities, thereby protecting digital assets. The following is a list of key risk reduction measures that should be considered.

To get started, companies should put in place solid technical controls and safety measures. This entails installing network security mechanisms to monitor and safeguard network traffic, such as firewalls and IDS/IPS. Access control measures should also be implemented, with the enforcement of robust authentication methods and adherence to the principle of least privilege for the purpose of restricting unauthorized access. Encryption and protection of data, both while the data is in transit and while it is at rest, help to reduce the danger of data being compromised. The security of devices that are linked to a network can also be improved by installing endpoint security solutions. Examples of such solutions include antivirus software, antimalware software, and host intrusion prevention systems (HIPSs).

The establishment of security awareness and training programs is also an essential component of the solution. Organizations have the ability to educate their staff and stakeholders on the most effective cybersecurity best practices by routinely conducting training sessions. This includes educating people about phishing scams, social engineering, and safe browsing practices, as well as raising awareness about these threats. It is also a crucial component of this plan to encourage employees to report any suspicious behaviors they observe swiftly and to cultivate a culture throughout the firm that places a high priority on security. It is equally necessary to create thorough plans for responding to incidents and recovering from natural disasters. Organizations can successfully prepare for potential cybersecurity issues by first developing an incident response strategy and then testing it on a regular basis. This includes defining roles and duties, setting up communication channels, and specifying the appropriate procedures that need to be performed in the event that there is a breach in security. In the event that a catastrophic event occurs, having a solid disaster recovery strategy in place ensures the quick restoration of both systems and data.

A fundamental component of risk reduction is the ongoing monitoring and evaluation of the efficiency of the controls that have been put into place. Organizations are able to detect potentially harmful activity and respond to potential security breaches if they make use of tools designed specifically for security monitoring. It is helpful to evaluate the effectiveness of controls and identify areas for improvement if frequent assessments, such as vulnerability scans and penetration tests, are carried out on a consistent basis. In conclusion, it is essential to stress the ongoing nature of the cybersecurity measures that are being taken. Continuous progress is required in order to remain flexible in the face of ever-evolving dangers and technologies. Maintaining an effective cybersecurity posture requires regularly assessing and updating risk mitigation methods, being updated about evolving cyber threats, and making control adjustments as necessary.

7.2.4 Plan Implementation and Monitoring

After the cybersecurity roadmap has been prepared, the next critical step is to ensure that the plan is being implemented correctly and that it is being continuously monitored. During this phase, it is made certain that the identified cybersecurity procedures and controls are put into effect in order to protect the organization's digital transformation projects and mitigate any risks that may be present. In addition to this, it entails keeping track of progress, making changes as they become necessary, and guaranteeing conformity with the goals and objectives that have been defined. The following actions provide an explanation of the most important parts of plan execution and monitoring.

7.2.4.1 Execute the cybersecurity roadmap

The execution of the cybersecurity roadmap requires a number of critical steps to be taken in order to guarantee the effective implementation of security measures and to secure the digital transformation activities being undertaken by the business. To get started, it is necessary to establish priorities and delegate activities based on the level of importance and immediacy they require. It is necessary to segment the roadmap into actionable initiatives and effectively communicate roles, responsibilities, and dates to the appropriate persons or teams. It is essential, in order to support the execution of the plan, to allow the appropriate resources, which may include the budget, the personnel, and the technology. Collaborating with the various stakeholders helps to secure the necessary resources and ensure that they are aligned with the objectives of the roadmap.

Following this, comprehensive implementation plans need to be prepared for each individual job or project outlined in the roadmap. These plans should include certain action stages, milestones, and dates, all of which should take into consideration dependencies and potential dangers. It is absolutely necessary for there to be effective communication and coordination among all of the parties involved in the execution process. Regular engagement with information technology teams, professionals in the information security field, business units, and executives helps preserve alignment and shared understanding. The cultivation of an open and honest working atmosphere is facilitated by the provision of progress updates and the resolution of concerns.

During the implementation phase, you will also be tasked with putting into place the required technological controls and safeguards that were outlined in the roadmap. This encompasses a wide range of operations, including the installation of security software and hardware, the configuration of network and system settings, the fortification of access controls, and the implementation of encryption technologies. Maintaining a close working relationship with IT teams allows for the seamless integration of security measures, which keeps digital transformation programs running smoothly. In addition, providing staff with cybersecurity training helps boost the understanding of recommended practices, common dangers, and individual responsibilities in the process of protecting digital assets.

The establishment of a plan for responding to incidents and the delineation of protocols for recognizing, reporting, and reacting to security breaches are also extremely important steps to take. It is helpful to validate the effectiveness of the incident response plan by testing it on a regular basis through drills and simulations. Establishing a reliable monitoring system paves the way for constant tracking of the effectiveness of security control as well as the discovery of potential security holes or weaknesses. The process of documenting the implementation, the lessons learned, and the results that were accomplished provide significant insights. Visibility for the purposes of regulatory compliance can be ensured for stakeholders, management, and other relevant parties by generating frequent updates on the status and efficacy of the roadmap.

7.2.4.2 Regularly review and update the plan

It is necessary to perform routine reviews and updates on the cybersecurity plan in order to guarantee its efficacy and ensure that it remains aligned with the ever-evolving digital ecosystem. Participation from relevant stakeholders is required throughout this process, as is the analysis of any shifts in the danger landscape, evaluation of control effectiveness, and determination of any necessary revisions. Organizations are able to proactively handle new risks and improve their security posture when they follow a disciplined approach to risk management.

For the purpose of obtaining an exhaustive analysis of the plan's efficacy, businesses should make it a point to involve all important stakeholders during the review cycle. These stakeholders should include IT teams, security specialists, and business leaders. It is essential to conduct an analysis of changes in the threat landscape in order to maintain awareness of the most recent cybersecurity threats and vulnerabilities. This includes keeping an eye on threat intelligence sources and reports from the industry, in addition to working with independent cybersecurity specialists from outside the organization. Organizations are able to identify areas that need to be strengthened or new controls that need to be adopted by reviewing the effectiveness of the controls and measures that have been implemented and putting them into place.

On the basis of the findings of the assessment, organizations are able to prioritize the necessary updates and enhancements to the cybersecurity plan. Any updates should be in line with the goals of the firm, any applicable regulatory requirements, and industry standards. It is essential to win the support and cooperation of key stakeholders before beginning the process of execution and to do so, you must first obtain their buy-in. After the revisions have been accepted, they ought to be implemented, with clear duties and timetables being allocated to the necessary parties. Continuous monitoring and measuring of progress, in addition to documentation and version control, are all important components that contribute to the upkeep of an accurate and efficient cybersecurity plan.

7.2.4.3 Monitor and track progress

Establishing KPIs that are aligned with the goals and objectives of the cybersecurity roadmap is required in order to monitor and measure progress. The effectiveness of the controls that have been introduced can be better understood by collecting and evaluating relevant data, such as reports of security incidents, results of vulnerability assessments, and audits of compliance. Audits and evaluations of the cybersecurity posture should be performed on a periodic basis in order to help detect any gaps or flaws.

In the context of monitoring, incident response and event management play a very important role. The timely identification and handling of potential dangers or security lapses are made possible by putting in place an incident response plan and monitoring security occurrences in real time. It is possible to keep tabs on incident response metrics such as mean time to detect (MTTD) and mean time to respond (MTTR) in order to determine how well issue-handling procedures are being carried out. It is crucial to communicate the progress that has been made and the current state of cybersecurity activities via regular reporting. The most important metrics, noteworthy events or incidents, risk assessments, and any changes or revisions to the cybersecurity plan should be highlighted in the reports. When reports are tailored to the audience for which they are intended, stakeholders are guaranteed to receive information that is both relevant and actionable.

In addition, monitoring makes ongoing development easier to do. Organizations are able to find opportunities for improvement in the controls that have been installed, the procedures that they use, or the employee training that they provide by examining the data that has been collected and getting insights through monitoring. It is essential to regularly revise and update the cybersecurity roadmap as well as any associated documentation in light of newly acquired knowledge and changing dangers. Participating in discussions with various stakeholders and requesting input from them both contribute to making the cybersecurity program more efficient.

7.2.4.4 Periodic risk assessments

Organizations are able to detect new risks, evaluate the effectiveness of current controls, and make educated decisions regarding risk mitigation methods, if they do periodic risk assessments and follow the guidelines. To begin, it is essential to routinely review and update the scope of the risk assessment, taking into account any changes in the organization's digital transformation projects, systems, technologies, and external factors. This should be done at least once every three months. Find out what assets, procedures, and data need to be evaluated so that you can be sure that you have full coverage.

Next, do an assessment of the possible dangers and openings that could put the digital assets and activities of the company in jeopardy. Maintain a high level of awareness regarding the most recent cybersecurity dangers, attack methods, and sector-specific risks. Assess both internal and external variables, including malware, social engineering, insider threats, regulatory compliance concerns, and supply chain vulnerabilities, among other potential dangers. Evaluate the likelihood and impact of the risks that have been discovered by taking into account the possibility that a risk event will occur, as well as the potential effects that this risk event could have on the organization's operations, reputation, financials, and compliance. Take into account the worth of the asset, the efficiency of the safeguards that are already in place, and the potential knock-on effects that could result from a successful assault.

Establish priorities for the risks based on their level of severity and criticality, ranking them according to the potential impact they could have and the likelihood that they will really materialize. This prioritizing makes it possible to allocate resources effectively and assists in concentrating on tackling high-risk areas first while also taking into consideration dependencies and interdependencies among risks. Develop appropriate risk mitigation measures depending on the risks that have been identified. These strategies should include a mix of technical controls, process enhancements, and training programs to address vulnerabilities and lower the possibility of potential threats as well as their potential impact. Maintain constant vigilance in monitoring and tracking the progress of risk reduction initiatives in order to guarantee the efficiency of controls that have been put in place. Document the findings of the risk assessment, including the risks that were identified, the measures to mitigate those risks, and the tracking of progress. The results of the assessment should be communicated to the relevant stakeholders in order to increase awareness and garner support for risk reduction actions.

7.2.5 Effective Stakeholder Communication and Reporting

Throughout the process of implementation, organizations may create collaboration, acquire support, and maintain alignment by engaging stakeholders and delivering transparent updates. To get started, it is necessary to determine who the important stakeholders are and to cater the communication to the individual requirements and worries of each group. It is important to utilize language that is both clear and succinct when communicating the findings of the risk assessment process, which should include a discussion of potential threats, vulnerabilities, and the impact these factors will have on digital transformation initiatives. The cybersecurity controls and measures that will be adopted to manage risks should be explained to stakeholders, along with the logic for these strategies and the anticipated benefits for the company. Stakeholders should be informed about these controls and measures.

It is important to present stakeholders with regular progress reports so that they are kept informed and engaged. These reports emphasize achievements in the implementation of cybersecurity controls and procedures, such as finished milestones and successful attempts to mitigate risk. It is important to discuss not only the difficulties that have been faced but also the measures that have been taken to overcome them. To demonstrate that cybersecurity initiatives are effective, metrics and data like the amount of time it takes to respond to an incident or the number of vulnerabilities that have been reduced should be included.

In addition to providing reports, organizations should also actively seek feedback and input from the stakeholders in their communities. This can be accomplished through the use of questionnaires, focus groups, or frequent meetings to collect their points of view, address any problems or suggestions, and solicit more feedback. Incorporating the comments of stakeholders into the cybersecurity roadmap not only indicates a commitment to continual development but also ensures that the plan continues to be aligned with the organization's ever-evolving objectives and priorities. Building trust and confidence in the organization's cybersecurity activities can be facilitated by promptly responding to the queries and concerns raised by stakeholders in an open and honest manner. Fostering collaboration and ensuring a united approach to safe digital transformation activities is something that can be accomplished when organizations properly communicate cybersecurity risks, progress, and mitigation actions. Mechanisms for regular reporting and feedback enable modifications, enhancements, and a proactive reaction to new threats to cybersecurity. Table 7.3 highlights the importance of each aspect and suggests actions that organizations should take to ensure successful implementation.

TABLE 7.3   Effective communication and engagement for cybersecurity initiatives

ASPECT	DESCRIPTION	ACTION REQUIRED
Stakeholder Engagement	– Identify important stakeholders and cater communication to their individual requirements and concerns.	Engage
	– Utilize clear and succinct language when communicating the findings of the risk assessment process.	Communicate
	– Discuss potential threats, vulnerabilities, and the impact on digital transformation initiatives.	Inform
	– Explain cybersecurity controls and measures to manage risks, along with the logic and anticipated benefits.	Explain
	– Inform stakeholders about the adopted controls and measures.	Inform
Progress Reports	– Provide regular progress reports to stakeholders to keep them informed and engaged.	Report
	– Emphasize achievements in the implementation of cybersecurity controls and procedures, including milestones and successful risk mitigation.	Highlight
	– Discuss difficulties faced and measures taken to overcome them.	Address
	– Include metrics and data demonstrating the effectiveness of cybersecurity initiatives, such as incident response time and reduction in vulnerabilities.	Include
Stakeholder Feedback and Input	– Actively seek feedback and input from stakeholders through questionnaires, focus groups, and frequent meetings.	Collect
	– Collect points of view, address problems or suggestions, and solicit more feedback.	Address
	– Incorporate stakeholder comments into the cybersecurity roadmap to demonstrate commitment to continual development and alignment with objectives and priorities.	Incorporate
Prompt Response to Queries and Concerns	– Respond promptly to queries and concerns raised by stakeholders in an open and honest manner.	Respond
	– Build trust and confidence in the organization's cybersecurity activities.	Build trust
Collaboration and Unified Approach	– Communicate cybersecurity risks, progress, and mitigation actions effectively.	Collaborate
	– Foster collaboration and ensure a united approach to safe digital transformation activities.	Foster
	– Mechanisms for regular reporting and feedback allow for modifications, enhancements, and proactive responses to new cybersecurity threats.	Modify/Enhance

7.3 EVALUATING AND ENHANCING CYBERSECURITY

In the quickly developing digital landscape of today, businesses are increasingly adopting digital transformation in order to improve their operations, provide better experiences for their customers, and drive innovation. This digital revolution, on the other hand, ushers in a slew of brand-new cybersecurity concerns and hazards that businesses and other organizations need to manage successfully. Within the context of digital transformation, enterprises are able to evaluate and improve their level of cybersecurity with the help of a complete framework known as the Digital Transformation Cybersecurity Roadmap. It comprises a wide range of essential components, such as threat detection and response, IAM, security awareness and training, compliance and governance, and risk assessment and analysis. By adhering to this road map, organizations will be able to conduct a methodical assessment of their present cybersecurity posture, locate any flaws, and prioritize activities to upgrade their security measures. The roadmap places a strong emphasis on the significance of connecting cybersecurity activities with digital transformation goals, assuring the safety of digital assets and infrastructure while simultaneously fostering a well-informed workforce and maintaining regulatory compliance.

This section's goal is to examine the assessment and improvement of cybersecurity in the context of digital transformation, with a particular emphasis on the Digital Transformation Cybersecurity Roadmap as the primary topic of discussion. When companies begin their travels toward digital transformation, it is absolutely necessary to have a thorough cybersecurity strategy in place so that sensitive data can be protected, important systems can be safeguarded, and the trust of customers and other stakeholders can be preserved. This section will delve into the important features of the Digital Transformation Cybersecurity Roadmap, which acts as a framework for reviewing the existing cybersecurity measures and implementing any necessary changes. The roadmap was developed in order to prepare for the digital transformation. Organizations are able to identify vulnerabilities, reduce threats, and develop a resilient cybersecurity posture that is aligned with their digital transformation efforts if they follow this plan.

7.3.1 Evaluating Current Cybersecurity Measures

It is essential to carry out a thorough review of the organization's existing cybersecurity measures before attempting to improve cybersecurity by utilizing the Digital Transformation Cybersecurity Roadmap. During this assessment, numerous facets of cybersecurity will be evaluated. Some of these aspects include security policies and procedures, the security of infrastructure and networks, data protection measures, incident response capabilities, and vendor and third-party risk management. By evaluating themselves in these categories, firms can determine the areas of the present cybersecurity framework in which they excel and in which they need improvement.

7.3.1.1 Assessment of the organization's current cybersecurity posture

An assessment of the current state of cybersecurity within the organization yields insights that can be used to secure digital assets and reduce the likelihood of cyberattacks. Standard procedures during an assessment consist of reviewing security policies and procedures, evaluating infrastructure and network security, assessing data protection measures, evaluating IAM practices, evaluating incident response capabilities, reviewing employee awareness and training programs, and reviewing vendor and third-party risk management practices. In addition, compliance with regulatory agency requirements is evaluated. A comprehensive analysis of the company's current security policies, processes, and controls is an essential component of evaluating its current cybersecurity posture. This section aids in determining the effectiveness of the currently implemented cybersecurity measures and identifies areas for improvement. The assessment includes an analysis of data protection regulations, security policies, acceptable utilization regulations, and incident response protocols. In addition, it evaluates the clarity and comprehensiveness of these policies, as well as the extent to which they are enforced across the enterprise (Figure 7.3).

The evaluation will also consider the company's infrastructure and network security. This will include an examination of the company's network architecture, firewalls, IDS/IPS, and secure network configurations. Due to this analysis, appropriate network segmentation and access controls will be implemented to prevent unauthorized access. The application of security patches and enhancements to the various infrastructure components is evaluated to ensure that a robust security posture is maintained. The evaluation places a heavy emphasis on the data protection measures, specifically the encryption mechanisms, access controls, and data backup and recovery procedures. This review focuses on the protection of intellectual property, personally identifiable information (PII), and sensitive data in the company's operations. In addition, it performs an analysis of the presence of data categorization and management methods to ensure that sensitive data is adequately protected.

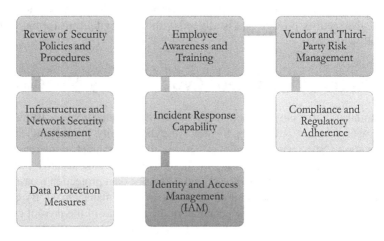

FIGURE 7.3   Evaluation of the organization's present cybersecurity position.

The practices of IAM are subjected to a thorough evaluation to determine the success of user access controls, authentication systems, and authorization procedures. The assessment also includes the administration of user accounts, including provisioning, deprovisioning, and periodic access assessments. Important systems and privileged accounts are undergoing a review of the use of MFA to strengthen security further. As part of this evaluation, the capabilities of the organization to respond to incidents, including the incident response strategy and processes, are being evaluated. It evaluates the organization's ability to respond to and recover from security incidents, as well as its incident detection and monitoring systems. Additionally, employee awareness and training programs are evaluated with the objective of ensuring that employees are aware of the most common forms of online attack, social engineering techniques, and the most effective methods for maintaining secure behavior. In the final phase of the evaluation, vendor and third-party risk management processes are evaluated to determine how well the organization analyzes and manages cybersecurity risks associated with external parties. In addition, compliance with applicable industry regulations, data protection laws, and privacy regulations is audited to ensure security standards are met.

7.3.1.2 Identification of strengths and weaknesses in the existing cybersecurity framework

In order to acquire a comprehensive understanding of the company's current security status, it is necessary to identify both the framework's strengths and weaknesses when conducting an analysis of the existing cybersecurity framework (Figure 7.4). Recognizing the organization's assets allows it to capitalize and expand upon its existing good practices. These characteristics can include personnel awareness and training programs, regular updates and patch management, effective incident response capabilities, comprehensive security controls, and adherence to applicable regulations and standards.

Identifying flaws, on the other hand, draws attention to areas of weakness or lacking components in cybersecurity measures. It is possible for weaknesses to manifest as

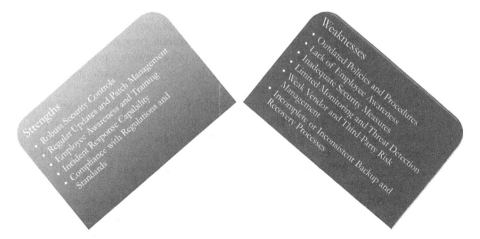

FIGURE 7.4 Several factors for identifying strengths and shortcomings.

out-of-date rules and procedures, a lack of staff awareness, inadequate security measures, limited monitoring and threat detection capabilities, ineffective vendor and third-party risk management practices, or insufficient and inconsistent backup and recovery procedures. The identification of these deficiencies is a prerequisite for both the detection of these vulnerabilities and the improvement of the broader cybersecurity framework.

In addition, it is necessary to conduct an analysis of the potential weaknesses and risks that are unique to the company's digital transformation initiatives during the evaluation. Due to the fact that digital transformation frequently entails the introduction of new technologies, networked systems, and expanded attack surfaces, it is necessary to conduct a more in-depth analysis of the associated risks. This analysis must account for a number of factors, including the migration to the cloud, the adoption of IoT, the use of mobile devices, remote work arrangements, and the integration of third-party systems. In addition, keeping abreast of new cyber threats and trends ensures that the organization is prepared to face evolving risks.

7.3.1.3 Analysis of potential vulnerabilities and threats in the context of digital transformation

In the context of digital transformation, businesses are confronted with a plethora of possible vulnerabilities and attacks that might put their cybersecurity at risk. It is absolutely necessary to carry out a detailed assessment of these dangers in order to devise preventative measures against them. When doing an analysis of potential vulnerabilities and threats, the following are some important topics to consider:

(A) *Increased Attack Surface*: Digital transformation often involves the adoption of new technologies, such as cloud computing, IoT devices, and mobile applications. Each of these technologies introduces additional entry points for potential cyberattacks, expanding the organization's attack surface. Analyzing the security implications of these technologies and assessing their potential vulnerabilities is vital.

(B) *Data Breaches and Privacy Concerns*: With the increasing volume and value of data being generated and processed during digital transformation initiatives, the risk of data breaches and privacy violations becomes a significant concern. Organizations must evaluate the security measures protecting their data, including encryption, access controls, data classification, and secure data storage and transmission.

(C) *Insider Threats*: Digital transformation involves organizational changes, such as new roles, responsibilities, and access privileges. It is crucial to assess the potential risks posed by insider threats, including malicious insiders, unintentional errors, and negligence. Evaluating access controls and user privileges and implementing monitoring mechanisms can help detect and mitigate insider threats.

(D) *Third-Party Risks*: Organizations often rely on third-party vendors, suppliers, and service providers for various aspects of their digital transformation initiatives. Assessing the security posture of these third parties, including their cybersecurity practices, data protection measures, and compliance with industry standards, is critical to mitigating potential risks associated with outsourcing or partnering with external entities.

(E) *Advanced Persistent Threats (APTs)*: APTs are sophisticated, targeted attacks that aim to gain persistent access to an organization's systems over an extended period. These threats can bypass traditional security measures and exploit vulnerabilities in the organization's infrastructure. Analyzing the potential risks posed by APTs, conducting threat modeling exercises, and implementing advanced threat detection and response mechanisms are essential to counteract these threats.

(F) *Compliance and Regulatory Risks*: Digital transformation often involves compliance with industry regulations, data protection laws, and privacy requirements. Failure to comply with these regulations can result in significant financial penalties and reputational damage. Organizations need to assess the potential risks associated with noncompliance, ensure appropriate controls and processes are in place, and regularly monitor and audit compliance measures.

(G) *Social Engineering and Phishing Attacks*: As digital transformation progresses, social engineering attacks, such as phishing and pretexting, become more prevalent. Analyzing the susceptibility of employees to such attacks, implementing robust security awareness and training programs and employing email filtering and other anti-phishing measures are crucial to mitigate these risks.

(H) *Supply Chain Risks*: Organizations relying on a complex supply chain face inherent risks related to the security practices of their suppliers and partners. Assessing the security posture of suppliers, conducting due diligence, and establishing contractual requirements for security controls are essential to mitigate supply chain risks.

7.3.1.4 Conducting gap analysis to identify areas for improvement

In the context of digital transformation, conducting a gap analysis is a necessary stage prior to analyzing and enhancing cybersecurity. The company's current cybersecurity procedures and practices are evaluated and compared to the industry's established standards, best practices, and regulatory requirements. By adhering to a methodical methodology that enables them to identify these areas, organizations are able to prioritize their efforts to strengthen those areas where their current cybersecurity framework contains gaps or flaws. To get started, businesses must establish the criteria that will serve as the benchmark for evaluating their cybersecurity precautions. This includes identifying the cybersecurity standards, regulations, and legislation that are relevant to their industry and operations. After establishing the criteria, the organization can conduct an audit of its extant cybersecurity processes. This audit will assess the organization's policies, procedures, technologies, and controls across multiple security domains. Table 7.4 presents gap analysis steps for enhancing cybersecurity.

When the company's practices are compared to the established standards, voids and deficiencies can be identified as a result of the evaluation. This investigation uncovers issues such as outdated software, inadequate encryption techniques, insufficient authentication mechanisms, and inadequate security awareness programs. Once the holes have been identified, the company can designate them a priority based on their potential impact and danger. This requires considering a variety of criteria, such as the likelihood that they will be exploited and the potential consequences of a security violation.

TABLE 7.4   Gap analysis steps for enhancing cybersecurity

STEPS	IMPORTANCE	RESOURCES NEEDED
Establish criteria for benchmarking cybersecurity	High	Cybersecurity experts, industry standards, and regulatory guidelines
Conduct an audit of existing cybersecurity processes	High	Internal IT team and audit tools
Compare practices to established standards	Medium	Industry benchmarks and best practices
Identify gaps and deficiencies	High	Gap analysis tools and evaluation frameworks
Prioritize gaps based on impact and danger	High	Risk assessment methodologies and expertise
Develop an action plan for addressing deficiencies	High	Project management tools and strategic planning
Assign roles, establish timelines, and set objectives	Medium	Project managers, team members, and timeline templates
Consider budget, resources, and priorities	Medium	Financial department and resource allocation framework
Implement an action plan and allocate resources	High	IT team, budget allocation, and necessary technologies
Monitor progress and track improvements	Medium	Monitoring tools and progress tracking systems
Evaluate and update strategy consistently	Medium	Evaluation criteria and periodic review process
Gain insights into the current cybersecurity posture	High	Data analysis tools and cybersecurity metrics
Prioritize efforts and create a roadmap	High	Strategic planning and roadmap templates
Strengthen defense and protect digital assets	High	Security technologies and encryption mechanisms
Preserve reputation in a complex digital landscape	High	Crisis management team and communication strategies

When businesses possess the prioritized gaps, they are able to develop an action plan that outlines the steps necessary to address each identified deficiency. In the strategy, roles should be assigned, timelines should be established, and measurable objectives should be outlined for each improvement initiative. It is also essential to consider factors such as budgetary constraints, available resources, and the business's priorities. When organizations implement and monitor progress, they are able to implement their action plan, allocate the necessary resources, and perpetually track the improvements that have been made. If the strategy is to effectively manage newly emerging threats and shifting expectations imposed on businesses, it must be evaluated consistently and kept up to date.

By conducting a detailed gap analysis and identifying areas that require attention and improvement, organizations can gain valuable insights into their current cybersecurity posture and identify areas that require attention and improvement. Within the context of their larger voyage toward digital transformation, this method enables businesses to prioritize their efforts, distribute their resources appropriately, and create a road map for enhancing cybersecurity. Ultimately, it enables businesses to strengthen their defense against cyber assaults, preserve their digital assets and data, and protect their reputation in an increasingly complex and interconnected digital landscape.

7.3.2 Enhancing Cybersecurity through the Digital Transformation Cybersecurity Roadmap

In the constantly shifting world of digital transformation, where innovation and connectivity are held in the highest esteem, the requirement for comprehensive cybersecurity measures has never been more vital. In the same breath that businesses recognize the potential of digital technologies to change their business processes, same businesses must simultaneously strengthen their defenses to ward off the ever-present dangers posed by the cyber realm. In this effort to review and improve cybersecurity, the Digital Transformation Cybersecurity Roadmap has emerged as an illuminating beacon of direction.

Within the context of digital transformation, the Digital Transformation Cybersecurity Roadmap is essentially a complete framework that equips organizations with the capabilities necessary to navigate the challenging landscape of cybersecurity successfully. It acts as a compass, pointing leaders in the direction of a digital future that is both secure and robust.

The first thing that needs to be done in order to get started on this journey toward transformation is to conduct an in-depth analysis of the organization's present cybersecurity posture. It is possible to make specific modifications after completing an in-depth study, which reveals both the strengths and flaws of the situation. When businesses are armed with this knowledge, they are better able to spot possible vulnerabilities and threats that are hiding beneath the surface of their digital projects, which enables them to secure their digital assets proactively.

As the roadmap is developed, solid security architecture and design will move to the forefront of attention. This foundation serves as a fortified bastion against cyber enemies, ensuring the continued safety of digital assets and infrastructure. Organizations build an unbreakable relationship between creativity and resilience by incorporating security into the core fabric of digital transformation projects. IAM provide the function of a diligent gatekeeper in the field of cybersecurity. A castle is only a complete stronghold with such a gatekeeper. For the purpose of preventing unauthorized access and thwarting malevolent conduct, these measures need to be strengthened immediately. The roadmap serves as a guide for enterprises as they create tight policies that provide seamless access to authorized users while also creating impenetrable walls against cyberattacks.

Threats, on the other hand, are continually shifting and adjusting as a result of the dynamic nature of the cyber landscape. The deployment of sophisticated threat detection and response mechanisms is one of the steps that the road map recommends taking to tackle this persistent foe and monitoring in real time, algorithms for ML, and intelligent automation work together to detect and eliminate threats with a level of speed and accuracy not previously possible. Organizations now have the ability to tackle cyber threats head-on, allowing them to stay one step ahead in the never-ending game of cat and mouse.

However, the fight to maintain cybersecurity is not fought exclusively in the world of technology; rather, it encompasses each and every person working for the business. Due to the fact that this is the case, the roadmap places an emphasis on the need for security awareness and training. Employees become the first line of defense when they are provided with the information and tools to recognize and respond appropriately to possible threats as a result of thorough training programs. Organizations can produce an army of cyber-savvy fighters who are resilient against the pitfalls and tricks of the digital world by cultivating a culture of cybersecurity within their ranks. In spite of this, the foundation of a safe digital environment is compliance and governance, which create the cornerstone of the complicated landscape that is cybersecurity. This roadmap provides organizations with information on how to navigate the regulatory landscape, ensuring that they conform to key rules and standards in the process. Not only do firms reduce their exposure to legal risk when they proactively address compliance needs but they also create an atmosphere that is more trustworthy and credible.

In this never-ending pursuit of superiority in cybersecurity, monitoring and ongoing quality improvements are of the utmost importance. The road plan encourages the construction of comprehensive monitoring methods, the tracking and monitoring of the effectiveness of cybersecurity measures, and the timely fixing of any gaps or weaknesses that are discovered. In addition to this, it inspires businesses to maintain their agility and adaptability by regularly analyzing and revising their roadmaps in order to bring them into line with the most recent technological developments and industry standards. When companies start down the road toward digital transformation, they have to realize that cybersecurity is not an afterthought but rather an essential component of the trip they are taking. The Digital Transformation Cybersecurity Roadmap acts as a guiding companion, shedding light on the path that leads to a digital future that is both secure and prosperous. Therefore, let us go forward, welcoming innovation while simultaneously strengthening our defenses, and in so doing, let us establish a digital universe that is secure, resistant, and unyielding to the powers of the cyber world. Let us achieve this by moving forward.

7.3.3 Monitoring and Continuous Improvement

Enhancing cybersecurity in the context of digital transformation is critically dependent on monitoring and making steady progress toward improvement. It is necessary for enterprises to build reliable monitoring procedures in order to guarantee the efficiency of their cybersecurity measures. This requires the implementation of sophisticated security monitoring tools and technologies, including IDS/IPS, SIEM solutions, and vulnerability assessments. Organizations are able to discover possible threats in a timely manner if they continuously monitor the traffic on their networks, the logs on their systems, and the security events that occur. Maintaining a proactive security posture also requires doing routine reviews of the Digital Transformation Cybersecurity Roadmap. Organizations are able to identify areas for improvement, incorporate lessons learned from security incidents, and update the roadmap to address growing cyber threats and industry best practices through periodic evaluations and engagement with stakeholders.

A culture of continuously improving cybersecurity is something that firms need to adopt in addition to monitoring their systems. In order to stay one step ahead of ever-evolving cyber dangers, it is necessary to integrate newly developed technology and established best practices. This entails keeping abreast of the most recent tendencies, threat intelligence, and industry standards. Participating in cybersecurity-related networks, forums, and conferences can provide access to important learning opportunities and valuable insights. It is possible to improve capabilities for threat identification and response by making use of cutting-edge technology such as AI, ML, and behavioral analytics. In addition, strategies for continuous professional development and training should be put into place to ensure that cybersecurity teams have the expertise and knowledge required to protect digital transformation initiatives properly. Organizations may reinforce their cybersecurity measures and prevent risks associated with digital transformation by combining proactive monitoring with a commitment to continuing development. This will eventually protect their digital assets and maintain a secure environment.

7.3.3.1 Establishment of monitoring mechanisms in order to keep tabs on the efficiency of existing cybersecurity measures

When it comes to tracking the efficacy of cybersecurity measures and having a solid security posture, establishing monitoring tools that are successful is absolutely necessary. To begin, businesses have an obligation to put into place cybersecurity metrics and KPIs, which offer measurable measurements of the organizations' respective security postures. These metrics can include the number of security events, the mean time to discover and respond, as well as the percentage of vulnerabilities fixed within a certain period of time. Organizations are able to evaluate their progress and determine the areas in which they need to make improvements if they first set baseline measurements and then regularly follow these indicators.

Second, enterprises are able to gather, correlate, and analyze security events from numerous sources in real time if they adopt comprehensive security incident and event monitoring systems such as SIEM. Because of this, it is possible to discover potentially malicious activity, anomalies, and violations of policy in a timely manner. In addition, tools for monitoring networks and computer systems, such as IDSs, IPS, and endpoint monitoring solutions, offer insights into the behavior of computer systems and networks, as well as potential dangers. Organizations are in a better position to detect and successfully respond to potential security breaches if they monitor and investigate these sources in a proactive manner.

In addition, by putting in place effective vulnerability management and scanning policies, firms are better able to keep one step ahead of possible attacks. Regular vulnerability assessments, penetration tests, and the use of automated scanning technologies are all helpful in identifying holes and prioritizing patching operations. In addition, by monitoring the behaviors of users and the credentials they have access to, businesses are able to identify any behavior that is either unlawful or questionable. Organizations are able to swiftly respond to problems and mitigate potential risks if they continuously monitor and manage user behaviors and vulnerabilities.

7.3.3.2 Regular evaluation and update of the digital transformation cybersecurity roadmap

It is essential to do routine reviews and updates on the Digital Transformation Cybersecurity Roadmap in order to guarantee its efficiency and continued applicability in the face of ever-evolving cyber threats and advances in technological capabilities. Organizations are able to proactively address emerging risks, align with industry standards, and optimize their cybersecurity posture in the ever-changing digital landscape if the Digital Transformation Cybersecurity Roadmap is evaluated and updated on a regular basis. This iterative strategy guarantees that cybersecurity measures continue to be robust and effective, thereby protecting the digital assets of the company and providing support for the firm's successful digital transformation goals.

(A) *Schedule Periodic Reviews*: Set a schedule for conducting regular reviews of the cybersecurity roadmap. The frequency of these reviews may vary based on the organization's risk profile, industry regulations, and the pace of technological changes.

(B) *Engage Stakeholders*: Gather input from key stakeholders, including cybersecurity professionals, IT teams, executive management, and other relevant departments. Seek their feedback on the effectiveness of the existing roadmap and suggestions for improvement.

(C) *Assess Alignment with Emerging Threats*: Evaluate the roadmap's alignment with the current threat landscape. Stay updated on emerging cyber threats, industry trends, and regulatory changes that may impact the organization's cybersecurity posture. Identify any new risks that need to be addressed or modifications required to existing controls.

(D) *Incorporate Lessons Learned*: Analyze past security incidents, breaches, or near-misses to extract valuable lessons learned. Identify any gaps or weaknesses in the existing roadmap that contribute to these incidents and determine how they can be addressed. Incorporate these insights into the roadmap to enhance future cybersecurity measures.

(E) *Evaluate Emerging Technologies and Best Practices*: Stay informed about the latest cybersecurity technologies, best practices, and industry standards. Assess whether any new tools, solutions, or approaches can augment the existing roadmap and provide better protection against evolving threats.

(F) *Update Goals and Objectives*: Based on the insights gathered from stakeholder feedback, threat assessments, lessons learned, and emerging technologies, revise the goals and objectives of the cybersecurity roadmap. Ensure they align with the organization's digital transformation strategy, risk appetite, and compliance requirements.

(G) *Review Implementation Progress*: Assess the progress made in implementing the roadmap's components and initiatives. Evaluate whether milestones have been achieved, controls have been effectively deployed, and compliance requirements have been met. Identify any areas that require further attention or adjustments.

(H) *Communicate Changes and Provide Training*: Communicate any updates or changes to the cybersecurity roadmap to relevant stakeholders. Ensure that employees, contractors, and third-party vendors are aware of the modifications and understand their roles and responsibilities. Provide training and awareness programs to educate the workforce about the updated roadmap and cybersecurity best practices.

(I) *Continuously Monitor and Adapt*: Establish mechanisms to monitor the effectiveness of the updated roadmap continuously. Regularly assess KPIs and cybersecurity metrics to track progress and identify areas for improvement. Be prepared to adapt the roadmap as new threats emerge or organizational priorities evolve.

7.3.3.3 Adoption of emerging technologies and best practices to stay ahead of evolving cyber threats

In order for enterprises to remain one step ahead of ever-evolving cyber threats, they need to adopt newly developing technology and execute industry best practices (Table 7.5). Because they take such a preventative strategy, they are able to effectively preserve their digital assets and keep the security of their digital transformation programs intact. In the first place, firms that embrace AI and ML are able to analyze enormous amounts of data and recognize patterns that are symptomatic of potential cyber threats. AI-driven anomaly detection and ML algorithms improve threat intelligence and automate incident response processes. This enables the identification and mitigation of security breaches to take place more quickly and accurately.

In addition, the deployment of User Behavior Analytics (UBA) assists organizations in detecting unusual behaviors carried out by users, which might be an indication of compromised accounts or insider threats. Patterns of user activity can be analyzed by companies in order to proactively prevent unauthorized access or malicious acts, which in turn ensures the security of the systems and data owned by the organization.

TABLE 7.5 Cybersecurity technologies and best practices

TECHNOLOGY/ PRACTICE	EXAMPLES OF TOOLS/ TECHNOLOGIES	IMPLEMENTATION CHALLENGES	EMERGING TRENDS AND INNOVATIONS
AI	Machine learning algorithms, anomaly detection systems	Data privacy concerns, false positives/ negatives in threat detection	Explainable AI, adversarial machine learning, and AI-driven threat hunting
Machine Learning	Predictive analytics and behavior-based analytics	Model training and updating, interpretability of ML algorithms	Federated learning, self-learning algorithms, and ML-based deception
UBA	User behavior monitoring, log analysis	Balancing false positives and false negatives and privacy concerns	AI-powered insider threat detection and user behavior anomaly detection
Containerization	Docker, Kubernetes, container security solutions	The complexity of managing container environments and potential vulnerabilities	Secure container orchestration, serverless containerization, and unikernels
Cloud Security	Cloud access security brokers (CASBs), cloud security posture management (CSPM) tools	Lack of control over cloud infrastructure shared responsibility model challenges.	Cloud-native security and cloud workload protection platforms (CWPP)
ZTA	Zero Trust Network Access (ZTNA) and identity and access management (IAM) solutions	Complexity of implementation and user experience challenges	Software-defined perimeter, continuous authentication, and AI-driven ZTA
Threat Intelligence	Threat intelligence platforms and information-sharing networks	Quality and relevancy of threat intelligence and trust and information sharing challenges	Threat intelligence fusion, AI-powered threat hunting, and dark web monitoring
Endpoint Security	Antivirus software, endpoint detection and response (EDR) solutions	Endpoint diversity and management and balancing security and user productivity	EDR advancements and cloud-based EDR
Red Team Exercises	Penetration testing tools and vulnerability assessment tools	Resource-intensive and coordination with internal teams and stakeholders	Automated red teaming, purple teaming, and threat simulation platforms

(Continued)

TABLE 7.5 (Continued) Cybersecurity technologies and best practices

TECHNOLOGY/ PRACTICE	EXAMPLES OF TOOLS/ TECHNOLOGIES	IMPLEMENTATION CHALLENGES	EMERGING TRENDS AND INNOVATIONS
Security Audits	Security audit frameworks and compliance assessment tools	The complexity of auditing processes and alignment with the evolving regulatory landscape	Continuous compliance monitoring and AI-driven audit analytics
Continuous Evaluation and Updates	Security information and event management (SIEM) solutions and threat intelligence feeds	Resource allocation, resistance to change, and organizational agility	AI-driven security orchestration and response (SOAR) and automated patch management

Containerization and cloud security are two essential elements that must be included in any effective cybersecurity plan. Protecting an organization's data and applications in the cloud requires that the organization put in place robust cloud security measures and make use of cloud-native security solutions. Technologies that utilize containerization offer applications for both isolation and security, thereby preventing both cross-contamination and unauthorized access.

Another recommended strategy to use is known as the Zero Trust Architecture (ZTA) approach. This concept does away with the traditional method of securing an area by erecting a perimeter around it and instead relies on stringent access controls, MFAs, and constant verification. Organizations limit the potential impact of breaches and lower the danger of unauthorized access by implementing the principle of least privilege and microsegmentation in their security practices. Organizations should also place an emphasis on improving threat intelligence and information exchange in order to bolster their defensive capabilities. When it comes to cybersecurity, forming partnerships with industry peers, government agencies, and cybersecurity suppliers facilitates the sharing of important threat intelligence and the development of coordinated defense tactics. Organizations are kept up to date on the most recent threat actors, techniques, and vulnerabilities if they participate in threat intelligence platforms and information-sharing networks.

In addition, enterprises should make endpoint security a top priority by putting in place advanced endpoint protection technologies and rigorous patch management policies. As a result of taking these precautions, malware, ransomware, and other types of endpoint-based attacks can be identified and stopped, hence enhancing the safety of devices that are linked to a network. Last but not least, it is essential to perform frequent red team exercises as well as security audits. While red teaming services imitate real-world intrusions to identify weaknesses, security audits evaluate whether or not an organization is compliant with industry standards and regulations. These actions provide significant insights that may be used to improve the security posture of the company and reduce the likelihood of potential issues.

Organizations are able to proactively protect themselves from growing cyber threats by embracing newly developed technologies and putting into effect industry best practices. These precautions allow for the early discovery and reaction to any security issues, which in turn reduces the risk of data breaches and disruptions to digital transformation activities. It is necessary to continuously evaluate and update cybersecurity strategy in order to manage new threats and harness novel solutions successfully.

7.3.3.4 Enhancement of cybersecurity measures on an ongoing basis, taking into account lessons learned and developments in the industry

In order for businesses to successfully protect their digital assets and remain responsive to ever-evolving threats, it is vital for them to upgrade their cybersecurity procedures continuously. In order to improve the overall cybersecurity posture, this approach comprises drawing lessons from previous events as well as changes in the sector. The first step for enterprises to take is to conduct postincident evaluations, during which they should examine the lessons learned from previous cybersecurity incidents and then distribute these insights throughout the organization in order to raise awareness and strengthen response capabilities. It is absolutely necessary to bring existing policies, processes, and guidelines up to date in light of newly discovered flaws in order to forestall the occurrence of future accidents.

One more essential component of continual improvement is making sure that you are up to date on the latest advances in your sector. Participating in industry journals, conferences, and communities can provide organizations with the information they need to proactively monitor trends, risks, and best practices in cybersecurity. Because of this, they are able to update their cybersecurity plans to take advantage of the most recent information and methods. In order to ensure compliance and ensure that cybersecurity practices are aligned with evolving requirements, it is equally vital to adapt to changing industry standards and regulatory regulations.

Performing routine risk assessments and adapting to changing circumstances are two of the most important steps in determining new dangers and openings. Organizations that carry out penetration testing, vulnerability assessments, and security audits are better able to proactively uncover holes, as well as prioritize the updates and security measures that are necessary. Programs of ongoing employee training and awareness are absolutely necessary in order to keep personnel up to date on the most recent dangers and protective measures. Employee readiness can be evaluated through simulated phishing attacks and security drills, which also help highlight areas in need of development.

Technology is playing an increasingly important part in the process of ongoing progress and enhancing cybersecurity measures through the analysis of new technologies and techniques and their subsequent adoption. Updating your security software, firewalls, and IDSs on a regular basis ensures that you have the most recent and effective defenses against ever-evolving threats. By maintaining relationships with technology vendors, service providers, and consultants, companies can guarantee that they are kept up to date on the latest security offerings and upgrades. Plans for responding to incidents and recovering from them should be periodically updated based on lessons learned, and plans for maintaining business continuity and recovering from disasters should be in line with the most recent cybersecurity risks and threats.

Efforts to increase cybersecurity are further strengthened when collaboration and partnerships are utilized. The free exchange of threat intelligence and recommendations for best practices is made possible through the sharing of information with other businesses, industry groups, and government agencies. By forming partnerships with cybersecurity vendors, managed security service providers, and consultants, businesses may harness the expertise of these third parties and stay current on the most recent security measures. Establishing efficient management and governance is crucial, including conducting frequent reviews and updates of cybersecurity policies, conducting internal audits, and engaging executive leadership to give supervision and assistance.

7.4 CONCLUSION

The Digital Transformation Cybersecurity Roadmap is an essential resource for companies that want to protect their operations in the ever-changing environment of Industry 4.0. Because of the rapid progress of digital technologies, the potential for the occurrence of cyberattacks has become more widespread. As a result, it is very necessary for businesses to place an emphasis on cybersecurity. Organizations are able to strengthen their defenses and secure their digital assets, data, and critical infrastructure provided they have an awareness of the specific cybersecurity problems posed by Industry 4.0, undertake comprehensive risk assessments, and regularly evaluate and improve their cybersecurity processes. The use of this road map gives businesses the ability to confidently embrace digital transformation while simultaneously minimizing cyber threats and maintaining the integrity and resilience of their systems. Organizations have the ability to succeed in the era of Industry 4.0 and maintain a competitive advantage in the quickly expanding digital world if they have an unshakable commitment to cybersecurity.

8 Performance Assessment

8.1 PERFORMABILITY: MEASURING SYSTEM PERFORMANCE AND RESILIENCE

Measurement of system performance and resilience needs to be given top priority by companies in the quick-paced environment of digital transformation. For organizations to succeed in the digital age, they need to be able to perform well as well as resist interruptions. The complexity of assessing performability within the context of digital transformation is explored in this chapter, which emphasizes its importance and offers insightful information. In order to overcome obstacles and take advantage of opportunities given by digital transformation, performance assessment is essential. Organizations may monitor and optimize their systems, find bottlenecks, and provide a seamless digital experience by accurately evaluating system performance. Performance evaluation also assists in reducing risks related to digital transformation, like outages, data breaches, and subpar user experiences. Organizations can gain important insights into the effectiveness, dependability, and user happiness of their systems by using metrics like reaction time, throughput, availability, and user experience.

In a time when disruptions are unavoidable, evaluating system resilience is equally important. Identifying key elements and potential weak points, doing vulnerability and risk assessments, and putting preventative actions in place to strengthen system resilience are all part of measuring system resilience. Strategies to improve resilience and lessen the effects of disruptions are covered in this chapter. It also examines several performance assessment methods and tools, including load testing, monitoring tools, and performance optimization methodologies.

Organizations can benefit from the difficulties encountered in digital transformation projects and effective performance evaluation initiatives by studying real-world case studies and best practices. Predictive analytics, cloud computing, edge computing, AI, and ML are some of the other cutting-edge developments and technologies that are being highlighted in this section since they will influence performance measurement in the future. Organizations may position themselves for success in the digital

DOI: 10.1201/9781003471226-9

transformation path by adopting these trends and best practices, assuring effective systems, strong resilience, and an amazing user experience.

8.1.1 The Role of Performance Assessment in Digital Transformation

Organizations face a variety of risks and problems in the ever-changing world of digital transformation as they work to adapt and prosper in a setting that is changing quickly. Success depends on maintaining the systems' optimal performance and resilience throughout this change process. This is where performance evaluation is crucial. Utilizing technology to fundamentally alter business procedures, operations, and customer experiences is known as digital transformation. However, there are a number of challenges and uncertainties that come along with this transformation path. Organizations need to make sure that their systems and applications are resilient enough to maintain high-performance levels in the face of mounting demands and potential interruptions, in addition to meeting the requirements of the digital era.

The activity of monitoring and assessing the effectiveness and resiliency of systems, applications, and supporting infrastructure is known as performance evaluation in the context of digital transformation. Organizations can learn more about the effectiveness, responsiveness, and efficiency of their digital systems by measuring performance. In addition, assessing resilience enables proactive efforts to improve system robustness and recoverability by revealing vulnerabilities, flaws, and potential points of failure.

Performance evaluation plays several different roles in the digital transformation process. First off, it gives businesses a thorough picture of how well their systems are operating in the digital sphere. This knowledge is essential for locating performance bottlenecks, inefficiencies, or problem areas. Organizations can identify opportunities for improvement and make specific efforts to improve performance by measuring important performance indicators, including response time, throughput, and scalability. Second, performance evaluation helps to guarantee the availability and dependability of digital systems. Organizations can monitor system availability and evaluate the effects of disruptions or outages using uptime and downtime metrics. MTTR measurements support attempts to reduce downtime and enhance business continuity by assessing the effectiveness of the recovery process.

Additionally, a crucial component of the digital revolution is user experience. Understanding how effectively digital systems conform to user expectations and requirements can be learned by measuring usability, user happiness, and customer retention. Organizations can improve user interfaces, streamline procedures, and improve customer experiences with the goal of increasing engagement and loyalty. Performance review goes beyond performance measurements and includes a system resilience assessment. This entails identifying potential points of failure, doing vulnerability analyses, and assessing risks. Organizations can proactively incorporate steps to improve resilience, such as redundancy, failover mechanisms, and disaster recovery plans, by identifying crucial system components and assessing their susceptibility to disruptions.

8.1.1.1 Understanding digital transformation and its impact on businesses

The integration of digital technologies across all facets of an organization, transforming how it operates and delivers value, is known as digital transformation. It has a significant and all-encompassing effect on businesses. It improves the client experience in the first place by offering individualized encounters, streamlined procedures, and practical self-service choices. Customer loyalty and satisfaction rise as a result. Second, digital transformation reduces manual labor, mistakes, and expenses while increasing operational efficiency through automation and optimization. It lets companies use data-driven insights to decide wisely, spot chances for expansion, and boost productivity. Additionally, digital transformation encourages creativity and agility, allowing businesses to react quickly to market changes, try out novel concepts, and acquire a competitive edge.

Digital transformation has its challenges, though, including integrating legacy systems, dealing with security issues, and overcoming cultural reluctance to change. The evaluation of system performance and resilience needs to be given top priority by companies in order to overcome these obstacles and guarantee a successful digital transformation. The measurement of performability is essential because it makes it easier to spot bottlenecks, foresee breakdowns, and deal with problems before they arise. Businesses may optimize the advantages of their digital transformation activities by maximizing performance and resilience.

Business processes can be optimized by efficiently assessing system performance and identifying opportunities for improvement. To do this, performance indicators, including response time, throughput, scalability, availability, and user experience, need to be evaluated. Additionally, companies need to assess system resilience to pinpoint vulnerable areas and probable failure spots. Proactive steps can be implemented to improve system resilience through vulnerability assessments and risk analysis. System performance needs to be evaluated and optimized using a variety of tools and methods, including performance monitoring, load testing, real-time analytics, and performance tuning. Furthermore, it is crucial to obtain knowledge from best practices and real-world case studies in order to understand effective performance evaluation methodologies in digital transformation programs.

Looking ahead, developing technologies will have an impact on performance evaluation in the context of digital transformation. The analysis and forecasting of performance trends will be greatly aided by AI and ML, while scalable and distributed architectures enabled by cloud and edge computing will have an impact on the measurement of performability. Organizations will be able to solve problems before they have an impact on operations thanks to predictive analytics and proactive performance management.

8.1.1.2 Key challenges and risks associated with digital transformation

For firms, digital transformation presents both opportunities and challenges. However, it is critical to recognize and take care of the main hazards and difficulties this process presents. The organization's cultural resistance is one of the biggest problems. People could be resistant to change and wary of implementing new procedures and technologies. Effective change management techniques, transparent communication, and the promotion of an innovative culture are necessary to overcome this reluctance. Technical debt and legacy systems present another difficulty. The introduction of new digital solutions needs to be improved by out-of-date and rigid systems, necessitating their upgrading or replacement. This procedure may be difficult, expensive, and time-consuming. To reduce disruptions, rigorous planning, risk assessment, and a phased approach are necessary.

Risks to data security and privacy in the digital transformation are serious. Organizations now face greater risks from data breaches, cyberattacks, and privacy violations as a result of the massive amounts of data being collected and processed. Critical factors to take into account include safeguarding sensitive data and maintaining compliance with data protection laws. To reduce these threats, effective cybersecurity protections, encryption, access controls, and routine security audits are required. Organizations frequently need help with skills and talent shortages as they undergo digital transformation. It is frequently necessary to acquire new skill sets and experience, yet this may not be possible within the firm. Progress may need more qualified personnel in developing fields. It becomes crucial to upskill current personnel or hire individuals with the requisite capabilities to drive effective digital transformation programs.

In order to solve the difficulties that arise during efforts to implement digital transformation, performance assessment is essential. By methodically assessing system performance and resilience, it offers organizations useful insights into the efficacy and efficiency of their digital activities. To begin with, performance evaluation helps in the detection of performance problems and bottlenecks that obstruct the efficient operation of digital systems. It is possible to identify specific areas that need improvement by carefully examining metrics like response time, throughput, and scalability. This makes it possible to take proactive steps to improve system performance and remove bottlenecks, such as code optimization, infrastructure tuning, or resource allocation. Additionally, performance evaluation substantially improves user experience. Usability, user happiness, and customer retention metrics provide priceless insights into the user's point of view. Organizations may pinpoint pain areas, solve usability issues, and raise user happiness by analyzing these characteristics. This information directs the creation of digital solutions, resulting in a favorable user experience that encourages user adoption and engagement.

Furthermore, performance evaluation is essential for minimizing downtime and guaranteeing continuous availability. Monitoring and analyzing availability indicators, including uptime, downtime, and mean time to recovery, become essential as digital transformation involves complex systems vulnerable to service interruptions. In order to reduce downtime and maintain continuous availability, businesses can use this to identify vulnerabilities, foresee probable failures, and put proactive remedies into place. Finally, performance evaluation helps create robust systems. Evaluating system resilience is crucial because digital transformation introduces new risks and difficulties like cybersecurity attacks and system malfunctions. Organizations can put steps in place to increase resilience by studying risk factors, conducting vulnerability assessments, and evaluating system components. This could include strong security procedures, redundant systems, and thorough disaster recovery plans.

8.1.1.3 Benefits of measuring performability in digital transformation initiatives

There are many benefits to measuring performability in digital transformation programs, many of which directly influence the success of their implementation. First off, it lets businesses increase system performance by locating and fixing bottlenecks, inefficiencies, and problem areas. Organizations may improve the speed, efficiency, and overall user experience of their digital systems while ensuring that transformation initiatives result in the expected results by carefully monitoring crucial performance indicators, including response time, throughput, and scalability.

Furthermore, performability measurement is essential for improving the user experience. Organizations can learn a lot about user preferences, problems, and expectations by analyzing usability metrics, user satisfaction levels, and customer retention rates. Armed with this information, businesses can decide on design and functionality with confidence, enhancing user experiences and increasing consumer engagement. Organizations can develop digital goods, services, or platforms that resonate with their target market by giving the user experience priority. This strengthens client relationships and promotes company growth.

Additionally, performability measurement greatly increases system toughness. Organizations can proactively detect weak points and potential failure modes inside their digital systems by vigilantly monitoring metrics for availability, reliability, and mean time to recovery. This gives them the ability to put into practice strategic actions meant to improve system resilience, reduce downtime, and guarantee a dependable user experience. Resilient systems are essential for ensuring continuous company operations and effective risk mitigation in today's interconnected and sensitive digital ecosystem.

Performability evaluation also makes it easier to identify and resolve issues before they become serious. Organizations can quickly spot performance degradation, anomalies, or looming difficulties using performance monitoring tools, profiling methodologies, and real-time analytics before they affect users or affect business operations. By allowing for prompt intervention, effective problem-solving, and effective mitigation techniques, early detection lessens the impact of disruptions and maintains system performance. Organizations may improve operational effectiveness, lower risks, and maintain the smooth running of their digital systems by proactively resolving concerns. Measuring performability in digital transformation programs provides high-importance benefits, including system performance improvement, enhanced user experience, increased system toughness, and early issue detection and resolution, all of which contribute to the success of digital initiatives (Table 8.1).

8.1.2 Key Metrics for Measuring System Performance

Performance metrics are essential for evaluating a system's efficacy and comprehending how efficiently it runs in the context of digital transformation. These metrics give important information about how well the system performs and can fulfill user demands.

TABLE 8.1   Benefits and importance of measuring performability in digital transformation programs

BENEFITS OF MEASURING PERFORMABILITY IN DIGITAL TRANSFORMATION PROGRAMS	IMPORTANCE
System Performance Improvement	High
– Locating and fixing bottlenecks, inefficiencies, and problem areas	
– Increasing system speed, efficiency, and user experience	
– Monitoring performance indicators (response time, throughput, and scalability) to ensure expected results	
Enhanced User Experience	High
– Understanding user preferences, problems, and expectations	
– Analyzing usability metrics, user satisfaction levels, and customer retention rates	
– Making informed design and functionality decisions	
– Enhancing user experiences and increasing consumer engagement	
Increased System Toughness	Medium
– Proactively detecting weak points and potential failure modes	
– Monitoring metrics for availability, reliability, and mean time to recovery	
– Implementing actions to improve system resilience and reduce downtime	
– Ensuring continuous company operations and effective risk mitigation	
Early Issue Detection and Resolution	Medium
– Promptly spotting performance degradation, anomalies, or looming difficulties	
– Using performance monitoring tools, profiling methodologies, and real-time analytics	
– Intervening early to solve problems and apply effective mitigation techniques	
– Minimizing disruptions and maintaining system performance	
– Improving operational effectiveness, lowering risks, and ensuring the smooth running of digital systems	

Response time, one of the performance metrics, gauges how long it takes a system to reply to a user request. Better system performance and user experience are shown by lower reaction times. Another crucial indicator is throughput, which measures how many transactions or requests a system can handle in a specific amount of time. Increased throughput indicates enhanced system scalability and performance. Scalability evaluates the system's capacity to manage expanding user demands and workloads and ensures that it can respond to changing business needs.

Metrics for availability are crucial for assessing a system's dependability and accessibility. Uptime indicates the amount of time a system is available to users and functioning, demonstrating the dependability and stability of the system. Downtime, which includes both planned maintenance and unplanned outages, is the period during which a system is not available. In order to supply services continuously, downtime needs to be kept to a minimum. The meantime it takes to return a system to normal operation following a failure or disruption is known as the MTTR. Faster recovery and greater system resilience are indicated by lower MTTR.

Metrics for reliability examine the system's capacity to function without errors and interruptions. The risk that a system's individual parts or the system as a whole will fail within a given time frame is measured by the failure rate. Mean Time Between Failures (MTBF) is a metric used to assess system reliability and pinpoint areas for advancement. It estimates the typical interval between two consecutive failures. The Mean Time to Failure (MTTF) is a calculation tool that helps proactive maintenance planning. It determines the typical amount of time a system or component can function before failing.

User experience metrics measure how happy and satisfied users are with their interactions with a system. Usability evaluates how user-friendly a system is to use, taking into account things like interface design and intuitiveness. User satisfaction, which is frequently gathered through feedback mechanisms, measures the degree of contentment consumers experience. Through evaluation of the value proposition and the entire customer experience, customer retention gauges the system's capacity to keep its user base over time. Organizations may learn a lot about the effectiveness, dependability, and user experience of a system by tracking and examining these critical parameters. These metrics offer a quantitative framework for assessing and enhancing the system's performance during the digital transformation process.

8.1.2.1 Performance metrics: response time, throughput, and scalability

When evaluating the efficacy and efficiency of digital transformation programs, performance measures are essential. We will examine three important performance indicators in this section: Response time, throughput, and scalability.

- *Response Time*: Response time refers to the duration it takes for a system to respond to a user request or transaction. It is a critical metric as it directly impacts user experience and satisfaction. Faster response times are generally desired as they contribute to improved customer satisfaction, increased productivity, and enhanced competitiveness. Measuring response time involves tracking the time it takes for a system to process a request, including network latency, server processing time, and any other relevant factors. By monitoring response time, organizations can identify bottlenecks, optimize system components, and enhance overall system performance.

- *Throughput*: Throughput measures the amount of work a system can handle within a given time frame. It represents a system's capacity to process and deliver a certain volume of transactions or data. Throughput is typically measured in terms of transactions per second (TPS) or requests per second (RPS). High throughput is desirable as it signifies the system's ability to handle the increased workload and deliver results efficiently. By monitoring throughput, organizations can identify performance limitations, optimize resource allocation, and ensure the system can scale to accommodate growing demands.
- *Scalability*: Scalability refers to the system's ability to handle increased workload or growing demands without sacrificing performance. It involves assessing how well the system can adapt and expand its capacity to accommodate additional users, data, or transactions. Measuring scalability requires evaluating the system's performance under varying workloads and stress conditions. It involves conducting load tests and analyzing how the system behaves as the workload increases. By assessing scalability, organizations can identify potential performance bottlenecks, optimize resource allocation, and plan for future growth.

8.1.2.2 Availability metrics: uptime, downtime, and MTTR

For evaluating a system's dependability and resilience during a digital transformation, availability indicators are essential. They reveal information about the system's capacity to continue operating, respond to user requests, and bounce back from errors. The most typical availability metrics are the following:

- *Uptime*: Uptime refers to the period during which a system or service remains operational and accessible to users. It measures the percentage of time that a system is available for use without any disruptions or failures. Uptime is typically calculated over a specific timeframe, such as a month or a year, and is expressed as a percentage. For example, an uptime of 99.9% means that the system experienced only 0.1% downtime.
- *Downtime*: Downtime represents the duration during which a system or service is not available to users due to failures, maintenance, or other operational issues. It includes both planned and unplanned downtime. Planned downtime refers to scheduled maintenance or system upgrades, while unplanned downtime is caused by unexpected failures, software bugs, or external factors such as power outages or network issues. Downtime is a critical metric that directly impacts user experience and business operations.
- *MTTR*: MTTR measures the average time it takes to restore a system or service to full functionality after a failure or disruption. It includes the time required to detect the issue, diagnose the problem, implement necessary fixes, and bring the system back online. MTTR is an important metric for assessing the resilience and recovery capabilities of a system. A lower MTTR indicates quicker recovery times and improved system availability.

TABLE 8.2   Availability indicators for evaluating system dependability and resilience in digital transformations

AVAILABILITY INDICATOR	DEFINITION	CALCULATION	USE CASE
Uptime	The period during which a system remains operational and accessible to users	Percentage of time the system is available without disruptions or failures	Measure overall system stability
Downtime	The duration when a system is not available to users due to failures or maintenance	Percentage of time the system is unavailable	Assess the impact on user experience and business operations
MTTR	The average time taken to restore a system to full functionality after a failure or disruption	Total downtime/ Number of incidents	Evaluate resilience and recovery capabilities
Error Rate	The frequency of errors or failures encountered by the system	Number of errors/ Total number of operations	Identify areas for improvement and system optimization
Scalability	The ability of a system to handle increasing workload or user demands without performance degradation	System response time under different load levels	Assess capacity to accommodate growth and changing demands
Redundancy	The presence of backup or duplicate components to ensure system availability in case of failures	Number of redundant components/ Total number of components	Enhance fault tolerance and minimize downtime
Service Level Agreement (SLA) Compliance	The extent to which the system meets the agreed-upon service levels	SLA compliance percentage	Monitor adherence to contractual obligations and customer satisfaction

Organizations use monitoring tools and systems to track system uptime and downtime, gather information on service interruptions and provide reports for analysis in order to assess these availability indicators efficiently. In order to improve availability and reduce downtime, these indicators assist organizations in identifying patterns, bottlenecks, and areas for improvement. Table 8.2 provides an overview of essential availability indicators used to evaluate the dependability and resilience of systems during digital transformations. These indicators play a crucial role in assessing a system's ability to remain operational, respond to user requests, and recover from errors.

8.1.2.3 Reliability metrics: Failure rate, MTBF, and MTTF

When evaluating the effectiveness and resilience of systems during the digital transformation process, reliability measures are extremely important. Organizations can learn more about the stability and dependability of their digital infrastructure by comprehending and measuring reliability. We will examine the failure rate, MTBF, and MTTF in this section.

- *Failure Rate*: The failure rate is a fundamental reliability metric that measures the frequency at which a system or component fails over a given period. It represents the likelihood of failures occurring within a specified time frame. The failure rate is typically expressed as the number of failures per unit of time (e.g., failures per hour, failures per year). By monitoring the failure rate, organizations can identify components or systems with high failure rates, enabling them to focus their efforts on improving reliability in those areas. A decreasing failure rate over time indicates improved reliability, while an increasing failure rate could indicate potential issues that need to be addressed.
- *MTBF*: MTBF is a reliability metric that quantifies the average time elapsed between consecutive failures of a system or component. It represents the expected time of continuous operation before a failure occurs. MTBF is calculated by dividing the total operating time by the number of failures experienced. MTBF provides insights into the reliability and robustness of a system. A higher MTBF indicates greater reliability, as it means that failures occur less frequently. MTBF is particularly useful for preventive maintenance planning and estimating system availability. By tracking MTBF, organizations can optimize maintenance schedules, reduce downtime, and enhance overall system performance.
- *MTTF*: MTTF is another important reliability metric that measures the average time a system or component can function before experiencing its first failure. MTTF is typically applicable to systems that are repairable and can be restored to an operational state after a failure. MTTF is frequently used to determine a system's estimated lifespan or to evaluate the dependability of specific system components. It offers useful data for planning replacements, estimating warranties, and improving designs. An increased MTTF increases the system's overall reliability by indicating a longer anticipated operating lifetime before the first failure.

Organizations can examine and track the dependability of their digital systems using reliability indicators like failure rate, MTBF, and MTTF. Businesses may increase the reliability and resilience of their digital infrastructure by monitoring these data, identifying areas for improvement, optimizing maintenance plans, and making knowledgeable decisions. The long-term effectiveness of digital transformation programs depends on using these metrics in performance evaluations. Evaluate reliability by measuring failure rate, monitoring MTBF and MTTF, and optimizing digital infrastructure based

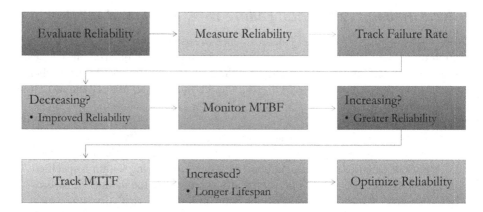

FIGURE 8.1   Evaluating and enhancing reliability in digital transformation.

on the outcomes to enhance overall reliability and resilience during the digital transformation process (Figure 8.1).

8.1.2.4 User experience metrics: Usability, user satisfaction, and customer retention

Metrics for the user experience are essential for determining a system's performance during a digital transformation. The first statistic, usability, is concerned with how well the system satisfies user expectations and is simple to use. It includes elements like user interface beauty, efficiency, memorability, and mistake prevention. Organizations may make sure that their systems are logical, easy to use, and able to support seamless interactions by assessing these factors.

The second indicator, user satisfaction, gauges a user's subjective assessment of their whole interaction with a system. It takes into account variables, including perceived utility, perceived usability, user comments, and personalization. Organizations can assess how well their systems meet user demands, encourage participation, and provide value by examining user happiness. Businesses can pinpoint areas for improvement and modify their systems to better match customer expectations by routinely gauging user happiness.

The third metric, customer retention, examines the system's capacity to hold on to consumers over time. User engagement, repeat usage, churn rate, customer lifetime value, and customer advocacy are all considered. A high customer retention rate shows that the users are dedicated to using the product and find value in it. Organizations may enhance the long-term effectiveness of their digital transformation activities and promote user loyalty by tracking and enhancing customer retention.

8.1.3 Strategies for Assessing System Resilience

Understanding the importance of resilience and its function in upholding the availability, dependability, and security of digital systems is necessary for assessing system resilience in the context of digital transformation. Organizations need to identify crucial system parts and potential weak spots in their infrastructure as part of this approach. Organizations can proactively correct gaps and minimize risks to improve system resilience by undertaking vulnerability assessments and risk analyses. The ability of the system to endure interruptions and recover rapidly is further strengthened by putting proactive measures like redundancy, failover mechanisms, strong backup and disaster recovery techniques, and rigorous security measures in place. Long-term maintenance and enhancement of system resilience depend on ongoing monitoring, improvement, and knowledge of market trends and best practices.

In general, evaluating system resilience in the context of digital transformation is a proactive and ongoing process that entails comprehending the architecture of the system, spotting vulnerabilities, performing risk analysis, putting resilience-enhancing measures in place, and continuously checking and enhancing the system's performance. Organizations may preserve business continuity and reduce the effect of interruptions and threats by implementing these techniques to assure the availability, dependability, and security of their digital systems.

8.1.3.1 Understanding system resilience and its significance in digital transformation

Organizations looking to succeed in today's technologically driven environment need to comprehend system resilience and its importance in digital transformation. The ability of a digital system to survive setbacks and recover rapidly, maintaining ongoing operations, is referred to as system resilience. Businesses rely on interconnected systems more and more, so any disruptions, errors, cyberattacks, or even minor mishaps can have serious repercussions. Organizations may reduce risks, guarantee business continuity, and uphold customer satisfaction by proactively assessing and improving system resilience.

For a number of reasons, system resilience is crucial to digital transformation. Limiting disruptions and supporting speedy recovery from failures or cyber disasters first ensures company continuity. Organizations can meet contractual responsibilities, avoid income loss, and protect their brand by sustaining uninterrupted operations—second, resilient systems aid in reducing the dangers connected to the digital transition. Organizations can lessen the risk and effects of cyber threats, data breaches, and technological dependence by detecting and addressing vulnerabilities. Businesses can install adequate security controls and create efficient incident response plans with the help of proactive resilience measures.

Additionally, companies can adapt to change thanks to system resilience. Significant adjustments to technological infrastructure, procedures, and operations are required for digital transformation. Systems that are resilient can adapt, scale resources to handle rising demands, and smoothly incorporate new technology. Organizations may successfully undertake and sustain digital transformation efforts by providing smooth transitions. Resilient systems also contribute to better customer experiences. Organizations can encourage customer pleasure, loyalty, and trust by providing seamless and dependable services—even during periods of high demand or unforeseen events. Additionally, system resilience helps firms comply with legal requirements. Data protection laws and industry standards are essential in the digital age. In order to protect sensitive data and uphold compliance, resilient systems employ strong security controls, data protection safeguards, and incident response methods.

8.1.3.2 Identifying critical system components and potential failure points

One of the most important steps in evaluating system resilience is identifying vital system components and probable failure spots. Organizations can better prepare for and minimize potential failures by knowing which parts of the system are most crucial to its operation and where potential vulnerabilities may exist. Here is a passage on the subject: It is necessary to identify the crucial system components and probable failure spots inside the digital transformation architecture in order to monitor performability and analyze system resilience efficiently. In this step, the system architecture and its dependencies are thoroughly analyzed. Organizations may prioritize their efforts and spend resources appropriately by recognizing the interdependencies and criticality of various components.

A detailed inventory of all the interrelated components of the system is the first step in identifying essential system components. This covers all important assets, such as hardware pieces, software programs, databases, and network infrastructure. Organizations can obtain a comprehensive understanding of the system's structure and pinpoint the essential elements that underpin its performance and operation by mapping out the complete system.

The next stage is to evaluate each system component's criticality and probable failure spots after they have been identified. A critical component is one whose failure would significantly affect the functioning of the entire system or halt efforts to implement digital transformation. These elements could be central programs, databases with essential information, networking tools, or specialized hardware. Organizations can prioritize their resources and implement focused strategies to improve their resilience by concentrating on these essential elements.

Organizations should perform a thorough examination of the system's vulnerabilities to pinpoint probable failure points. Analyzing potential hazards such as hardware malfunctions, software problems, cybersecurity dangers, and capacity restrictions is part of this. It is crucial to take into account both internal and external variables that could result in system failures. Risk analysis, threat modeling, and vulnerability assessments are just a few of the methodologies that can be used to conduct this analysis. Organizations should also take into account dependency on outside systems or third-party services into account. These dependencies could bring about extra hazards and sites of failure that need to be considered. Understanding the overall performability of the system requires evaluating the dependability and availability of these external components.

Organizations can improve the resilience of their infrastructure for the digital transition by proactively identifying key system components and potential failure sites. This could entail creating failover methods, enhancing security procedures, enhancing backup and recovery plans, or implementing redundancy measures. Organizations can construct a more robust and effective digital infrastructure that can survive any disruptions and support their digital transformation goals by having a thorough grasp of the system's weaknesses and important components.

8.1.3.3 Conducting vulnerability assessments and risk analysis

Measurement of performability during digital transformation requires vulnerability assessments and risk analyses. Organizations can improve the performance and resilience of their systems by proactively identifying potential vulnerabilities and dangers. Critical system components are first identified, and after that, potential threats that might have an influence on the system are evaluated. Assessments of vulnerabilities are carried out to find flaws like obsolete software or lax access controls. Organizations may prioritize their mitigation efforts thanks to risk analysis, which assesses the likelihood and effect of each vulnerability. Implementing security updates, upgrading disaster recovery plans, and tightening access controls are examples of mitigation techniques. The effectiveness of mitigating measures is regularly tested and monitored, and thorough documentation aids in decision-making and future evaluations.

Organizations can detect possible weaknesses in their systems and take proactive action to improve performance during digital transformation by conducting vulnerability assessments and risk analyses. Critical system components are carefully identified during this procedure, and possible threats are evaluated. Following rigorous examinations, which include examining system design and configurations, vulnerabilities are discovered. Organizations are able to prioritize mitigation measures depending on severity thanks to risk analysis, which assesses the possible effects of each vulnerability. Then, in order to fix vulnerabilities and reduce risks, mitigation measures are used. These include putting in place security updates and improving access restrictions. Continuous testing, observation, and recording guarantee the ongoing efficacy of mitigating measures and serve as a basis for upcoming evaluations.

Organizations can proactively address potential vulnerabilities and hazards by conducting vulnerability assessments and risk analyses, which will ultimately improve the performance of their systems during digital transformation. Identifying crucial system components and evaluating potential risks are the first steps in this approach. Finding flaws like obsolete software or incorrect setups is made easier with the aid of vulnerability assessments. Organizations can prioritize mitigation activities by using risk analysis to evaluate each vulnerability's impact and likelihood. Implementing security measures, bolstering redundancy, and enhancing disaster recovery plans are some examples of mitigation tactics. Regular testing and monitoring guarantee that these safeguards remain successful, and thorough documentation makes decision-making and future evaluations easier. Table 8.3 enables organizations to proactively identify vulnerabilities, assess risks, prioritize mitigation efforts, and continuously monitor and improve system performance and resilience.

8.1.3.4 Implementing proactive measures for resilience enhancement

In order to guarantee that systems will function as intended during the digital transformation process, proactive measures for resilience augmentation need to be put into place. Organizations can maintain a high degree of system performance and availability by taking proactive measures to reduce the effect of probable failures and disruptions.

TABLE 8.3 Performability measurement and mitigation framework for digital transformation

ASPECT	ACTIONS	BENEFITS	TOOLS/ TECHNIQUES USED
Step 1: Identification of critical system components	Identify crucial system components during digital transformation	Enables focused attention on critical areas	System mapping and analysis
	Determine the importance of each component	Prioritizes allocation of resources	Stakeholder consultation
	Document the identified components for future reference	Facilitates knowledge sharing and continuity	Documentation management systems
	Assign priority levels to each component based on its criticality	Guides the order of mitigation efforts	Risk assessment frameworks
Step 2: Vulnerability assessments	Conduct vulnerability assessments on the identified components	Identifies potential weaknesses and flaws	Vulnerability scanning tools
	Identify potential weaknesses and flaws in the system	Helps in preemptively addressing vulnerabilities	Penetration testing
	Perform rigorous examinations of system design and configurations	Enhances system understanding and visibility	Code review
	Discover vulnerabilities such as obsolete software and incorrect setups	Allows for targeted remediation actions	Configuration auditing
Step 3: Risk analyses	Evaluate the potential threats and risks associated with each vulnerability	Provides a holistic view of system risks	Risk assessment frameworks
	Assess the likelihood and impact of each vulnerability	Guides prioritization of mitigation efforts	Probability- impact matrix
	Prioritize mitigation measures based on severity and potential impact	Maximizes the effectiveness of resources	Risk prioritization techniques

(Continued)

TABLE 8.3 (Continued) Performability measurement and mitigation framework for digital transformation

ASPECT	ACTIONS	BENEFITS	TOOLS/ TECHNIQUES USED
Step 4: Mitigation techniques	Implement security updates to address vulnerabilities	Strengthens system security and resilience	Patch management systems
	Enhance disaster recovery plans and redundancy	Improves system readiness for potential disruptions	Business continuity planning
	Tighten access controls and improve security measures	Reduces the likelihood of unauthorized access	Access control systems
Step 5: Testing and monitoring	Regularly test the effectiveness of mitigation measures	Validates the efficacy of implemented measures	Security testing tools
	Monitor the system for any new vulnerabilities or risks	Enables proactive identification of emerging threats	Security monitoring systems
	Continuously observe the performance and resilience of the system	Facilitates prompt response to system issues	System monitoring tools
Step 6: Documentation	Maintain thorough documentation of all assessments, analyses, and actions taken	Supports informed decision-making	Documentation management systems
	Use documentation as a basis for decision-making and future evaluations	Enables continuous improvement	Knowledge management platforms
	Ensure that documentation is easily accessible and organized	Simplifies knowledge sharing and collaboration	Documentation templates

To find potential flaws and problems in the system design, one method is to conduct risk assessments. Organizations can effectively manage risks by implementing techniques like redundancy, failover mechanisms, and disaster recovery plans on a regular basis. To respond to changing threats and guarantee system resilience, it is crucial to evaluate and update these measures continuously.

A strong infrastructure design is yet another proactive step to improve resilience. Systems should be designed with fault tolerance and redundancy in mind by organizations. Single points of failure can be avoided, and system resilience can be enabled by distributed designs, load-balancing techniques, and high-availability settings like clustering and replication. Utilizing virtualization and containerization technology also enables scalability and quick deployment.

Continuous monitoring and warning systems are essential for spotting potential problems before they get out of hand. To monitor system performance and health, organizations should put in place comprehensive monitoring systems and make use of real-time analytics. Organizations can react quickly to degradation or anomalies by creating proactive alerting methods and setting thresholds for KPIs. Systems for automating incident response can speed up recovery times and reduce downtime.

The regular use of simulation and testing has a big impact on building resilience. System behavior is evaluated through performance testing, load testing, and stress testing. Organizations can assess a system's resilience and recovery capabilities by simulating failure scenarios. Results from tests help system configurations be improved and optimized. Additionally, proactive activities in risk identification and risk mitigation are encouraged via staff training and establishing a culture of ownership and responsibility.

8.1.4 Tools and Techniques for Performance Assessment

A variety of methods and strategies are used in performance evaluation in digital transformation to measure and improve system performance accurately. These tools include tools for performance monitoring and profiling, which gather and examine data to spot bottlenecks and problems with resource utilization. Examples include Dynatrace, Datadog, and New Relic. To identify system performance limits and potential failure mechanisms, load testing and stress testing approaches replicate various user situations and stress conditions. For these goals, tools like Apache JMeter and LoadRunner are frequently utilized.

Dashboards and real-time performance analytics offer the most recent information about system performance. They gather and display performance data, enabling stakeholders to track important indicators, spot anomalies, and solve problems quickly. Elasticsearch, Splunk, and Grafana are among the more well-known tools in this category. Targeted changes to system configurations, code, or infrastructure are made as part of performance tuning and optimization efforts. Organizations can enhance responsiveness and lower latency by optimizing database queries and server settings or putting in place caching systems and CDNs.

Organizations should mix these technologies and strategies to attain high performance. In order to guarantee that system performance satisfies the requirements of digital transformation initiatives, continuous monitoring, analysis, and optimization are essential. Organizations can proactively address problems and improve their systems for optimum performance in the digital age by utilizing performance evaluation tools.

8.1.4.1 Performance monitoring and profiling tools

In the context of digital transformation, performance monitoring, and profiling tools are essential for evaluating and maximizing system performance. By recording measures like CPU usage, memory utilization, network latency, and disk I/O, these tools offer real-time visibility into the health and performance of the system. Organizations can proactively detect bottlenecks and make data-driven decisions to improve system efficiency by studying this data. Profiling tools allow for a thorough examination of how an application is being executed and the identification of potential problem code regions. This enables programmers to enhance the performance of key portions of the system.

Additionally, alerting and notification mechanisms are provided by performance monitoring technologies to alert stakeholders to performance anomalies or deviations quickly. To enable preventive actions to avoid or alleviate performance concerns, administrators can configure threshold-based alerts for critical performance parameters. These technologies also keep track of performance information over time, enabling reporting and historical analysis. Organizations can monitor performance trends, evaluate system upgrades or setbacks, and produce reports for interested parties. Planning for capacity, recognizing seasonal patterns, and assessing the effects of system modifications all depend heavily on historical data.

Performance monitoring technologies interface with well-known DevOp tools and frameworks to conform to DevOps principles, enabling seamless integration into the development and deployment pipelines. Performance monitoring is made to become an inherent part of the development and deployment processes thanks to automation capabilities that automate performance tests, data gathering, and analysis. Additionally, these solutions support distributed systems, enabling businesses to track requests across many components and spot speed and latency issues from beginning to end. Additionally, they provide customized metrics and insights tailored to cloud and hybrid systems.

8.1.4.2 Load testing and stress testing techniques

In order to assess the effectiveness and durability of systems during the digital transformation process, load testing and stress testing are crucial methodologies. In order to assess the system's behavior and performance under typical operating settings, load testing entails simulating realistic user loads. This includes creating test scripts, maintaining test data, executing distributed load testing, and testing for scalability. The objective is to make sure the system can manage the projected volume of users, transactions, or data without degrading.

Contrarily, stress testing entails putting the system through harsh workloads or situations in order to assess its resilience and stability. Such methods as peak load testing, soak testing, spike testing, and failover testing are included. The goal is to determine the system's breaking point, analyze how it responds to stress, and assess its capacity for recovery. Organizations can use stress testing to find performance bottlenecks, foresee problems during periods of high usage, and guarantee data integrity and business continuity during important events.

Organizations can learn important lessons about system performance and resilience by using load testing and stress testing approaches. They can proactively identify and deal with possible bottlenecks, scalability constraints, and stability difficulties thanks to these strategies. This then helps to maximize efforts for digital transformation and guarantees a positive user experience even in difficult circumstances. Stress testing and load testing give organizations the assurance that their systems can withstand upcoming workloads, maintain performance, and recover quickly, which helps to make their path through digital transformation successful overall.

8.1.4.3 Real-time performance analytics and dashboards

In the context of digital transformation, dashboards and real-time performance analytics are essential tools for assessing and tracking system performance. These technologies enable organizations to make data-driven decisions and proactively solve performance concerns by giving quick insights into the health and effectiveness of digital systems. Through continuous monitoring and analysis of system metrics and KPIs in real-time, real-time performance analytics enables stakeholders to spot bottlenecks, spot anomalies, and act quickly to fix them. These technologies gather information from multiple sources, use sophisticated algorithms to process and analyze it, and then display the results in enticing dashboards, charts, and graphs.

System performance is tracked and examined via real-time performance dashboards, which act as a central center. They offer a consolidated picture of important performance data and insights in a style that is simple to understand. These dashboards give stakeholders a quick overview of system performance by displaying crucial KPIs like response time, availability, error rates, and resource use. Additionally, they offer drill-down capabilities for more in-depth research and can be tailored to match the individual demands of various stakeholders. The establishment of alerts and notifications based on predetermined thresholds or anomalies is also possible with real-time performance dashboards, ensuring that quick responses be taken to address performance issues and reduce risks. Additionally, they could have historical analysis features that let users compare present performance to historical trends and monitor performance advancements over time.

8.1.4.4 Performance tuning and optimization strategies

For assessing and improving system performance in the context of digital transformation, performance tuning and optimization are essential. Organizations should use a variety of efficient tactics to get the best results. First and foremost, it is critical to locate performance bottlenecks using in-depth analysis and profiling tools. This makes it possible to identify the underlying factors that contribute to delays and inefficiencies, such as database queries, network latency, CPU usage, and memory usage. When bottlenecks are located, resource allocation can be fine-tuned based on demand patterns and by using techniques like load balancing, parallel processing, and resource pooling.

Another important factor is optimizing database performance. Organizations can speed up query response times by enhancing their query and indexing procedures.

Additionally, examining and improving database schema design reduces duplication and increases the effectiveness of data access. Utilizing caching techniques lowers the number of times a database is accessed, enhancing overall efficiency. Another key step is code optimization, which involves removing duplicate operations and superfluous computations and optimizing algorithms and data structures. Effectively addressing code-level performance issues requires utilizing compiler optimizations and performance profiling tools.

Organizations should also concentrate on data management and caching. Implementing caching mechanisms, CDNs, and data compression methods lowers network bandwidth usage, latency, and disk I/O operations. I/O and network optimization are equally important. Organizations can reduce latency and improve responsiveness by optimizing network setups, protocols, and asynchronous I/O activities. Another factor to take into account is scalability; by designing systems for horizontal scaling, using load-balancing methods, and utilizing auto-scaling mechanisms, it is possible to handle growing loads successfully.

For sustainable performance increases, ongoing monitoring and tuning are crucial. Performance issues can be quickly identified and resolved with the help of proactive alarm systems, analytics, and real-time performance monitoring. The measurement of system performance, comparison to benchmarks, and identification of improvement areas are all aided by routine performance testing and benchmarking. Organizations may guarantee optimal performance throughout their digital transformation activities by regularly reviewing performance indicators and making the appropriate improvements.

8.1.4.5 Future trends and emerging technologies

Future trends and developing technologies are expected to significantly increase the assessment of system performance in the context of digital transformation. Evolutionary changes are being made to performance evaluation approaches so they can adopt a more thorough and linked strategy. Holistic, end-to-end assessments that take into account the combined influence of multiple system aspects on performance and resilience are replacing outdated techniques that concentrated on individual components.

The future of performance evaluation will be significantly influenced by AI and ML. These technologies provide groundbreaking capabilities for substantial real-time data analysis, pattern recognition, bottleneck detection, and performance issue prediction. Organizations may proactively solve possible issues before they affect users by utilizing AI-driven predictive analytics. Additionally, by learning from past data, ML algorithms may constantly improve system performance and robustness.

It is necessary to pay attention to the impact of edge and cloud computing on performance measurement. The expansion of edge devices and the widespread use of cloud services call for the modification of performance assessment approaches. Tools and methodologies that offer insights into the performance of distributed systems across several locations need to be tailored to hybrid and multicloud setups. Additionally, new methods are needed to assess performance and resilience at the network edge as edge computing brings computational power closer to data sources.

8.2 ANALYTICITY: LEVERAGING ANALYTICS FOR DATA-DRIVEN DECISION-MAKING

Data-driven decision-making has become crucial for firms looking to gain a competitive edge in the fast-paced business environment of today. With so many opportunities and difficulties presented by the advent of digital transformation, using analytics to guide wise decision-making is now necessary. The integration of digital technologies into an organization's operations is known as "digital transformation," and it profoundly alters how firms operate, engage with consumers, and generate value. Technological improvements, changing client expectations, and the need for agility and innovation are driving this paradigm change. The capacity to utilize data and derive useful insights becomes increasingly important for sustainable growth and staying ahead of the competition as firms start their digital transformation journeys.

Analytics is at the heart of digital transformation, enabling businesses to utilize their data fully. Businesses may extract valuable insights from massive datasets and turn those insights into actionable intelligence by using a variety of analytical approaches and tools. The enhancement of overall performance, process optimization, improved customer experiences, and informed decision-making are all made possible by these insights. The use of analytics, the creation of performance evaluation frameworks, and the application of analytics to measure and evaluate the results of digital transformation initiatives are all covered in this section's exploration of the idea of analyticity within the context of digital transformation.

8.2.1 Role of Analytics in Digital Transformation

In order for enterprises to harness the power of data and make wise decisions, analytics is essential to the process of digital transformation. With the spread of digital technologies and the enormous volumes of data they produce, analytics offers a way to gain insightful information and influence company results. Organizations can gain a competitive advantage, improve operational effectiveness, and provide individualized consumer experiences by utilizing analytics.

Different analytics have different applications in decision-making. Organizations may interpret past data and spot patterns using descriptive analytics, whereas diagnostic analytics reveals the causes of certain results. Prescriptive analytics goes beyond predictions to offer suggestions for the best course of action. Predictive analytics projects future patterns. These analytic methods enable firms to streamline operations, reduce risks, and take proactive action.

There are many advantages to integrating analytics into digital transformation programs. It makes it possible to make data-driven decisions, boosts operational effectiveness, improves customer experiences, and gives businesses a competitive edge. However, data quality, privacy, and hiring skills are needed. By assuring data integrity, putting in place strong security measures, building a culture that values data, and spending money on IT infrastructure, organizations can overcome these difficulties.

8.2.1.1 Introduction to analytics and its significance in digital transformation

Organizations are flooded with enormous amounts of data produced from several sources in the continuously changing landscape of digital transformation. This data has a huge potential for revealing insightful information and promoting reasoned decision-making. Analytics is crucial in this situation. Organizations can extract significant patterns, trends, and correlations from their data by using analytics, which is the systematic examination and analysis of data, to make data-driven choices.

Analytics offers firms a framework for converting their unprocessed data into useful insights. Organizations can better understand their operations, consumers, and market dynamics by implementing advanced analytical approaches like data mining, predictive modeling, ML, and AI. They can see opportunities, streamline procedures, and promote innovation thanks to this insight.

Analytics take on even greater importance in the context of digital transformation. By utilizing the vast amounts of data generated through digital interactions, transactions, and activities, it serves as a catalyst for digital transformation. Organizations may make sense of this data using analytics, and they can use the insights to inform their digital initiatives. Organizations can use analytics to determine client preferences, personalize experiences, optimize supply chains, reorganize workflows, spot irregularities, and forecast future trends. These data-driven insights are crucial for directing strategy and fostering innovation.

Additionally, analytics aids businesses in navigating the complexity and unpredictability of the digital environment. It gives businesses a data-driven compass so they can track their progress, evaluate their performance, and adjust their strategy as necessary. Organizations may evaluate the success of their digital projects, pinpoint areas for development, and make data-supported decisions to streamline their transformation journey by regularly evaluating data. However, using analytics in digital transformation has its own set of difficulties. Data-driven decision-making involves not only technical prowess but also a cultural shift. To properly leverage the power of analytics, organizations need to invest in developing analytical capabilities, creating strong data governance and quality management procedures, and implementing the appropriate IT infrastructure.

8.2.1.2 Different types of analytics and their applications in decision-making

Decision-making processes benefit greatly from various types of analytics, which give businesses insightful information and enable data-driven initiatives:

- *Descriptive Analytics*: Descriptive analytics focuses on summarizing historical data to understand what has happened in the past. It involves analyzing and interpreting data to gain insights into patterns, trends, and relationships. Organizations use descriptive analytics to assess historical performance, identify areas of improvement, and track key metrics. For example, analyzing sales data to identify the best-selling products or analyzing customer feedback to understand common pain points.

- *Diagnostic Analytics*: Diagnostic analytics aims to determine why something has happened by drilling deeper into the data. It involves examining various factors and variables to uncover the root causes of specific outcomes or events. Diagnostic analytics helps organizations understand the factors influencing their performance and identify opportunities for optimization. For example, analyzing customer churn rates and conducting root cause analysis to determine why customers are leaving.
- *Predictive Analytics*: Predictive analytics leverages historical data and statistical modeling techniques to make informed predictions about future outcomes or events. It uses patterns and trends identified in historical data to forecast future behavior or trends. Organizations use predictive analytics to anticipate customer behavior, optimize inventory levels, or predict market demand. For example, using predictive analytics to forecast sales for a new product launch or predicting maintenance requirements for industrial equipment.
- *Prescriptive Analytics*: Prescriptive analytics takes predictive analytics a step further by suggesting optimal courses of action based on the predicted outcomes. It uses advanced techniques, such as optimization and simulation, to generate recommendations for decision-making. Prescriptive analytics helps organizations determine the best strategies, actions, or interventions to achieve desired outcomes. For example, optimizing the allocation of marketing budgets across different channels based on predicted customer response rates.
- *Diagnostic Analytics*: Diagnostic analytics aims to determine why something has happened by drilling deeper into the data. It involves examining various factors and variables to uncover the root causes of specific outcomes or events. Diagnostic analytics helps organizations understand the factors influencing their performance and identify opportunities for optimization. For example, analyzing customer churn rates and conducting root cause analysis to determine why customers are leaving.
- *Text Analytics*: Text analytics involves analyzing unstructured data, such as customer feedback, social media posts, or survey responses, to extract meaningful insights. It uses NLP and ML techniques to analyze text and identify patterns, sentiments, and themes. Organizations use text analytics to understand customer opinions, sentiment analysis, or extract key information from large volumes of textual data. For example, analyzing customer reviews to identify common product complaints or extracting customer preferences from survey responses.
- *Spatial Analytics*: Spatial analytics focuses on analyzing geographic or location-based data to understand patterns, relationships, and trends. It combines geographic information system (GIS) technology with data analysis techniques to gain insights from spatial data. Organizations use spatial analytics to optimize supply chain logistics, identify new market opportunities, or analyze the impact of location on business performance. For example, analyzing customer demographics and location data to identify the best locations for opening new stores.

8.2.1.3 Benefits and challenges of incorporating analytics in digital transformation initiatives

There are many advantages to incorporating analytics into digital transformation programs. First off, it facilitates better decision-making by offering insightful information and data-driven intelligence. Decisions made by organizations can be more timely and well informed which improves operational efficiency and gives them a competitive advantage. Second, by comprehending consumer behavior, preferences, and wants, analytics improves the customer experience. By personalizing offers, adjusting marketing tactics, and providing a superior customer experience, firms are able to increase satisfaction, customer loyalty, and revenue. Analytics also promotes process optimization by highlighting inefficiencies and potential opportunities for development. Organizations can obtain cost savings, higher productivity, and improved performance by streamlining workflows and automating tasks. Additionally, analytics-driven digital transformation encourages data-driven innovation, giving companies the ability to spot market trends, create cutting-edge goods and services, and outperform the competition. By foreseeing outcomes, reducing risks, and ensuring that digital transformation initiatives are implemented more smoothly, it also helps with risk management.

Nevertheless, there are difficulties in integrating analytics into digital transformation. Organizations need to manage many data sources, assure accuracy, and put efficient data management policies into place to overcome the considerable challenges posed by data quality and integration. Businesses increasingly rely on data for analytics, raising questions about data privacy and security that need strict data governance procedures and security safeguards. Another area for improvement is the talent and skill gap, as businesses look for qualified data scientists and analysts who are adept with analytics software. The incorporation of analytics may need to be improved by cultural opposition and problems with change management, needing a change in company culture and successful change management techniques. Concerns about scalability and infrastructure develop as businesses improve or create the infrastructure that can handle massive amounts of data and complicated computations.

8.2.2 Building Analytic Capabilities

For enterprises to effectively use analytics for data-driven decision-making and to accelerate digital transformation, it is imperative to invest in strong analytical capabilities. This entails fostering a data-driven culture, putting in place solid data governance procedures, equipping the staff with analytical abilities, and utilizing the right technologies and tools. Organizations may build a strong foundation for effective analytics deployment and increase the value obtained from data by concentrating on five key areas.

Building analytical capability begins with creating a data-driven culture. This entails encouraging staff members to use data in their regular jobs and cultivating a mindset that values data. Developing a data-driven culture requires strong leadership, excellent education, and communication, as well as encouraging cross-functional teams and collaboration. Putting into place solid data governance procedures is similarly crucial. Defining their data architecture, ensuring data quality management through data profiling and cleaning, and addressing data security and privacy issues are all necessary for organizations. Strong data governance guarantees the accessibility, accuracy, and reliability of data for analytics, laying the groundwork for sound judgment.

For businesses to fully benefit from their analytics projects, it is essential that the employees develop analytical abilities. This can be done by encouraging cross-functional collaboration, implementing training and upskilling programs, and hiring people with analytical skills. Organizations may enable their employees to analyze data, comprehend insights, and make data-informed decisions by investing in the development of analytical skills. Utilizing tools and technology is yet another essential component of developing analytical talents. For data integration, visualization, and predictive analytics, organizations should assess and adopt the proper analytics platforms and tools. Analytical capabilities can be further improved by ensuring scalable infrastructure, investigating automation, and using AI-driven analytics to extract important information.

8.2.2.1 Establishing a data-driven culture within the organization

Organizations need to invest in developing strong analytic capabilities if they want to use analytics for data-driven decision-making and to accelerate digital transformation. This entails cultivating an analytical workforce, putting in place strong data governance policies, fostering a data-driven culture, and utilizing the right technologies and tools. Organizations may maximize the value generated from data by concentrating on four key areas and laying a strong basis for effective analytics deployment.

The first step in developing analytical capabilities is creating a data-driven culture. This entails encouraging people to use data in their regular job by cultivating a data-centric mindset. The key elements of developing a data-driven culture include leadership commitment, effective education, and communication, encouraging cooperation, and cross-functional teams. Adopting strong data governance techniques is similarly crucial. Organizations need to specify their data architecture, manage data quality by profiling and cleaning their data, and address data security and privacy issues. A solid foundation for decision-making is provided by strong data governance, which guarantees the availability, integrity, and quality of data for analytics.

For businesses to maximize the benefits of their analytics projects, developing analytical capabilities within the workforce is essential. This can be accomplished by implementing programs for skill upskilling and training, hiring people with analytical experience, and encouraging cross-functional cooperation. Businesses can empower their staff to analyze data, comprehend insights, and make decisions based on that data by investing in the development of analytical abilities. Another crucial component of developing analytical talents is utilizing tools and technology. Companies should assess and adopt the best analytics platforms and tools for data integration, visualization, and predictive analytics. The ability to further improve analytics capabilities, enable real-time decision-making, and unearth important insights can be achieved by ensuring scalable infrastructure and investigating automation and AI-driven analytics. Figure 8.2 outlines the key areas necessary for organizations to develop strong analytic capabilities.

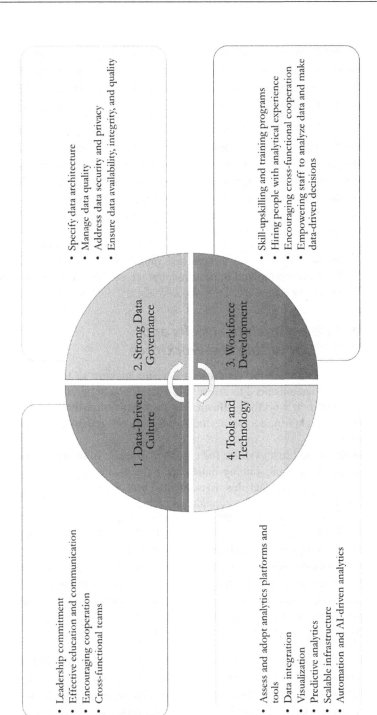

FIGURE 8.2 Key areas for developing analytical capabilities.

8.2.2.2 Data governance and data quality management for effective analytics

Effective analytics and decision-making in the context of digital transformation require the management of data governance and data quality. In order to manage data assets and ensure data integrity, security, and compliance, data governance entails developing rules, policies, and processes. It includes things like developing data policies and standards, putting in place data management procedures, and creating a committee for data governance. These procedures offer a framework for upholding data usage, access, and quality requirements, allowing businesses to utilize their data assets effectively.

The goal of data quality management is to make sure that the analytics-related data are accurate, complete, consistent, and relevant. It incorporates tasks like data profiling and assessment to comprehend data properties and spot difficulties with quality. Processes for standardizing data forms and structures, as well as addressing mistakes and inconsistencies, are known as data cleansing and standardization. During the integration of different sources, data integration and validation assure data integrity and ongoing data quality monitoring and improvement processes help discover and proactively address data quality issues.

8.2.2.3 Developing analytical skills and capabilities within the workforce

To successfully use analytics for data-driven decision-making in the age of digital transformation, organizations need to invest in the development of analytical skills and competencies within their workforce. Businesses can fully utilize their data assets and generate valuable insights by equipping their staff with the required knowledge and skills.

Organizations should first evaluate the current skill levels of their staff to find any gaps and then customize their training initiatives. Surveys, interviews, or skill evaluations can all be used to conduct this assessment. Then, thorough training programs encompassing both technical and nontechnical components of analytics should be made available to improve analytical skills. While nontechnical training might concentrate on critical thinking, problem-solving, and data-driven decision-making techniques, technical training may encompass data analysis, statistical modeling, data visualization, and ML. It is crucial to adapt training curricula to the unique requirements of the many job functions within a business. While operations personnel may need training in process optimization and predictive analytics, marketing professionals may need instructions in consumer segmentation and campaign analytics. Employees can maximize the impact of training programs by developing the skills most pertinent to their roles through customized training.

Organizations should encourage staff to keep up with the most recent trends and developments in analytics in order to promote a culture of continuous learning. Webinars, workshops, industry conferences, and online courses can all be used for this. Employees can experiment with new analytical tools and methodologies when resources and support are made available for self-directed learning. The development of analytical communities or centers of excellence also promotes employee engagement and knowledge sharing, enabling the discussion of concepts, best practices, and lessons learned. Employee skill development can be further supported by mentoring and coaching programs that link new hires with seasoned analysts or data scientists. These mentors can offer advice, share relevant experiences, and aid staff members in acquiring useful skills. For tracking success and finding areas for growth, regular feedback and performance reviews are crucial.

Organizations enable staff to develop and use their analytical talents by giving them access to analytical tools and technologies. This involves granting access to cloud-based platforms, data visualization tools, and analytics software. Employee experimentation and exploration of these technologies promote practical experience and a better understanding of their uses. The last thing that businesses should do is create a system for rewarding and recognizing individuals who excel at analysis or who provide insightful data analysis. Employees are encouraged to consistently enhance their skills by being recognized and rewarded for their analytical prowess, which also fosters a culture of data-driven decision-making.

8.2.2.4 Leveraging technology and tools for analytics implementation

Organizations may access a wealth of data in the modern digital era, which can provide insightful information and aid in making well-informed decisions. However, in order to use this data effectively, it is necessary to adopt the right technologies and tools for data collection, processing, analysis, and visualization. Organizations need to carefully select and use the appropriate technology and tools when employing analytics for performance assessment within the context of digital transformation. Data integration and collecting need to be given top priority by enterprises. This entails locating essential data sources and putting in place strong integration procedures to mix data from diverse sources, guaranteeing data dependability and consistency. Additionally, before doing analysis, companies should make use of data quality management tools to guarantee the reliability and correctness of the data.

Organizations should then think about their data management and storage techniques. The establishment of a central data warehouse or data lake provides effective data organizing and storage. Cloud-based solutions can also be helpful because they offer scalability and affordability when managing massive amounts of data. Furthermore, during the analytics implementation process, firms need to put data governance procedures in place to protect data security, compliance, and privacy. Another crucial component is choosing suitable analytics platforms and tools. Users can examine data, create interactive dashboards, and generate reports to visualize performance assessment measures using user-friendly business intelligence (BI) tools. Tools for data visualization provide simple and eye-catching representations of data, aiding in understanding and interpretation. Furthermore, modern analytics platforms with features like predictive modeling, ML, and AI assist in identifying trends in the data and extracting deeper insights.

Moreover, finally, businesses should place a strong emphasis on automation, process management, and scalability. By streamlining data collection, integration, and transformation, automated data pipelines increase productivity by minimizing manual work. Workflow management tools make it easier to orchestrate and monitor the analytics process, ensuring efficient teamwork and successful execution. To accommodate the rising data volumes and easily integrate analytics, scalable infrastructure and seamless interface with existing systems are essential.

8.2.3 Performance Assessment Framework

An essential element for assessing the efficacy and impact of digital transformation activities is the performance assessment framework. It offers a methodical way to gauge and evaluate an organization's performance over the course of the digital transformation process. Employing a strong framework enables firms to make data-driven decisions that promote continuous improvement while gaining insightful information about the efficacy of their efforts.

The performance assessment's goals and objectives within the context of digital transformation are distinctly defined at the outset of the framework. Then, KPIs are chosen to gauge development and success. These KPIs should measure both quantitative and qualitative performance characteristics and be in line with the organization's strategic objectives. Effective data collection processes are built using data from both internal and external sources to ensure accurate assessment. Enterprise systems, customer reviews, market analysis, and social media analytics are a few examples of these sources. To preserve data accuracy, completeness, and timeliness, data governance practices are put into place. Following data collection, relevant techniques and tools are used to analyze the data, including descriptive, diagnostic, predictive, and prescriptive analytics.

At various points along the way, the performance of digital transformation efforts is tracked through routine performance evaluations. The outcomes are evaluated against benchmarks or industry standards and interpreted in the light of clearly specified goals and objectives. Key stakeholders are notified of findings in a clear and simple manner, facilitating informed decision-making and promoting ongoing development. Figure 8.3 describes the performance assessment framework for evaluating the efficacy and impact of digital transformation activities.

8.2.3.1 Defining performance assessment in the context of digital transformation

The systematic review and measurement of an organization's progress, efficacy, and results in adopting and implementing digital technologies and practices is referred to as performance assessment in the context of digital transformation. It entails evaluating how well operational efficiency, customer experience, and the overall impact on corporate growth are improved as a result of digital transformation activities. To analyze the efficacy of digital transformation activities and direct decision-making along the transformation path, a thorough performance assessment framework is necessary.

A strong performance evaluation framework includes a number of essential elements. The first step in strategic alignment is to assess how much the organization's digital transformation projects contribute to its strategic goals and competitive advantage. Second, operational efficiency gauges how well resources are used, how much money is saved, and how much productivity is increased as a result of digital technology

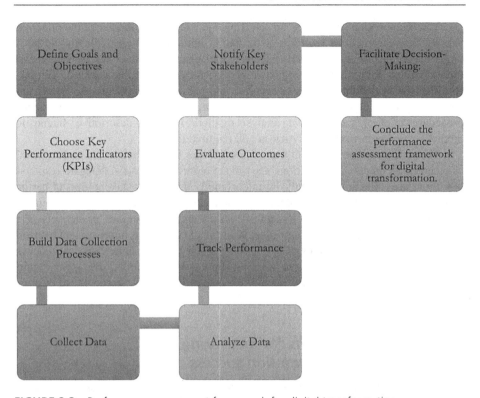

FIGURE 8.3   Performance assessment framework for digital transformation.

and procedures. Third, the evaluation of the customer experience takes into account elements like user engagement, personalization, and responsiveness to the needs of the consumer. Fourth, the organization's capacity for fostering innovation, adjusting to market changes, and seizing new opportunities through digital transformation is evaluated. Fifth, data utilization looks at how well data and analytics are used in decision-making. Finally, organizational culture and change assess elements like employee participation in supporting and embracing digital transformation and change management.

Organizations create pertinent metrics and KPIs that are in line with their goals in order to undertake performance assessments in the context of digital transformation. They apply analytics tools, set up data collection methods, and routinely review and evaluate performance data to produce useful insights.

8.2.3.2 Components of a robust performance assessment framework

A strong performance evaluation framework is made up of a number of crucial elements that are crucial for assessing the efficacy and success of initiatives for digital transformation. To provide the evaluation process direction and concentration, it is first and foremost necessary to create specific objectives and targets. These goals should be SMART, and they should be in line with the organization's broader digital transformation strategy.

The framework also depends on selecting and using KPIs that gauge the effectiveness and advancement of digital transformation initiatives. These KPIs should be in direct accordance with the stated objectives and goals since they act as benchmarks in comparison with which the organization's performance can be assessed. To make sure that the evaluation process is accurate and reliable, it is essential to gather and analyze pertinent data. Establishing data-gathering methods, putting data governance procedures in place, and using data analysis methods, including descriptive, diagnostic, predictive, and prescriptive analytics, are all required for this.

The performance assessment framework includes regular monitoring and reporting as essential elements. Organizations need to set reporting intervals, delegate responsibility for data collection and analysis, and promptly inform key stakeholders of performance findings. With the help of data-driven adjustments to their digital transformation programs, enterprises are able to identify issues and opportunities proactively. The framework also encourages firms to adopt a culture of continuous improvement by using performance assessment findings to pinpoint problem areas, hone their approaches, and implement remedial measures. Gaining support and promoting teamwork require including important stakeholders, such as executives, managers, workers, and customers, at every stage of the process.

8.2.3.3 Metrics and KPIs for measuring digital transformation success

Setting up precise measurements and KPIs that are in line with the organization's strategic goals and desired outcomes is necessary for measuring the effectiveness of digital transformation. These KPIs and indicators offer a quantitative means to gauge the success of digital transformation efforts and monitor development over time. Digital revenue growth, customer acquisition and retention, conversion rates, cost reduction, time-to-market, employee productivity and efficiency, data quality and utilization, innovation and experimentation, customer satisfaction, and Net Promoter Score (NPS) are some important metrics and KPIs for gauging the success of a digital transformation.

An essential criterion for measuring the success of digital transformation initiatives in fostering corporate growth is the rise of digital revenue. The ability of the company to draw in and hold onto customers in the digital environment can be evaluated by keeping track of the number of new customers acquired through digital channels and the rate of customer retention. Conversion rates give information on how well digital marketing and user experience work to increase conversions. Cost-reduction measures, which indicate efficiency gains and cost advantages, quantify the savings realized through digital transformation activities. Time-to-market measurements gauge how soon a firm can deliver value. Website traffic, social media interactions, and app downloads are tracked by digital consumer engagement metrics to determine customer engagement levels. Metrics for employee productivity and efficiency measure changes brought about by digital transformation projects, such as less manual work and better teamwork. Metrics for data quality and use guarantee accurate data-driven insights for decision-making. Metrics for innovation and experimentation keep tabs on the organization's dedication to innovation and capacity for change in response to new technologies. Metrics on customer satisfaction offer information on the whole experience of the customer and the effects of the digital transformation on satisfaction levels.

The measurements and KPIs used for the organization undergoing digital transformation should be specific to its goals and objectives. These indicators are regularly monitored and analyzed to assist in pinpointing problem areas, monitoring development, and guaranteeing the success of digital transformation programs.

8.2.3.4 Data collection and analysis techniques for performance assessment

Techniques for gathering data and analyzing it are essential for determining how well digital transformation programs are performing. Organizations need to use a variety of data-gathering techniques in order to gain insightful information on how effective their efforts are. Applying internal data sources like customer databases and operational logs, including external data sources like market research studies and industry benchmarks, and applying digital analytics technologies like web analytics and social media analytics are all examples of this. Organizations using IoT devices also have the ability to record real-time data on operational elements and customer interactions. Organizations may accurately track progress by defining KPIs that are consistent with the objectives of the digital transformation and setting baselines. By quickly identifying and resolving performance issues, real-time monitoring systems support rapid decision-making.

Utilizing several methodologies is required for data analysis. Through data visualization, trend analysis, and dashboards, descriptive analytics offers a historical view of performance. By carrying out correlation studies and root cause analyses, diagnostic analytics assists in determining the causes and factors affecting performance. Statistical models and ML algorithms are used in predictive analytics to forecast future performance based on historical data. By advising the appropriate course of action to maximize performance using optimization algorithms and decision support systems, prescriptive analytics goes beyond prediction. Performance data is presented via data visualization techniques like charts and graphs, and detailed stakeholder insights are provided by performance reports.

An important component of performance evaluation is continuous improvement. Customer and employee feedback channels are examples of feedback mechanisms that provide insightful data. Organizations can adapt their data collecting and analysis methods through iterative analysis in response to customer feedback and shifting business requirements. With this iterative approach, performance evaluation procedures can be continuously improved and refined, enabling companies to make data-driven decisions that will help them succeed in the age of digital transformation.

8.2.4 Leveraging Analytics for Performance Assessment

Organizations are conscious of the significance of data-driven decision-making in the age of digital transformation. This chapter explains "analyticity" and explains how to use analytics for performance evaluation. In order to fully realize the potential of the digital revolution, analytics is essential for gleaning useful information from massive amounts of data. Organizations can create the necessary analytical capabilities, such as data governance, quality management, and the development of analytical talents, by developing a data-driven culture. For assessing the effectiveness of a digital transformation, a strong performance assessment methodology that is in line with strategic objectives is crucial. Organizations can monitor KPIs, gauge employee productivity, and assess customer satisfaction, operational effectiveness, and revenue growth. Ethics and other problems with data privacy need to be dealt with, and a culture that welcomes change should be promoted. Organizations advance in the digital age by using analytics to acquire a competitive edge, make wise decisions, and produce significant commercial outcomes.

Analytics is essential for monitoring and assessing the results of digital transformation projects. Organizations can evaluate the performance of their digital projects in real time and make data-driven changes to their plans by measuring and monitoring progress. Additionally, analytics aids in spotting patterns and trends in data, allowing firms to comprehend the effects of changes brought on by digital transformation and align their decisions with consumer desires and market demands. Additionally, analytics gives businesses the ability to foresee outcomes through predictive analytics methods, enabling proactive planning and decision-making.

Another crucial element of digital transformation is value generation and ROI, and analytics gives us the tools to measure the effects of digital activities. Organizations can evaluate the financial performance, operational effectiveness, customer happiness, and market share produced by their digital transformation activities by examining pertinent data and indicators. These insights aid in defending expenditures, setting priorities, and promoting ongoing development throughout the process of digital transformation. By locating bottlenecks, inefficiencies, and improvement opportunities, analytics also makes continual improvement and optimization possible. Organizations may maximize the efficiency of their digital transformation programs by refining plans, improving procedures, and fostering innovation through the collection of feedback and performance monitoring.

8.2.4.1 Use cases and examples of analytics-driven performance assessment in different industries

Organizations from a variety of industries are using analytics to evaluate and improve their performance through digital transformation initiatives in today's data-driven world. Analytics are essential to client segmentation in the retail sector since it enables businesses to customize marketing campaigns, offer focused incentives, and make specialized product suggestions. Furthermore, by predicting demand patterns and analyzing real-time sales data, analytics help merchants manage their inventory levels and boost supply chain effectiveness. Analysis of consumer behavior, rival pricing, and market dynamics are further areas where analytics-driven performance assessment aids merchants in maximizing profitability and customer happiness.

Analytics are used in the healthcare sector to evaluate patient outcomes, spot treatment trends, and streamline workflows. Healthcare providers can lower costs and enhance service quality by evaluating patient data. Healthcare practitioners may predict epidemics, identify high-risk populations, and put preventive measures in place thanks to analytics, which also helps predictive modeling for disease prevention. Hospitals and healthcare systems may optimize resource allocation, streamline operations, and improve the patient experience overall with the use of analytics-driven performance reviews.

Analytics are used in the financial services sector for fraud prevention and detection. Financial institutions use cutting-edge analytics tools to spot and stop fraud in real time, safeguarding consumer funds and upholding confidence. Risk assessment and credit scoring are also made possible by analytics, giving banks and lenders the ability to assess borrowers' creditworthiness, manage their loan portfolios, and make wise lending decisions. In the very competitive financial services sector, analytics-driven performance assessment also helps predict customer attrition, develop targeted retention initiatives, and nurture customer loyalty.

8.2.4.2 Analytic models and techniques for assessing organizational performance during digital transformation

Making data-driven decisions while evaluating organizational performance during digital transformation necessitates the adoption of rigorous analytical models and approaches. Organizations can use analytics to monitor the performance of their transformation programs, identify areas for development, and receive insightful information about their digital transformation initiatives.

Descriptive analytics is a crucial strategy that entails looking at historical data to comprehend prior performance and trends. Organizations can accurately analyze their existing situation by identifying patterns and correlations by evaluating data from numerous sources. On the other side, diagnostic analytics focuses on figuring out the underlying reasons for particular results or problems. Organizations can gain insights into the factors affecting their performance and take corrective action through data mining and root cause analysis.

Another useful method is predictive analytics, which uses past data to forecast the future with accuracy. Organizations can predict the effects of their digital transformation activities and identify potential hazards or resource needs by using statistical modeling and forecasting approaches. Prescriptive analytics goes a step further by offering suggestions that can be put into practice. Organizations can choose the optimal course of action to boost performance during digital transformation by combining historical data, predictive models, and optimization strategies.

Real-time or near-real-time data analysis is essential for gaining quick insights and making quick decisions. Organizations may proactively adjust and respond to changes along their digital transformation journey by monitoring performance metrics and spotting abnormalities. Additionally, benchmarking enables businesses to assess their performance in relation to industry norms or rivals, revealing gaps and establishing reasonable goals for growth. Making informed decisions and fostering a data-driven culture are made possible by data visualization and interactive dashboards, which show performance indicators and insights in an attractive and accessible way.

8.3 USABILITY: CREATING USER-CENTRIC DIGITAL EXPERIENCES

Organizations from all industries are adopting digital transformation as a way to stay competitive and provide top-notch user experiences in today's quickly changing digital market. The idea of usability, which refers to how easily intended consumers can use, comprehend, and enjoy a digital product or service, is at the center of this transition. For businesses pursuing digital transformation projects, developing user-centric digital experiences is a core goal. Businesses may increase consumer pleasure, engagement, and success in the digital sphere by putting users at the center of their design and development processes. Figure 8.4 illustrates the key components and relationships in the context of organizations adopting digital transformation and prioritizing user-centric design and development processes.

8.3.1 Understanding Usability in Digital Transformation

Organizations across industries are experiencing a digital transformation to increase their competitiveness and fulfill the constantly changing expectations of their users in the quickly changing digital landscape of today. The idea of usability—creating user-centric digital experiences that are intuitive, effective, and engaging—is essential to the

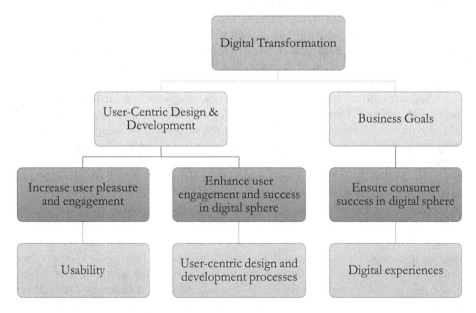

FIGURE 8.4 Digital transformation and user-centric design.

success of any program for digital transformation. In the context of digital transformation, usability refers to how effectively, efficiently, and satisfactorily a digital product or service can be used by its intended consumers. It includes a variety of elements like navigation, information organization, interactivity, user interface design, and overall user experience. By placing a high priority on usability, businesses can make sure that their digital solutions satisfy the needs and expectations of their target market, resulting in increased user adoption and satisfaction and, eventually, the achievement of their transformational goals.

Usability and digital transformation work together harmoniously. Usability is at the center of the attempts to undergo a digital transformation; it is not only an afterthought or a surface-level layer of design. By giving usability first priority, businesses effectively put the user at the center of their digital operations, taking into account their wants, preferences, and pain points. This user-centric strategy is essential for developing seamless, enjoyable, and capable of generating meaningful interaction digital experiences.

Initiatives for digital transformation that are successful need to be driven by usability. Organizations may improve user satisfaction, boost productivity and efficiency, increase user adoption, and gain a competitive edge in the market by putting a strong emphasis on usability. Users should be able to do their activities, locate information, and navigate through digital interfaces without difficulty, thanks to usability. As a result, there is a rise in user satisfaction, trust, and brand loyalty. Usable digital experiences improve productivity and efficiency by streamlining procedures, reducing complexity, and minimizing user errors. Usability-focused digital experiences are more likely to be welcomed by users, which will increase user engagement and adoption rates. Additionally, by providing outstanding experiences that stand out in the market and draw in a bigger user base, businesses that prioritize usability in their digital transformation initiatives get a competitive edge.

Organizations need to invest in user research, persona development, user journey mapping, information architecture, user interface design, and usability testing in order to apply usability in digital transformation effectively. By identifying customer wants, problems, and preferences, these activities enable businesses to develop digital experiences that appeal to their target market. Organizations may use the power of usability to offer transformative digital experiences and accomplish their goals for digital transformation by putting the user at the center of their digital activities.

8.3.2 Usability Assessment Framework

In the context of digital transformation, the Usability Assessment Framework is a systematic method for assessing and enhancing the usability of digital experiences. It is made up of several important parts that work together to make sure that user-centric design concepts are applied to the creation process. User research and persona building are the first steps in the framework, during which qualitative and quantitative data are gathered to comprehend user demographics, behaviors, goals, and pain areas. User journey mapping is then used to depict the entire user experience, pinpoint key touchpoints, and examine user motives and emotions. The framework also assesses the clarity and usability of the information architecture and navigation, as well as the consistency and esthetic appeal of the user interface design. In order to validate design decisions and acquire user feedback and suggestions, usability testing and user feedback gathering are done last. The components of the framework are as below:

- *User Research and Persona Development*: User research involves gathering insights and understanding the target audience's needs, goals, and preferences. This component helps in creating accurate user personas that represent the various user groups and their characteristics. Persona development aids in building empathy and guiding decision-making throughout the design and development process.
- *User Journey Mapping*: User journey mapping visualizes the end-to-end user experience, highlighting key touchpoints and interactions. This component helps identify pain points, areas of improvement, and opportunities for enhancing the user experience. By mapping out the user's journey, organizations can gain a holistic view of the user's interactions with the digital product or service.
- *Information Architecture and Navigation Assessment*: Information architecture focuses on organizing and structuring content in a way that is intuitive and easy for users to navigate. This component assesses the effectiveness of the information architecture, including menu structures, labeling, and categorization. Evaluating navigation systems ensures that users can easily find the information they need and navigate through the digital experience seamlessly.
- *User Interface Design Evaluation*: The user interface (UI) design evaluation component assesses the visual and interactive elements of the digital product or service. It examines factors such as visual hierarchy, typography, color scheme, use of imagery, and consistency across the interface. Evaluating the UI design ensures that it aligns with user expectations and enhances the overall usability and esthetics of the digital experience.
- *Usability Testing and User Feedback*: Usability testing involves observing and gathering feedback from representative users performing specific tasks on the digital product or service. This component helps identify usability issues, discover user pain points, and assess overall user satisfaction. Usability testing methods include moderated testing, unmoderated testing, and remote testing. Gathering user feedback through surveys, interviews, and feedback forms also provides valuable insights for improving usability.

8.3.3 Performance Metrics for Usability Assessment

In the process of digital transformation, evaluating usability performance is essential for developing user-centric digital experiences. Establishing performance measures that offer insights into user happiness, engagement, behavior, and task completion rates is crucial for conducting a successful evaluation of usability. Organizations may make wise decisions to increase the usability of their digital products and services by keeping an eye on these measures.

User happiness, task success rate, duration on task, and mistake rate are KPIs for usability assessment. Indicators like NPS, Customer Effort Score (CES), and user engagement indicators like time spent on the platform or frequency of visits can be used to gauge customer happiness and engagement. Tracking indicators like the click-through rate (CTR), conversion rate, and bounce rate allows you to assess the efficiency of the digital interface and suggest adjustments. Additionally, measuring job completion times, mistake rates, and user flow analysis help pinpoint usability problems and improve the digital experience by measuring user involvement and task completion rates.

It is also critical to track metrics related to inclusion and accessibility. This includes monitoring inclusion measures like user demographic data and assessing accessible compliance with standards like WCAG 2.1. Performance evaluation requires both qualitative and quantitative data collection. Usability tests can be used to observe user behavior, usability surveys can be used to obtain qualitative input, and analytics tools can be used to collect quantitative data on user interactions and engagement metrics.

Organizations can better understand the advantages and disadvantages of their digital experiences by including these performance metrics in usability studies. During the digital transformation process, this knowledge enables data-driven decision-making, empowers iterative improvements, and supports the development of user-centric digital solutions. In the end, a performance assessment-centered approach improves usability, which results in higher user happiness, more engagement, and successful digital transformation initiatives. Performance metrics can be used to evaluate usability, measure user happiness and engagement, identify usability problems, track inclusion and accessibility, and make data-driven decisions to improve the digital experience (Table 8.4).

8.3.4 Tools and Techniques for Usability Assessment

A variety of methods and approaches are used in usability testing to collect insightful information about user experiences. Usability testing, which involves seeing consumers engage with a digital good or service, is one widely utilized technique. With the use of resources like screen recording software, eye-tracking gadgets, and remote collaboration platforms, usability testing may be carried out both locally and remotely. Gathering user feedback is a key component of usability assessment. Surveys, questionnaires, interviews, or focus groups can be used to gather this information, which offers insightful information on user perceptions and preferences. While analytics and data visualization tools assist in tracking KPIs and offer insights into user behavior and performance metrics, eye-tracking and heat map analyses provide visual representations of user attention and interaction patterns.

There are many solutions available for remote usability testing and monitoring, in addition to usability testing and user feedback gathering. Utilizing functions like screen sharing, video recording, and real-time data collection, these systems allow researchers to study user interactions from a distance. These tools include UserTesting, UserZoom, and Lookback as examples. Even when users are spread over various geographical regions, these solutions enable effective data collecting and analysis. Additionally, eye-tracking technology and heat map analyses offer visual representations of user attention

TABLE 8.4 Usability performance metrics and insights for user-centric digital experiences

PERFORMANCE METRICS	DESCRIPTION	DATA COLLECTION METHODS	ACTIONABLE INSIGHTS
User Happiness	Measures the satisfaction and happiness of users with the digital experience	Usability surveys and qualitative feedback	Identify areas for improvement based on user feedback
Task Success Rate	Measures the rate at which users successfully complete tasks within the digital interface	User testing and task analysis	Identify usability issues and optimize workflows
Duration on Task	Measures the time taken by users to complete tasks within the digital interface	User analytics and task tracking	Identify bottlenecks and streamline user journeys
Mistake Rate	Measures the frequency of user errors or mistakes made while interacting with the digital interface	User analytics and error logging	Identify problem areas and enhance error prevention
Net Promoter Score (NPS)	Indicates the likelihood of users recommending the digital product or service to others	Surveys and feedback forms	Measure overall customer satisfaction
Customer Effort Score (CES)	Measures the ease of use and convenience experienced by customers when using the digital interface	Surveys and feedback forms	Identify areas for reducing customer effort
Time Spent on Platform	Measures the amount of time users spend on the digital platform or application	User analytics and session tracking	Gauge user engagement and content relevance
Frequency of Visits	Measures the number of times users visit the digital platform or application within a specific timeframe	User analytics and session tracking	Assess user loyalty and repeat usage
Click-through Rate (CTR)	Measures the percentage of users who click on a specific element or link within the digital interface	User analytics and click tracking	Evaluate the effectiveness of call-to-action elements
Conversion Rate	Measures the percentage of users who complete a desired action, such as making a purchase or signing up	User analytics and conversion tracking	Optimize user flows and increase conversion rates

(Continued)

TABLE 8.4 (Continued)   Usability performance metrics and insights for user-centric digital experiences

PERFORMANCE METRICS	DESCRIPTION	DATA COLLECTION METHODS	ACTIONABLE INSIGHTS
Bounce Rate	Measures the percentage of users who leave the digital interface without further interaction or exploration	User analytics and session tracking	Identify landing page or content issues
Job Completion Times	Measures the time taken by users to complete specific tasks or workflows within the digital interface	User analytics and task tracking	Streamline processes and reduce task completion time
User Flow Analysis	Analyzes the path and sequence of user actions within the digital interface to identify usability problems	User analytics and user behavior tracking	Optimize user journeys and remove pain points
User Demographic Data	Includes data on user characteristics such as age, gender, location, and other relevant demographic information	User surveys and user registration information	Understand user segments and tailor experiences
WCAG 2.1 Compliance	Assesses the adherence of the digital interface to accessibility standards for individuals with disabilities	Accessibility audits and compliance testing	Ensure inclusivity and accessibility for all users

and interaction patterns, enabling researchers to pinpoint focus areas, gaze durations, and navigational courses. For conducting in-depth user behavior analysis, a variety of eye-tracking technologies, whether hardware-based or software-based, are available. Utilizing software like Hotjar, Crazy Egg, or Google Analytics, heat map analysis can be done.

Analytics and data visualization tools are essential for gaining a thorough insight into user experiences and for helping people during the digital transformation process make wise decisions. Users' behavior, conversion rates, and page performance can all be better understood by using web analytics solutions like Google Analytics, Mixpanel, or Adobe Analytics. With the use of these technologies, researchers can track KPIs that are connected to user engagement and assess the effectiveness of usability advancements over time. Additionally, the data presentation capabilities offered by these technologies assist in making the data intelligible and esthetically appealing, assisting stakeholders in understanding crucial usability indicators and making data-driven decisions.

8.3.4.1 Usability testing methods and tools

During the process of digital transformation, usability testing is a crucial component of evaluating and enhancing the usability of digital experiences. There are numerous techniques and resources available to carry out usability testing successfully. In contrast to remote usability testing, which enables researchers to evaluate participants who are located in separate locations via video conferencing or screen sharing, in-person usability testing entails monitoring people in a controlled environment. Utilizing software tools, automated usability testing compares designs to usability heuristics, determines accessibility compliance, and gathers usability metrics and analytics. Surveys and questionnaires collect user feedback on satisfaction and usability, while eye-tracking and biometric techniques offer insights into user attention and emotional responses.

The project goals, budget, and resources should all be taken into consideration when selecting a technique and tool combination for usability testing. While remote testing is more convenient and has a wider participant pool, in-person testing provides for direct user behavior observation. Eye-tracking and biometric techniques enable more insightful evaluation and data collection than automated testing does. Subjective feedback is provided by surveys and questionnaires. Digital transformation initiatives may guarantee user-centric design and continuously improve the usability of digital experiences by using these techniques and resources.

8.3.4.2 User feedback collection techniques (surveys, interviews, etc.)

In order to evaluate usability and guarantee user-centric digital experiences, user feedback needs to be gathered. Many methods can be used to acquire insightful data. A large number of users can submit feedback through rating scales, multiple-choice questions, and open-ended responses in surveys, which provide a quantitative method. Interviews provide qualitative data and allow for a deeper analysis of user experiences, wants, and expectations. Group talks are facilitated by focus groups, which use the dynamics of interaction to produce in-depth insights. Users have a handy option to submit their ideas and suggestions by using user feedback forms that are embedded into digital goods or services. Real-time observation of user interactions during usability testing reveals user pain points and potential improvement areas. Social media listening is keeping an eye on online forums to compile user opinions and thoughts. Companies may interact with people directly, get insightful user insights, and improve the usability of their digital experiences.

8.3.4.3 Eye-tracking and heat map analysis for user behavior evaluation

Strong methods are used to assess user behavior and obtain an understanding of how users engage with digital interfaces, such as eye tracking and heat map analysis. The movement of a user's eyes while they interact with a digital interface is measured and recorded by eye-tracking technology, which provides insightful information on visual attention, gaze patterns, and fixation points. While participants complete particular tasks, this data is gathered using specialized equipment, such as eye-tracking glasses or desktop eye-trackers. We may next use software tools to evaluate the obtained eye-tracking data and understand the gaze plots, heat maps, and areas of interest (AOIs) that are produced. We may identify visual hierarchy, define areas of interest, evaluate the success of visual cues and call-to-action components, and comprehend any usability problems with regard to visual attention by studying this data.

On the other hand, heat maps offer graphic representations of compiled user engagement data. Warmer colors denote places with high user engagement, whereas cooler colors denote areas with lower involvement. They use color gradients to express the strength of user interactions. By monitoring user interactions like clicks, mouse movements, and touch gestures, heat maps are produced. We can evaluate the success of layout and design decisions, find popular locations or features on a website or application, and spot patterns or trends in user activity by examining heat maps. Additionally, to acquire a more comprehensive understanding of user behavior and interactions, heat maps can be integrated with other data, such as eye-tracking or scroll depth. Informed design decisions may be made based on this research, and user interfaces can be optimized to increase engagement, CTRs, and conversion rates.

Organizations may develop user-centric digital experiences that are in line with their aims for digital transformation by using eye-tracking and heat map analysis, which offer unbiased and data-driven insights into user behavior. Organizations may maximize usability and improve user experiences by analyzing where users focus their attention and how they navigate around a website or application. These methods assist in identifying areas for improvement, prioritizing design changes, and validating the efficacy of user experience improvements.

8.3.4.4 Remote usability testing and monitoring tools

In the area of user experience research and design, remote usability testing and monitoring solutions have grown in popularity. With the help of these tools, researchers and designers may acquire insightful data about how users engage with and use digital goods and services without having to do in-person interviews. They provide an easy and affordable option to perform usability tests, particularly when participants are spread geographically or face-to-face sessions could be more practical. There are numerous remote tools for usability testing and monitoring, each with its own special functions. The following is a list of frequently used tools in this category:

- *UserZoom*: UserZoom is a comprehensive user research platform that offers remote usability testing and monitoring capabilities. It allows researchers to create and conduct remote usability tests, collect quantitative and qualitative data, and analyze the results. UserZoom also provides features like screen recording, heatmaps, and clickstream analysis to gain deeper insights into user behavior.
- *UserTesting*: UserTesting is a popular remote usability testing tool that enables researchers to gather user feedback through video-based recordings of participants' interactions with a digital product. It offers a large pool of participants, allowing researchers to recruit individuals who match their target audience quickly. UserTesting also provides features like think-aloud protocols, task-based testing, and survey integration.
- *Optimal Workshop*: Optimal Workshop specializes in remote usability testing tools for information architecture and navigation assessment. It offers

tools like Treejack for card-sorting exercises, Chalkmark for first-click testing, and OptimalSort for creating and analyzing online card-sorting studies. These tools provide valuable insights into how users navigate and find information within a digital interface.

- *Lookback*: Lookback is a remote usability testing tool that allows researchers to conduct moderated and unmoderated testing sessions. It supports live video streaming of user interactions, allowing researchers to observe participants' facial expressions and hear their thoughts in real time. Lookback also offers features like screen sharing, time-stamped annotations, and collaborative note-taking.
- *Hotjar*: Hotjar is a remote user behavior analytics tool that provides insights into user interactions through heatmaps, session recordings, and feedback polls. While it is not specifically designed for usability testing, it can be used to monitor and analyze user behavior on websites and web applications. Hotjar's heatmaps visualize where users click, move their mouse, and scroll, helping designers identify areas of interest or potential usability issues.

The features, usability, participant recruiting choices, data analysis capabilities, and pricing of the tool should all be taken into account when choosing one for remote usability testing and monitoring. Additionally, it is critical to confirm that the tool fits your unique research goals and the requirements of your digital transformation project.

8.3.4.5 Analytics and data visualization tools for performance assessment

Tools for analytics and data visualization are crucial for evaluating the usability and effectiveness of user-centric digital experiences. Organizations can watch user interactions and spot opportunities for development thanks to Google Analytics, which offers detailed data on website traffic, user engagement, and conversion rates. In order to identify trends and areas for optimization, heatmap tools like Hotjar and Crazy Egg provide visual representations of user activity. A/B testing tools like Optimizely and Google Optimize make it easier to conduct tests to evaluate various iterations of digital designs and identify the most successful ones. These solutions support enterprises in continuously improving their digital experiences by offering data-driven insights.

The transformation of raw data into visual representations using data visualization tools like Tableau, Power BI, and Google Data Studio makes it possible to spot trends, patterns, and outliers. These solutions' interactive dashboards and reports provide a comprehensive perspective of important usability performance indicators, facilitating effective insight sharing and monitoring development over time. Organizations can identify usability problems and areas for improvement by using session replay technologies like FullStory and Hotjar records, which offer detailed visualizations of individual user sessions, including mouse movements and clicks. Tools for collecting customer feedback and surveys, such as Qualtrics and SurveyMonkey, collect qualitative information to supplement quantitative data and offer a thorough picture of user experiences.

Organizations should create clear objectives, define pertinent KPIs, and routinely evaluate the data to draw useful insights in order to use analytics and data visualization technologies effectively. Organizations may improve user-centric digital experiences, make well-informed decisions, and accelerate successful digital transformations by utilizing these tools. Organizations may develop a thorough understanding of usability and set priorities for changes by combining quantitative statistics from tools like Google statistics and heatmap tools with qualitative input from customer surveys and session replays. By using data visualization tools, data may be represented visually, making it easier to see patterns and trends.

8.4 CONCLUSION

The important facets of performability, analysis, and usability are examined in this chapter. It focuses on the significance of monitoring system resilience and performance, utilizing analytics for fact-based decision-making, and giving user-centric digital experiences the first priority. Organizations may pinpoint areas for development by tracking performance, and analytics empowers reasoned decision-making and optimization. Making usability a top priority guarantees that digital interfaces live up to user expectations. When taken as a whole, these components give businesses the tools they need to prosper in the digital age and get the most out of their digital transformation initiatives.

Index